In the House of War

RELIGION AND GLOBAL POLITICS SERIES

Series Editor
John L. Esposito
University Professor and Director
Center for Muslim-Christian Understanding
Georgetown University

ISLAMIC LEVIATHAN
Islam and the Making of State Power
Seyyed Vali Reza Nasr

RACHID GHANNOUCHI
A Democrat Within Islamism
Azzam S. Tamimi

BALKAN IDOLS
Religion and Nationalism in Yugoslav States
Vjekoslav Perica

ISLAMIC POLITICAL IDENTITY IN TURKEY
M. Hakan Yavuz

RELIGION AND POLITICS IN POST-COMMUNIST ROMANIA
Lavinia Stan and Lucian Turcescu

PIETY AND POLITICS
Islamism in Contemporary Malaysia
Joseph Chinyong Liow

TERROR IN THE LAND OF THE HOLY SPIRIT
Guatemala under General Efrain Rios Montt, 1982–1983
Virginia Garrard-Burnett

IN THE HOUSE OF WAR
Dutch Islam Observed
Sam Cherribi

In the House of War

Dutch Islam Observed

SAM CHERRIBI

UNIVERSITY PRESS

Oxford University Press is a department of the University of Oxford.
It furthers the University's objective of excellence in research, scholarship,
and education by publishing worldwide.

Oxford   New York
Auckland   Cape Town   Dar es Salaam   Hong Kong   Karachi
Kuala Lumpur   Madrid   Melbourne   Mexico City   Nairobi
New Delhi   Shanghai   Taipei   Toronto

With offices in
Argentina   Austria   Brazil   Chile   Czech Republic   France   Greece
Guatemala   Hungary   Italy   Japan   Poland   Portugal   Singapore
South Korea   Switzerland   Thailand   Turkey   Ukraine   Vietnam

Oxford is a registered trade mark of Oxford University Press
in the UK and certain other countries.

Published in the United States of America by
Oxford University Press
198 Madison Avenue, New York, NY 10016

© Oxford University Press 2010

First issued as an Oxford University Press paperback, 2013.

All rights reserved. No part of this publication may be reproduced, stored in a retrieval system,
or transmitted, in any form or by any means, without the prior permission in writing of Oxford
University Press, or as expressly permitted by law, by license, or under terms agreed with the
appropriate reproduction rights organization. Inquiries concerning reproduction outside the scope of
the above should be sent to the Rights Department, Oxford University Press, at the address above.

You must not circulate this work in any other form
and you must impose this same condition on any acquirer.

Library of Congress Cataloging-in-Publication Data
Cherribi, Sam, 1959–
In the house of war : Dutch Islam observed / Sam Cherribi.
   p. cm.—(Religion and global politics series)
ISBN 978-0-19-973411-5 (hardcover); 978-0-19-997185-5 (paperback)
1. Islam—Netherlands. 2. Muslims—Netherlands. 3. Islam—Europe.
4. Muslims—Europe. 5. Netherlands—Ethnic relations. 6. Europe—Ethnic relations.
I. Title.
BP65.N4C44 2010
297.09492—dc22   2009034600

Printed in the United States of America
on acid-free paper

For my mother, Aicha, and my daughters

Acknowledgments

This book owes much to many people. The first to whom I am in debt is the eminent philosopher and sociologist Pierre Bourdieu, who was my mentor beginning in the 1980s. This book is my tribute to him and his vast store of knowledge and experience. If I have found a way to analyze and better understand any group of people, it is because Bourdieu showed me the great breadth and depth of humanity. The world, to me, it seems, is a slightly less magnificent place since his death in 2002.

I also wish to acknowledge the kindness, patience, sharp insights, and brilliant advice of my mentors and friends in Europe, the United States, and Africa. I am extremely grateful to be able to stand on the shoulders of such giants as Mohamed Arkoun, Abram de Swaan, and Johan Goudsblom.

I also am thankful for the help of Holli Semetko, Doris Graber, Kevin Barnhurst, Roberto Franzosi Ivan Karp, Cory Kratz, Loic Wacquant, Aaron Sicourel, Gayatri Spivak, John Boli, Frank Lechner, Robert Agnew, Karen Hegtvedt, Gordon Newby, Kees Schuyt, Hans Sonneveld, Jose Komen, Dale Eickelman, Willy Jansen, Thierry Flamant, Michel Laguerre, Amitai Etzioni, Jonathan Gitlen, Michael Rohdes, Saji Girvan, Chef Rafih Benjelloun, Samir and Ouail Mahir, Nicolaas van Vliet, Mohamed Boudoudou, Driss Boujoufi, Mohamed Charouti, Mattias Duyves, Abdou Mnebhi, Fouad Laroui, Chazia Mourali, Anil Ramdas, Abdelhak Bouargane, Adelhak Filali, Nadia Bouras, Bouchaib Dihaj, Omar and Abdellatif Mdibeh, Simohamed,

Fatiha, Leila, Ab, and Adil Cherribi, Omar Radi, Stephan Sanders, Brieuc-Yves Cadat, Karim Traida, Teun van Dijk, David Theo Goldberg, Philomena Essed, Dick Herwig, Joke Madsen, Katinka Bijlsma-Frankema, Michael Peletz, Khedija Ghadoum, Juan Diez Nicolas, Marijke Jansen, Aaron Collett, Christophe de Voogd, Whitney Easton, Geet Bhatt, Edward Asscher, and Frits Bolkestein. I would also like to thank Dean Robert Paul of Emory College for his support and generosity.

This book would have been impossible without the superb editing skills of Stephanie Francienne Ramage, a journalist in Atlanta, Georgia, whose attention to detail and sense of tone and nuance are apparent on every page.

Finally, I would like to dedicate this book to the memory of my mother, Aicha Filali Cherribi, and to the future of my beloved daughters. My mother gave me the thing most precious to her: a loving, peaceful Muslim heritage. My daughters turned my attention to the world in which they would have to live and awakened in me a keen anxiety that prompted me to write this book. I want them to be safe. I want them to be proud of being women, to be proud of their Moroccan lineage, and to nurture the seeds of tolerance I hope their European and American upbringing has instilled in them.

Contents

Introduction: Confessions: The Composite Relationship of the Secular and the Religious, 3

1. The Established Outsiders of the European Integration?, 23

2. Immigration without Integration, 57

3. How Europe's Secularism Became Contentious: Mosques, Imams, and Issues, 83

4. Prisoners of the Mosque, 105

5. Pim Fortuyn versus Islam: Muslims, Gays, and the Media's Reliance on Conflict, 133

6. The Public Intellectual versus Islam: A Year of Sex and Rhetoric, 155

7. Riding Pim's Wave: Islam, Women, the Sacred, and the Naked, 187

Conclusion: The Vanishing Muslim Individual, 217

Notes, 233

Bibliography, 257

Index, 269

In the House of War

Introduction: Confessions

The Composite Relationship of the Secular and the Religious

How it was I quote before Pim with Pim after Pim how it is three parts I say it as I hear it

—Samuel Beckett, *How It Is*

Before Pim

For much of its history, the Netherlands has set the bar for social progress in Europe. For centuries, its neighbors have looked upon it with a mixture of horror and awe, and sometimes puzzlement. "Only the Dutch," they've said, and the Dutch have echoed with a note of pride, "Yes, only the Dutch." And so the events at the beginning of the twenty-first century in that most progressive country have been particularly troubling. For while the Netherlands has been swept by the same forces of change that have swept the rest of Europe—consolidation of the European Union (EU), a massive influx of Muslim immigrants, and the rising voice of Islamic fundamentalism—this small country has amplified those forces, allowing an observer to view the whole of Europe through a Dutch lens. But understanding how to use that lens is crucial, not only for those of us who have participated in this chapter of Dutch history but also and especially for those who must learn from it as a secondhand account.

How, then, do we tell the history of what happened in Europe, and particularly in the Netherlands, to our children without allowing emotions to distort the story?[1] What we are studying, after all, is part of the world we live in. It's not something kept in a petri dish in a sterile lab. I hear the voice of Pierre Bourdieu telling me that if you're not going to draw on your own experience in a real, personal way right from the beginning when talking about something so close to you, your own social world where you have been an actor and have also been acted upon, then you have nothing new to offer in terms of insight. This book draws on many sources, one of which is my own experience. And since I know personally most of the players in the field discussed here, even Pim Fortuyn and Theo van Gogh, as well as Geert Wilders and Hirsi Ali and all those who have written about them, from politicians to journalists, I must confess as to my role in all of this, however insignificant.

It's not easy to write a firsthand account of my life as a Moroccan, a Dutchman, and now a permanent resident of the United States. However, a way to gain distance from the people and events discussed in this book, a way to find perspective, is through scholarship, and it is this approach that I attempt to use, as a sociologist and an immigrant, in navigating a deeply personal narrative in the pages that follow.

The Trifecta of Coercion

The *academic* purpose of this book is to explore the historical, geographical, political, cultural, and sociological contexts sometimes missing from observations of tensions surrounding the Islamic community in Europe, and in the Netherlands in particular. Within those contexts, I have observed three major developments since the 1960s: (1) the movement of rhetoric from inside to outside the mosque, as well as the emergence of more persistent claims of Muslims to European society; (2) the crisis of models of integration and incorporation in Europe, complicated by Europe's own integration within an enlarged EU configuration (the EU, after all, has challenged individual national identities); and (3) the globalization of Europe's Muslim "problem." All three developments—greatly facilitated by the media—laid the foundation of the present renaissance of fundamentalist Islam.

It is this renaissance, coupled with my own unique history and the inquiries of my young students into that renaissance and that history, that has led me to write this book. There are many others, more formidable scholars than I, who have lent their considerable genius and talents to this field, but my life and the people I love have moved me to contribute the experience and insight I have, however limited, to hopefully enlarging an understanding of the field. This work is an academic and personal examination of the conditions that, beginning in the 1950s, paved the way for the tragedy of September 11, 2001, as well as its aftermath.

So much focus has been given to the United States and the Middle East that the prevalent view has lacked a firsthand political and academic narrative of how Islam in Europe has shaped the present image of Islam in the world. This book seeks to assist in filling that void. I hope to do that largely through the exploration and explanation of a simple model that I call the trifecta of coercion: coercion of Europe's Muslim migrant community from below, from within, and from above.

Coercion from below is how one's migrant status affects common and even universal pressures—the pressure to make a living, to succeed in one's profession, to have a place in one's community—but the way this coercion occurs among migrant imams and the influence that the imams consequently have throughout the European Muslim community are strongly significant to the issue of integration. The second part of the trifecta is coercion from within, which refers to the pressure within the Muslim European individual, as well as within his or her community. This coercive pressure is produced by the conflict of messages put forth by the larger society and the Muslim religious establishment. Coercion from above, the third part of the trifecta, is twofold. It is exerted by official Islam through embassies and government programs and by radical unofficial Islam through a message of Muslim transnationalism and anti-Western activism. Radical, unofficial Islam uses official Islam—governments, civic organizations, and their programs—as vehicles to gain access to poor, uneducated, and isolated immigrants. For radical unofficial Islam, Europe is a hunting ground, and its quarry is the disenfranchised seeking empowerment. This coercion is also brought to bear against well-educated and affluent European Muslims through the Muslim migrant underclass, whose very presence at times makes their more economically advantaged or more literate fellows feel guilt or estrangement; there is within them the ancient question, "They are Muslims and I am Muslim, but surely we are entirely different individuals?"

The trifecta of coercion acts as a pulverizing machine that destroys the individual who happens to be Muslim and reconstitutes him or her as someone who is only a part of a larger, alienated, monolithic entity, in this case the "Muslim threat." The trifecta may be seen in any migrant context, among Mexican and Central American migrants in the United States—who become reconstituted as part of the "brown threat"—as well as among sub-Saharan migrants in North Africa (the "economic and cultural threat") and any other migrant group anywhere in the world. The very heartening fact is that it is entirely possible to dismantle the trifecta of coercion simply by removing or substantially alleviating any one of the sources of pressure or conflict. For example, by reducing the conflict between the religious message and the message of the larger society, or by diminishing the pressure exerted by radical unofficial Islam, the individual Muslim is given a little more critical breathing room, enough freedom to reject violent so-called solutions. Any lessening of coercions within the trifecta is like snipping a connecting wire in a bomb. Alleviate the pressure, and dismantle the apparent threat. For this, the Netherlands provides a kind of bomb-dismantling guide with cautionary tales of what not to do, as well as some hopeful intimations of approaches that seem to work.

With that in mind, in the seven chapters that follow, I use transformative trends and pivotal events as a road map to the place of Islam in the Netherlands at the start of the twenty-first century. These trends and events include the introduction of Muslim guest workers in the 1960s and 1970s; the appointment of, first, uneducated imams and, later, more radical imams to European mosques in the 1990s; the emergence of Abu Jahjah in neighboring Belgium; the rise of Pim Fortuyn; the terrorist attacks on former New Amsterdam on September 11, 2001; Fortuyn's assassination in May 2002, followed by the celebrity of Hirsi Ali; the murder of Theo van Gogh in 2004; and the anti-Muslim immigration campaign of Geert Wilders.

Of Headlines and Hittists

After working on this for years, all the while wondering what more I could add, in a scholarly sense, that would be worthy of those like Mohammed Arkoun whose shoulders I stand upon, the will to finally make a real go of it, an understanding of my personal role and my academic responsibility, crystallized for me on the morning of February 20, 2007.

That morning, I walked across my lawn in Atlanta, Georgia, to pick up my newspapers. This little ritual, performed every day by millions in the United States, is almost a symbol of the American dream, but the headline I saw emblazoned across the *New York Times* pulled me, with sharp recognition, back into my adolescence in Morocco and what has become a seemingly inescapable nightmare for Arabs, Europeans, and Americans. The words "North Africa: A Staging Ground for Terror" blared above an article about the fear that grips the West when terrorists and their new recruits use North Africa's arid, mountainous landscape as a base from which to launch attacks against targets in Europe.

The headline thrust me into the distant past, because in the post-9/11 world, the staging grounds of North Africa are old news. The area's nearly ubiquitous poverty and the presence of a massive population of restless, unemployed youth—called Hittists, a derivation from the Arabic word for "wall," because they are so often seen leaning against walls, waiting for anything that will change the empty monotony of their lives—is, today, a well-known image.

In the mid-1980s, when Islamists from North Africa—specifically from Algeria—mounted a wave of terrorist attacks on France's subway system, neighboring European countries were concerned that terror would be imported to their own soil. Algeria itself was little more than a forced accessory to the crimes, having been brought to its knees by violent Islamists, terrorists trained in Afghanistan. Until that time, the distinction between the citizens of certain states and the Islamists who dominated them escaped many onlookers; European consciousness of Islam as a political force was vague, the Europeans only just having adapted to the idea of their former colonies having their own sovereignty.

But the Algerian Civil War, when bearded Islam lost its innocence in the very public conflicts of North Africa and the attacks they spawned in Europe, changed that: suddenly, Islam exploded on European consciousness in a way it had not since the Ottoman Empire's soldiers battered the gates of Vienna. Since the terrorist attacks in France in the 1980s, Islam as a whole has been considered a security threat on some level by nearly every public personality or organization in the Western world. Consequently, its adherents in the West, desperate to live in peace without stigma, have felt compelled to differentiate themselves from each other by delineating just what kind of Islam they practice. Some, like Rachid Mimouni, one of many Algerian intellectual émigrés who fled to nearby Morocco and Europe, refined their Islamic distinctions in a very public way by writing critical and expository articles about the emerging Islamists.[2]

Much more recently, as detailed in a July 1, 2008 *New York Times* article titled "A Threat Renewed: Ragtag Insurgency Gains a Lifeline from Al Qaeda," this history and these distinctions, as well as their significance in the Arabic and European societies, are set to take on a fresh importance in the years that lie ahead.

"Just as the Qaeda leadership has been able to reconstitute itself in Pakistan's ungoverned tribal areas, Al Qaeda's North Africa offshoot is now running small training camps for militants from Morocco, Tunisia and as far away as Nigeria, according to the State Department," the *Times* reported, and went on to say that in April 2008 the State Department "categorized the tribal areas and Al Qaeda in the Islamic Maghreb as the two top hot spots in its annual report on global terrorism. The threat is felt most acutely in Europe."

The Binary Social Reality of the Migrant Community in Europe

I am from the Maghreb (North Africa), and I am a bit like other Muslim migrants except for four important distinctions: I am a European citizen, I am a former member of the Netherlands Parliament, I am a resident of the United States, and most important for this story, I am a secular Moroccan who grew up in that country's Muslim culture.

I attended college in France in the early 1980s, when tensions between North Africans and the French made it a fairly uncomfortable place for anyone who might be mistaken for an Algerian. In Amsterdam, where my uncle and many cousins lived, I was treated well. So, I decided to move there. I loved to feel and smell the city that is a kind of seventeenth-century open-air museum, with its canals and legions of antique bicycles. The professors at the University of Amsterdam were not formal and cold, as my French professors had seemed to me. The French approach, of course, was not unfamiliar to me; it was the system that I had grown up with in Morocco.

Through the University of Amsterdam, I became immersed in the cultural and artistic institutions in the heart of the city. I was the first Moroccan in the University of Amsterdam's sociology department. Moroccan university students were so unusual that there were no Moroccan student organizations. My singularity gave me an enormous push in my professional life. After three months of preparation, I earned my Dutch degree of proficiency, and I was accepted at the university.

Eventually, I found a job at the Amsterdam Center for Foreigners established at the historic house of the French philosopher Descartes. Then, I found a position at the Dutch Broadcasting Company to work on minority programs. Simultaneously, I freelanced for the International Broadcasting Service's French and Arabic programs because I spoke both fluently. So far, my life in Amsterdam was rich and joyful. I never felt like a foreigner. I was seen as an individual, perhaps in large part because there were no others like me in my department, and there were very few other Moroccans working in broadcasting at that time.

And my intellectual diet was a feast. Abram de Swaan, the famous Dutch sociologist, introduced me to the reflexive and critical approach to one's own community. Pierre Bourdieu himself, whom I had met in France, inspired me to work on universalizing the access to the universal for those who are denied access or don't have the right tools to enter it. For me, these were not merely academic discussions. In Amsterdam, I was divided between two worlds. I regularly popped in to see my uncle's family, my cousins, and their friends who were living the lives of guest workers. All through my first year as a student in Amsterdam, while I circulated among brilliant scholars and worked on broadcasts at the radio station, I also worked in a French restaurant where my cousin Omar was the chef. My family was proud of my getting into the university and helped me in every way they could. No matter how much I felt like a part of things on campus, I knew when I spent time with my family that ultimately, they were me and I was them, and I wanted them to have equal access to the beautiful, fascinating world I had discovered in the city where they took the jobs that no one else wanted. I have always thought, and I still think, that mastering the language of one's adopted culture and learning about its history are keys to becoming mainstream and escaping from the margins of society where migrants reside. As I moved fluidly between Amsterdam's glittering academic circles and the gritty, hardworking world of the Moroccan migrants, all I wanted to do was help the migrants, including my family, to become full citizens.

Eventually, I became a Dutch citizen, and in 1994, with a lot of support from my friends and the faculty at the University of Amsterdam, I was elected to the Dutch Parliament. By then, helping to fully integrate the migrants had become my raison d'être, and it was the major plank in my campaign platform. For eight years, I did the work of politicians everywhere: my days were days of negotiations and compromise, I endured the spotlight of the media with a hollow feeling in the pit of my stomach as I waited to see how what I had said would look to my constituency, regretting, hoping, trying, failing, occasionally prevailing, but all the while being part of a very real, living sociological lab.

With Pim

Just one year before I was reelected to Parliament in 1998, I had a fax exchange with a popular newspaper columnist named Pim Fortuyn. The exchange was prompted by my critical review of his now famous book, *Against the Islamization of the Netherlands*. He asked me to meet with him for further discussion of the book,[3] which I had opined was not a productive dialogue with Muslims. I did not realize then that Pim Fortuyn, and the legend of Pim Fortuyn, would come to play a much bigger part not only in the life of the Netherlands but also in the life of all of Europe.

One of the worst days of my own life and certainly the most tense, awful day of my political career occurred about four years after that fax exchange on May 6, 2002. Just minutes after 6 P.M. and just a week before the election that would change the country forever, Pim Fortuyn was shot five times in the parking lot of a broadcasting company in Hilversum following a radio interview. He was shot in the head and the chest. At 7 P.M. he died. I, like most Dutch citizens, was glued to the TV, wondering how this could have happened in a nation where the prime minister biked to work and the Parliament building had no metal detectors.

The next day, there was what looked like a revolution in the streets. On the sidewalks, the atmosphere was electric with shocked grief and simmering anger. At Parliament, the atmosphere was downright frightening. In the cafeteria, two guards from Surinam, who were Hindus, told me anxiously that they hoped the killer was not a migrant. The killer, as it turned out, was a Dutch animal rights activist, but the fact that he was not a migrant would be, for all intents and purposes, forgotten in the months that followed. The next day, I went to Rotterdam, Fortuyn's hometown, where a large demonstration was taking place. The BBC *News Night*'s anchorman, Jeremy Paxman, asked me live, on camera, about the atmosphere of hate that was so unusual in the traditionally tolerant Netherlands. For the first time, I felt real panic about what I should say. I felt for the first time in my life—despite all of my years of devotion to the Dutch system and culture, despite my public service to Holland, despite my very real, official citizenship—that my Dutchness was questioned by the crowd. I knew that when they looked at me, they saw a Moroccan.

A little later, just before I was interviewed live by Nick Gowing on BBC *World News*, the same tension was still evident in the crowd. I was rattled. I had a drink with a columnist from the Dutch newspaper *Trouw*, who thought that Fortuyn was the best thing that had ever happened to the Netherlands, and then I went back to Amsterdam, thinking about how easy it is to destroy social cohesion and how vulnerable societies are to populism. The Netherlands, this little paradise created by the Dutch and not by the gods—this little country that had built one of the greatest empires in the history of the world (and the Dutch had never been as prosperous as they were at the time of Fortuyn's emergence), as well as one of its finest intellectual legacies—had, within days of a national tragedy, it seemed to me, descended into social anarchy.

This was all the more shocking because everything is so well designed in the Netherlands: the water system, the levees, even the land itself is divided so neatly it looks as if it had been carefully drawn with a ruler. The Dutch are not accustomed to riots; they are accustomed to negotiation and the politics of accommodation for all minorities. When Pierre Bourdieu had visited me in 1995 in the Dutch Parliament, he had been flabbergasted: "This is the democracy of proximity," he had said with visible admiration. "In France, we talk about it, but the Dutch do it."

And yet, less than a decade later, and in the space of less than three years between May 2002 and November 2004, the Netherlands witnessed the murders of first Pim and then Theo van Gogh and was rocked by riots. Mosques were burned, and Muslims were openly reviled by the public and the media. It was, perhaps, a sort of democracy, but certainly not the orderly kind that had won Bourdieu's praise.

After being voted out of Parliament in 2002 in the antimigrant furor that had engulfed the Netherlands, I, like so many immigrants before me who were seeking refuge from political turmoil, went to the United States. It seems a silly thing now to have worried about at the time, but my full name is Oussama. It's a fairly common Muslim name, but one that has become quite loaded with connotations since 2001. Coming to the United States, I was worried about how people would react to my name, and since some of my family members and friends had long since gotten used to calling me Sam, I simply took that nickname as my name.

It turned out to be an unnecessary precaution. My students and colleagues at Emory University have been absolutely wonderful. And while it is true that at border control in the first year after 9/11, I did get more than one SSSS on my ticket (that means "severe control"), I was treated properly. It is also true that since 2004 I have not endured any profiling at customs because of my Arabic name and face.

But the dynamics that led to the unrest in the Netherlands were also clearly in evidence even in the United States. The renaissance of fundamentalist Islam is ubiquitous. You will find it around the world.

A few years after my arrival in the United States, on that particular morning in February 2007, the *Times* headline served as the final catalyst in resolving my own internal debate. I knew I could no longer avoid writing about how deeply my own life and struggle for personal freedom has been entwined with the evolution of Islamism and the bittersweet relationship between Arabs and the European cultures that they so often inhabit. My Moroccan origin provides me with a vantage point from which to view this tender, passionate, and perilous relationship—Morocco's relationship with the West, after all, is a microcosm of Islam's relationship with the Judeo-Christian world.

Islam from the Hypersecular Perspective: The Shadow of Voltaire

I grew up in Kenitra, Morocco, which in the 1960s and 1970s was home to the Mehdia U.S. Naval Air Station, the largest U.S. military base in Africa until it was effectively closed, along with many other U.S. military bases, during the Carter administration. (An agreement allowing the United States to retain some use of the base was hashed out with the Reagan administration in 1982.)

Many of my memories include the Americans who worked on the base and lived in my neighborhood. Their books, donated by the thousands, lined the shelves of the municipal library where I spent my days reading, and their music, broadcast from a radio station run by the soldiers on the base, provided an eclectic soundtrack of rock, jazz, blues, Motown, and the venerable Frank Sinatra for my evenings. Yet, beneath the charming oddities of an imported American culture was a local economy that was almost entirely dependent upon the base's business. I remember the day the base endured its largest budget cut—that day was like a day of mourning for the thousands of people who benefited from subsidiary employment as servants, cleaners, chauffeurs, babysitters, and schoolteachers for the Americans. We never really thought of the base as a military installation, although clearly that's what it was. Today, things are often too simplistically dismissed as "imperialism," without a thought for what such seeming imperialism might mean in practical terms to real people. For me, my family, and my friends, for example, the American base was a business that brought our community many positive things—among them, quite frankly, economic stability and educational opportunities beyond those offered by the French. I have maintained friendships with some of the Americans I met then, even after all these years. Strange as it may seem, even now, while attending meetings with former President Jimmy Carter, whose center is just a few minutes from Emory University, I still find myself fighting the urge to ask him how he could have closed down an economic generator on which a whole town had become dependent. But that question is really only an introduction to a much bigger question: why, in the wake of independence from European colonizers, were we and other Arab states still lagging behind the West to such a degree that we remained dependent on Europeans and Americans?

I came of age in Morocco about twenty years after it assumed its liberty from France, at a time when religious questions were limited to those dealing with the problems posed by modernity and progress, problems familiar to Christian scholars. By contrast, the most important and passionate question posed in Islam's academic circles was "What went wrong with us?" Centuries before Western Europe's Renaissance of classical Greek ideas, the Arabs had reveled in an almost unequaled dominance. Our language was the lingua franca of scholars, particularly of scientists and philosophers, and our technology provided us with a standard of living far beyond that of Europeans. So how was it possible that the Europeans had managed to eclipse us in terms of learning, technology, and quality of life in the centuries that followed? These questions are still asked. Reading Bernard Lewis's *What Went Wrong* prompted me to ask: Was it really Islam that kept us backward? Or was it our evident inability to make a distinction between the political and the religious? Can we still continue to blame colonialism even now, decades after Arab and Islamic states were granted their independence by European colonizers? Why have we not been able to reform our societies and civil codes, and adapt the role of religion to our modern lives? Why do the Muslim establishment and religious elite still refer to the time of the Prophet Muhammad as the ideal time period that must be re-created in the future? Why is it that the religious establishment deems an agnostic or, for that matter, a nonpracticing Muslim to be a pernicious influence rather than simply a neutral, unrelated presence? Why is the great diversity of thought within Arab society—the presence of liberals, Marxists, conservatives, reformists, and counterreformists—never acknowledged?

When I was a student at the University of Rabat, there were more Marxists and Communists in academia than there were comparatively moderate liberals. It was a time when the neo-Marxist theories explained by Samir Amin in *Underdevelopment and the Impasse of the Third World* were popular. In 1980, in Europe, Louis Althusser strangled his wife, and therefore his career—and a notable cadre of the French intelligentsia—died soon after: Nicos Poulantzas (1980), Roland Barth (1980), and Michel Foucault (1984). A French Algerian named Jacques Derrida was left to pick up the pieces, put them back together, and take them apart again, something he made an art of doing. His ascension also marked the beginning of the intellectual detachment of the Maghreb from the Arabic hegemony of the Middle East that North Africans called "Machrek"—a culture and heritage that had its center in Egypt. For decades, all cultural goods had come from France or Egypt. In the 1980s, when the literature of Jacques Berque and Naguib Mahfouz was popular, North Africa finally started to produce its own intellectuals again, among them Mohamed Jabri, Abdelkebir Khatibi, and Fatima Mernissi.

What we think of today as "Islamists" were virtually nonexistent, and those who did exist were rare and timid creatures. I remember an incident in Morocco in 1982, when a bearded student wearing a Moroccan djellaba asked for more inclusiveness of dissident Islamic voices in the student community. The student organization's response was that as long as he did not begin his presentation with verses from the Koran, he was welcome to share his group's opinions. Only six years later, while I was studying in Europe, did the Islamic movement become the most dominant at numerous Arab campuses, not exclusively in Morocco, but in all of North Africa. Shortly thereafter, beginning in the early 1990s, at the end of what is commonly recognized as the North African migration period, the Islamic movement spread to Europe. At about that time, as part of my study in sociology, I interviewed Moroccan guest workers. Each interviewee recounted a story similar to that told to me by Aziz, a Moroccan waiter: "When I left Morocco in the late '60s, I was wearing jeans and listening to American and European music. Twenty-five years later, I returned to Morocco on vacation. The customs officials were astonished to see me with a beard and a djellaba. . . . The customs officials said to me, 'We sent you to Europe with jeans and you've come back more Muslim than us.'"

Many Muslim scholars say that when compared with Europeans, who seem to have, for the most part, successfully carved out separate places for the religious and secular in their lives, Muslims appear to cling to their religious identities as their central identities. This may be a way of demonstrating that they are distinct and will continue to live with a religion that has persisted without interruption for centuries. Most Muslim academics attempt to approach the gap between religion and philosophy from a perspective that emphasizes the reconciliation of religion and rationality. This identity association is evident in the trend of reinterpreting ancient Arab philosophers, like Averroës, so that their work appears to be more within the boundaries of orthodox Islam. It amounts to an exercise of balancing between reason and the religious dogma without giving an inch for the primacy of reason.[4]

Clearly, the tense relationship between Islam and secularism is not new. It has been a cause for debate throughout history, as intellectuals have sought to minimize the impact of religion on politics and society. It was the European colonizers who first sought to separate religious—in this case, Islamic—influence from the political process. One major obstacle to their plans was the traditional status of some Arab rulers, such as the Moroccan king who is also "the Commander of the Faithful" because of his descent from the Prophet Muhammad. He has both religious and political authority. Because of the European occupiers' efforts, religious laws have not been the basis of legal order in Morocco since the colonial period. Instead, Morocco's legal order is a combination of customary law, Napoleonic law, and a small part of sharia, the last applied only to inheritance and marriage. This model was widespread in most Arab countries except those on the Gulf, Yemen, and Saudi Arabia. Yet even in those countries, the "divine right"—the practice of propping up royal regimes with the Koran—found its way into legislation.

Another complication of attempting to separate the religious from the political arises from the definition of *secularism* itself. The translation of the Arabic word for "secularism," *ladiniya*, which means only "nonreligious," shifted over time to *ilmaniya*, which means "worldly." The separation of church and state and the perception of secularism as a worldly experience devoid of spiritual value are two significant factors among many others that explain the rejection of secularism in the Islamic world. Bernard Lewis explains that the relationship between Caesar and God in Christendom fostered the notion of a separation of church and state, which consequently made it easier for citizens of the Roman Empire to accept secularism alongside Christian doctrine. Gayatri Spivak asserts that one of the reasons secularism is rejected by Hindus and Muslims is because it is viewed as an extreme aspect of Christianity (although Spivak also notes that it is necessary for Hindus and Muslims to adapt to modernity by devising their own secular ethics).[5]

As a high school student in a country recently freed from French domination, I was impressed by two related ideas: Cartesian doubt and the passionate egalitarianism of Rousseau, Diderot, and Voltaire, the philosophy underlying the French Revolution. If Descartes himself had erected a sort of wall between the spirit and the body, and if God himself did not play favorites but instead endowed humankind with the capacity for self-determination, then it was reasonable to me that a Jeffersonian wall could be built between Arab political institutions and Islam. I was not the only one thinking this. A whole generation of Moroccans understood that secularization for European societies had been achieved through a painful process during the pinnacle of Christendom's power, and with that as our model, we moved forward, determined to intellectually do for our country what others had done for theirs. At the university in Rabat, this movement centered on ideas about how to create a secular space free of religious dominance. We believed that our secular utopia was possible because up until the late 1970s, there was no religious student movement at Moroccan universities. We daydreamed about the French advanced notion of secularism—*laïcité*, a total separation of church and state made possible by the subversion of the church.[6] At the same time, many students were chased by the police and jailed, not for their secular ideas but for their belief in Marxist revolutionary ideals. Many were members of a Qaeda or Qaidyyin movement that was communist, not extremist Islamic as the one associated with Bin Laden. I personally was not a member of any student organization.

The Extraordinary Moroccan Case

Religion came to my family exactly as Salman Rushdie would later say it came to his own, "like an ache in their bones"—a rheumatism at the end of their lives.[7] My parents never imposed a particular religious ethic upon anyone at home, though I sometimes would see my mother discreetly praying. My father used to distrust anyone who used "Allah" or other Islamic references in conversation when buying something in the *souk*, the marketplace. He even distrusted those traders with the so-called religious beard, and he would say to us, when one of them would begin to grow out his beard, "Now it's time to find another vendor."

Islam, as practiced in Morocco in the 1970s and early 1980s, was basically tolerant, despite some rigid social codes and laws that were common in the more traditional, and usually rural, areas. Clifford Geertz says most Moroccans "alternate between religiousness and what we might call religious-mindedness with such a variety of speeds and in such a variety of ways that it is very difficult in any particular case to tell where one leaves off and the other begins."[8] Most Moroccan city maps, even as late as the 1970s, showed a French quarter or a European section and a Muslim section called the *medina*. The European section allowed bars, and women were seen freely going about their business, but in the *medina*, the public sale of any alcoholic product was prohibited, and there were more forms of social control designed to diminish the freedom of girls and women. Most North Africans lived in this atmosphere of dual-personality dichotomy, in a world of two constantly conflicting ideological forces, modernism and traditionalism, crammed into a shared physical space. Symptoms of this cultural split personality are evident in the nature and use of their language. Moroccans allow themselves to say certain objectionable things in French but not in the overserialized Arabic.

Morocco's relationship with modernism is very complex. After forty years of independence, French is still the second language of the country and the language used by the elite, the bourgeois, and those who would like to be elite but achieve only being bourgeois. In many ways, Paris remains the intellectual hub for the Maghreb (the North African community). Morocco's proximity—it's only fifteen kilometers from Gibraltar to Spain—makes it the gateway to Europe for all sub-Saharan citizenship candidates and an unavoidable stop in their clandestine migration. Geographically, Morocco resides on the line between two cultural influences, and because of this, as Clifford Geertz explains in *Islam Observed*, Morocco is a deeply religious country despite its relative modernity. The Moroccan sociologist Paul Pascon spoke of his own country when he spoke of a composite society where tradition, superstition, animism, and modernity can all reside in one place. Morocco now is at the crossroads of Europe and Africa—Europe, with its dreams of modernity and welfare, and Africa, with its problems of poverty and youths fleeing to Europe through Morocco. This crossroads comes into view against the rise of Islamism in the Islamic world and among some of Morocco's own children—the children of émigrés living in Europe.

From Radical Secularism to Humanistic Secularism:
The Echo of Spinoza

During my studies at the University of Rabat, I summered in Amsterdam with my uncle's family, who had lived there since the 1960s. Upon completion of my bachelor's degree, I made the decision to emigrate from Morocco because of the wealth of opportunities to be found in Europe. Besides the familiarity that came with having spent time in the Netherlands, I was fascinated by the country's cosmopolitan intellectual heritage and its traditions of tolerance. My undergraduate degree, in fact, was in philosophy. The seventeenth-century French philosopher and mathematician René Descartes found refuge in Amsterdam, as did his contemporary, Baruch Spinoza, who was born in Amsterdam to Portuguese-Jewish parents. As a liberal secular Moroccan, I firmly believed, like Descartes, in a separation between the physical and the spiritual. Like Spinoza, I also believed in the separation of religion and the state.

For many years, I worked in the Descartes House, a center that functions as an interface between migrants and the City of Amsterdam. Prominently displayed in my office bookcase was a book titled *Descartes Is Not Moroccan*.[9] I was well aware of the difference between Descartes' metaphysical rationalism and the Enlightenment's idealist rationalism. But my fascination with Spinoza grew when I read his writings against the intolerance of religious authorities in his own era, whether Jewish, Catholic, or Protestant. Spinoza, like other descendents of the Marranos, Jews of Spanish and Portuguese origin, was tolerated in Holland and, upon his rejection of Judaism, was tolerated more in Dutch society than within his own Jewish community.[10]

At the University of Amsterdam, I learned from great thinkers, including Norbert Elias, Johan Goudsblom, Abram de Swaan, Mohammed Arkoun, and Pierre Bourdieu. Bourdieu and I became close friends. He was my mentor and a member of my PhD committee. My dissertation was an analysis of the sermons of Arabic-speaking imams in Europe and their views on Western society in the early 1990s.

It wasn't until 2001, while I was serving as a member of the Dutch Parliament, that I realized that those sermons had been a big part of the mosaic that paved the path toward extremism for some Muslims in Europe. In the first few months after 9/11, tensions were very high between the Jewish, Christian, and Muslim communities in the Netherlands. It was important to address this rumbling pressure, and so I brought together rabbis, pastors, and imams at a public forum at Amsterdam's Felix Meritis, the Netherlands' cultural debate chamber.

What I had learned from my research in the 1990s was that imams in Europe had a strong online presence that encouraged interactions between computer-savvy young people and religious leaders on a variety of topics, including marriage, sexuality, rituals, and problems pertaining to integration and assimilation. European Muslims also used call-in radio programs and live television broadcasts on local cable stations to disseminate their messages. I found that because of this interaction with various publics, both Muslim and non-Muslim, Islamic religious leadership had become more visible, accessible, and transformable. After the events in the United States on September 11, 2001, these forums, which had formerly been casual opportunities for cross-cultural discussions, became sensitized.

Yet, it was bound to happen. September 11 may have hastened the realization by Muslim and non-Muslim Europeans alike that their social landscape was dramatically altering, but it is unlikely that they would have been able to ignore it much longer. The evidence was all around them. When you take the train from Amsterdam to Paris, through what the French call the *banlieues*, you can see the poverty of the old housing projects, the lasting scars of violence in graffiti and destruction increasing as you travel south from the Netherlands to Belgium and France. Because these were, and are, the neighborhoods of Muslim immigrants, the passing landscape also serves as an indication of how exclusion based on religion or ethnicity emerges in even the most secular of societies. The European Union is seen as a constructed space of Europeanness with its own historic, cultural, and political solidarity, and a crucial observation involves recognition that different models of integration, based on soft or hard versions of secularism, shape policies and expectations and claims of minority groups. Just five hundred kilometers from Amsterdam, where in certain Islamic schools teachers and students are obliged to wear headscarves, Parisian schools ban headscarves entirely, and Islamic schools are not funded. This is a telling commentary on the meaning of citizenship and unity in the European Union.

Perhaps more important, these measures are themselves measures of how illiberal theocratically oriented Islam has transformed what most of the world thinks of as Europe. After all, Europe is not simply a landmass—it is an idea. The idea of Europe is one of openness, tolerance, and a secularism that is open to and tolerates religion while resolutely denying it the power of government. Is this still the case? Has not the European fear of Islam and its obsession with Muslims driven it to impersonate the very culture it despises? Has fear and fascination with Islam shaped Europe's laws over the past decade to the point that France and Holland do a credible imitation of countries where religion requires that certain dress be eschewed, that certain types of education be prohibited, that certain people be treated as suspects? Isn't this the very spirit of extreme Islam, and hasn't it thoroughly possessed the body of Europe? If these violent and virulent Islamists destroy Europe's joie de vivre, its moral courage, its devout determination to live openly in a suspicious world, then they will have no more need for bombs.

After Pim: The Echo of De Tocqueville, or the Triumph of the American Model

After the 2002 election in the Netherlands, when the far right revolution inspired by Pim Fortuyn was achieved, the media's continuous drone against Muslims accelerated into a Dutch nationalist xenophobia. At that time, I was married to an American, and we moved to her home country. I took a position in the sociology department of Emory University, where I was impressed with the campus and facilities that made European universities pale in comparison. I was even more fascinated by the fact that Emory is a Methodist university located in the historically conservative South, and yet posters that admonished students to "Get a Faith" were posted next to posters supporting sexual diversity and organizations for gay, lesbian, bisexual, and transgender individuals. There is even a campus organization called "the All-Faith Church," and its services begin with recitations from the Bible, the Koran, the Talmud, and various other scriptures.

My office is located in the basement of Emory's Tarbutton Hall, a building that bears the name of an old Southern family who made their fortune in the railroads that served middle Georgia's kaolin mines. Yet, it was here one Friday at noon, on a campus scattered with such family names and canopied by towering oaks, that I heard something I hadn't heard in many years. It was the Muslim call to prayer. It transported me back to the *medina* of Fez, where I had awakened to it each morning at my grandmother's home. It was emotionally overwhelming. I followed the sound to the Quad. It was coming from the clock tower, the school's best-known landmark. Muslim students stopped and gathered while they listened, and non-Muslim students reacted with deference while going about their own business. It was Ramadan, and the university was showing its respect for the faith of the Muslim students during the holy month. It occurred to me that a scene like this would probably not be tolerated on the campus of a European university. But as part of a broader picture, U.S. presidents have an even more integrated connection between the secular and the religious. Former President Jimmy Carter is a self-described "born-again Christian." Yet, in his book *Endangered Values: America's Moral Crisis*, he cautions the reader to be wary of the erosion of the Jeffersonian wall that separates the church and state in the United States.[11] President George W. Bush, whose public image is at least partly entwined with America's religious right, has made a point of reaching out to the country's Islamic community and, when put on the spot regarding his religion, usually demurs by saying only that he believes in God and prays for guidance.

As De Tocqueville stated clearly, American society is religious, but the federal state defends the core political principles of secularism. From this American example, I learned how the United States is better equipped, as the French writer and philosopher Bernard Henri Levy admits, to ensure a superior form of secularism, one that tolerates religion, than is the case for France or other European countries.[12] A secular society should not obstruct those who view religion as a temporal enforcement of a private spiritual contract. Secular society presents, however, a great obstacle for those who see religion as a mandate ordained by God regarding what should happen, not simply for them within their own private spiritual devotion, but for a country or even the planet. For these people, religion is not a personal experience but the basis for public policies. However, between such adherents and their secular American counterparts, there is a growing rift, something that almost mirrors the chasm between secular Europe and its community of devout Muslims. This divergence in America's view of the religious and the secular is evident in the 2001 American Religious Identification Survey, which found that the three categories with the greatest membership gains since 1990 were evangelicals ("born again" Christians) with a 42 percent gain, "non-denominationals" with a 37 percent gain, and "no religion" with a 23 percent gain. This would seem to indicate that as a nation, the United States has moved toward becoming more polarized, with a combined gain of 60 percent for those who do not adhere to any particular religion or no religion at all, and a gain of more than 40 percent for those who view themselves as evangelicals, a group that is usually self-identified as fundamentalist. So we see the developing gap throughout the West.

This polarization makes the role of secularism even more critical to religious equality. Secularism, a condition that is neutral to religion as opposed to antireligious, provides a decompression chamber for religion, ensuring that antireligious factors or those factors that play favorites among certain religions cannot act to galvanize potentially violent sects. It seems to me that real religious equality can exist only within a secular environment. Any society that recognizes religion beyond its right to exist and to conduct itself peacefully must favor one creed over another—a situation that necessarily marginalizes minority religions. When we speak of a society that is religious, we are really discussing a theocracy. My colleague at Emory, Abdullahi Ahmad An-Na'im, explains: "Religion needs secularism to mediate relations between different communities (whether religious, antireligious, or nonreligious) that share the same political space or space of public reason."[13] That is why Europe's secularism, to a certain extent, also acts as a buffer between its historically Christian society and its newer, numerically significant Muslim community.

Living in the United States has given me the necessary distance to reconsider dynamics in Europe. When I look at it today, from across the pond, what I see is an ideological bullfight—an appropriately Spanish oeuvre, considering that nation's densely mixed religious history that owes so much to Islam. In this bullfight, Islam is the bull, goaded and provoked by politicians and pundits who want to make themselves famous matadors by exaggerating the fierceness of the bull against whom they have chosen to pit themselves. He can be dangerous; he is, after all, a bull. He is also no match for their intellect; he is, after all, a bull, and this is their arena, their game, about which he knows little and appreciates less. That is not to say that Islam or its adherents are without guile, but Islam is only a religion, just as a bull is only a bull. By focusing so much on this religion, and indeed on religion in general, we lose sight of our responsibilities as individual human beings, while the matadors make their reputations on a beast of their own creation.

As Sartre says, human societies don't need to be atheist or religious in order to have the same norms of honesty, humanism, and progress.[14] The thing that might well bring greater understanding and peace between the West and Islam is an understanding of the role of secularism in the Islamic world. Consider this: imams in tenth-century Baghdad were more open and liberal than twentieth-century imams in London and Amsterdam.[15]

As Descartes would say, I read the grand book of the world, and I was fascinated by the European history of ideas and recognized in it the contribution of Arab Islamic thinkers like Al Mutazillah, Averoës, Al Kindi, and later Ibn Khaldun. In the *lingua franca* of their time, Arabic, their philosophies reflected the diversity and richness of their civilization. The fate of peace in our world rests with the fate of such Muslim intellectualism, preserved in the decompression chamber of secularism.

I

The Established Outsiders of the European Integration?

Only Islam seems to be unpalatable in the Netherlands and elsewhere in Europe.
—Abram de Swaan, *Bakens in niemandsland: Opstellen over massaal geweld*, 190

"A spectre is haunting Europe." This is not the spectre of communism to which Marx and Engels were referring but rather the spectre of Islam and Islamic "terrorism."
—Jack Goody, *Islam in Europe*

On January 1, 2000, I visited my halal butcher on east Amsterdam's Van Woustraat. He was vociferously unhappy. It was the first day of the official use of the euro, and he groused that "this euro has no *baraka* [divine grace]. This is bad for business."

From the very beginning, the euro triggered strong emotional reactions—and most of them were not good. The Dutch lost their colorful money and adopted a new way of counting change. The guilder had been based on a system that included a 25-guilder bill. When the guilders were exchanged in the new system, the 25-guilder was replaced with a 20-euro. Even on its face, there was a loss. This aspect of the transition to the euro had been reviewed and discussed well in advance, but what had never been fully anticipated was the emotional impact, the feeling that the Dutch were being expected to give up their identity for something vague, a sort of European nonidentity. There was no central rallying point or concept to the European Union; there was no one shared ideology; there was nothing, as far as most citizens could see beyond a hoped-for economic advantage in the form of shared currency.

But money has a far greater emotional significance than is immediately apparent. It buys flowers for lovers, shoes for babies taking their first steps, chocolate for aging parents who may have been feeling neglected, books for long-awaited college classes, or perhaps a plane ticket to vacation on the Mediterranean with friends whom one has not seen in years. All of these make up the fabric of life, and the currency that affords them down through the centuries becomes a kind of common ground within a given culture. There are well-worn phrases that rely on the shared recognition of national denominations of money. Consider, for example, the *dubbeltje* in the Netherlands. A common phrase among the Dutch is "Als je voor een dubbeltje geboren bent, word je nooit een kwartje," meaning, "If you are born as a dime, you'll never become a quarter." Now such a limitation is of no consequence because neither the *dubbeltje* (the world's smallest coin in use) nor the *kwartje* exists. The euro denominations that have taken their place do not carry the same cultural freight. The exchange of national monetary denominations for the euro is a metaphor for the exchange of national cultures for the nonspecific culture of the European Union. As for the European Union's identity, in the words of Gertrude Stein, "There is no there, there."

At the very time that the void of the EU nonidentity yawned open, and perhaps as a result of that void, Europe's Muslim population, with its very distinct identity, became more visible than ever before. With the Dutch, the French, the Germans, and the others feeling as though they were losing themselves, the newly emerging Muslim identity became amplified and appeared to be a greater threat than might have otherwise been the case.

Understanding the Place of Islam in Europe

In 1957, the first plans for the European Union were put on paper, at roughly the same time that Europe's former North African colonies were assuming responsibility for their independence. At the time, it seemed that these two cultures had painfully decided to pursue divergent paths, but soon it would become apparent that their fates were inextricably entwined and utterly interdependent. The idea that the Islamic crescent, which stretches across North Africa from Morocco into the Middle East, could keep its distance from Europe, separated from it only by the Mediterranean—and by only nine miles of the

Mediterranean at the straits of Gibraltar—is a notion that has never withstood the test of time. In 1683, the Ottoman Empire's forces trudged all the way to Vienna before being forced back. Now, once again, Europe is under a sort of Islamic siege, but this time the siege is primarily social and political and, most significantly, of Europe's own making. This siege has ramifications not only for Europe but also for all of the West.

More than fifty years since its inception, the EU now anticipates expanding beyond its current membership of twenty-seven countries to include Turkey, with its 83 million majority-Muslim population, but that possible inclusion is the source of much tension in the EU. Like Turkish delight, the Turkish dilemma is sticky for Europeans. Once welcomed in theory as a strong buffer state between Europe and the East, it is now viewed as an enclave of Muslims, and that is not something that Europe, seeking an identity of its own and increasingly afraid that its identity is being Muslimized, can accept. Ironically, Europe, viewed for so long by Americans as a much older, more sophisticated society, now finds itself awkwardly young—both in terms of its status as the European Union and in terms of its burgeoning young Muslim population, two factors that are undermining its sense of self and raising the specter of long-feared "Eurabia." By comparison, the United States is more mature by 180 years, and its culture is seemingly only in danger of officially recognizing its most recent influx of immigrants from south of its border—many of whom already identify themselves as Americans.

Some years ago, European newspapers made predictions that in 2050 there would be a Muslim majority in all of Europe's major cities. The easily recognizable Islamic appellation "Mohammed" is already the most popular name in many of Europe's metropolitan areas.[1] The renowned Princeton historian Bernard Lewis recently told the German newspaper *Die Welt* that Europe will be Islamic by the end of this century.[2] European Union Commissioner Frits Bolkestein has predicted that Europe will implode from the sheer volume of its Muslim citizenry if Turkey becomes a member of the EU.[3] Yet, the Muslim influx was not sudden. It developed over many decades.

It was during the height of what would become known as the North African diaspora, an exodus that brought millions of Muslims to Europe, that I began my fieldwork quite by coincidence. In the early 1990s, it happened that, because of my Moroccan background, I was asked by several immigrant organizations and the City of Amsterdam to put together a course for thirteen Arabic-speaking imams, twelve Moroccans and one Turk. The aim of the course was to teach the imams about the Dutch language and culture. It was to serve as a kind of orientation.

Almost immediately, a fascinating division among the imams became apparent: some chose to adapt to their Western environs, and others did not.

I wondered about the motivations of both the adapters and the nonadapters and soon found myself working on what would become my doctoral dissertation. With the permission of the imams, I recorded their sermons over a period lasting from 1991 until 1993. I created a typology based on their life histories. What I describe as "the revolutionary" imam, for example, was a type that was openly anti-Semitic and homophobic and called on his followers to fight for Muslim rights in Bosnia. But while the topics of Jews and homosexuality were a priority for a minority of imams, they all shared a lively interest in democracy, the media, and women's role in society.

I also observed something very peculiar and particular to mosques in Europe that is absent from churches, temples, and synagogues: the problem of leaders who are, themselves, illegal immigrants. Their precarious status, along with the secrecy and paranoia it breeds, makes some imams prisoners in their own mosques. They live in fear of leaving the mosque, getting caught by the police, and being sent back to their home countries. And because they live in fear and distrust of the Western world around them, these shepherds lead their flocks toward fear and distrust as well. What would otherwise be a culture with certain aspects that more religious types might simply judiciously avoid instead becomes a culture that is, in their eyes, rife with spiritual danger, a landscape of immorality fraught with traps designed to damn one's soul and, of course, get one deported to a more moral, but economically stricken land. These imams saw their European tenure and that of their congregations as a temporary exile in a "perverse" society, and they saw their role as that of navigator in perilous terrain to guest workers and their children.

Yet, at the other end of the continuum, there were, and are, many sophisticated religious leaders: one imam entrepreneur made ironic observations about his own people in the Dutch society; a Moroccan imam who attended a gay pride meeting in Amsterdam urged his fellows not to persecute homosexuals and made it clear that his mosque would not exclude them; and numerous imams do social work that resembles that of the well-respected outreach programs of American Christian churches.

The differentiation of these two groups of imams—those who integrate and those who don't—is determined by four factors that, in turn, will determine the future state of Islam in Europe: first, the establishment of guest workers in their new societies; second, the guest workers' interaction with the state, its institutions, and the media; third, the enlargement of Europe, as an experiment in globalization;[4] and fourth, the global impact of pan-Islamism.

Since the 1950s, European countries have allowed or even encouraged immigration from Muslim countries to suit their individual purposes. The United Kingdom opened its doors to Asian Muslims from its former colonized states in India and Pakistan; France brought guest workers from freshly decolonized Algeria, Morocco, and Tunisia; and the Netherlands, though it had no colonial ties to Turkey or Morocco, brought in guest workers from those countries to fill lower level, menial jobs. The Netherlands had been a destination for job-seeking Indonesian Muslims for many years by then.

The Male Dominance of Islam in Europe

In the 1960s and early 1970s, Europe's Muslim guest workers were overwhelmingly males from rural areas where the most orthodox and male-centric forms of Islam reside. Thus, the guest workers became defined by a certain testosterone-driven exclusion. This gender vacuum only enhanced the European perception of Islam as misogynistic. The group was treated accordingly, with no social programs aimed at serving women and families, making it more difficult for the Muslim women who would immigrate later, in the 1980s, to find an independent role in their new Euro-Muslim world. Understanding these women would also prove to be a challenge for Europeans. Some were not especially proud of some aspects of their culture, but Europeans who looked at the Muslim migrant workers as a monolithic group might have missed the gender nuances.

Alain Touraine explains: "The principle obstacle [facing emancipation] is the control of sexuality, obligation of sexuality and its control ... and, after the wedding night, by the exhibition of a piece of cloth stained with blood. Women are more scandalized by this control of their intimacy than by arranged marriages."[5]

A chain of the blind leading the blind was created, as culturally and linguistically isolated imams counseled men in their mosques who were equally isolated, and those men, in turn, tried to navigate the European world for their wives and daughters. The male-centric view of Islam engendered in the male-only communities of the early period of the North African diaspora would prove to be the key to understanding the malefication and the aggression and fear that define Islam as lived by many Muslims in Europe.

This gender dynamic is key to understanding, Alain Touraine reiterates, the isolationism of Muslim communities in Europe. "Muslim women suffer from many prohibitions thrown at their sexuality and suffer also from the contradiction imposed on them by belonging to a family and a community [stigmatized and problematized] at one hand and on the other hand the expression of their desire in the quest of individual happiness."[6]

Enter the Amicales

The Muslim migrant workers' gender imbalance fostered a cultural isolationism that was already ensured by two powerful factors: first, the myth of return, the migrants' belief that they would work most of the year in Europe and return each summer to their home countries, eventually retiring to their home countries; and second, the vested interest their home countries had in continuing to control them. The Moroccan, Turkish, Algerian, and Tunisian governments were terrified that leftist factions living in exile in Europe would influence migrant communities and that their doctrines would find their way back into the Islamic crescent, along with financing provided by paychecks earned in European jobs.

To keep this from happening, the North African governments formed *amicales*, groups charged with the responsibility of controlling the migrants—spying on them in Europe and, if the spying revealed possible leftist contacts, threatening them and their families each summer when they came home.

This tactic ensured that the migrants continued to take a partisan interest in the political events of their home countries and distracted them from taking an interest in their own European political destiny. Moroccans, for example, were quickly caught between two camps, those who supported King Hassan II and those who opposed King Hassan II. The Turks, similarly, found themselves pressured to state some kind of loyalty to either the Turkish government and its complement of "Grey Wolves"—an *amicale* that took as its mission making sure that immigrant money found its way back to Turkey—or the government's leftist opposition. A little later, the governments of the home countries, Morocco, Turkey, and others, sent official imams to strengthen migrant ties to the home governments as a way of ensuring that money would return to the home country.

The official imams' congregations, often already out of step with the larger European society around them because of linguistic, economic, and cultural factors, were empowered by their imams, who told them that not only was this estrangement okay but also it was, in fact, desirable and even holy. The pressure to remain plugged into the political aims of their home countries made it harder for migrants to civically and politically integrate in their new European home—a circumstance that benefited the Turkish and Moroccan political groups who wanted their money. But their continued allegiance to the causes of their countries of origin spawned problems for them in Europe: their European neighbors viewed them with suspicion and saw them as failing to make a commitment, and an investment, in Europe. This was compounded by Europe's brand of secularism, one that views religiosity itself with some suspicion; as the immigrants continued to rely on their mosques as a way of socially connecting and fostering their ties to their countries of origin, the Europeans began to view the mosques themselves as anti-European. The more Europeans identified the mosques as the source of separatism, the more migrants viewed the mosques as a source of identity—they clung to their mosques and imams like rafts in a sea of European influence that threatened to dissolve and absorb them. The convergence of these two factors—the need of politicians in their home countries to secure their allegiance and the suspicion this allegiance fostered among Europeans—galvanized a Muslim community that might otherwise have adapted peacefully to its Western environment.

In the scenario I've just described, we see all three parts of the trifecta of coercion. First, we see coercion from below in the form of imams who were reliant on pleasing their employers, the governments of Morocco, Turkey, and other Muslim home countries, for their professional promotion and economic well-being. With that coercion acting upon them, these imams taught that alienation from the larger society was desirable. Though most imams today are not migrants, the earlier anti-integration ideology has shaped Muslim culture in Europe and remains a staple of the community. We see the second part of the trifecta, coercion from within, in the pressure within the Muslim individual in Europe, as well as within his or her community, produced by conflicting messages put forth by the larger society and the Muslim religious establishment. This is evident in the vast number of Web sites and television and radio talk shows designed to provide guidance to Muslims regarding interactions with the larger European society. For example, a Google search of the question "May I participate in a company dinner where pork and wine are served?" produces many results, but nearly all counsel Muslims to beg off and not participate. Yet, clearly there is a desire to be part of one's professional community, or such questions would not be posed. Pressure within the larger society to abandon Islam takes the form of government regulation that prohibits any sign of religious devotion in one's dress. A headscarf might only be a headscarf in another context, but the decision to cover one's head in Europe carries official significance. In the middle is the individual trying to live according to his own moral tradition between the standards of his inherited culture and his adopted culture. The factors that exert coercion from within are both prosaic and profound; they deal with the mundane, but the mundane shapes individuals and their world. Finally, we see coercion from above in the form of official Islam—the *amicales* of the 1970s and 1980s and the imams deputized by their home countries' governments. And radical unofficial Islam would play a part only a little later. Removing or substantially alleviating any one of these factors would have effectively disarmed the mechanism that would lead to so much violence, tension, and inequality later.

As Europe's establishment became increasingly uneasy regarding what it perceived as the misplaced loyalties of immigrant communities, the status of the mosques was elevated within migrant communities. For the first generation of Muslims, the mosque was seen as a relocated part of their country of origin, the place to heal the *ghorba*, the burning nostalgia of exile.[7] For members of the second and third generations, it has become the place where they speak their language of origin, where they read the Koran, where they first encounter their own cultural traditions, and where they first experience civic and social engagement. The most recent generation of Muslims in Europe sees the mosque as a symbol of their own alienated identity. They associate the mosque with distant lands of minarets and souks. These lands are not their own, they are their grandfathers', and like the shadowy, foreign countries of all immigrant progenitors, they have become mythologized. These countries—Algeria, Morocco, Tunisia, Turkey, Egypt, Lebanon, India, Pakistan—have become idealized, a place where life, though impoverished, appears across the distance of a generation to have been morally more cohesive and less confusing. With this vision of an Islamic Promised Land—a realm defined by ideology rather than actual geographic boundaries—a new leadership fed by this myth and alienation within European society has emerged, even as the original immigrants have aged and died. The result is a new social and religious configuration intent upon acquiring and asserting political power, not dissimilar in style to that of the African American religious leaders who birthed the American civil rights movement. This admiration of the American civil rights movement will define the religious makeup of new Muslim leadership in Europe because it, like the African American model, relies heavily on the personalities and devotion of its leaders.

An American Comparison

In *The Dignity of Working Men*, Michèle Lamont[8] compared low-skilled workers in the United States and France and analyzed how they used their moral standards to make distinctions between groups, to draw boundaries between themselves and others, to include and to exclude. She studied the world inhabited by white working-class men and how they legitimize "racism" through drawing various kinds of symbolic boundaries. Her work provides new insight into understanding the position of blacks in the United States and the position of Muslim immigrants in France in the minds of white working-class men in both countries. Lamont's research shows how the exclusionary practices of the upper classes identified in the earlier work of Pierre Bourdieu and those of the working classes described by Norbert Elias and John L. Scotson in *The Established and the Outsider* remain pertinent.

In an earlier study, *Money, Morals, and Manners*, Lamont uses interviews conducted in the late 1980s to compare how French and U.S. upper-middle-class white men define members of their class. Her work is interesting not only because of the insights she provides into the French and American upper-middle-class male cultures but also because she shows how the mechanisms of exclusion continue to operate by establishing "symbolic boundaries" through the labels men use to describe one another as "worthy" or "unworthy." In Lamont's words, the study "analyzes the relative importance attached to religion, honesty, low moral standards, cosmopolitanism, high culture, money, power and the like, by Hoosiers, New Yorkers, Parisians and Clermontois." Her study calls for more research on how the "salience of boundaries" changes over time. Although other studies in the United States show that "boundaries based on class-related characteristics (such as education, familiarity with high culture, etc.) are gaining importance over those based on universal traits (e.g., race, gender, religion)," Lamont finds that "moral and socioeconomic boundaries" or "symbolic boundaries" are "increasingly used to euphemistically draw boundaries based on gender, race, and ethnicity."[9]

In the Netherlands, for example, it is common to hear "allochtoon" a word that has come to mean "For a Moroccan [or Turk], he speaks perfect Dutch"—essentially a euphemism used by Dutch non-Muslims that plants a seal of approval on its object. The symbolic boundary is language, and by saying that someone speaks it well in spite of his ethnicity—even though the person in question may have lived in the Netherlands all his life and there should be no question of his ability to speak the language—is really a way of saying "he's agreeable in spite of his ethnicity" or, more to the point, "he's not so Muslim." Lamont specifies how three types of symbolic boundaries are used to maintain distinctions between individuals and groups: moral boundaries, socioeconomic boundaries, and cultural boundaries.[10] The first of these concern such qualities as "honesty, work ethic, personal integrity, and consideration for others." The second concerns judgments about "people's social position as indicated by their wealth, power, or professional success," and the last are "drawn on the basis of education, intelligence, manners, tastes, and command of high culture." This last and most exclusive tier is particularly difficult for most Muslim immigrants because they lack the linguistic ability to access advanced education or high culture. There are exceptions, but like all exceptions, they serve only to draw attention to the rule.

Therefore, understanding how Muslim guest workers and their children view themselves and the world will enable us to understand how they draw different boundaries among themselves as a group, within their group, and also between themselves and the rest of the society. Amplifying the "muted voices"[11] of this population is important in understanding the complexity and the plurality of their voices beyond the polarization that has triggered a generalized social myopia.

This myopia is manifested in a ubiquitous way among the Muslims of Europe. Those who observe the rituals of Islam as part of their routine, as well as those who are secular and merely culturally Muslim and those who are devout, all feel as if they must always explain that they are not terrorists or fanatics. After the killing of the Dutch filmmaker Theo van Gogh by a young man of Moroccan descent, a Dutch writer who was also of Moroccan descent described how he couldn't enter a café without being looked at as somebody who might be hiding a weapon under his belt. The methodical drumbeat of the media and politicians against Muslims beginning in the aftermath of September 11, 2001, succeeded in placing European citizens of Middle Eastern and North African descent into the role of an internal threat, like that constructed by the U.S. media and politicians against Japanese Americans during World War II. The result is that "Muslims" have to publicly express their disgust for radicals and their love, affection, and gratitude for the country in which they live, in a way not required of others. Despite the fact that the majority of second- and third-generation Muslims have been born and raised in Europe, their loyalty and European identity are constantly subject to doubt. One of the historical leaders of the guest workers' emancipation in the Netherlands, a Muslim immigrant himself, said, "I refuse to be Islamized."[12] Allowing freedom of expression of religious identity, or the lack of a religious identity, is a privilege of advanced democracies because their foundational tenet of the separation of church and state is intended to provide a shield from manipulation by the religious community, a circumstance that does not exist in most Islamic countries.

Over the course of the 1980s and 1990s, as the population of immigrants and their children and grandchildren in European societies grew, various European languages offered expressions to describe what was happening, but the fact that these terms have developed is a vivid indication of how widely acknowledged the phenomenon is. Just as some particularly isolationist Americans refer to their culture's "browning," the Dutch refer to *verkleuring* and the French call it *la banlieusisation*. *Verkleuring* refers to the coloring of Holland's population, and *la banlieusisation* refers to the ghettoization of France's inner cities and suburban enclaves. Together, these two terms capture how Europeans see the impact of growing populations of first-, second-, and third-generation immigrants of color over the past two decades in major metropolitan areas of many European countries. The majority of these immigrants are Muslim or claim an Islamic identity, which represents a startling shift away from their previous self-identification in the 1970s and 1980s as Moroccans, Turks, Tunisians, Algerians, and Pakistanis. The Muslim identity of immigrant workers was an invention of European anxiety. Prior to the 1990s, the immigrant workers were often referred to in Dutch as *allochotonen* (which at that time simply meant not indigenous), *buitenlanders* [foreigners], and *minderheid* [minority] and in French as *étranger* [stranger], *maghrebins* [from the Maghreb], and, for the second generation, *beurs* [an anagram of "Arab"]. The German word *Scheisse* [shit] is used in many combinations like *Scheissaraber* [Arab], *Scheissauslaender* [foreigner], *Scheissmusleme* [Muslim], *Scheissschwartze* [all non-Europeans], *Scheissneger* [black], *Scheisskanake* [Turks], and *Scheissfidschi* [Asians].

Islam, despite its varying ethnic origins, traditions, and diversity of expressions even within any one given European metropolitan area, is now described monolithically as "Europe's second religion" and as "the fastest growing religion in Europe."[13] Islam has become more visible in European public spaces in recent years, not only because of the growth in the sheer number of Muslims, mosques, and, in some countries, Islamic schools but also because of the high media profile of contested issues such as Islam's view of homosexuality, the role of women, and the perception of certain Muslim components of dress, like headscarves and djellabas. These tensions and frictions in European societies have to do with the belief that Muslims' cultural characteristics are not compatible with the European way of life. Despite the fact that demographic research on fertility and childbearing shows that second- and third-generation immigrant women are postponing their childbearing years and having fewer children,[14] which makes them more like their indigenous European counterparts, and the fact that marriage between Muslim immigrants and non-Muslim Europeans is increasingly common, popular rumors about accelerated Muslim birthrates and marital exclusivity persist. One of the most evocative scenarios claims that by 2050 there will be whole areas of European countries that are entirely "Muslimized."[15] In view of this, indigenous Europeans are understandably concerned about maintaining the norms and values of their societies, especially on those occasions when their values come into direct conflict with so-called Muslim values.

Sex and Islam in Europe

When we consider the values of Islam and the values of European societies, the greatest differences can be found in themes of sexual liberalization. With few exceptions, divorce is so socially accepted that it is a nonissue in most European countries, abortion is legal, prostitution is tolerated or state-regulated, and individuals are not to be discriminated against on the basis of their sexual orientation. Public attitudes toward gays and lesbians have become much more liberalized in Europe, as well as the United States, over the past decade.[16] The European Charter of Human Rights and European states' constitutions include protection of religious freedom and nondiscrimination on the basis of gender, race, ethnicity, and sexual orientation. In the context of a discussion about such value conflicts in European societies, it is worth noting that as recently as 1994, the Dutch Parliament passed a constitutional amendment specifically protecting the rights of "minorities" regardless of their religious affiliation, including "ethnic" and "sexual" rights, and implying the freedom not to practice a religion as part of the freedom of religion. However, the Dutch amendment has not been emulated elsewhere in Europe.

The conflict between Europe and Islam is reified in the lack of female emancipation within Islam and the assumption of female emancipation in European culture. The Turkish sociologist Nilufer Gole thinks that Islamic women are central in understanding the conflict with the West and also in understanding the conflict between modernists and traditionalists in the Islamic world itself. Turkey is a vivid example of authoritarian secularism, where the state and its apparatuses see the veil as an oppression of women. Gole gives the example of a female member of the Turkish parliament who was not only denied entry to the parliament as sacred secular space because she was wearing a headscarf but also stripped of her Turkish nationality.[17] However, the question of women's emancipation in the Islamic world goes beyond the veil issue: it deals with polygamy, repudiation, and the segregation of men and women. In many countries in the Islamic world, we see a kind of self-imposed reveiling by women who have never been veiled before.

In Europe, the opposition to Islam appeals to the feminist interests of women. There is, even as Nulifer Gole says, a kind of feminization of Europe. By focusing on the veil and the masculinity of Islam, the Europeans have imposed an Islamized misogynist identity on guest workers and their children. This conflict of values can be seen on a larger, global scale. According to Ronald Inglehart and Pippa Norris,[18] it is eros rather than *demos* that is the main point of contention between Islamic and Western societies. The public in Islamic countries, for example, is supportive of democratization, but in respect to beliefs about gender equality, they remain quite conservative. The subordinate position of women is reinforced by traditional religious values and laws in Islamic countries.

Is it possible that the acculturation of Muslims in Europe will bring change to their backward attitudes toward women? Based on their analysis of World Values Survey data from seventy-five countries between 1981 and 2001, Inglehart and Norris formed the following conclusion:

There is a persistent gap in support for gender equality and sexual
liberation between the West (which proves most liberal), Islamic
societies (which prove most traditional), and all other societies (which
are in the middle). Moreover, even more importantly... the gap has
steadily widened across all indicators as the younger generations in
Islamic societies remain as traditional as their parents and grandparents.
The trends suggest that Islamic societies have not experienced a back-
lash against liberal Western sexual mores among the younger generations as some popular accounts assume, but rather that young Muslims
remain unchanged despite the transformation of lifestyles and beliefs
experienced among their peers living in post-industrial societies....
These predominant beliefs and values matter, not just for cultural
attitudes, but also for the actual conditions of men and women's lives.[19]

Their study was designed to address differences between societies, but what they identify on a global scale is also important for our understanding of the developments within European societies during the past two decades. It is during this same time period—the 1980s, 1990s, and the early years of the twenty-first century—that the demographic changes within European societies have been so dramatic.[20]

Apart from a few recent studies in which immigrant populations in Europe are described in general terms or with reference to particular examples, and primarily in country-based chapters,[21] there is little in the way of research on the different generations of Muslims in European countries. Are younger Muslims in Europe remaining "unchanged" from their traditional parents in terms of sexual mores and values, as Inglehart and Norris suggest? Are they rejecting their parents' values outright and opting for the norms in the countries in which they live? Or are they creating a new set of values and norms? Inglehart and Norris say little about the contribution of Islamic religious leadership to the maintenance of traditional values in Muslim societies, although it is certainly part of why young people in Muslim countries today are as traditional in many ways as their parents and grandparents.

From Srebrenica to New York: The Construction of Islam as Race

The fall of the Iron Curtain in 1989 made it possible for many Eastern European countries to join the European Union. Some of these, like Yugoslavia and Albania, constituted the biggest historic challenge to the stability of Europe since World War II. In that same year, Slobodan Milošević was elected president of Yugoslavia, and the country soon faced an accelerated ethnic disintegration centered on

Kosovo and its Muslim population. This crisis manifested itself in the lack of a unified European defense identity able to settle conflicts in the neighboring former communist countries. Europeans could not do it alone, so the Americans and NATO were called on to stop Miloševic's ethnic cleansing in the Balkans. That led to air strikes in Serbia and Kosovo in March 1999, and thus were revealed continued tensions within Europe itself, aggravated by hundreds of thousands of refugees—most of them Muslim—fleeing to neighboring countries in the EU.

The Yugoslav crisis brought with it political turmoil for Europe as a whole and for the Netherlands in particular. The massacre of at least 6,000 Muslim men and boys while under the protection of a Dutch-UN peacekeeping force at the Muslim enclave of Srebrenica in July 1995 is now seen as a national conscience-crippling experience, second only to the betrayal of the Jews who sought refuge in Holland in World War II, in terms of its long-term psychic impact.

The murkiness surrounding the atrocities committed at Srebrenica was an early sign of a deepening identity crisis and the end of a number of old certainties about the future. The Dutch government asked the Netherlands Institute for War Documentation (NIOD) in 1996 to set up independent research into the events that took place before, during, and after the fall of the enclave. When the NIOD report was finally released on April 10, 2002, after being postponed for more than a year, Prime Minister Kok announced six days later, on April 16, 2002, that his government would bear full responsibility for the massacre, and he and his cabinet subsequently offered their resignations.

The aftershocks of Srebrenica still continue today, although the trauma has now been overshadowed entirely by the fear of Islamic terror in the Netherlands.[22] No one asked if perhaps an Islamic threat were needed to numb the shame of what had happened at Srebrenica, but the threat, needed or not, had already presented itself in the events in New York on September 11, 2001, seemingly absolving many Dutch citizens of something they'd rather not think about anyway.

National parliamentary elections were held just weeks after the resignation of the prime minister and his cabinet, on May 15, 2002, which ushered in the new outsider party, the Lijst Pim Fortuyn (LPF) with 26 seats, making it the second largest party in the parliament, despite the assassination of its leader by a Dutch animal rights activist just a week before the election. Fully 79 percent of voters cast their ballots, nearly 6 percent more than had voted in the previous national election in 1998.

The Srebrenica investigation findings and Dutch frustration about the challenges to the Dutch educational, health, and welfare system posed by Muslim migrants, which were often the subject of negative stories in the press, formed the background against which public discontent deepened in the country as Pim Fortuyn and his new political party, LPF, moved ahead in the polls by preaching populist politics based on ethnic distinction and exclusion. The patterns of ethnicization of Islam and Muslims, as in the Balkans, though without the physical violence, were duplicated in many European countries without, it seems, any awareness that ethnic distinction was being used in almost the same way that it had been used politically by the Serbs. Europeans were oblivious to the fact that the construction of Islam as a race would have long-term, inescapable, and broad disintegrative effects.

The breakup of Yugoslavia and the ensuing civil war in the mid-1990s had dispersed thousands of Bosnian Muslim political refugees across Europe (as well as to the United States, Canada, and Australia). Those who had been relocated to western European countries were sent back to Bosnia when the war ended, despite their often successful integration by learning the local language and sending their children to local schools, and despite some protests from concerned European citizens.[23]

Illegal immigration in Europe soon became the top issue among all European leaders, particularly at the European Summit in Seville in June 2002. At the summit, prime ministers from all of Europe agreed that immigration was such a major problem that it could no longer be addressed effectively at the national level and had to be dealt with by the European Union.

At the same time, within the discussion of immigration, the alleged lack of integration of legal immigrants, especially Muslim migrants from North Africa and Turkey, and the ways in which they lived in Europe became an increasingly important issue frequently featured in the media. Consequently, Europe in the 1990s and the early twenty-first century saw an emphasis on populist appeals and the growth of support for populist political parties with strong anti-immigrant policies, including Filip de Winter's Vlaams Blok in Belgium; Jorg Haider in Austria; Pia Kjaersgaard's Danish People's Party (DPP) in Denmark; the Republican Party (REP), German People's Union (DVU), and National Democratic Party (NPD) in Germany, with no dominant leader; Jean-Marie Le Pen's Front National in France; Makis Voridis's Hellenic Front in Greece; Umberto Bossi's Northern League and the National Alliance in Italy; and Pim Fortuyn's LPF in the Netherlands.

Politicians often take their cues from the media and shape public policy accordingly. The increase in public support for far right parties cannot be seen in isolation from the demographic changes in Europe's major cities over the past two decades and the subsequent media coverage of those changes. A recent comparative study of neopopulism in its variety of forms in societies around the world shows how the media are instrumental in the rise and fall of populist parties and leaders.[24] Some researchers have found a connection between support for the far right and one's daily news diet. In particular, there seems to be a correlation with one item on the menu: crime news, a topic easily sensationalized and often linked to the poor and uneducated—a population in Europe that is usually mostly Muslim.[25] In Austria, for example, scholars have established a link between the type of newspaper one reads exclusively, and support for far right-wing populists such as Jorg Haider.[26]

Estimates of the Muslim population in Europe vary widely because it is difficult to collect the data on population characteristics via routine channels, as many countries either do not have a census or do not ask the questions necessary on the census to register one as a Muslim. In France, the last time a question on religion was asked in a census was 1872.[27] There is also the question of whether one can capture Muslim identity in a survey question about one's religion.[28] A report by France's High Council on Integration made the crucial point that the people mentioned in the report on Islam should not be considered "of Islamic faith" because:

> Religious identity is not stable or fixed data. Converts, religious disengagement or returning to the faith are all phenomena for which it is difficult to quantify the effects. We need to analyze with caution the reality which is extremely diverse, which covers the religious feeling, the individual experience which can be translated in a variety of attitudes in practicing the faith, within the Islamic communities which must construct their identity in a secular society where their faith is a minority.[29]

There are only two ways to understand Islamic belonging: If one is born to Islamic parents, he or she is a Muslim, and, in theory, everyone who says the *shahada*, the Islamic profession of faith, is also a Muslim, since the act of declaring "There is no God but God, and Muhammad is the messenger" is "the supreme manner of affirming Islamic faith."[30] It is therefore difficult to obtain exact figures because official statistics do not take into account the freedom of individuals to say or not to say the *shahada*.[31] A 2001 IFOP survey of Muslims in France conducted for *Le Monde* found that 78 percent described themselves as Muslim "believers," 16 percent said they were of Islamic descent, and 6 percent described themselves as without religion.[32] From this, we see that even those who identify themselves as Muslim do not always think of themselves in terms of the Islamic faith.

North Africans and Turks are the most common Muslim immigrant groups in Europe, but there are also other nationalities. "Islam in the Republic," a report produced by the French High Council on Integration (http://www.hci.gouv.fr/)

in 2000, provides the following breakdown of France's 5.98 million Muslims: 155,000 Algerians, 1 million Moroccans, 350,000 Tunisians, 350,000 Turks, 350,000 from other Arab countries, 250,000 from sub-Saharan African countries, 40,000 converts, 350,000 asylum seekers, 100,000 Asians, and 100,000 from other origins. Muslims accounted for about 9 percent of the total 62.3 million inhabitants of France. The French example reveals the kind of variety that can be found within Europe's immigrant communities originating in the Muslim diasporas.[33] There are 1.6 million Muslims in the United Kingdom, 2.8 percent of its 58.8 million people. In Austria, there are 339,000, which is just over 4 percent of the total 8.2 million in the general population. In Belgium, 400,000 Muslims make up 4 percent of the total population of 10.3 million. In Denmark, there are 170,000 Muslims or about 3 percent of the 5.4 million Danes. In Germany, most of the 3 million Muslims are Turks, and they are 3.6 percent of Germany's total population of 82.5 million. In Italy, there are 825,000 Muslims, who make up 1.4 percent of Italy's total population. In the Netherlands, there are 945,000 Muslims or 5.8 percent of the 16.3 million Dutch. In Spain, there are 1 million Muslims, accounting for 2.3 percent of 43.1 million Spaniards. And Sweden's 300,000 Muslims are 3 percent of that country's total population.[34]

In May and June 2005, the European Union referenda on the EU constitutional treaty—or, as framed by the media and politicians, "the EU constitution"— yielded a "no" in France and the Netherlands because, among many other reasons, the French and the Dutch were afraid of Turkey, a majority-Muslim country, joining the EU. The French and Dutch "no" votes are very significant for the future of the EU, because these two countries are seen as two of the founders of Europe; they were the most stable identities in the 1960s, when Germany was still divided between East and West, and Belgium was divided along linguistic lines. When France and the Netherlands are unhappy with the idea of a European constitution, what can we expect for the rest of Europe? Both France and the Netherlands have felt a decline of influence in Europe since the EU admitted ten new member countries in May 2004.

A general anxiety regarding migrants characterized the six years preceding the EU's expansion to include the ten new members, most of them in Eastern Europe, in 2004 and, later, the addition of Romania and Bulgaria in 2007. The contentious issue was that these countries were the source of large populations of migrants to Western Europe, and already France, the Netherlands, Denmark, Italy, Spain, and Germany had large migrant populations, specifically of Muslim migrants. Anxieties were heightened by the deteriorating economic situation after the introduction of the euro in 2000 and the influx of Polish workers eager to take jobs in Western Europe. These feelings were evidenced in the dramatic rise of the far right. In France, Jean-Marie Le Pen, a candidate who said the best place for Muslims was in their countries of origin, made it into the second round of the French presidential elections in 2002. In the Netherlands, Pim Fortuyn, a newspaper columnist who preached that Islam was backward, led a political revolution that same year, well before the killing of Theo van Gogh by a Dutch Muslim of Moroccan descent in 2004.

The Maghrebian Diaspora in Europe

Much of my fieldwork focused on one group of the Maghrebian diaspora, the Moroccans, and their interaction with others. Europe's Moroccan community provides an ideal lens through which to view the migration of Muslims in general into Europe because their self-identification with Islam and their economic and social interaction with their European environment is representative of a majority of Muslim immigrants. Moroccan immigrants appear in almost every European country, but they have higher concentrations in France, the Benelux countries, Spain, and Italy, with lower concentrations in Germany, Austria, Denmark, Sweden, Finland, the United Kingdom, and Portugal. Moroccan populations tend to cluster in larger metropolitan areas, with the exception of Spain and Italy, where they are found working in rural areas as agricultural laborers and small business entrepreneurs. There are Moroccan or North African enclaves in many major European cities, including Barcelona, London, Málaga, Paris, Marseilles, Lyon, Hamburg, Frankfurt, Brussels, Antwerp, Gouda, Enschede, The Hague, and Amsterdam. These enclaves include Moroccan grocery stores, bakeries, butchers, restaurants, other small businesses, and banks headquartered in Morocco, as well as Moroccan mosques.

Most Moroccans living in Europe share the tradition of returning home to Morocco during the summer holiday season. In the summer months, 3 million Moroccans living abroad return home to visit family and friends. From Germany to Holland, France to Spain, the highways become crowded with Moroccan motorists driving home for the holidays. The Moroccan government makes a major issue out of this annual ritual. Major banks in Morocco display posters advertising special events for Moroccan families visiting from Europe, and advertising campaigns on television, on radio, and in the press are geared toward them and their disposable income. In the past, Morocco earned its income from fishing, agriculture, and mining phosphates, but now the main source of revenue for the state is the income generated by emigrants who return on annual visits and who send money to the homeland throughout the year. According to the World Bank, the amount of money pumped into

Morocco's economy by its emigrants is greater than the sum produced by its tourism, and it is so substantial that the government uses projected emigrant remissions as collateral against corporate bonds. In any week in July and August, village streets throughout Morocco look as though they belong in the Netherlands or France on account of the predominance of license plates from these countries.

The journey itself seems to be a test of loyalty to the homeland. It can be treacherous for families trapped on hot, congested European highways for many hours at a stretch. By the time they reach Spain, they may find tents along the road with Moroccan doctors and nurses providing water and medical treatment. A few years ago, when there were too few ferries to support the flood of people returning home, some young Moroccan children died from overexposure to the sun while they waited in line for ferries. Many European countries publish brochures in Arabic to instruct people on the dangers of this journey. They encourage a vaccination program against tuberculosis and hepatitis. When the emigrant visitors finally arrive by ferry in Morocco in the hot summer months, they often find themselves met by state-sponsored camera crews. The resulting live interviews are broadcast across the country to dramatize the importance of coming home and to perpetuate the idea that their tenure in Europe is a visit rather than relocation.

The Moroccans constitute the most widely dispersed Arabic-speaking population in Europe. Although many of those who settled in the Netherlands and Germany are Berbers from the Rif and speak Berber more often than Arabic, most Moroccan households in Europe have a satellite dish to enable them to watch Arabic-language television channels, and Moroccans easily interact with other Muslims from other Arabic-speaking countries. Many families and people coming from the same villages in Morocco are dispersed across different European countries, creating the same kind of pan-European prevalence of certain family names that resulted from the Jewish diasporas. For example, there is the Alami family,[35] scattered across many European countries, including the Netherlands, France, Spain, and Belgium. Moroccan family reunions during the annual homecoming ritual, in which former members of a Moroccan village return together, have the feeling of an international summit, with the cacophony of European languages spoken by their children blending into one patched and improvised patois.

During these family gatherings, family members or former village neighbors can exchange stories about what life is like in their new countries. Many will have become citizens of a European country, but this newly acquired citizenship may be of little value if they want to bring their grandparents to visit children and grandchildren in Europe.

The procedures and paperwork for obtaining travel visas vary in difficulty from one country to another. Spain, for example, is more prone to granting travel visas to Moroccan relatives of their citizens than is the case in France or the Netherlands, where restrictions are so rigid that Moroccan applicants camp out at the French and Dutch embassies in Morocco for the months that it takes to attain a visa. This is part of why the ritual return home has become so important, for it is often the only time that grandparents can be reunited with their loved ones.

This annual pilgrimage reinforces Moroccans' strong national bond, not only because it renews an attachment to a cultural and ethnic homeland but also because although the emigrants may become citizens of their European countries of residence, the Moroccan government always considers them Moroccan. As recently as early 2007, the Netherlands felt the impact of this when a Dutch citizen who was born in Morocco was elected to the Dutch cabinet, along with a member who had been born in Turkey. Having two of the cabinet's twenty-five members wielding such dual citizenship raised fear in the Netherlands regarding the potential for divided loyalties.

The duality also becomes a complicating factor when there are transnational disputes over policies that pertain to private life.[36] Divorce and remarriage, for example, are not so simple for Moroccan women in most of Europe. Different rules apply in different European countries. France and Belgium have bilateral agreements with Morocco, which require that they recognize repudiation as divorce for marriages performed under Moroccan law.[37] The rest of northern Europe has so far chosen not to make bilateral agreements on divorce, largely as a result of lobbying by immigrant Moroccan women against the French and Belgian examples.[38]

With such public influences being exerted in such private matters, Moroccan religious leaders and Moroccan mosques[39] play a central role in the practice of Islam in Europe. There are many mosques in Europe, but no official count takes into consideration the foreign national origins of the mosques. There are also no statistics on the many unofficial or illegal mosques found in basements, hidden rooms, and other spaces. The many Moroccan mosques in Europe are often frequented by other Arabic speakers, including Egyptians, Syrians, Iraqis, Algerians, and Tunisians, as well as Muslims from sub-Saharan Africa. A number of Moroccan mosques also have imams from these Arabic-speaking countries rather than from Morocco. Many Moroccan imams can be found in European mosques that cater to Algerians and Tunisians. In France, for example, 40 percent of the imams are Moroccan, and Moroccan imams work in mosques in communities of people from the different Maghreb countries.[40]

The Netherlands as Europe's Pinnacle of Contested Issues

The Netherlands provides a fascinating context for the study of social cohesion and social change, especially concerning religion and values. The high population density and the comparatively small geographic size of the Netherlands also make it a more manageable laboratory for the social researcher.

The Dutch are known for their "tolerant" society, a reputation earned by Holland's role as a refuge for Jews during the Spanish Inquisition and for Huguenot Protestants who left France after the revocation of the Edict of Nantes in 1685. Amsterdam is a model city for certain social parameters and is arguably the most tolerant city in the world in terms of the use of drugs, public displays of sexuality, and acceptance of all sexual orientations. Consequently, one of the most contested issues between Muslim immigrants and their Dutch communities is sexual morality. The contrast between Muslim and Dutch norms on this issue is particularly pointed in Amsterdam, which has a well-deserved international reputation for its "safe sex" red light district, a state-sanctioned business district where partially clothed women display themselves in windows and sex is overtly for sale at state-regulated prices. By contrast, prostitution in much of North Africa, and certainly in Morocco, is covert, religiously prohibited, and socially denied. The hypocrisy regarding prostitution in Morocco is obvious in tourist areas, where sex workers can be seen soliciting visitors, mostly from the Persian Gulf countries.

Amsterdam is perhaps best known in recent years for its openness on the issue of sexual orientation, another area of contention between Muslim immigrants and other Dutch citizens. The first official homosexual marriages in Europe were held in Amsterdam's city hall at the stroke of midnight as the country's gay marriage law went into effect in April 2000. Two couples (two gay men and two lesbian women) married before the world press. There is an unusual openness among the gay community in Amsterdam, which is especially noticeable on Gay Pride Day, when the canals are filled with boats on parade, and millions of gay Dutch citizens and visitors participate in more displays of public nudity than is usual for Amsterdam. In Dutch public opinion, there is a clear preference for homosexual civil liberties and overwhelming support for nondiscrimination on the basis of sexual orientation.

The gay community also maintains an important visible presence in almost all national political parties (with the exception of the small fundamentalist Christian parties), as well as in positions of political power. Additionally, there are important cross-party political alliances on the basis of sexual identity at the local and national levels. In Amsterdam's March 2002 city council elections, for example, two women from opposing parties took out one advertisement in the local newspaper that displayed each of their smiling faces with the caption "Vote for Your Lesbian Candidate."

That same month, in an interview with a leading newspaper, Pim Fortuyn, the gay politician and then leader of a small but successful local party called Leefbaar Nederland (LN, which translates as Livable Netherlands), called for an amendment to the Dutch Constitution removing the protection accorded to Islam as a religion because, he argued, Islam discriminated against constitutionally protected homosexuals.[41] Making the conflict between the practice of Islam and the practice of homosexuality a contested constitutional issue led to Fortuyn's almost immediate expulsion from LN by the board of the party. Then, within only weeks of a national election, Fortuyn immediately embarked on a successful personal campaign to form his own party list, Lijst Pim Fortuyn (LPF), which swept into power in the May 2002 election, just over a week after Fortuyn was gunned down by an animal rights activist.

A year later, in the March 2003 Amsterdam city council elections, Geert Dales, the successful local leader of the VVD, the free-market liberal party, campaigned on the promise that, if elected, he would organize a regular monthly reception (*borrel*) for gay and lesbian civil servants. During that city council election campaign (which also happened to coincide with the Islamic holy month of Ramadan), he publicly invited imams in the city to go with him into some of the city's homosexual bars and meeting places.

For practicing Muslims, all of this is anathema. Homosexuality, by most traditional interpretations of the Koran, is an abomination against God. Although condemnation of homosexuality varies within the community—and even from imam to imam—culturally, it is still definitely not widely accepted.

With these juxtapositions in mind, the Netherlands offers a microcosm of how individuals and groups live together within the context of heightened social conflict over fundamental values and is therefore of paramount importance to understanding the future direction of European Islam.

Multiple Perspectives on European Islam

European Islam is still being defined; it takes distinctive forms in different European national and local contexts while sharing some common elements. When considering European Islam and its development, it's necessary to understand the differing European and Muslim attitudes regarding generational, gender, and class divisions, as well as differences between those who are active and passive in the public arena. Another view of its development stems from European political elites who are concerned about the growth of the Muslim population in their own countries. This is a multifaceted perspective that varies not only between countries and regions but also across political parties and even among individual political notables. A third view is that of observers of contemporary society, those who tell us daily what of importance is happening in the world: journalists and academics are both observers and participants in the public discussion of Islam, with the media providing the backdrop against which many contested issues are discussed. Sometimes the media provide the impetus for public debate by highlighting certain topics or revealing controversial stands. Last but by no means least are the perspectives of the indigenous publics who are described in the various European languages with special terms to indicate their Germanness, Swedishness, Dutchness, Danishness, Frenchness, or Italianness. These publics also include the active and the passive, the interested and uninterested, the educated and uneducated, and those who may or may not be prejudiced against those who look different or speak a different language.[42]

Academics, particularly those who study religion and politics, challenge our traditional ways of thinking about the boundaries of disciplines because the discussion of Islam is no longer the discussion of the sociology or anthropology of religion but is instead a discussion of religion in politics and society.

Theorizing Migration, Islam, and Social Change in Europe

The topic of Muslims in Europe is part of the larger topic of migration, a subject that has attracted the attention of scholars from a range of disciplines. Migration encompasses a wide range of policy and political topics[43] and has been approached differently in different disciplines.[44] Migration and the comparative policy study of the regulation of immigration reveal that, from a global perspective, states continue to think about it in "a unilateral, sovereign manner," as if the state is "untouched by the massive domestic and international transformations that are increasingly reconfiguring states and the interstate system."[45]

Different academic perspectives exist on the extent to which immigration is changing the nation-state. One such perspective compares post–World War II politics of immigration control and integration in Britain, Germany, and the United States and argues that the nation-state has proven to be quite resilient in the face of immigration.[46] Another perspective warns that when EU countries increase immigrant participation in EU citizenship while allowing dual nationality, the principle of an essential singular nationality underlying the nation-state is shaken, and in this way the policy responses to migration—both those that restrict and those that are more lenient—are gradually transforming state political institutions.[47] For example, in 2006, Spain passed legislation allowing citizens of Latin America who have Spanish ancestry to immigrate to Spain and become citizens at roughly the same time that it also granted amnesty to up to 1 million illegal immigrants, including thousands of Muslims.[48] The former group may have been intended to balance the effect of the latter on Spain's culture.

Regardless of the numerous approaches one might use to examine the topic of migration and Islam, as long as those approaches are confined to legal, institutional, and rights-based perspectives, the crux of the anxiety felt by the general public might not be grasped because it is the product of something beyond all of these.

Bourdieu's beautifully written ethnography of Algeria, is based on his fieldwork in that country in the 1950s. Significantly, Mohammed Arkoun, a professor of Islam at the Sorbonne and an Algerian himself, describes Bourdieu's study as the uncontestable starting point for any understanding of contemporary Algeria.[49] First published in 1958 and republished in 1962, it is probably Boudieu's least cited work, even though many of the terms and concepts he employs in later publications stem from this seminal study. The book discusses the situation in French Algeria in the late colonial period during the 1950s, specifically focusing on the change from a traditional peasant society to an industrial society with paid laborers and the consequences of rural-urban migration within Algerian society. Migrants from the villages to the cities left to find jobs in factories or to do other manual labor. The migrants brought with them their own traditions, which included a strong emphasis on religion. Bourdieu reveals that Islam became a very important indicator of difference when the village migrants came into contact with white French society. In *Sociologie de l'Algérie* Bourdieu sets forth five important laws for understanding the process of change that develops when migration occurs and migrant communities develop in new social contexts:

- The law of unequal opportunity. Certain aspects of the cultural systems, things like demographics, economics, and technology, are transformed rapidly, while other aspects like beliefs, traditions, and practices change slowly. This disjuncture brings a profound disequilibrium.
- The law of differential compatibility. This law defines the limits of what can and cannot be borrowed from the host culture and incorporated by the migrant community.

- The law of context. What is borrowed from the host culture is reinterpreted by the migrants in a new context that results from their perception of and contribution to the host society.
- The law of the scale of change and the change of the code of reference. Cultural aspects are altered and change their significance in the new cultural environment of the host society because of the presence of migrants.
- The law of interconnection. Cultural elements, some details of which have been altered, can have a significant impact on bringing about a radical change in positions of members of both communities, the host and the migrant[50]

Each of these laws has an application to the situation of Muslim immigrants in Europe, not only at the time of their arrival en masse in the 1960s but also today. The colonial situation in Algeria in the 1950s is analogous to the situation of Muslim immigrants in Europe. In the 1950s, Algerian villagers moved from small rural settings into growing urban centers, where they found work. There they found the imported capitalized system, a new sophisticated system of production involving factories and mass production. The confluence between the Algerian village migrants and the French entrepreneurs led to an acceleration of change within both the North African and European worlds. The normal evolution of society was altered by the economic necessity of this migration. In more recent decades, they have encountered the same circumstances in Europe, though amplified and consequently with more amplified results. In both contexts, the new social-economic-linguistic situation forced new social practices. Both the past and the present reveal that the first points of contact, the process of adaptation of the immigrants to their new situation, and the changes experienced by parents and their children all determine how their presence will shape the culture around them.

Stigmatization, Exclusion, Culture, and Contentious Politics

Bourdieu spent part of his life in Algeria's Kabilie region, where he developed much of his oeuvre regarding the integration of European and Muslim societies. He was so moved by his experiences there that in the early 1990s, he called on other academics raised in the Muslim world, including the philosopher Jacques Derrida (though he was not Muslim, he was nonetheless a native of the Muslim sphere) and the writer Salman Rushdie, to help refugee intellectuals from Islamic communities under the auspices of Villes Refuges [Cities of Refuge], an initiative that provided funding and safe houses for those who had formerly taught in universities in the Muslim world.

In the summer of 1995, Derrida and Bourdieu met in Portugal with other academics for the first annual Writer's Parliament. I was there as Bourdieu's guest because I had collaborated with him at College de France, and we had continued a working relationship after my election to Holland's Parliament, thanks in part to the political impact of immigration issues. One evening, as we traveled by bus from dinner on the outskirts of Lisbon to our hotel, Derrida, by then in his sixties, turned to me and remarked on the couscous that the restaurant had served us, "My mother's was better"—a statement that prompted a conversation about the food of our childhood. Bourdieu contributed recollections of the food he had enjoyed during his stay in Algeria, and the exchange brought to light the seemingly mundane, yet profoundly important cultural differences that are as deep and mysterious as one's DNA. Among us, the conversation was a touchstone, but to our fellow passengers, we must have sounded like a group of North Africans seeing importance in something that was only, after all, a meal. Because we could rely on each other for reassurance concerning our identity as academics, fully integrated in our European environment, their view of us had little effect. But for those Muslims who are cut off from their European environs, either by their own choice or by other difficulties like language, the effect of such outside scrutiny may very well change the trajectory of their lives.

The most superficial glance at Europe's culture will bring to light the stigmatization of Muslims. Phrases like *geitenneuker* [goatfucker] and *kut Marokkanen* [cunt Moroccans] in Dutch or *boungoule* in French are used with a frequency and consistency that Paul Sniderman, a political scientist at Stanford University, has said are critical in creating prejudice against immigrants. He notes that it is not the degree of negativity but this consistency that actually builds prejudice.

An Italian Example

The need to categorize for the purpose of distinguishing those who are not like ourselves is the subject of a program of research conducted by Sniderman and his colleagues. In *The Outsider: Prejudice and Politics in Italy*, they use experimental survey methods to discuss "the social construction of the concept of the outsider."[51] The book is important not only because the Italian case has characteristics that reflect the party systems, immigrant groups, and media coverage of immigrants in other European countries but also because the authors show how deep and widespread prejudice is in Italy and make a compelling argument that it could become much worse there and in other European countries in the future if certain practices continue. Sniderman and colleagues define *prejudice* as "a readiness to attribute negative characteristics, or correspondingly, to decline to attribute positive characteristics to a group."[52] They specify that "the more consistently a person attributes negative characteristics, or alternatively, declines to attribute positive characteristics to a group, the more prejudiced he or she is."[53] They approach the subject from the perspective of previous work on race in the United States, with the idea that race is "especially stigmatizing" in Europe,[54] and note that Italy is an interesting case because of the difference in attitude toward "white" immigrants from Eastern Europe versus "black ones from Africa," and they also distinguish between those from North Africa, such as Morocco, Tunisia, or Algeria, who "are not considered black by themselves or by Italians." These three immigrant groups, Eastern Europeans, Africans, and North Africans, also represent key immigrant groups in other Western European countries.

The Sniderman study provides several important findings. First, no matter where the immigrants come from, substantial majorities of Italians are willing to blame them for social problems, specifically crime, unemployment, and public health lapses. Majorities of Italians find fault with immigrants, attributing negative characteristics (such as laziness or violence) to them or failing to attribute positive characteristics (such as honesty) to them.[55]

In the independent Italian film *Through the Eyes of Another*, the protagonist is a Kurdish refugee, yet in one scene, the film's writer shows a group of Italian youths referring to him as a "Moroccan"—a descriptor that conveys someone who is an undesirable outsider who should not be having a relationship with an Italian woman.

They did not know his race, but his appearance, which they associated with Moroccans, was enough to convince them of his unworthiness. Simply put, race is not the primary basis for prejudice in Italy, and all three immigrant groups, as well as a fourth group (southern Italians), were found to be seen in equally negative terms. Second, "two explanatory mechanisms, one expressive and the other rational, lie behind categorization and thereby lie behind prejudice."[56] Specifically, "The more likely that Italians are to believe that other people cannot be trusted, the more likely they are to categorize immigrants as the other. Similarly, the more importance that Italians attach to economic security as compared to either liberty or equality, the more prejudiced against immigrants they are."[57] Third, they show that prejudice has the power to potentially "reshape the ideological equilibrium."[58] This is because intolerant attitudes have the built-in political constituency of those "who subscribe to the values of the right" in which "authority values" are important, such as "a belief in the indispensability . . . of strictness and discipline; of sacrifice and self-denial, and the aggressive enforcement of order and the assurance of stability." Yet they show that the appeal of these authority values is not confined to the political right and that there is indeed "a large constituency [for these values] on the left, particularly among the less educated, which makes up the bulk of the left in Europe."[59] Fourth, their analysis of the vote in the 1994 Italian general election showed that hostility or prejudice toward immigrants continued to be a significant influence on vote choice, even after controlling for demographic characteristics and the voter's ideological perspective on the left-right scale. They state that it was surprising to find that "hostility" or "prejudice" remained a significant influence on vote choice in that election because immigrants and immigration were not a major issue in the campaign but rather one issue among many others, including political corruption. They argue that if hostility or prejudice toward immigrants can be an important predictor of the vote in an election in which immigration was not a major issue, then it could become a profoundly important influence on vote choice in an election in which immigration was a major issue.

Anti-Immigration and Winning Elections

The Netherlands general election campaign in May 2002 was just such an election, and the result was exactly as Sniderman and his colleagues would have predicted. The party with the strongest anti-immigrant stand easily won, despite having been created only months before the election. With immigration as its sole issue, Pim Fortuyn's Lijst Fortuyn party, even with its namesake recently deceased (or perhaps because its namesake was recently deceased), handily gained 26 seats in a 150-seat Parliament. With this example in mind, it may be deduced that Sniderman and his colleagues, despite their pioneering approach to understanding intolerance and its contribution to political change, fail to address one very important characteristic that contributes to the social construction of outsiders: religion. Sniderman and his colleagues also recognize this drawback to their own work and call attention to it in their concluding chapter:

> There are a number of issues that we recognized as important, but lacked the means to address in this particular study. Perhaps the most important of these is the question of religion. The place of Muslim practices, particularly in public institutions like schools, has become a major source of friction, arguably different in kind than resentment over other forms of difference. It is different in kind because, to take France as an example, a normative consensus on tolerance may itself be at odds with the public expression of religious

practice. Religion may divide more deeply because it stands as a marker not merely of different beliefs but of opposing ways of life.[60]

Immigration Crisis as a Catalyst for Social Problems in Europe

Immigration in Europe has been a subject of considerable importance to political elites for the past few decades. Gary Freeman argues that the immigration crisis in the EU in the 1980s served to hinder progress toward advanced political and economic integration leading up to the Maastricht Treaty, one of the foundational agreements of the organization of the European Union.[61] The vast majority of immigration has been legal, with migrants arriving in Europe as guest workers in the 1960s and bringing their families afterward. The public perception is that the size of this population is growing among younger cohorts of society. In Amsterdam and Oslo by 2001, for example, news reports mentioned that the most popular newborn boy's name was Mohammed. There are similar trends in a number of other European cities. However, Muslims also account for many of the illegal immigrants, temporary workers, and asylum seekers and refugees. In recent years, it has been hard to avoid the compelling visuals of refugees and asylum seekers washing ashore on Europe's beaches. As one English intellectual recently said to me, "It's not easy to always keep in mind the many distinctions between Muslims: the asylum seekers, the illegals, the secular Muslims, the moderates, the fundamentalists, and then of course there are the terrorists."

A Brief Overview of European Attitudes and Policies

Freeman compares different states' capabilities to regulate migration and shows that there is considerable variation across them, which fluctuates cyclically. He makes a very useful distinction between four areas of migration policy: "managing legal immigration, controlling illegal migration, administering temporary worker programs, and processing asylum seekers and refugees."[62] Muslim immigrants fall into each of Freeman's four categories.[63] Freeman demonstrates the importance of uniting historical considerations with specific examples of policies and their outcomes for immigrants. His work emphasizes the way in which political elites control decisions about immigration policies and how these are, for the most part, hidden from public scrutiny.[64] He claims that migrant-friendly immigration policy is the product of pro-immigration lobbying from families, antiracist movements, lawyers, intellectuals, and the media.[65] These "client politics" help explain differences and similarities across countries in terms of immigration and integration policies.

Strikingly, European attitudes and policies are aimed at those whose families, in many cases, have lived in European countries for generations. It's important to remember that when examining official government policies.

Thus programs designed to foster the integration of migrants generally apply to Muslim migrants. The following subsections draw on government and private nonprofit policy summaries, media reports, and the Washington-based Pew Global Attitudes Project of 2006 to compare attitudes and programs aimed at Muslim migrants among four European countries: Germany, Great Britain, France, and Spain.

Germany's National Integration Plan

Germany has a Muslim population of more than 3 million, and Muslims make up a third of all foreigners in the country. Most are of Turkish origin—about a third of all naturalizations involve Turkish migrants.

According to a representative survey among German Muslims, the majority of Germany's Muslim population regards itself as German: 82 percent want to stay in Germany, and two-thirds want to be naturalized (Survey of the Islamic Archive, 2002). The same survey, conducted two years later, found that 89 percent think that it is important to integrate, and only 5 percent opposed doing so.

However, naturalizations of Muslims in general have steadily decreased since 2001, which is due, in no small way, to discouraging public discourse primarily concerned with terrorism—discourse that became amplified following later terrorist attacks in Madrid in March 2004 and in London in July 2005.

Following the London bombings, Christian Wulff, the head of Germany's Christian Democratic Union party in Lower Saxony, proposed video surveillance of mosques to prevent a possible similar attack in Germany. His response to the London attack and the support his response received from many Germans illustrated how closely terrorism and Islam are linked in the German consciousness. In the towns of Osnabrück and Braunschweig in his province, the identities of all attendees of the Friday services at mosques were checked. The mosques were searched, entry and exit from a predominantly Muslim neighborhood were blocked, and identities of its residents were checked.

A 2006 study conducted by the University of Bielefeld's Institute for Interdisciplinary Research on Conflict and Violence revealed that 39 percent agree with the statement: "Due to the many Muslims living here I sometimes feel like a foreigner in my own country"—an increase from the 35 percent who felt that way in 2004. According to the Pew Research Center, the proportion of

Germans who think that relations between Muslims and Western countries are generally bad is the highest of all Western countries, 70 percent.

In "Der unheimliche Muslim," published in the journal *Soziale Welt Sonderband* in 2006, Werner Schiffauer explains that a "growing number of naturalisations turn Ausländer [foreigners] into citizens and threaten to change the balance of power between what Elias calls the 'established' and the 'outsiders.'"[66] He refers to the idea of "moral panic" raised by Stanley Cohen in the early 1970s and points out that such a panic is characterized by an "exaggerated presentation of the threats for society, by a generalised atmosphere of distrust and by a widespread tendency to witch-hunt."

In an effort to close the widening gap between migrants and other Germans, in July 2007, German Chancellor Andrea Merkel unveiled her National Integration Plan (NIP), designed to give officials throughout the government, from the smallest hamlets to major metropolitan areas, a framework for conducting migrant programs. The NIP is based on the EU's Common Basic Principles, and like it and most other government documents, it doesn't mention Muslims per se, but Germany did officially address the issue of Muslim immigration in the Islamkonferenz (Islamic Conference), which met for the first time in September 2006. According to the Washington-based nonprofit Migration Policy Institute, Germany's Islamic Conference identified specific needs that would have to be addressed in order to promote immigration. They include language courses geared toward the specialized needs of targeted immigrant groups—such as separate classes for women—and better educational opportunities for immigrant youth, with the specific goal of ensuring that more immigrants enter the upper educational tracks and have a better chance to enter universities.

The Washington-based Pew Global Attitudes Project, which posed questions to Muslims and non-Muslims about each other in fifteen countries in 2006, included selected responses in a section devoted to differences in attitudes toward Muslim migrants across all the countries. In that section, Stefanie Mates, a psychotherapist in Berlin, is quoted as saying, "Education and integration is the key. Being able to speak German is essential for integration and understanding the culture and values. Learning the language is so important. Yet so many live in tightly organized families who do not speak German."

Britain's Exceptionalism

As early as the fourteenth century, Muslims were presented as being familiar to the English. In his *Canterbury Tales*, Geoffrey Chaucer writes about a physician who had been educated in the sciences as taught by Arabic philosophers, including Averroës. About 600 years later, during World War I, more than a million troops—many of them Muslim—were transported from India to fight on Great Britain's behalf. In early 2008, "Pavilion Revisited" an emotionally startling exhibit by the British photographer Said Adrus (whose own father fought for Britain in World War II) reminded attendees at Woking's Lightbox Gallery that a popular dog-walking site, Horsell Common, was once the designated burial ground for Indian-British soldiers, mostly Muslim, killed in World War I. The graves were moved to a site in Surrey in 1969, after vandals desecrated them. Sadly, that site, Brookwood Cemetery, has also been violated by anti-Islamic vandals. The 1930s saw a particularly large influx of Pakistani Muslims to Britain, as pressure from an emerging independent India made many of them seek a livelihood and peace away from their homeland.

Various works, including *Islam in Britain, 1558–1685* by Nabil I. Matar, *The Infidel Within: Muslims in Britain since 1800* by Humayun Ansari, and the indispensable *Cultures in Conflict: Christians, Muslims and Jews in the Age of Discovery* by Bernard Lewis, offer excellent explorations of Islam's centuries-old relationship with the English.[67] This book does not attempt to do so and, for the sake of brevity and pertinence, limits its scope to Muslim immigration beginning after World War II.

Like West Germany, Great Britain faced a shortage of labor after the war, so workers from the Muslim corners of its former empire were encouraged to immigrate. In his 2003 paper Philip Lewis[68] offers a glimpse into integration efforts among Britain's Muslim religious leadership. "If in Germany," notes Lewis, "there is communication, discussion but no interaction, in Britain we see real attempts within the Muslim communities to encourage social, political interaction with wider society; and to legitimize that islamically and that is new. . . ." Lewis continues:

> British Muslims have become aware that wider society is not inhospitable to many of their concerns. Britain allows more space for
> Muslim self-expression than most other European countries: a State which comprises four nations, which has gradually made institutional space for denominational diversity since the Reformation, and which enjoys the relatively plastic category "British" allowing some measure of multiple identities—British Jews—has gradually extended to Muslims the same rights enjoyed by other faiths.
>
> Because public and civic life is permeated with Christian influence—with the existence of an established Church—British society is

proving increasingly responsive to the religious concerns of Muslims. Theology departments have been extended to include religious studies. All new religious education syllabi used in State schools have to reflect the social fact of religious diversity. Because the State funds religious schools that provide education for more than 20 per cent of all children, this category has been extended since 1998 to include a handful of Muslim schools. Any religious group can found a private school. There are now more than 80 Islamic private schools. In September 1999 the Prison Service appointed the first Muslim Adviser and there are now a growing number of Muslim chaplains in prisons and hospitals. Public service broadcasting has always included explicit religious slots, which now include Muslim voices.

This is the context within which we can now detect a willingness by some Muslims to acknowledge and tackle pressing social problems, as well as professionalisation or clericalisation of religious leaders, who are exploring the institutional spaces for religious personnel in British society.

Yet, according to the findings of the Pew Global Attitudes Project in 2006—three years after Lewis's paper was written and one year after the July 7, 2005, terrorist bombings in London—though non-Muslim Britons were generally more tolerant of Muslims than the non-Muslim citizenry of other European countries, British Muslims held far more negative views of non-Muslims than did Islamic minorities elsewhere in Europe. As reported by the *Guardian* newspaper, "a significant majority viewed western populations as selfish, arrogant, greedy and immoral. Just over half said westerners were violent. While the overwhelming majority of European Muslims said westerners were respectful of women, fewer than half British Muslims agreed. Another startling result found that only 32 percent of Muslims in Britain had a favourable opinion of Jews, compared with 71 percent of French Muslims."

The July 7, 2005, bombings apparently had little impact on British views of Islam: the poll found that 63 percent of the general population in the United Kingdom had a favorable opinion of Muslims, down only slightly from 67 percent in 2004. Attitudes in Britain were more positive than in Germany and Spain, where the view of Muslims suffered markedly (it should be noted that Spain endured a terrorist attack in March 2004), and were about the same as in France. Yet, British Muslims were more pessimistic than their counterparts in Germany, France, and Spain about the ability of devout Muslims to live in a modern society. Only 17 percent of British Muslims believed that Arabs were involved in the September 11, 2001, attacks, as compared with 48 percent of French Muslims. Nearly half of British Muslims blamed non-Muslims in the West for the tension between Muslims and non-Muslims, and more than a quarter of their non-Muslim neighbors agreed with them. By comparison, in Germany and France, both communities blamed each other in roughly equal measure. Less than a third of British non-Muslims said they viewed Muslims as violent.

Among its featured responses in the United Kingdom, the Pew Project included that of a health worker named Shahedah Vawda:

> After the bombings on 7 July last year I was surprised by how fantastic Londoners were, and how many people were able to look beyond what had happened. . ... Of course it's not a perfect society, but I was expecting the backlash to be a lot worse. . ... Where we are at the moment? We have two sides that don't understand each other particularly well. And I think both are equally responsible. I think the Muslims need to be introspective and look at their community from within and put their house in order. We do have a serious issue in terms of the miseducation of youth about Islamic practices, what's acceptable and what is not. We have to look at the importation of foreign imams.

France

In France, more than in any other nation surveyed as part of the Pew Global Attitudes Project, both non-Muslims and Muslims overwhelmingly (74 percent and 72 percent, respectively) believed that there is no conflict between living as a devout Muslim and living in a modern society.

2

Immigration without Integration

All European societies are now faced with Islamic diasporas that disturb established ways of dealing with religion in the public space.
—Danièle Hervieu-Léger, 203

Muslims are clearly present in a secular Europe and yet, in an important sense, absent of it.
—Tallal Assad, *Formations of the Secular: Christianity, Islam, Modernity*, 159

After tension between the Dutch and Moroccan communities (keeping in mind that many of the latter were, in fact, Dutch citizens) reached a boiling point in fall 2002, the Dutch government felt it had to do something to combat the negative image that surrounded the Moroccan community. A small company called Attacom was hired to do a proactive campaign to improve the image of Moroccans.

The Ministry of Justice commissioned the firm to develop a national campaign, and by November 4, 2002, the "Leuke Marokkaan!" was born. *Leuk* translates as amusing, funny, or entertaining and is colloquially often used simply to mean "nice." The Nice Moroccan campaign included a Web site and brochures, as well as posters in most tramways and buses. One of the posters was of a young man saying: "I love boerenkool [farmer's cabbage], but with lamb!" A total of 42 cities, 25 major municipalities, and 17 smaller ones adopted the campaign. An Attacom staff member noted that the aim was "to project a positive image of Moroccans because they are so often painted negatively in the news."[1] In the brochure, which was called "Hoe leuk zijn de Marokkanen?" ["How nice/fun are the Moroccans?"], the men and women were all young and attractive. One woman wearing a scarf, identified as "Fouzia Kassi, 25," was featured saying: "This scarf is part of my identity." Clearly, this was Attacom's attempt to alleviate pressure within the second part of the trifecta of coercion—the pressure felt by a Muslim individual or community when Islam and the larger society send conflicting messages. Attacom was attempting to integrate the directive of Islam to dress in a certain way with the message of the larger society, that is, to be tolerant of how people dress.

But the response to the national campaign was not what Attacom had hoped. Its reception among intellectual circles was made clear in the left-wing weekly news magazine *De Groene Amsterdammer*'s headline on November 16, 2002: "Hoe leuk zijn kut-Marokkanen" ["How nice are cunt Moroccans?"]. The "cunt" reference was an intentionally ironic tip of the hat to a popular rap song by a Moroccan. The subhead was franker: "I can't stand to hear the word Moroccan anymore"—which summed up the way most people I spoke with thought of the publicity campaign.

Similarly, many studies involving sociological fieldwork, survey research, and opinion polls show that perceptions of Muslims are far from positive, thanks largely to the trickle-down effect of a constant media drone on the topic—though usually not a drone that carries the good intentions of Attacom's campaign. Michèle Lamont shows in *The Dignity of Working Men* that "French workers associate the alleged weak work ethic of Muslims with a parasitic nature"[2] and "immigrants are viewed as the ultimate slackers."[3] Through the eyes of French workers, the resistance to assimilation by their Muslim immigrant coworkers is even more intolerable than lack of self-reliance or lack of civility. French workers see their immigrant coworkers' religious homogeneity—a cohesiveness that is born of an attention to detail in Islamic practice that is intrinsic to Islam itself—as resistance to assimilation. These "ethnoracial" differences, as viewed by French workers, are taken for granted, naturalized through cultural explanation that makes Muslims incompatible with the French.[4] For example, Muslims have "barbarian habits"; they kill sheep during Ramadan.[5] Michèle Lamont explains that the French need to assimilate Muslims springs largely from the French perception of France's civilization-forming role in the world. With this in mind, the French have traditionally been protective of their national identity, resenting the threat of foreign influences. The lower status of Muslim immigrants has to do with a castelike system that the French maintained with former colonies; this "caste relationship is particularly strong because of the traditional salience of Islam as a French nemesis."[6]

Many reports and studies on the representation of Muslims in the news media and politics show the stigmatized image and place of Muslims in European societies.[7] There is a tendency in Europe to ethnicize and Islamize social problems, a tendency that is evident in the way, for example, that riots in 2005 in France's *banlieues*—the public housing projects north of Paris—were characterized as Muslim immigrant-related events.[8] The root cause of the riots was unemployment and its attendant restlessness, something that could be found anywhere in the world, regardless of the presence of any Muslim immigrant community, but the two topics—unemployment and Muslimness—have become intertwined in the media and in politics.[9] There is a grain of truth in the stereotype if we look at the numbers of unemployed people of Muslim descent.[10]

To understand this phenomenon, it is desirable to go back to the beginning of the establishment of Muslim communities—the arrival of guest workers. A long-term perspective illuminates the context of present controversies and problems in societies and also how the image of Muslims in Europe has changed as they have been transformed from guest workers to citizens and finally to Muslims, having rediscovered their faith through the outside pressure of the European environment. The history of the present multiple identifications of Muslims has to do with the changing political and social context of Europe and its own evolution under the pressures of globalization. Arkoun speaks of the "history-problem," forgetting the past because of the pressure of the present, a circumstance that leads to the construction of imagined identities.[11] Arkoun urges us to study the European societies from an anthropological and historical perspective in order to deconstruct the mythical and ideological constructions surrounding Islam and Muslims in Europe. The reconstruction of this culturally forgotten history is essential to shed more light on present conflicts. Today especially, Islam makes waves in the media and triggers social controversies daily everywhere in Europe.[12]

Islam in Modern Europe

The starting point of a significant Islamic presence is found even before the multiplication of mosques across the continent. As early as the 1960s, the first wave of North African guest workers in Europe began informally organizing groups based on political allegiance to the ruler of their homelands. In some cases, the exiled opposition formed its own groups. This initial configuration would produce two forms of Islamization that act simultaneously on the immigrant population. One form is an Islamization through official Islam that trickles down to the workers through the presence of imams and even outright spies sponsored by the governments and embassies of the Islamic home countries; another type of Islamization is created by the influence of political refugees, those who had been exiled from their home countries, many of whom were and are fundamentalists. This latter, radical form of Islamization is the result of the exile from Egypt of groups like the Muslim Brotherhood and their affiliates, who disseminated their doctrines in Algeria, Afghanistan, Pakistan, and India, where it was adopted by those who would emigrate to France and England.[13]

This transplantation spawned a new ideological interpretation of Islam carried out by some forms of translational Dawa that has as its goals active Islamic missionary work and indoctrination in traditions, as well as political power. Both types of Islamizations rely on the naïveté of a European culture that defined itself as secular and therefore not vulnerable to religious influences. Talal Assad explains that Muslims "are included within and excluded from Europe at one and the same time in a special way, and that this has less to do with the 'absolutist Faith' of Muslims living in a secular environment and more with European notions of 'culture' and 'civilization' and the 'secular state,' 'majority,' and minority.'"[14]

A long-term historical perspective will shed more light on the sociogenesis of the actual state of Islam throughout Europe. However, Mohammed Arkoun has made a remarkable contribution toward a comprehensive understanding of Islam by limiting his focus to France alone. He posits that the Mediterranean is more or less a lake, the shores of which have become Christianized or Islamized, depending on political whims. He compares modern guest workers to the Arabic medical doctors who traveled to Europe during the Middle Ages. The role of Muslims was decisive during World War I and World War II in shaping the French army.[15] In total, the Maghreb sent 280,000 soldiers, a little more than 2 percent of its population to join the French army to fight against Germany in World War I, and 340,000 fought in World War II.[16] Many cemeteries in Europe like the one in the southern Netherlands feature crescent insignia and Arabic epitaphs. They are visible archives of the involvement of Muslims in freeing Europe. Paris's first mosque was built by Morocco in 1926, another was built in Fréjus in 1928, and in 1930, a French-Muslim hospital was built. There has always, according to Arkoun, been an ongoing exchange of people and ideas between Europe and North Africa. He presents the two societies as evolving in tandem but believes that North Africa's development was retarded by the politicization of Islam, specifically its use by North African rulers who sought to legitimize their authority. Indeed, it was this politicization that prevented the Arab world from participating in Europe's enlightenment. By co-opting Islam, the political powers also muted ideas about self-determination, effectively smothering inquiry.

In *Islam in Europe*, sociologist Jack Goody writes: "Islam was always the formidable Other since the eighth century."[17] But the frequent neglect of the role of Islam in Europe has to do with the balance of power reinforced by Orientalism, the view that Islam is exotic and irrational, and therefore not to be taken seriously.[18]

Based on a series of lectures Clifford Geertz gave at Yale University, *Islam Observed* is Geertz's seminal work and an early attempt to "break away from the conventional disciplinary boundaries" of history, religion, and anthropology in order to understand Islam as a "world religious tradition" from a comparative perspective.[19] His work helps us understand various expressions of Islam and the reactions they elicit in European countries due to historical contexts and cultural practices. This explains why the plethora of integration directives issued by the EU have not harmonized EU policy toward Islam: each country deals with its Muslim population differently. In the Netherlands, Islamic schools are financed by the state. In Belgium, Islam is recognized by the state. But in France, neither the headscarf nor Islamic schools are allowed by the state. *Islam Observed* offers perhaps the clearest articulation of the work done on migration and citizenship policies, because Geertz posits that religion as an "idea and practice" is significant to those regimes despite the secular European environment where Muslim migrants are living. It takes only an hour and a half to travel by train from Brussels to Paris, and two and a half hours from Brussels to Amsterdam, yet a Muslim making that trip will traverse three different sets of public policies aimed at him and his fellows.

Policies of Integration

The perception of assimilation or forms of integration among guest workers in European societies can be contrasted with how belief can form a kind of resistance to some European policies. In reviewing scholarship in the field of migration and ethnic relations, Koopmans and Statham[20] identify three types of citizenship policies:

- "Ethnic" or "exclusive." This policy makes access to the political arena very difficult or impossible. Until recently, when it changed its requirements for citizenship, Germany was exemplary of this—effectively shutting out immigrants from achieving citizenship and therefore political power. This form still typifies Austria and Switzerland.

- "Republican," used in the French sense of the term, or otherwise described as "assimilationist." This policy provides comparatively easy access to citizenship via, for example, automatic citizenship if one is born in the country. The former melting pot approaches to integration of France and the United States, which held sway until the mid-1960s, are examples here, but this policy, according to Koopmans and Statham, "requires from migrants a high degree of assimilation in the public sphere and gives little or no recognition to their cultural difference."[21]
- "Multicultural" or "pluralist." This policy offers easy formal acquisition of citizenship, as well as the rights of citizens to maintain their cultural difference. Examples of this type of pluralist citizenship policy include the contemporary United States, Canada, Australia, Britain, and the Netherlands.

While acknowledging its existence, Koopmans and Statham criticize this threefold typology for its two-dimensional view of citizenship: "If indeed there are two dimensions to citizenship, one—ethnic versus civic—defining the formal criteria of access, and another—multicultural versus assimilationist—defining the cultural obligations which such citizenship entails, we end up with four, not three models...."[22] What they mean is that a model must be accorded each criterion: ethnic, civic, multicultural, and assimilationist. They also note that the threefold typology obscures "both the dynamic aspects of the process of migrant integration, and the important differences within states, both among the integration approaches advanced by different political actors, and among those applied to different categories of migration...."[23]

They then compare several European countries with some pertinent historical detail.[24] Their analysis shows that there can be considerable variation even among countries that have been described as fitting within the same categories. For example:

> Britain and the Netherlands' "multicultural" approaches to migrant incorporation have had their own problems. Here the problem has not been a lack of policy instruments ... based on ethnic, cultural or racial differences, but rather that these instruments have sometimes reinforced and solidified the very disadvantages they were supposed to combat.... Particularly in the Netherlands, the combination of these factors has led to a vicious circle in which state policies have reinforced the image of migrants as a problematic, disadvantaged category in need of constant state assistance—not only in the eyes of the majority population, but also in those of many migrants and their representative organizations. To the majority populations, migrants

thus appear as a group deserving help, respect, tolerance and solidarity, but not the kind of people that anyone in his or her right mind would want to employ or would want one's child to be in school with.[25]

Aside from giving a precise description of how public policy can bolster the very discrimination it is designed to dislodge, Koopmans and Statham also remind us that the discussion of citizenship in generalizations like those they make can, in fact, obscure the considerable distance between policy and those who are expected to be governed by it. For example, with respect to policy concerning political asylum seekers, the researchers note that such people (migrants) "everywhere tend to be subjected to a segregationist regime." This has led to some major within-country differences between the situations of those who arrived as guest workers and those who arrived through colonial ties.[26] For example:

> [In] France and the Netherlands, which have both had guestworker programmes and have experienced massive post-colonial migration, there have been important differences, at least initially, between the respective incorporation regimes that [are intended to] make newcomers feel part of the mainstream in society. The contrast was perhaps largest in the Netherlands, where guestworker (non) incorporation initially proceeded along much the same ethnic segregationist lines as in Germany and Switzerland, while the regime for post-colonial migrants was much more inclusive. Germany's incorporation of Aussiedler is an interesting and rather pure case of an ethnic assimilationist approach. Despite their often important cultural and linguistic differences from the German majority society, the inclusion of Aussiedler is based on the presumption that they are ethno-culturally Germans. As a result, Aussiedler are in fact confronted with strong assimilation pressures. They have to become what they were already unambiguously supposed to be on entry, that is, Germans, and have to give up what they supposedly never had, that is, the Russian, Polish or Romanian parts of their cultural identity.[27]

The Dutch example is unique in Europe for three reasons: the historical tolerance that minorities have enjoyed,[28] which gave birth to the multicultural approach toward immigration in the 1980s, an approach that resulted in giving migrants the right to vote in municipal elections, as well as the radical change toward intolerance vis-à-vis the Muslims.

A Dutch History of Islam

To truly understand the impact of Islam on Europe, it is necessary to focus on one country, as Arkoun has focused on France. In the Netherlands, for example, the presence of Muslim immigrants who came from North Africa in the 1960s offers us an example that is more different from, than similar to, France. Comparing the Netherlands and France is almost like comparing two extreme examples. In, *Islam Observed*,[29] Geertz compares two countries outside Europe that typify the two extremes in the Islamic world—Morocco and Indonesia. He never suggests that these two examples of Islamic societies might come together in any way, and yet they have in the Netherlands. The Netherlands offers not only an important example of how a European postcolonial society has dealt with Islamic issues in the past five decades and deals with them in the present but also the Dutch example helps us update and "restore" Geertz's approach to understanding contemporary Islam; his work looks at two Muslim societies a world apart, but today those two worlds have collided in the globalized Netherlands. Having maintained colonial rule in Indonesia for centuries, the Netherlands has a considerable population of Indonesian immigrants, as well as a substantial population of Moroccans who immigrated as guest workers in the 1960s.

The Dutch met Islam as traders, as masters of the sea, and as colonizers of the largest Islamic country in the world, Indonesia. Historically, the Dutch have been confronted directly with Islam as a factor of major importance. In 1854, the Dutch colonial administration in Southeast Asia issued a decree that gave the governor general the power to prohibit any Christian missionary activities because they understood that these activities could undermine Dutch trade interests. Only the regions in which Islam had already established itself as the leading religious force were still open to Christian missionaries. The Dutch East Indies Tea Company feared that any provocation of Islam could hinder their commercial activities.

In 1880, X. Van Hoevell, a member of the Netherlands Parliament, said that the Christian churches in Sumatra should no longer receive subsidies from the Dutch state. In 1891, the Dutch Indies embarked on their own Islamic politics by appointing a Muslim adviser to the consul general, Snouck Hurgronje, who occupied this position from 1891 to 1898. The son of a Calvinist pastor in the Reformed Church, he had a good name in the Islamic world, especially with the ulama of Mecca, where he had lived for many years under the Islamic name Abd al-Ghaffar. Access to Mecca at that time was entirely forbidden to non-Muslims. As Abd al-Ghaffar, he wrote extensively about his travels and life in this sacred city. He later became interested in the Dutch Indies. He spoke not only Arabic but also the dialects, as well as many languages of Southeast Asia, including

Malay and Javanese. In Batavia, he was the attaché to the Ministry of Colonies, and he wrote many reports on Islam in Java. Socially, "he behaved as a Muslim."[30] His perspectives on politics, society, and religion in Southeast Asia were based on three central points: first, the Dutch administration should not interfere in the religious affairs of the Muslims; second, religious activities in the area should be monitored closely; and third, the state has to intervene in attempts to develop Islamic societies, in order to transcend the religious system. He courageously concluded one of his reports to the Dutch government with a comment about the difficulty of attaining cultural emancipation of Muslims in Indonesia under Dutch rule, and he criticized the mercantilism of the Dutch state.

In 1931, this same Abd al-Ghaffar, now much older, wrote a report for the French government about the Berbers of Morocco. He was fascinated by "the international meaning of Islam."[31] He drew parallels between Calvinism and Islam and came to a conclusion that remains relevant today: the Calvinist religion distinguishes rigorously between law and grace, between the obligations put forward in the Old Testament and the notion of liberation put forward by the New Testament. Because Islam does not allow liberation from older laws, emancipation is through development of a supplemental moral system. In this sense, Islam, when interpreted as a set of religious obligations, becomes part of a moral system that is amendable, refutable, and adjustable and that can be the subject of rational and cultural emancipation.[32] Throughout his life, Abd al-Ghaffar believed that emancipation of Muslims within the Dutch kingdom (including the colonies) from the weight of religious traditions was possible—that they would recognize a separation between the state and the religion.

With this look back in time, it becomes easier to understand the initial positive attitude toward the Indonesian Muslim newcomers in Holland. In comparison with other European colonial powers, the Dutch had more experience with Islam and its development in other societies. The University of Leiden has an extensive collection of manuscripts from the Islamic world, in large part through Dr. Snouck Hurgronje, who called for a gradual assimilation of Muslims into Dutch society as early as 1900.

Moroccan Muslims in the Netherlands

Moroccan sociologist Paul Pascon wrote in 1954 of the migration of Berbers from the Atlas Mountains in southern Morocco to Casablanca as the birth of the Moroccan proletariat. He later described this migration as comparable to the migration of the Berbers from north Morocco to Europe in the 1960s. These Berber mountain dwellers, who originated in the poorest regions of Morocco, were not changed by the experience of migration in terms of their attitude toward their faith. They continued to respect Islam, lived by the severity of tradition, and continued to be immune to the seductions of urban life. Women, for example, continued to adhere to traditional values.

But in the Netherlands, a central pillar of the Mahgreb's Islamic culture was swapped out: the imams in Amsterdam offered[33] a new interpretation of Islam. The new interpretation rejects the mediator role that some figures like the marabou, the sharif, or the ancestor were held in as a stable symbol of continuous tradition that colored the local practice of Islam in North Africa,[34] and these imams instead refer to themselves as occupying that key role of leader in the political sense of the word.

Moroccan migration has increasingly become the focus of media and research as Morocco itself has become a magnet for sub-Saharan African migrants and other candidates for illegal migration to the EU. It has also been an object of interest because of the rise of Islamism and the al-Qaeda-inspired or -related bombings in 2005 and 2007. The origins of Europe's Moroccan community lie in the migration of male guest workers to the Netherlands in the early 1960s. During this period, the guest workers were certain that they would work only for a short time in Europe and then return permanently to their homeland and their families. There were no mosques in the Netherlands, no place for them to practice their faith, and initially no expectation that the men would be here for the long term.

Between 1965 and 1976, the guest workers began to see their working and living in the Netherlands as something more permanent because members of their immediate families were granted visas to join them. The first mosque was built. Children were born in the Netherlands or immigrated there. Doubt regarding a permanent return to Morocco surfaced as returning to Morocco became an annual ritual for families rather than an end goal.

Over the next ten years, tensions began to emerge within the Moroccan community, as well as between the Moroccan community and other communities in the Netherlands. The period from 1986 to the present day is usually described as the period of compromise and relative emancipation for the Moroccan community.

Although the uniquely Dutch form of social organization known as pillarization[35] largely came to an end in the 1960s, the integration of Islamic and various other immigrant communities over the past thirty years has brought about what can be seen as the beginnings of repillarization.

Hidjra *of the Guest Workers*

The relationship between the phenomena of emigration and immigration is a dialectic one. When translated into Arabic, the two terms share one word: *hidjra*, which would indicate a journey with an implicit return home. Only in recent years have Arabic sociologists come up with a term that describes only the leaving of one's country, or emigration: *muhadjara*. But in political and religious discourse, the term *hidjra* is still the only one that is used. This word went through an evolution of meaning, still retaining a sublimation of the Prophet Muhammed's departing from Mecca and going to Medina in the year 622. The *hidjra* consequently embodies the powerful imagery of both Islam and migration, and it emphasizes the place of Islam in the immigrant experience, as well as the place of immigration in the Islamic experience.

The dialectic between emigration and immigration also explains the forms that immigration takes in specific periods. I refer to these periods with the words of Abelmalek Sayad: "ages of immigration." Each era, or age, carries a distinctive characteristic of the condition of the migrant, stemming from a particular mode of relationship between a social group of migrants, the group's country of origin in the case of émigrés, and the host country in the case of immigrants. A new category of immigrants emerges with particular modes of relationship among these three terms—migrants, émigrés, and immigrants—in a given period or age. The mirages of migration, social, economic, cultural, and political, are collectively shared by three complicit partners: the society of emigration, the society of immigration, and the immigrants themselves.

A unique aspect of Moroccan emigration to the Netherlands, in comparison with other ethnic groups from Greece, Spain, and Italy, is not only its Islamic character but also the rural character that underlies it. The Moroccans have mostly come from the Berber Rif mountain region. This is in contrast with Moroccan emigration to other places in Europe, which stems historically from the urban areas in Morocco like Casablanca and Rabat. The Netherlands has a different type of Moroccan immigrant. As geographer Paolo de Mas said, "They come from a region which has a periphery character, economically and geographically, and they have been accustomed to moving." Prior to emigration to Europe, they moved within Morocco or to neighboring countries like Algeria for work on the land. Dutch employers wanted non-European—therefore, less expensive—manual laborers. By bringing in some from the Rif, many more, accustomed to moving for work, emigrated from the region. Most of these migrants came with special working contracts, imported to do specific jobs. This led to concentrations of Moroccan immigrants in Dutch cities and towns such as Gouda and Enschede.

The arrival of Moroccan migrants in the Netherlands was an innovation in the country's immigration policy because there was no history of working relationships with Morocco. Moroccans usually went to France because most already spoke the language.

Though Moroccans had emigrated earlier to the country for work, the first official convention written to govern recruiting manual laborers from Morocco to the Netherlands was signed May 14, 1969, by the Ministry of Employment and Social Affairs in Rabat and the Ministry of Social Affairs and Public Health in Den Haag. This convention has twenty-seven articles in which both countries' responsibilities to the migrants are discussed, along with the type and condition of work, duration of job, and housing possibilities. This first phase of recruitment fostered word of mouth from the first groups of workers, which, in turn, led to more migration from the same regions, which created groups characterized by the same dialect, local cultural habits, and religious practices. Frictions between different groups in the country of origin were brought over to the host country, so separation persisted, as one group would concentrate in one city and others in another city.

Moroccans emigrated for economic reasons.[36] Apart from the social trajectories prior to the migration and the conditions that pushed the people to migrate, the predispositions of the host city also determined how they integrated into the Dutch culture. The ages of migration are, first, the establishment of individuals (here I mean the guest workers); second, the birth of new organizations, both secular and religious, for cultural incorporation; and third, the construction of the transnational community.

Conflict is a common element in each age, and through its examination, we can understand the entire history of the institutional approach to cultural incorporation.

The Age of Doubt, 1965–1976

The first Moroccan migrants to the Netherlands in the 1960s immediately became socially, religiously, and linguistically disoriented. With this came a feeling of alienation. Haunted by the idea of making a lot of money, with which they could return to Morocco permanently, they made do in the short term with the annual ritual of returning by car for the long summer holiday. This ritual return was also the opportunity for reproduction, since the workers returned to be with their wives and often conceived children during these summer months. They referred to the rest of the year, spent in the dormitories and factories in northern Europe, as *jahilia*, an Arabic term that is used to mean both "obscurity" and the period before the advent of Islam. It was a time when one was so forgotten, or overlooked by the Europeans, that one forgot oneself, that one began to doubt one's very existence. With the problem of language, the lack of halal food, and makeshift or no mosques, it was a time of stunning isolation and doubt.

In the beginning, the immigrants were not introduced to the existing forms of social organization in the country and were entirely unfamiliar with trade unions and other institutions. In the nineteenth century, the city proletariat in Amsterdam was afraid of competition from cheap laborers from the countryside. In the mid-twentieth century, the Dutch trade unions themselves feared losing their base if they helped the new immigrants. Over time, however, the Dutch population began to open its eyes to the conditions of the guest workers. Outside factories, one could observe the presence of some Dutch people helping guest workers, often through Christian organizations. In the early 1970s, the immigrants who were most fluent in Dutch also began to participate in these benevolent groups. They lobbied for improvement in the basics, such as salary and social benefits. Eventually, they began talking about the conditions of housing and about ending the dormitory system. Between 1967 and 1973, the guest workers were officially given temporary worker status. The Dutch state did not develop interventionist policies for these temporary workers and dealt with problems on a case-by-case basis. In 1973, the first quasi-governmental organization specializing in assisting immigrants was founded. The first organizations were semiofficial and created by worker groups that took the official status of nonprofit foundations (*stichtingen*) for foreign workers. With the help of government subsidies, these foundations proliferated.

In 1974, Minister of Social Affairs Jaap Boersma and Minister of Justice Dries van Agt presented the first draft of legislation to establish the Dutch state as a caring state (*zorgmaatschappij*) responsible for helping immigrants obtain social status. This law was intended to forge a social partnership between the quasi-governmental organizations dealing with immigrants and the immigrants' own organizations—the first of which would spring up the following year, in 1975. This was the starting point for an increasing amount of legislation concerning immigrants and immigration. In response to these political and legal developments, a new actor came into the field: the Committee of Moroccan Workers in the Netherlands (KMAN). The KMAN had a dual objective: helping immigrants and guest workers obtain answers to questions about laws that influenced their lives, while at the same time building an organization that could mobilize Moroccan immigrants. Similar organizations emerged for other immigrant groups from Turkey, Portugal, Spain, and Italy.

Alongside all of these institutional developments came a third: *amicales*. *Amicales* were the organizations created by the home country to control their citizens abroad. The first *amicales* were directly connected to the state of origin and represented the Moroccan dynasty.

It is important to mention the role of churches and philanthropic associations. From the beginning of the 1970s, they organized guest worker solidarity on a voluntary basis, at a time when churches found their congregations diminishing. Church administrators began to orient their charity work toward the immigrant communities, taking social action to help immigrants. The Council of Churches (Raad van Kerken) coordinated assistance to immigrants and put cooperation with immigrant organizations very high on their agenda. This explains concretely why many leaders in the immigrant organizations found jobs with the Council of Churches. The leader of KMAN, for example, also worked with the Council of Churches.

The churches were the first organizations to create free spaces for Muslim immigrants to pray. Prior to this, there was no official space—in other words, no space recognized by authorities—for Muslims to pray. This shift opened the possibility for ecumenical work, which can be seen in the slogan "Samen leven samen bidden" ["Live together, pray together"]. The origin of this initiative was the Moses and Aaron Church in Amsterdam, which has been seen as a progressive force in the city. It is just a short walk from the historical Jonas Daniel Meijerplein, which symbolizes Dutch workers' resistance to Nazism in the World War II. For the immigrant organizations, these ecumenical efforts were a practical demonstration of Christian charity and provided a context for mutual understanding between Muslims and other faiths. So, the Moroccan community developed through the intermediary of institutions related to the dynamic of emigration-immigration and religion.

The Age of Community Building and Conflict, 1976–1986

In 1975, there were approximately 7,000 Moroccan guest workers in Amsterdam, mainly men. In the first period, there were two types of organizations within the Moroccan community—*amicales* and the KMAN—and even though they were opposed to one another politically, with the former on the right and the latter on the left, both focused more on the home country and the myth of return than on their Dutch environment. The status of Moroccan guest workers in the various European countries was of great importance to King Hassan II for both economic and political reasons. *Amicales*, created by the Moroccan government to control the guest workers and their paychecks, aimed in particular to "protect" them from the Marxist ideology that was widely perceived as a threat to the Moroccan royal family.

By contrast, KMAN was led by Abdou Mnebhi, a Moroccan who had been active in the French communist trade union movement (CGT) and whose goal was to extend worker protection to guest workers in Holland though an organization that was both independent from and critical of the Moroccan state.

In 1975, a number of Moroccans who had no passports were helped by KMAN to obtain passports and bring them out of migrant status and into normal immigration status. This procedure was replicated across Holland in Eindhoven, Utrecht, Rotterdam, and Amsterdam, and groups of Moroccans mobilized by KMAN were assisted by the progressive Christian left. Thus, KMAN obtained legitimacy despite the fact that it openly opposed the authority of the Moroccan king, with whom the Dutch government was on friendly terms, openly claiming that the mosques in the Netherlands were instruments of monarchical indoctrination controlled by Hassan II, with the majority of imams protected by the Moroccan Consulate.

In the 1970s and the early 1980s, KMAN launched a number of working committees on education, solidarity, labor problems, and other social issues. KMAN became very active in offering free consultations to guest workers with housing problems or other issues, and it used the consultations as opportunities to offer information about political developments in Morocco. KMAN also organized activities in Holland against *amicales*, in coordination with KMAN's sister organizations in France and other European countries. KMAN started to behave as a mass organization with its own magazine, the *Marokkaanse Arbeider [Moroccan Worker]*, published ten times annually—it didn't publish in the months the workers were on holiday in Morocco—in Arabic and Dutch.

Developing in parallel opposition to KMAN were the Moroccan *amicales*, which were much like other contemporary organizations developed by political factions in Yugoslavia, Greece, and Turkey. Usually considered "cultural organizations," the Moroccan *amicales* had bases in every locale in Europe with a concentration of Moroccan residents. They became very active in the Netherlands in 1975, when the migration laws were tightened. The *amicales* were usually run by immigrants who were illiterate and less adept at navigating in their host country; not surprisingly, their allegiance lay with their home country. Actually rather naïve, they had the reputation of being the link to a repressive regime, a reputation that imbued them with a sinister image that they themselves would not have recognized. The organization's letterhead displayed, in capital letters, the words "ALLAH, NATION AND KING." The *amicales* organized social events such as feasts during religious festivities or national occasions, as well as counterdemonstrations when the KMAN was on the streets. They sought their recruits at mosques, Moroccan butcher shops, other small businesses, and schools.

In 1975, there was a major summit in Rabat with all of the *amicales* worldwide. One of the most important requests was that customs formalities be eased for immigrants returning to Morocco during the annual summer holiday.

Other requests were for the Moroccan government help build mosques in Europe and send imams to lead these mosques, as well as, in the case of Holland, open a consulate and make special ID cards that displayed the colors of the Moroccan flag. All of these points were honored by the Moroccan government, with the notable exception of sending imams.

Amsterdam's largest mosque, Al Kabir, played a very important role in the history of the struggle between individuals and organizations from these two camps, *amicales* and KMAN. The emergence of the mosque in the Netherlands helped the immigrants create a new home. In 1973, a foundation called De Moskee was created in Utrecht. Its mission was to advise city authorities on the practicalities of Islamic culture, including such topics as halal food in local hospitals, the development of Muslim cemeteries, and the ritual circumcision for boys between the ages of two months and seven years.

In 1997, the Union of the Moroccan Mosques (UMMON) was founded in Amsterdam. UMMON's initial objectives included the uniformity of the time of Ramadan so that Muslims in the Netherlands could fast on the same days, the establishment of abattoirs according to Islamic law, the uniformity of time of prayer, the creation of Muslim cemeteries, and visiting the sick who have no family. But the main objective was to create new mosques. UMMON, which today is responsible for more than one hundred mosques in Holland, experienced a great deal of internal conflict between individuals and groups. There were people working for *amicales* in UMMON, but there were also people opposing *amicales* who were very active in the organization. KMAN remained outside this sphere because of its stated role as a secular trade union.

In the field of immigration, there were and are also Dutch organizations specifically designed to help immigrants. Two of the best known were the Foundation for the Welfare of Foreigners (SWB) and the Netherlands Center for Foreigners (NCB). By 1980, there were fifteen such organizations. This number nearly doubled over the next decade, with each organization supported by subsidies from the Dutch national government until the late 1990s, when the provinces began monetarily supporting them. This network of organizations performed what was called "categorical" work, helping one category of the population. Over time, a dichotomy emerged in the welfare system: the general approach and the categorical approach, or a universalist approach versus a particularistic approach. Categorical aid was reserved for a certain category of people, the guest workers. In 1981, these centers or organizations had to switch their orientation from what the Dutch call a "frontline organization," helping individual migrants, to a "second-line organization," helping immigrant organizations. This aid or help was in the form of providing advice and information and coordinating specific projects that had to be implemented by immigrant organizations requesting assistance. This shift from individual to organizational assistance did not operate efficiently because many of the people working in the Dutch organizations were not trained to do the kinds of work that they were now expected to do, and a consequence was that many of these organizations were focusing more on their own internal problems than on the problems of the migrants, according to Gijs von der Fuhr,[37] a prominent adviser of migrant organizations in Amsterdam.

Social research on the (Dutch) *autochtoon* and (non-Dutch) *allochtoon* institutions dealing with immigrants in Holland began only in the 1980s. Most of the research subsidized by the state focused on Moroccan and Turkish organizations, which in general had traditional leadership. These organizations represent for the guest worker a kind of lifeline to the country of origin when they feel isolated in the host country. Mosques play a very important role in giving the guest workers this connection. Social and cultural organizations are responsible for planning various activities, such as feasts, meetings, and educational events. Political organizations such as KMAN, even if they do not have many members, can nevertheless mobilize the masses, and they were especially adept at doing so up until about 1986, when prominent politicians rushed to the mosques to win the votes of the migrants who were granted the right to vote that same year, decreasing the need for KMAN's mobilization These three types of organizations—religious, social-cultural, and political—also can be described in terms of a hierarchy of importance for the guest workers. The organizational culture itself was very different across these three types, all of which contrasted markedly with their counterparts devoted to the same concerns among the native European population.

Between 1975 and 1986, there was a major struggle over who would control the field of migrants and who would be the legitimate voice of the immigrant guest workers. In a way, the Dutch organizations working with migrants were forced by tension within the Muslim guest worker community to choose between these three types of migrant organizations, so that they were no longer neutral players in the field. In Amsterdam, KMAN, a political organization, tried to assert its legitimacy as the representative of the workers through local municipal governments, as well as through the political parties on the left. KMAN's struggles for primacy against *amicales* were sometimes violent. Newspapers sometimes reported heavy fighting between supporters of *amicales* and KMAN during KMAN demonstrations. Meanwhile, the religious organizations continued to build mosques. The KMAN and *amicales* both developed strategic relationships with Dutch organizations, mostly social-cultural, working with migrants, though KMAN had a much larger network. Occasionally, KMAN workers would work for a Dutch organization in the field. The government changed its politics on immigration in the aftermath of the tragic hijacking of a Dutch passenger train on December 2, 1975, by angry young Ambonese men protesting against Dutch immigration policy. The hijacking, in which some hostages were killed,[38] was the first time that foreign immigrants had demonstrated such power over Dutch authorities, and it traumatized the country. By 1981, immigration policy had become the responsibility of the Ministry of the Interior, whereas previously it had been the responsibility of the Ministry of Social Affairs: the focus thus shifted from social work to internal security. This policy was elaborated in a government document stressing the importance of a tolerant multiethnic society that made efforts to compensate for the social disadvantages of immigrants. This policy document considers the development of the cultural identity of every group of immigrants as essential. It is interesting to see that until 1981 the family reunion policy was not restricted, as had been the case in other European countries, even if the government wanted to restrict the numbers of immigrants coming into the country under this policy.

In the second half of the 1980s, a policy document on *allochtonen* was developed that insisted on the necessity of giving attention to the newcomers and helping them learn the Dutch language to facilitate a better place for immigrants in Dutch society. The word *integration* was noticeably missing. In the public discussion that followed the publication of this document, the topic of quotas in the labor market emerged and, with it, the idea that immigrants would be given the opportunity to fill some particular public-sector municipal-level positions in the area of social work, subsidized by the state. This was intended to combat all the forms of social exclusion faced by immigrant communities. Large cities received a great deal of attention from the government, not least because they fostered the development of new phenomena such as what came to be described as "black schools," schools that have a majority of pupils from non-Dutch or immigrant origin. In 1994, the new government decided to appoint a special secretary of state to deal with the problems of big cities, specifically to deal with integration, education, and employment problems. After the 1998 election, the continuing coalition government elevated this position to ministry level, and it became the Ministry of Integration and Large Cities. It is also worth noting that after the 1994 elections on September 1, the law on ethnic and sexual minorities was passed, which banned discrimination in any form against ethnic minorities and homosexuals.

The Age of Urban Compromise and the Rise of Ethnic Politics, 1986–2007

The age of urban compromise was characterized by compromise between organizations working with immigrants in the cities, as well as by a confrontation between organizations residing in different cities (for example, Amsterdam versus Utrecht). Variables in the organizational development of the Moroccan community also emerged. In the 1980s, three were important.

First, a new type of immigration to the Netherlands started that was more selective and included many North African students, with most coming directly from Morocco or from Morocco via France and Belgium. These students would energize the secular organizations and present a challenge to the religious organizations.

The second was the emergence of a problematic second generation, with many dropouts and issues with delinquency and petty theft. The media, particularly in Amsterdam, began to focus on the problems of Moroccan youth in that city, and it was the first time in Dutch history that Moroccan immigrants were the topic of front-page news. They attracted the attention of politicians and were seen as a symbol of delinquency.

The third was the formation of small councils of migrants within the different cities to play an advisory role for local government. Some of these became official recognized organs with the "right of reply" (*inspraakorgaan*) to any actions taken by the Ministry of Interior. The Ministry of Interior's goal was to subsidize one organization for each of the country's immigrant communities. A second goal of the government with respect to the Moroccan community was to marginalize the KMAN, because of its left-wing politics. The unexpected outcome of this government effort in the Amsterdam Moroccan community was that it instead developed new lines of conflict within the community.

The government's stated aim led to the end of the long-standing conflict between the religious organizations (what was left of the *amicales*) and the KMAN. For the first time, these two Moroccan organizations, which had struggled against one another for years, began to work together. In Amsterdam, UMMON (the religious organization) and the KMAN formed the most important partnership with the city council, called the Urban Moroccan Council (Stedelijk Marokkanse Raad, SMR), subsidized by the city but not by the ministry. In Utrecht, however, the organizations opposed Amsterdam's new dynamic and instead created a new group, Samenwerking Marokkanen en Tunisiers [Moroccan and Tunisian Guest Workers], or SMT, which excluded KMAN, was subsidized by the Ministry of Interior, and continues to be seen by the ministry as the official representative of the Moroccan community. The Tunisians, according to one civil servant in the ministry, were added to this group because "we should not reduce these organizations to Moroccan-only, since Tunisians and Moroccans are almost the same."[39]

Different views of the Other persisted within these organizations. The members of KMAN said they refused to be marginalized by serving on a board for the ministry. The SMT, on the other hand, thought that KMAN wanted to be the only player and to monopolize power, while KMAN members believed that members of SMT could not represent the Moroccan community because they were subsidized by the ministry. The line of conflict within the community was drawn between those who were seen as anti-Dutch-government (SMR, which involved antigovernment KMAN) versus those who were pro-Dutch-government (SMT). Despite the work of a committee of wise men to solve the problem between the two organizations, which proposed that two councils be created, one for Amsterdam and the north of the country (SMR) and the other for the rest of the country (SMT), the government did not accept this proposal. The SMR emerged from this conflict saying that they would tone down radicalism and focus on policy that promotes "vital interests of the Moroccan community" using "minimal cooperation." Within the SMR, the religious component (the UMMON) leaders explained to followers in the mosques why they had cooperated with what they had previously described as the "Marxist Devil," the KMAN, using the same "vital interests" language. This cooperation between UMMON and KMAN within the SMR in Amsterdam was a major development and led observers to ask how it was possible that a pro-King group (UMMON) could work with an anti-King group (KMAN). Both organizations had, in fact, betrayed their principles. The KMAN, with its few members, lost ideological support on the left but was hoping in return to have access to the social basis of the mosque and hence potential fertile ground for politicization. And the UMMON nourished the hope that it would be accepted by the left and no longer associated with the *amicales*. The two organizations defined the general interests of the Moroccan workers by making a distinction between the interests of the Moroccan nation and the interests of the Moroccan state. They were for the former and against the latter. The KMAN began to be less critical toward the Moroccan state, and the UMMON distanced itself and criticized the *amicales*. A new unity with new consequences had been forged—welding political, social, and religious aims together.

This historical compromise in Amsterdam and the SMT compromise in Utrecht bring us to see two major changes during this period. The first is the unification of immigrant organizations run by the immigrants themselves, and the second is the centralization of the Dutch organizations working with migrants. The news of the SMR, the UMMON-KMAN union, was described in the press as a bombshell for the municipality, the Ministry of Interior, and the Moroccan community. A civil servant at the Ministry of Interior qualified this union as an act of "total opportunism." We see in these words that he recognized the potential effectiveness at the level of organization brought about by this unexpected alliance. The age of compromise began with shared or common projects and ended the years of quarrels between religious organizations and secular organizations. In this alliance between the secular and the religious, with the secular represented by the KMAN and the religious represented by the UMMON, an unintended result was to emphasize the Muslimness of the Moroccan community. There was also a relative failure of the Dutch and Moroccan governments to control these organizations.

The KMAN wanted to be an autonomous organization with a fundamental image of being activist and militant. Between 1975 and 1985, it opposed almost all Dutch organizations working with immigrants by saying that it represented the Moroccans and that the Dutch organizations did not. But KMAN had two problematic goals: its leaders wanted to preserve its autonomy, while at the same time be recognized by the host society.

Immigrants in Politics

In 1994, the Dutch Parliament had, for the first time, three MPs of Moroccan origin, one in PvdA (Labor), one in VVD (Liberal), and one in the Green Left (GL). With representation in government, the discourse of most Moroccan organizations changed from emphasizing Moroccan identity among migrants to emphasizing citizenship.[40] With this, the polarization between the secular and religious organizations ended entirely. The second half of the 1990s saw the end of opposition to Morocco from within the Moroccan community in the Netherlands. It is interesting to see that the leader of the KMAN lived for twenty-three years in exile in the Netherlands, never returning to Morocco until the 1990s, when he and other exiles returned to Morocco to launch projects that linked the two countries together.

In 1996, there was a schism within KMAN due to generational conflicts and its autocratic form of management. As a result, KMAN lost credibility with Dutch organizations, as well as with the Moroccan community. It is worth noting that by the late 1990s, most of the people who had been in leadership positions in KMAN in the 1970s and 1980s, with the exception of the leader himself, had gone on to hold high positions in the Dutch public sector as civil servants and city government officials, social workers, television and radio broadcasters, and elected members of municipal councils and the national Parliament.

It is also significant that following the loss of these leaders from immigrant organizations, those who remain are predominantly religious leaders who might not have been capable of making such career shifts. New organizations formed in the late 1990s include those for students of Moroccan origin, as well as small cultural organizations, such as those devoted to Berber culture. Because many second-generation immigrants speak only Berber and Dutch, they feel isolated when visiting Morocco because they do not speak Arabic. There is now, according to Paolo de Mas,[41] the idea that "the Rif is a suburb of Amsterdam" and is closer to Schipol (the airport of Amsterdam) than to the airport of Morocco, where they feel like strangers because nobody speaks one of their two languages, Berber or Dutch. When they land in Casablanca, they are greeted in Arabic or French.

The 1990s also witnessed the emergence of a Moroccan cultural elite in the Netherlands, primarily writers and cultural producers who were born in Europe or who immigrated there when they were very young. These writers, actors, poets, and others have a degree of distance from, and disdain for, their Moroccan cultural heritage, as well as Dutch culture. In comparison with other immigrant groups, such as the Turkish, the Surinamese, and the Antilleans (the latter two groups have the advantage of speaking the Dutch language because their homelands were Dutch colonies), there are more—and more prominent—writers from the Moroccan second generation.

In the 1990s, Dutch policy toward immigrants was seen by neighboring countries to be successful and progressive. There were expansions of the rights of immigrants and elevation of their legal status, obtaining Dutch nationality was simplified, and social welfare benefits remained comparatively generous. There were also major government efforts made to combat the social disadvantages of migrants, including efforts to improve the Dutch language skills of immigrants and their opportunities in the job market, although these efforts did not achieve all of the desired outcomes. In 1994, the law to improve employment opportunities for *allochtonen* was passed with the cooperation of the governing coalition (PvdA, VVD, and D66) and the opposition (Green Left). The law provided tax incentives to employers if they provided jobs to *allochtonen*, but this law was not compulsory and ultimately was not taken up by a significant number of businesses. In 1997, this legislation was replaced by a law referred to as "Together" (Samen), which was intended to establish partnerships between the public and private sectors to bring unemployed immigrants back to work.

Immigrants Adapting to the Law

In the process of the emancipation of immigrants in this transition to citizenship, many immigrants began to understand how the Dutch system works and how the law works. They began to use Article 23 of the Constitution to build their own confessional schools, because it provides for the freedom of schools to be created on the basis of religious or pedagogical ideology. Article 23 guarantees the respect of "otherness" and also protects the religious identity of a specific group. This law was criticized by those who saw it as the coup de grâce for pillarization as a system of pacification and accommodation of minority claims and the beginning of what Michel Laguerre and Jan Rath called "minorization,"[42] to describe the process by which minorities are kept in a marginalized position. Pillarization had been seen as a very important step and a central experience to the evolution of social and special interest groups in Dutch society. The Dutch ideal of the process of emancipation of the individual begins first within one's own group, with having a strong feeling of one's own individual and group identity, and then one proceeds to function as an individual in the wider Dutch society while at the same time being a member of an ideological and social pillar such as Catholic, Protestant, or public institutions.

The introduction of television played a decisive role in triggering the process of depillarization in the Netherlands, despite the complex corporate character of public service broadcasting, in which different ideological pillars in the society were represented by their own broadcasting organization, which aimed programs at audiences in the group. Liesbet Van Zoonen argues that the arrival of the technology of television in mass through the public sphere meant that a kind of social mixing developed that had not occurred before.[43] For example, when one family on the street had a television set, everyone on the street went to watch, so Protestants, Catholics, and others were together watching the same programs.

The emergence of satellite dishes and broadcasts of Arabic and Turkish TV in the beginning of the 1990s played a very important role in the crystallization of an Islamic transnational identity. Had such technology not been available, the guest workers would have continued to watch Dutch-language television, just as their Dutch neighbors did. But Arabic television, which told them more about their countries of origin than about their host country, made Islam synonymous with ethnicity. This ethnicization derived from the dynamics of migration and the establishment of Islam as a transplanted religion in Europe. Add to this the political Islam that also found refuge in Europe as clandestine opposition to Islamic states through refugee networks—which makes the situation more complex and confusing. Not only did Islam became a politicized ethnic marker but also some researchers said that the bureaucratic pressure on Islamic organizations in Europe pushed them to work toward developing an ethnic identity.

In the 1960s, there was an assumption that pillarization was ending (although the national political and media institutions continue to operate along the logic of the pillarized society in the ways that they are subsidized by the state). The Muslim migrants who arrived in the 1960s, at the supposed end of the system of pillarization or *verzuiling*, later saw the benefits of the model of *verzuiling* for their own communities. During the 1980s and 1990s, the number of Muslim schools began to multiply, from 1 to 42 between 1986 and 2005, without taking into account all of those organizations that continue to apply for official status as Islamic schools but have not yet been granted that status.

Conclusions: The Rise and Fall of Migrant Secular Organizations

Guest workers came to the Netherlands for economic reasons originally. The family reunions, when guest workers decided to bring their wives and children to the Netherlands began in 1973, the year of the oil crisis, and continued until the 1990s. Lotty van den Berg-Eldering was the first Dutch anthropologist to study Moroccan families and their establishment in the Netherlands. She described the anxiety of the guest workers and their families coming to the Netherlands, how the extended absences of the husband as a guest worker had repercussions on the relations within the family and also on the children's education, and the reproduction of the role of the father through the eldest son, noting that because of the rigidity of village traditions, it was not easy to accept change. One of the conclusions of her book was that immigration of guest workers brought money to help elevate the status of the family in Morocco but at the same time had very negative influences on the boys, especially the older sons, and their education. According to van den Berg-Eldering, the family reunion was seen by the guest workers as a way of solving the problem of their children's poor school performance back in Morocco and in some cases even school expulsions.[44]

In the 1990s, policies affecting minorities in the Netherlands changed dramatically. No more was there the soft approach to integration, with each community keeping its own cultural identity, as was the case in the past. The emphasis came to be on the fact that some immigrants needed to become familiar with Dutch norms and values and to become linguistically and culturally integrated in Dutch society. In the mid 1990s, the citizenship contract (*inburgeringscontract*) was therefore created with the aim of guaranteeing that those who come to the country through family reunions or marriage, and rely on the support of the social security system, become familiar with Dutch society. These newcomers were asked to take citizenship and language courses. Throughout the 1990s, the emphasis on the importance of learning the Dutch language became stronger, not only because it was felt that this had not been emphasized enough in the 1970s and 1980s but also because of the increasing number of minorities in the large cities and the growing number of Islamic schools.

Over the course of the different phases of Moroccan immigration—the age of doubt, the age of community building and conflict, the age of urban compromise and relative emancipation—the guest workers shifted from being total outsiders in Dutch society to becoming a group with an ethnic religious identity within Dutch society but not taking on the Dutch nationality or identity.

The mobility of the professional secular elite was more artificial because it was mainly subsidized through the system of welfare that promoted minority social workers to work with minority communities. Many minority members made careers in social work. Independent entrepreneurs opening grocery stores or butcher shops or working as translators, legal experts, and advisers also played an important role as intermediaries with the Dutch institutions. It is interesting that the entrepreneurs were looking for clients in the mosques, and we see the development of a whole arsenal of intermediary organizations that emerged to answer the demands of the guest worker immigrants without the linguistic skills to defend their own interests. For the average guest worker, it was always difficult to go to a Dutch organization existing for the sole purpose of helping immigrants, not only because of a lack of awareness of their existence but also because of a lack of feeling of proximity of these intermediaries. In the 1960s and 1970s, the immigrant secular organizations that are nonreligious were predominant in the Dutch public arena for two important reasons. The first is the structure of the social help and welfare dominated by social workers. The second is the general policy that was based on the separation of the church and state, which meant that mosques were not seen as client organizations needing help with their members. The mosques and religious organizations were subsequently marginalized in part because many believed that they were connected to the Moroccan regime.

Just before the Berlin Wall fell in 1989, the secular organizations began losing ground, and also lost the attention of Dutch national politics, which began to recognize as important the growing mosques and Islamic schools and the general importance of religious organizations. Secular organizations came to be viewed by the Dutch state as having no followers, whereas religious organizations were seen to have many. From this point onward, religious organizations competed with secular organizations for state subsidies for nonreligious activities. It is interesting that leaders of religious organizations, only some of whom were imams, became visible, competing with the secular leaders for space in the public arena. Secular organizations also organized more and more religious activities, such as events or feasts connected with religious holidays or Ramadan, so that one could speak of an Islamization of the agenda of the secular organizations.

Secular organizations have depended on the help of some imams. An example is the organization of public demonstrations against the introduction of the Schengen Accord, because of the difficulties Moroccans living in the Netherlands would face in traveling through France without a transit visa. Secular organizations also mobilized them in demonstrations against the Gulf War and against ethnic cleansing in Bosnia. The religious elite in the early 1990s became more visible in the public arena as they aimed for social and political recognition of Islam. Official recognition would mean that the Dutch state would have to treat Islam as it treats other religions, which would require state subsidies for, among other things, pastoral work, homes for the elderly, religious schools, and religious universities. This increasing visibility of the Islamic religious elite in the public space goes hand in hand with a series of major external events, including the fatwa against Salman Rushdie, the Gulf War, the war in Chechnya, and, according to Gilles Kepel,[45] the emergence of religious fundamentalism in different religions and countries around the world.

During the decade of the 1990s, in different Dutch institutions of higher education, Arab and Moroccan student groups formed and articulated their sympathies with Al 'adl wal-Ihsane, which was an organization in Morocco devoted to bringing Islamic fundamentalism to the forefront in that country and whose leader was often under house arrest until the death of King Hassan II in 2000. At Dutch mosques on Fridays during that period, one saw many of his followers distributing pamphlets from organizations that were illegal and forbidden in their countries of origin. This continues to be the case today, though the banned organizations may have changed and the Internet is increasingly a forum for reaching a younger transnational public.

As these examples illustrate, there is a transnational emphasis that comes with the Arab and Muslim identity. All of the new youth organizations of second-generation Moroccans in the Netherlands, the children of the guest workers, are also interested in questions of identity, and they do not reject religion entirely. Religion is always present. One need only look at some of the Web sites (such as http://www.maroc.nl and http://www.magreb.nl) to see that these second-generation immigrants define themselves as Moroccan, Muslim, and/or "Mocro," a hip term for "Moroccan." Being citizens of the Netherlands is just part of their legal status and identity.

3

How Europe's Secularism Became Contentious

Mosques, Imams, and Issues

It befitted not to a man that God should address him except by revelation (*wahy*) or from behind a veil, or He sends a messenger to reveal what He will by His leave. Lo! He is exalted, wise. And thus, We have revealed to you (Muhammad) a Spirit of Our Command while you did not know what the Book is, nor what the faith. But We have made it a light whereby We guide whom We will of Our worshipers. And lo! You verily guide unto a right path.
—Qur'ân, 42, 51–52

Surely, We have sent down to you the Book with the Truth, so that you may judge between the people by that which God has shown you.
—Qur'ân, 4, 105

In every major European city, there is a street known as Satellite Dish Street.

It happens that my relatives' neighborhood, the one I used to visit between college classes, has since become that street in Amsterdam. There, the air is filled with the scent of anise, saffron, roast lamb, and grilled fish. The sidewalks are filled with veiled women and djellaba-wearing men, and lined with shops selling such veils and djellabas. The shops open their doors next to the doors of mosques. Arabic script dances across banners and shouts from the cases of Arabic DVDs in the windows of video stores, as Arabic music drifts from passing cars. Above all this hustle and bustle, shimmering like the inverted domes of small mosques, are satellites—row upon row of them. Every apartment has its own.

With satellite access to international media, Moroccan and Turkish immigrant households can, and often do, almost exclusively watch Arab and Islamic entertainment from television stations around the world.[1] Television also gives access to religious services broadcast every Friday from Mecca, which means television is a source of competition for the local mosque. If the mosque-goers stay home during the Friday congregational sermon, less money will be collected to fund mosque activities. The level of income contributes to the prestige of the imam.

Along with access to international Islamic programs comes access to Western programming that many devout Muslims find offensive: pornographic shows that are an accepted part of the broadcast schedule in Europe, programs that focus on the equality of women, and comedy offerings that ridicule Islam, among other material that a majority of imams find objectionable. Ironically, it is in television that Islam and Europe are most integrated; on the screen, Muslim-centered content shares intermittent space with Western entertainment and news. There is a certain democracy to television access.

Television has also been the subject of many sermons in the mosques of Amsterdam. The imams are largely of the same opinion. In the words of one imam: "The European media are perverse. Television and media in general are the pulpit of perversion." If there has to be television, then the imams would like to see authentic Islamic television with only Islamic programming and with only Islamic entertainment, such as songs about the Prophet.

The Dutch government, on the other hand, has used television as part of its orientation for new immigrants. In a video that functions as a kind of shock inoculation to Dutch culture, produced by the Ministry of Integration, the government features typical Dutch television content, including scenes of homosexual couples kissing. The summary statement is, in effect, "If this bothers you, you might not be happy in the Netherlands."

Escaping the Trap of Orientalism versus Occidentalism

Satellite Dish Street serves as a metaphor for the isolated immigrant, still connected to his land of origin. But it's important to remember that Satellite Dish Street is not a dead end; it's an avenue that leads us back to the Western culture in which such streets have developed. The study of Islam today, particularly in Western societies where Islam is a minority and not a majority religion, challenges our sociological theories' capacity for grasping the reality of the practiced faith—the daily devotions that are the underpinnings of the Islamic community, without which the Satellite Dish Streets would not exist.

Islam has been discussed with a capital *I* by historians and Islamologists,[2] and although these general discussions are insightful and extremely valuable, they do not distinguish between the complexity of the religion and its interaction in contemporary society. As sociologists, we have to begin with a new epistemological perspective in approaching Islam in the West. To escape the trap of Orientalism versus Occidentalism—essentially the concept of a realm of fundamentalist fantasy pitted against that of rationalism and modernity—we need a new philosophy that subsumes both.

Pierre Bourdieu, who developed much of his theoretical arsenal in Muslim societies and then used it in the West, and Norbert Elias, with his long-term historical perspective in the study of European civilization, offer complementary insights that can be brought to bear on understanding the development of Islam in the West.[3] To address the complex issue of Islam, with all its various shades, one needs both Bourdieu's concept of field and Elias's concept of configuration. Together, these two concepts allow us to grasp the interdependencies between different spheres of influence. This marriage between the reflexive sociology of Bourdieu and the figurative sociology of Elias provides the most comprehensive approach to understanding the development of Islam in Europe and the West.[4]

In Western European societies, until fairly recently, we have been thinking of religion in secular terms and have not recognized it as a major factor in the public space. As Edward Said explained, ". . . Islamic doctrine can be seen as justifying capitalism, socialism, militancy as well as fatalism, ecumenism as well as exclusivism, we begin the tremendous lag between academic descriptions of Islam (that are inevitably caricatured in the media) and the particular realities to be found within the Islamic world. . . ."[5]

After the fall of communism, European societies began to experience the return of religion in the public debate.[6] The whole debate in Europe about multiculturalism and ethnic identity began to have more religious overtones, especially including the topic of Islam, the religion brought by the migrant workers to Europe in the 1960s. The configuration of Islam in Europe varies from one European country to another, with the accents that every ethnic group gives to the local content of this religion. The different shades of Islam across Europe can be described in terms of what people say they want from the society: there are those who are militant and want their own Islamic Parliament in Bradford, England, for example; others elsewhere in Europe are moderate and just want the opportunity for their children to attend good-quality Islamic schools.

The commonality is that in these migrant communities, the affirmation of Islamic identity happens only through religion. The only security is religion. The sermon plays a significant role in potentially mobilizing or demobilizing a set of positions or demands for the community. Different Islamic communities in Europe are influenced by different types of Islam: pan-Islamic, Saudi Islam, militant Islam, Libyan Islam, Pakistani Islam, the Milli Gurus Islam, and more. The key source of influence is the imam.

The imam occupies an especially powerful role in the relatively youthful and growing immigrant communities in Western Europe, which now account for some 7 million Muslims. He is an influential opinion maker. Without the imam, the mosque as a place of worship ceases to function. Yet most, if not all, of the research that has been done in contemporary societies either has been theological in focus or has not involved any fieldwork inside the mosques.

Moroccan Mosques of Amsterdam in the Pre–Theo Van Gogh Era

The city of Amsterdam is a unique laboratory in which to observe the clash between advanced modernity and traditional imams. It also allows insight into the radicalization process of some imams and their congregations. Amsterdam, after all, is where Mohammed Bouyeri, the Dutch-born Moroccan Muslim killer of cinematographer Theo van Gogh, took his first steps to a radical ideology of Islam. It was in the At Tawhid mosque that Bouyeri consumed the doctrine that would lead to his murder of Van Gogh, who had made the anti-Islamic film *Submission*.

I had the privilege of doing sociological fieldwork in the 1990s in all fifteen Moroccan mosques of the city of Amsterdam and of interviewing some famous imams in the Netherlands. With some help from my colleagues, I collected on audiotape a random sample of ninety sermons given in the fifteen mosques in Amsterdam between 1992 and 1995. I attended most of the services to listen to these sermons, and associates audiotaped those that I could not attend. I also attended many of the lessons held by the imams during the week between prayers and audiotaped many of these. These lessons are largely a form of rehearsal for the Friday sermon. A number of radio and television discussion programs between 1991 and 1996 that were aired in Amsterdam on Dutch broadcasting outlets that gave time to minorities also became part of the basis for this chapter. I also draw on tracts and books by imams, for example, a book available only in mosques of Imam Alkhamlichi, written in Arabic, *The Path to Paradise: 1995*, which is a 727-page collection of eighteen years of his sermons in the Netherlands.

To study the process of the establishment of a religion of outsiders within just one city—their motivations to construct a specific mosque, the problems this presents in the public space in regard to strategies, financing, interdependent relationships, and the psychological and social processes involved—allows more insight and understanding than the superficial descriptions of a catchall study. The sociogenesis of a mosque is a process of transplantation of the Islam of the Moroccan diaspora in the Netherlands.

Most of the mosques are large and sober spaces, comparable to modest churches, without any form of decoration. The mosques have Arabic names, also written in Latin letters, for example, Al Kabir, Anour, Al Ihssan, Attawihid, and Asoena. Most of the time, there is no translation of the Arabic names. Van Bommel, a Dutchman who converted to Islam and who became an imam said: "These Arabic names are a symbol of distance for the immigrants, both Moroccan and Turkish, the distance between the Dutch society and the migrants."[7]

The mosque is both a sacred and secular (profane) space, which functions as a place of cult contemporaneously with cultural and commercial activities, where identity expressions take place that could interfere with its religiosity. For Muslims, it is the house of Allah and the Umma because, according to one imam, it is the place in the world where "the light of faith shined for the first time. The mosque will remain the origin of the sunrise throughout the ages. In the mosques, Ulamas studied to fill the world with the light of equality, sciences and knowledge." That is why, according to another imam, "The mosque is our school, our university, it is the place where the good is." These opinions reflect those of a group of imams and emphasize the educational role of the mosque. Another said, "The mosque is a place of learning, of unity, which permits one to become one who is chosen by Allah. There they learn to pray to Allah, unified and facing Kibla [in Mecca] in a line, there is no better unity than the one of the followers in collective prayer behind one man [the imam] for one Allah. They read one book. They direct themselves towards Kibla [Mecca]. They bow in prayer, and the people who fill the mosques are those who adore Allah." In the words of another imam, "Because in the mosque the believers are hand in hand, the people recognize one another, and there is a union of hearts . . . the mosque is the best platform for Muslims to have meetings and prayer." If we look to another group of opinions, from imams with an expansion mission, we see "the mosque is a parliament. The members of parliament are the believers." The mosques have a function of Islamization on the global level. According to the imams who represent this view, the mosque is just a platform to launch Islamizing missions. One of the quotes from my dissertation, "The Imams of Amsterdam," which includes a corpus of sermons I collected in the early 1990s, says:

> The role of the mosque is to form the mujahidin [jihadist] and the fatihun [Muslim leadership that "conquers" a new country] who have a universal mission [because] this house of Allah is an institution to call for Allah, it is a university for the conservation of the divine Sharia, it is an Islamic center, a paradise on earth, a zone of honor and sanctity. Why not? There where the name and the word of Allah are repeated. It is a place where you learn the Koran and the rituals. In the mosque the angels descend with mercy. The sky and the earth are happy in such occasions. God gave us the order to build mosques in time and space according to our needs and capacity . . . because building mosques is an obligation of capacity. If some people in a neighborhood build a mosque the other people are not obliged to build another one, but if no one does it Allah will punish all of them . . . if your village has only three Muslims, you need to have a mosque because the collective prayer makes Satan disappear.[8]

In fact, we can hear certain strong expressions from the same corpus of sermons like "from the mosque come the *fatihun* [the conquerors] and the *mujahidin* [the combatants] to liberate humanity from slavery and spread the cult of Allah." To realize this goal, the immigrant mosque-goer has to go to the mosque as many times as possible every day and stay there as long as possible in prayer. It is the only way to get to the row of the "good-doers." The good-doers are the people whose names are displayed on a special board as core givers to the mosque.

There are also different rows for the level of givers marked in different colors (red, yellow, blue). Imams want followers to come often to the mosque to establish a tradition of giving by stimulating them to visit the mosques as much as possible, especially the five times each day when Muslims are required to pray. An empty mosque is something imams have to discourage. Again, another quote from the same corpus:

> You have to increase the number of steps to the mosque. Prayer is a union between you and Allah [the Ribat—the term *ribat* comes from the verb *rabata*, to tie a knot, in this case between oneself and Allah, and the one who fulfills *ribat* is called *murabit*]. The *murabit* is the one who guards or protects the frontiers of the Islamic country [the mosques], to stop the infiltration of enemies. You faithful, you are the *murabit* in this mosque. Is there anything better in life than to wait for the next prayer after finishing the first prayer?

These groups of opinions of imams attach great importance to the mosque itself. For them, the mosques are all beautiful and equal. For them, there is no difference between a big mosque and a small mosque, a big minaret or a small minaret. "What gives the value to a mosque? Is it the height of the building? Is it the architecture? Is it the ornaments? Is it the carpets? No the value of the mosque is the quantity of honor the grandeur you give to it." According to these imams: "Any mosque is more beautiful than the palaces of kings and presidents. God wants mosques to be constructed, and we burn incense and make them sacred." Why? "The mosques are directed towards Allah. They are full of faithful who believe in God and the last judgment." The three groups of imams share the same point of view when it comes to the organization of the mosque. "The mosque is the house of God and the Umma, and has three pillars: the *djma'a* [the council of the mosque], the imam, and the faithful who fill the mosque. And these three pillars have to play their role, no more and no less, according to the Koran and the Sunna." The psychological impact of these comments from sermons explain in a way the desire for the multiplication of mosques in the Netherlands. Van der Veer explains that the religious practice in immigration helps to Islamize the whole question of assimilation and ethnicity.[9] In that perspective, building mosques is an increase in the degree of Islamization of guest workers and their families. In religious communities, the sharing of rituals, through prayers and Ramadan and the days of fasting, plays a crucial role in shaping a group identity among individuals. In postcolonial immigration, religious organization has formed a collective life for migrants; paradoxically, their immigration into a country of "nonbelievers" and "infidels" has reinforced their religious engagement, and the mosques and temples, for example, are symbols of cultural pride and resistance against racism.[10] But how can we explain the motivation of the Muslims in the beginning of their arrival to the Netherlands, when they began building mosques even before the family reunions and even before the recruitment of imams, at a time when they did not speak the local language? How was the first mosque built? What is the story behind the first mosque?

Mosques and the Emergence of the Politics of the Sacred

In the first period of immigration, the guest workers prayed and had religious rituals in their living quarters, in factories, and even on the streets. An individual played the role of the imam and conducted the prayer. These activities, in the absence of professional imams, were done in harmony because everyone was voluntarily devoted to prayer without hierarchical pressure. The first

Moroccan mosque opened its doors in Amsterdam in 1972, after a major political battle. An employee of the Dutch postal service, a man of Moroccan origin, played the role of mediator between the municipality and the faithful who wanted to buy a building to be used as a mosque. This employee spoke Dutch and wanted to help his fellow Muslims. One of the founders of this first mosque told me: "You [Dutch civil servants] put all the Muslims in one glass and then put your hand over the glass, just like when a bee gets in a glass and you suddenly cover the glass. This is the case of the Muslims without mosques: it's like a bee without oxygen." He and others worked together to make a convincing case to the municipality of Amsterdam. The construction of this first mosque constituted a very important field of struggle between individuals and organizations in the history of the city and the history of the migrants in the country. The struggle over the construction of the first Moroccan mosque was characteristic of the struggle that other Muslim ethnic groups experienced in the country. The completion of the first Moroccan mosque in Amsterdam marked a new phase in the construction of the Moroccan identity in Holland. Symbolically, it constituted the emergence of the role of the sacred in shaping religious and ethnic identity. The founding of this first mosque corresponds with the beginning of family reunions. These two important phenomena gave more visibility to Moroccan migration.

In the book *Moslem in de Polder*, a series of interviews on Muslim immigration to the Netherlands, Beerehout, a Dutch Muslim convert, makes the observation that the first thing Dutch migrants in Canada did was build a church.[11] There are also parallels between religious behavior among migrants from Morocco and Turkey and the behavior of Catholic villagers in Brabant in southern Holland, who until recently were listening regularly to the advice of the priest.

Jacques Waardenburg, an eminent Dutch Islamologist, thinks that the Muslims look with envy to the privileges of the Christians in the Netherlands, even though there is a strict separation between church and state. He said:

> Christians and Jews had support from the state in constructing churches and synagogues, but the Muslims, in the most crucial moment of their lives, at the beginning of their immigration, never had any help. Thus, Christians and Jews have the most beautiful churches and synagogues but the Muslims have to pay from their own pockets to use garages, barracks and schools for their worship services, etc., in order to practice their religion. A part of the mistrust of the migrant towards Dutch society can be explained by the politics of the government on immigration in the 1970s.[12]

The citations from the sermons of the imams show that the mosque has a particular role in immigration. Even if every imam defines in his own way the importance of the mosque—it is a university, a house of Allah, a permanent parliament, a school for the mujahadeen (combatants), and so on, these citations from the sermons open up a new semiological space where it's possible to compare mosques and the positions of the imams. They show us that the space of the sacred is also a space of competition and conflicts. From a historical perspective, the conflict was always part of the structure of the religious field. External factors also greatly influenced the mosque and the religious field.

On Friday, November 19, 1993, visitors to the city's largest mosque, Al Kabir, found copies of an open letter to the administrative board of the mosque distributed near the front entrance. The authors asked for the return of an imam who had been forcibly expelled. They wrote: "We always want to unify the *djma'a* around the world of Allah, in the house of Allah, and make the mosque a place of gathering and unification and not a place for quarrels and disobedience to God." The police had closed the mosque and organized a mediation committee after dramatic incidents in the mosque involving knives and even guns. Consequently, September 18, 1993, is one of the darkest days in the history of the Muslim community in Amsterdam: the faithful were prohibited from entering the mosque on Friday, praying together, and listening to the sermon. The leaflet accused the president of the administrative board:

> You did not respect the agreement and you postponed finding a solution. You dribble [bounce the ball]. You thought only of your personal interests and you made us believe that the problems were solved. Your presence in the mosque kills the spirit of the mission of the mosque, which is to keep the torch of Islamic learning. This place is for our sons, daughters, and women, in a world full of degeneration far from the world of Allah and the *sunna* of our prophet. The mosque in the time of the Prophet was favorable for gathering, for prayer, for it was a popular university where the faithful came to be cultivated spiritually and culturally. You are obstructing the activities of the mosque. Take, for example, the revenues of the shops: you yourself said that it is in the order of thousands of guilders. You spend left and right without thinking of the general interest. You abuse the goods of the Muslims. You bought a car for 30.000 to 40.000 Dfl, without the consent of the *djma'a*. You rented other buildings belonging to the mosque. Restore the trust to the mosque, as you promised the police.[13]

The president of the mediation committee proposed a committee for controlling and monitoring how the council operates. Three points were proposed:

1. Give voting rights to all the faithful who come to the mosque, as was suggested by the council's opposition, because the faithful constitute the total of the Muslim community, so that everyone who comes into the mosque can vote on its issues.
2. No decision could be taken on activities in the mosque without agreement from the majority of those who pay the weekly or monthly *shart*. (The number of the faithful in the mosque on Friday is almost 1,500, but there are only 225 individuals who contribute regularly to the mosque's finances and whose names therefore appear in prominent places in the mosque. The others contribute only sporadically.)
3. The president of the mediation committee must accept that the imam would return to the mosque, and that the council would also remain.

Imams, according to the president of the mosque's council, are often guilty of "forgetting that they are employees and I am the employer, the boss." Imams want to lead. They are dependent on the contributions of the faithful, which means that there is a working relationship, and as long as the imams refuse the employee-employer relationship, the problems will remain. To elaborate this case further, when there are problems such as these between the imam and the board or the faithful contributors, the solution is often to bring in a sheikh to remediate the situation. In this very complex situation in Amsterdam, even the sheikh's intervention was not accepted, and he felt as if his authority was undermined, despite being known and respected in the community. In some cases, they even ask the consulate from the country of origin to mediate. This means that a foreign country becomes a part of the conflict. In sum, different mediators have been used: the Dutch police; the sheikh, who is a mediating figure in the country of origin, where he plays the role of judge; and even the country of origin itself, which is represented by consulates and embassies that may get involved in the conflict.

Mosque, Conflict, and Hierarchy

Conflict is a principle of structure in the migrant Muslim communities where sometimes there are neither winners nor losers. The congregational traditions and implicit rules on how to behave in various circumstances constitute strategies of containment, so that even when a conflict erupts it can be quickly brought under control. There is, in any given moment, an equilibrium resulting from the spontaneously created solidarities and sometimes from rational choices made by the parties in conflict. The actors find themselves in the moral dilemma of having to choose between one party and another party; to remain silent is seen as a sign of complicity. Even if the meaning of the conflict is not entirely grasped by the actor, he is perceived as partisan. Marcel Gauchet is right when he thinks that conflict creates a moment of collective reflexivity, in an unconscious way, and guarantees a reflexive function that excludes the conscious choices of the actors.[14] In other words, the political compromise within the mosque adapts itself to the juridical compromise brought about by Dutch law in order to guarantee the social compromise between the imam and the community. The apparatus of the welfare state guarantees the achievement of these compromises by allowing the community a humane option—the imam can be fired, and the community knows that the state will take care of him in the form of benefits. Such conflicts bring on a war of strategies, positions, and stands and open a new field of negotiations amid heightened tensions. By conflict, I refer to the rival forces struggling for power and the structured opposition of antinomic visions of the collective expectation of what one has to be. The organizational scheme in this case is ideological. The struggle for power is not always visible. It is beyond that. There are double agendas of community leaders that mask realities and make the conflict difficult to grasp and to understand. The reality is presented in a spontaneous way through visible characteristics but with a deeper meaning that is visible to only a select few. There is a mosque in the Netherlands where the president of the board declared in the presence of his imam:

> We are the only mosque that has never had a problem for more than seventeen years. The faithful like me a lot and listen to me. During this Ramadan, we didn't have any subsidy, but for the sacred night the faithful and *djma'a* bought 200 kilos of meat, 150 liters of milk, 120 loaves of bread, at least 5,000 guilders in expenses. Every day of Ramadan, we make the *harira* [soup] for at least 200 people, with dates, bread, and *shabakiyya* and other sweets. It is not Morocco paying for that; it is not Holland. The faithful and others pay the *shart* every month.[15]

Despite the conflicts that may emerge in any mosque through the course of a year, during Ramadan, the Moroccan mosques are transformed into restaurants where everyone is welcome, both Muslims and non-Muslims. Ramadan is a month-long break from internal conflict within the mosques, which display their best traditions of hospitality. The previous quote from the president of the board to the new imam in his mosque was, in fact, a warning to the imam to not get involved in politics; the president urged the imam to continue the tradition of this mosque as one without internal conflict.

Mosques in the European diaspora are echo chambers for the social problems of the community. In this sense, the mosque is both an open place and a closed place to the power games played by the different actors within it. Unlike the mosque in the countries of origin, the European mosque, year-round, contains a marketplace selling fruit, vegetables, bread, and meat. It also often has a café, a newsstand, bookstalls, and sometimes even a travel agency, all catering to the local male Muslim community. The mosque is structured by the rhythm of prayer, five times a day, and the Islamic calendar, and also by the configuration of its functions.

The main (men's) entrance of the mosque is often a grand hall, with shelves along the walls for storing shoes, which are not allowed to be worn inside. On one side of the grand hall is a large room with men's toilets. These are not standard European pissoirs because it is not appropriate in the mosque to have one's private parts visible to others in any way. Instead, there are individual closed compartments, and within each is a fifteen-centimeter hole in the ground, a faucet with running water, and a bucket for cleaning the area and the body. Plastic sandals are available for everyone to use in these toilets, so that bare feet do not get wet. After relieving oneself and cleansing oneself in the appropriate fashion with the water available, one crosses the room to a wall of faucets. There, men sit on stools performing ritual ablutions: washing their hands, mouths, noses, faces, and lower arms, and with their fingers and hands, passing water across their foreheads and hair. The ritual is completed with the washing of the feet. One begins always with the right hand, and each of the aforementioned parts of the body is washed with water three times. Water is seen as a source of cleanliness and purity. Once this process is complete, men move into the main room of the mosque, which is often carpeted with Arabic motifs and is often adjacent to a library full of Korans that have been donated by various countries and Islamic organizations. From the large main room, it is also possible to enter a smaller room where the imam usually prepares his sermons, and where he sometimes sleeps overnight in the mosque. At the periphery of this main room, there are also classrooms for teaching Arabic and the Koran on the weekends and after school hours during the week. All of this space is accessible only to men. Young girls may be brought in by their fathers, but by age twelve at the latest, they are expected to enter only through the women's entrance and then remain in the parts of the mosque that are reserved only for women.

During the feasts and religious holidays, the mosque is transformed into an enormous space for unlimited hospitality. It is important to note the distinction between large and small mosques. There are mosques that can accommodate fewer than 500 people and larger mosques that can accommodate up to 2,000. Working at a large mosque is more prestigious than working at a small mosque. The majority of the people who work in the mosque are volunteers, with the imam usually the only paid staffer. An example of a prestigious volunteer position is the muezzin, the man who performs the call to prayer. The imam appoints the muezzin. To maintain his position as the muezzin, he has to be at the mosque almost all the time it is open. Otherwise, others will quickly volunteer to conduct the call to prayer. Some volunteers are responsible for the food: for cooking it and bringing it in to be served. When the imam is absent or sick, the volunteer who replaces him is seen to have the most prestigious function one can have.

How all of this is financed has ramifications for the mosque's political leanings, as well as for the funding's hold on its staff and members. Many mosques are financed by Gulf states, particularly by Saudi Arabia. The Saudi state also aids Islamic schools, sometimes even covering the children's transportation costs for youngsters who live in communities that are not near a school. Muslim children in Roermond, a city in the south of the Netherlands near Maastricht, for example, are taken by bus to an Islamic school some thirty kilometers away; their trip is paid for by a wealthy Saudi. The Gulf states are not the only supporters of mosques and Islamic activities in the Netherlands. In Utrecht, a Libyan-financed mosque provided subsidies for many activities until 2001, when the imam was expelled by Dutch authorities for espionage. There are also a number of mosques with close links to Islamic organizations in Pakistan. Other mosques are supported by Turkey, Morocco, Egypt, and other countries or organizations in those countries.

There are also opposition movements within the countries of origin, and these are usually religious fundamentalist movements, which are working to strengthen their influence in Europe. The result is that mosques often can be identified as belonging to one camp or another, from a particular country or movement, either being in support of an existing government in the country of origin or in support of a fundamentalist movement that opposes the existing government. One mosque is described as the Saudi mosque, for example, and another as the Daw'a mosque, which refers to the fundamentalist opposition to the Saudi government.

Mystic and magic "healing" sects may also be evident, such as the l' Alawiyya sect, whose leader is an Algerian living in France who often comes to Utrecht to meet with his followers in the Netherlands. People come from as far away as Germany and Denmark to see him in Utrecht. He's the Benny Hinn of North Africa. None of these healers or mystics, or the sects that they have produced, are seen by the Islamic leadership in Europe as legitimate representatives of the religion, and they are mostly seen as not being religious.

Every mosque has its own space for selling books, cassettes, and videos made by the imam or obtained from the Arab world, with recorded sermons and readings from the Koran. In the past, people preferred the Egyptian way of reading the Koran, which was viewed as the classical style of reading. Today, however, the most popular way of reading or reciting the Koran is the Saudi style, which is more emotional than the Egyptian, or classical, style. This is noticeable not only in Amsterdam but also in all the European capitals and throughout much of the Muslim world. This is a very significant and important development for the pan-Islamic movement because it involves a recitation of the Koran that is a direct emotional plea. Such emotionalism, with its play on deep-seated gestalt, can explain the rise of fundamentalism or Islamic revival. A parallel can be made with the songs that accompanied the Bolshevik revolution in order to stimulate adherence to the new ideology.

A New Interpretation of Islam

The Muslim communities are, in fact, confronted with a new interpretation of Islam in Europe, in which the imam is the holder of the symbolic capital. He defines the normative rules of behavior. By contrast, the majority of the Moroccan immigrants are from villages (from the Rif), where the marabou, the tribe, and the family play a very important role.[16] In Europe, the imam finds himself confronted with a local interpretation of Islam, the national and international interpretation of Islamic movements, and the ideologies of transnational Islam. All these factors have to be considered to understand the structure and nature of the religious field. Juridical, political, and economic factors are each important to understanding the mechanics of how this field functions and its degree of autonomy, particularly whether it is economically autonomous. From this perspective, we can better understand the sociogenesis of the mosque.

Until now, the sociogenesis of the mosque has never been the subject of study. The mosques are studied in an external way or in a very conventional way—the architecture, the history, or the styles in different Muslim countries, such as Pijper's study of the Javanese mosque—but no systematic study of the mosque as a community, as a space that is both sacred and political. Only in 1998 in the Netherlands, for example, were there two monographs, one on a Moroccan mosque in Tilburg and another on a Turkish mosque in Rotterdam, and in 2002 in France, a monograph about the French mosques was produced by Xavier Ternisien.[17] These studies stress the difficulties of establishing and building the mosque, as well as the opposition of the non-Muslim indigenous population toward the construction of the mosque and the problems of migrant communities in local politics. In Rotterdam, the city council could not budget money for the entire cost of a mosque and approached Saudi Arabia to cofinance the restoration of an old church to be used as a mosque. There is also a comparative study on a number of Turkish mosques in Holland and Germany to address questions about the institutionalization of Islam in those two countries. In his book *From Carpet to Minaret*,[18] Nico Landman describes in general terms the parameters of the Muslim community in Holland based on a review of literature, without any fieldwork. Xavier Ternisien discusses the politics and counterpolitics around the emergence of mosques in France.[19] Gilles Kepel's 1987 study of Islam in the suburbs touches on almost the same issues that can lead to mobilization of young Muslims in France and their vulnerability to the influences of the revival of extremist Islam worldwide.[20]

Hidjra and Legitimation

Before discussing the content of some of the sermons delivered in the mosques in the Netherlands in the early to mid-1990s, I need to discuss the historical context of one of the key concepts that structures the religious imagery and discourse: the *hidjra*. Defined historically, the *hidjra* is the migration of Muhammad (who was not yet established as the Prophet) from Mecca to Medina. The *hidjra* also demonstrates the distance between the representations that structure the imagery of the group, the social immigrant group, and the social realities interpreted by these representations.[21] Over the centuries, the layers of interpretation of the *hidjra*, without ever being reflexive or critical, have given the contemporary imam the possibility to legitimate almost anything with the use of the concept.

Muhammad, the legend goes, left his tribe and his social network as a fugitive. Medina became majority Muslim when Muhammad came to live there. This moment has been seen as the beginning of Islamic history, but it has also been mythologized. Almost all of the Moroccan imams who live in Amsterdam, for example, liken their migration to Europe to Muhammad's migration to Medina, with the caveat that they and their followers, in order to be good Muslims, must return to their country of origin regularly and ultimately be buried there. But the metaphor goes further. Some imams say that their followers in the Netherlands should live as the companions of Muhammad did in Medina; in other words, the imams suggest that they are the contemporary guide to salvation, like the Prophet was in his time.

Hidjra is a very important identity marker because it is a term used almost daily to refer to the immigrant community of Moroccans in the Netherlands. It is now used by the migrants themselves and by the Arabic-language media to refer to the migrant communities. One of the imams of Amsterdam even referred to walking to the mosque as *hidjra*, because one migrates through the non-Muslim public space to get there.

Migration versus Integration

The structure of the Islamic myth about *hidjra* can be depicted in a diagram, illustrating the relationship between migration on the one hand, and integration on the other hand, based on sermons and interviews with the imams. On one side, we see the path to Heaven. On the other side, we see the path to Hell. The path to Heaven is shown with only three ovals or steps. The first is to imitate the real Muslims—in other words, the Prophet and his companions—in all deeds and actions. The second is to pledge allegiance to Allah. The third and final step is to remain a good Muslim with all the positive consequences, including eternal salvation. On the other side of the diagram, we see five steps. The first is to imitate the non-Muslims, the second is to pledge allegiance to the non-Muslims, the third is to become a non-Muslim, the fourth is to be excommunicated and be a nonbeliever, and the fifth and ultimate final step is integration. Integration means *perte absolue*, an absolute loss to the Muslim community.

The possible path to Hell is often the subject of sermons. There are many temptations. An example of a common temptation is taking Dutch citizenship and getting a Dutch passport. This was simply not acceptable to the imams. According to one imam: "People who have a weak mind and weak reasoning think that naturalization is interesting or attractive ... the ulama of the Zeytuna Islamic University in Tunisia [which is like the University of Qarawiyin in Fez, Morocco, one of the oldest in the Islamic world] in the time of French colonialism in North Africa had a fatwa against converts and against people who had been naturalized so that they would not be treated as Muslims and to prevent them from being buried in Islamic cemeteries." Up to 1996, Moroccans in the Netherlands were the least likely immigrant group to take Dutch citizenship.

Moroccan imams in Amsterdam generally stayed away from using the word *integration* and instead used the term *cohabitation* or *coexistence*. They stimulated parents to send their children to exclusive Islamic schools; consequently, the number of such schools multiplied during the mid-1990s.

Rights for Women—and Everyone Else

Three issues featured prominently in the Amsterdam imams' sermons during my fieldwork in the early to mid-1990s. One was the issue of women working outside the home. The second was the issue of women wearing the veil. And the third was the issue of divorce.

WORKING OUTSIDE THE HOME. Many of the Moroccan imams in Amsterdam were hostile to the idea of women working outside the home if doing so meant working with men. Even work delivering newspapers—work that takes place alone and usually on bicycles—was not deemed appropriate. There were a variety of shades of commentary by imams on women and teenage girls working outside the home; the most extreme statement, from an imam who could be considered a revolutionary because of his extreme views on most issues, was: "By letting your daughter deliver newspapers or do other kinds of work, you force them into prostitution." Only one of the fifteen Moroccan imams in Amsterdam expressed approval of women working outside the home, but only in certain circumstances and in honorable professions.

WEARING THE VEIL. Although the issue of the veil is not the major issue in the Netherlands that it has been in France, there was a lot of public debate in Holland in the early 1990s about the repercussions of the French discussion. A program on Dutch national television aimed at minorities brought on an alim, not an imam but one who has been trained in interpreting the Koran, from the United Kingdom. He advanced a very liberal position: "wearing a veil is not an obligation." According to his interpretation, individuals can decide for themselves whether to wear a veil, and it would not affect one's fate. No one from the Netherlands was invited to offer an opposing opinion, and on the following Friday, many sermons included this as their topic. Based on my analysis of the sermons at the largest mosques, and subsequent interviews with imams whose sermons I did not tape on any particular Friday, I found that all but one of the fifteen imams in my study heavily criticized this liberal perspective. They agreed that Muslim women should wear a veil. One imam expressed it this way in his sermon: "The veil is not a question of *idjtihad* (religious intellectual endeavor). Science or intellectuals have nothing to say on this question. The Koran was very clear on this point. Putting the veil on your head is an obligation. In the Arabic language everything which covers the head is a veil. In the pre-Islamic period, women were wearing a scarf on their head, but their chest and their neck were not covered. The Koran asks for a veil to cover the neck, shoulders and the chest." Another imam said to his followers: "Parents have to accept this choice prescribed by the Koran for their daughters."

DIVORCE. *Repudiation* refers to the Islamic process of divorce, when the man says, "I divorce you," and the woman cannot challenge the decision. With the exception of one imam, all of those I studied were solidly behind the most conservative position, which gives women no rights whatsoever in the matter of divorce. One imam summed up the position this way: "The sharia (Islamic law) does not have to adapt to the modern world because these are divine laws. People have to bend to the sharia." In 1992, when I organized a public discussion on the topic with twelve imams, and even today, when Moroccan migrants divorce in the Netherlands, the divorce is not recognized in Morocco. There are more than six thousand divorced Muslim women in the Netherlands who are still considered to be married by the government of Morocco. This continues to be an important issue in Morocco and has been a major policy point for the new King Mohammed VI. He wants to improve the position of women, and as part of a larger package of policy initiatives, steps are being taken to have Parliament consider passing laws on these matters, but progress was stalled in March 2000, when hundreds of thousands of Moroccans demonstrated against reforming the Code of Personal Status, called Moudawana, Morocco's family law. This was the subject of major demonstrations in Rabat, organized by feminists, and counterdemonstrations in Casablanca, organized by fundamentalists.[22] In Amsterdam, the imams supported the fundamentalist perspective and circulated petitions to prevent any change to the law.

With the issue of the equality of women came the issue of democracy, which is also often the subject of sermons. As a whole, the imams were largely of a similar opinion on democracy: real democracy is in Islam. Islam, in their view, offers another type of democracy, which is the rule of the word of Allah. All Muslims are equal. Through the Shura principle, there is regular consultation among Muslims about the Koran and the prophet Muhammad; some say this demonstrates that there is an alternative to Western-style democracy.

They believe that democracy in Western societies gives too much liberty to marginal groups to dictate what has to happen in the public sphere. They are horrified in Amsterdam, for example, by the coffee shops where hashish and other drugs are sold, by the open toleration of prostitution, by the visibility of pornography on television, and by nudity and issues of sexual identity—which can be found even in Dutch children's television.[23] They are also taken aback by the sometimes bold and almost routine displays of homosexuality on the streets and in advertising; if groups to which these pander are minorities, then how, they ask, is the Netherlands a democracy?

Yet they praise the social welfare state in the Netherlands for its caring role. The level of provision for immigrants, in terms of housing and health care, is often complimented. One of the imams put it this way: "Holland could be the best Islamic country in the world if the Dutch became Muslim and got rid of all the sex and drugs on the streets."

A Discourse of Insiders and Outsiders

Islam in the Netherlands in the 1990s was preached as a distinctive exclusionary faith. The sermons of the imams give us insight into the development of the configuration of the religious field in contemporary Europe. Despite the different types of economic and religious capital identified among the imams, their sermons revealed far more similarities than differences when it comes to taking stands on controversial social issues. Had I focused on religious sermons or sermons of theological value, I may have found differences among the imams that could have been traced to their particular stores of knowledge, so that those who had formal training might have differed in their discussion from those who had no formal training. But as this chapter suggests, one's religious or economic capital, or one's level of education or formal training, appears to have had no bearing on one's opinions on controversial social issues stemming from the new society in which these transplanted imams found themselves in the early to mid-1990s. The imams observed the Dutch society in which they live and expressed their opinions openly in their sermons. They spoke to their followers, those who are within an inner circle, who are already predisposed to listen. When they spoke outside the mosque, they were, almost without exception, speaking to their followers in their own language (Arabic), usually on a television channel or program that was aimed specifically at Muslim audiences, and with journalists who were part of the Muslim community and who showed them the respect that they believed they deserved.

The content, functions, variations, and vision of the messages of the Moroccan imams are still not sufficient to understand the social universe that produced them. I studied the messages of imams in sermons related to integration and Dutch society. These messages should not be seen as entirely representative of the Islamic tradition, though they display some attitudes among many of the Muslims living in Europe. These messages in the sermons, especially the message of the *hidjra*, are developed by strong subliminal imagery in the absence of historical awareness and knowledge. The imams, as new interpreters of a new social reality where Islam is a minority, produce a discourse that encloses the Muslim community and excludes outsiders. The sacred is metamorphosed by interpretations that are not inclusive of the lived reality.

Imams decontextualize and recontextualize in an ahistorical way, always referring to the time of the Prophet as if the Muslim migrants living in the beginning of the third millennium still lived as the contemporaries of the Prophet. They reiterate the words of contemporary militants, notably the word *djahiliyya*, meaning the pre-Islamic period (or the time before the Islamic "enlightenment" that started with the revelation and the migration of the

Prophet from Mecca to Medina), which is already condemned by the Koran, to qualify Western societies as anti-Islamic. According to the imams, Islam is a synonym of liberty and good, for the past and for the future. There is no real liberty or real doctrine outside the realm of Islam. The views of the imams concerning integration, assimilation, naturalization, the rights of women, the role of television, and the value of democracy are a reproduction of models of interpretation that were propagated through the writings of orthodox militants and contemporary Muslim preachers who try to instill public fervor, but in this case with a transnational public.

Note also that these religious messages, sermons, and lessons accentuate the call for more high ritual and expanded prohibitions. These prohibitions, based on hadiths attributed to the Prophet or on Koranic verses, serve to found and legitimate the operation of *tahlil*, which is the action of rendering something religiously acceptable, and the *tahrim*, which is the action of rendering something religiously forbidden. The transgression of these prohibitions can lead to *takfir*, excommunication. Even if the imam has no judicial authority to exclude Muslims from the Islamic sphere or to declare them excommunicated or non-Muslim, nevertheless, by using these instruments of *tahlil* and *tahrim*, the imam wins more symbolic power. The degree of popularity of these interpretations may determine whether the imam's position among his public is dominant or weak.

There are differences that mark the public space in the Islamic world and the tensions that are accepted or tolerated by others. These tensions reverberate in the behavior of the imams, and as a consequence, they may influence the behavior of their public in Europe. I observed that the imams are unable to make an analysis or a distinction when it comes to the history of the public space in Europe. They react uniquely but with dogmatic simplified definitions about what Islam has said. For example, they prohibit miniskirts even for toddlers, as well as the pierced earring for men. They prohibit adult women from working in the same places as adult men. They ask Muslims not to have parties or feasts with non-Muslims, where, in the words of one imam, "There is a risk that one may drink, dance, or sing, with the possible consequence of becoming a victim of 'impure seductions.'" For these imams, good Muslim women have to wear scarves, yet in the same city, Muslim women who still call themselves Muslim are displaying their bodies freely in the red light district.

There is a conflict of symbolic representations in the minds of the imams. The imam does not see the public space in Europe as a plural space, where there are cinemas, coffee shops, synagogues, mosques, red light districts, and a Parliament. The imam appears to forget that there are people from all faiths, as well as atheists, who decide what is possible in the democratic public space in Europe. The imam speaks entirely against this reality, and this is his way of helping the Muslim deal with this plural society.

The imams I studied were confronted with difficult Muslim teenagers. Teenage boys with identity issues and problems of integration and assimilation were, and continue to be, a serious problem for the community. These youngsters are not completely integrated or assimilated in the Netherlands; they remain caught between their country of origin and Dutch society. When these youngsters experience emptiness or a void born of alienation and helplessness, the imam's words give them something to hold on to. But we do not know that what they give these youngsters will help them share the ideals of the pluralistic society in which they live. We do not know if the imams have further complicated the situation of these youngsters by offering them a refuge in the traditional concept of roles in contemporary Moroccan society rather than contemporary European society. Nevertheless, the Moroccan community in the Netherlands needs the imam because they need a voice that speaks their language. Thus the principle of the sermon is positive, the function is necessary, but the result may be very complicated. The complications stem from the fact that there are many social issues on which the imam takes a stand, and there are many ways in which members of his audience may react. The imams are not prepared to advise one to tolerate many of the defining characteristics of the public space in the pluralistic Dutch society.

I found that the discourse of the sermons functions in what might be called a no-man's-land. It is a discourse that is far away from the society in which the imams live. The Mufti of Marseilles, Soheib Bencheikh, reached the same conclusion about imams preaching in France with respect to their distance from French society. He said in 1998 that there is a large gap between the migrant youth in France and the imams who preach about subjects that are far away from French society, who are against the integration of Muslims in French society, and who push skepticism rather than citizenship. The Mufti even went so far as to describe most of the imams in France as "charlatans" who misuse the sincere naïveté of their followers with a venomous discourse to extract their money.[24]

Conclusion

The imam occupies what is perhaps the most important place in the Muslim immigrant community in Dutch society. Whereas citizens of Dutch extraction may turn to their therapist, their minister or priest, their local government official, their member of parliament, or even their local pub for assistance or advice, for immigrant Muslims in the Moroccan community in Holland, the imam is the first port of call for every problem in the family. The people feel at home in the mosque and rely on the imam. But there is no evidence that the imans' attempts to help their followers contribute to the upward mobility of the Moroccan Muslim community. This is because, as we will see in chapter 4, the vast majority of Moroccan imams lack linguistic capital and knowledge about the pluralistic society in which they live, and because the vast majority of them are not sufficiently educated to be able to practice the *idjtihad*, the religious intellectual endeavor.

4

Prisoners of the Mosque

The religious passions that the Koran inspires are said to be, for us, hostile, and that it is better to let them extinguish in superstition and ignorance through lack of jurists and priests. That would be a great imprudence, because when religious passions exist in a people, they always find those who will conduct them for their own profit. By allowing the natural and sincere interpreters of religion to disappear, you will not remove religious passions, you will only hand over the discipline to furious impostors.
—Alexis de Tocqueville, "De la colonie en Algérie"

Every Wednesday, beginning in the early 1990s, I used to visit the imam of one of the mosques in what is called Amsterdam-West, and my visits continue to this day whenever my schedule permits. Our friendship developed from my role as a translator of sorts. Between bites of semolina cookies and mint tea, I would translate Dutch documents for him and, at his request, explain to him the kind of rights the documents indicated he had. One of his conundrums was that he was hesitant to ask for a day off from his job as an imam for fear of offending his congregation-employer, even though Dutch law guaranteed him a day off. His timidity in pressing the issue was part and parcel of his precarious place in society. At that time, he seldom left the mosque unless he was invited for dinner by a community member, or for births and funerals. He had come to the Netherlands from the Rif in the mountainous north of Morocco. His background was rural, and he would have been considered provincial even in Morocco. This background combined with his uncertain citizenship status—he was, during the 1990s, an illegal immigrant—to create a wariness of the culture around him that is unexceptional among the imams of many European cities. Of course, Europe had not counted on him or others like him.

Europeans did not expect that the arrival of temporary Muslim immigrants would also herald the transplanting of their faith, in a very significant way, to the heart of Europe. To a historical observer, it may have seemed that in the 1980s the drawbridge of a fortress had been lowered to allow in a Trojan—or, in this case, an Islamic—horse. After all, some claim that the European identity was constructed as a bulwark with which to defend the Christian culture from the Muslims.[1] As European leaders speak about "Christian Europe," and Turkey persists in its efforts to join the European Union, the battles of Poitiers and Vienna are summoned to the minds of those Europeans who are aware of their history.

With the import of Islam came the import of imams, community leaders from Muslim countries, most without any significant history of democracy, elections, or a free press. Imams were not able to speak freely in their sermons in Muslim countries; their texts were controlled and vetted by ministries of religious affairs that concerned themselves with preventing inappropriate interpretations of the Koran or language—*inappropriate* meaning that such interpretations might not be in the interests of the government. This does not mean that there were never any critical voices from the pulpit, but those voices were ultimately silenced. Imams in Muslim countries are fully aware of the constrained conditions under which they work.

Large numbers of imams moved to Europe in the 1970s and 1980s in response to the need for religious services for guest workers and for their families, who followed them in the 1960s. The imams often moved to Europe without any knowledge of the language and customs of the society to which they were emigrating. Once there, not only did they know less about the new society in which they found themselves than the thousands for whom they were expected to provide guidance but also they had less sympathy for the norms, values, and customs of those societies than did many of their followers.

It was often the case that these imams had moved from a cloistered environment in a Muslim country where they were actually handed their sermons by the government. They had only to read to their congregations what civil servants in the ministry of religious affairs had printed for them, or to rely on manuals of classic sermons—all of this while living in countries where Islam was the religion of the vast majority. Many imams have little or no education; others are highly educated from notable families with many famous religious clerics. Whatever the path that led them to their profession as an Islamic preacher, the outcome was the same: to be an imam, one does not have to be a creative writer or even an adequate public speaker; one must only be able to work within the constraints of the job.

Moving to Europe brought these imams certain freedoms. One of the most challenging was the freedom to produce one's own sermon, which had to be adapted to the new environment: Islam was no longer a majority religion; they were living in the Dar al Harb (taken from the Arabic that means literally "house of war" but is colloquially used as "the land of the unbelievers"), and they were confronted with new issues every day. The imam was the exalted teacher, the protector of the values and morals, and the adjudicator of conflicts between members of the immigrant community. Even the reluctant imam was thrust into this multifaceted leadership role; it came with the new job.

More challenging than issues of dress and dietary adherence in a European environment was a newfound political helplessness. Whereas in their home countries imams had functioned almost as an arm of government, European governments often gave preference to secular organizations and paid little or no attention to the Islamic religious leaders and Islamic religious organizations. In fact, there was a division of opinion within the immigrant community: the secular left-wing immigrants who were in the minority stood apart from the majority of the religious "conservative" immigrants. The secular immigrants were often in better social positions, having made the transition from guest workers to lower-middle-class professionals in social work and community organizations. The religious organizations and Islamic religious leaders suffered from the stigma that they were supporting Muslim regimes that perpetrated human rights violations, a stigma given to them by the secular immigrants and the society at large. This situation persisted until the mid-1980s, when governments and political parties began to realize that Islamic religious organizations were capable of mobilizing more people than the secular Muslim organizations. Secular Muslim social workers had to go to the mosques when they wanted to find people for projects and activities. By the mid-1980s, the mosques had become the symbol of the Muslim immigrant community.

A dramatic change was signaled in 1986, when immigrants in a number of European countries were given the right to vote in local municipal elections. In the Netherlands, this opportunity resulted in a visit from Dutch Prime Minister Lubbers, along with other party leaders, to mosques where they actually spoke in Arabic or Turkish and asked those in attendance to vote in the municipal elections. This active campaigning in the mosques led King Hassan II of Morocco to tell his subjects specifically not to vote in the municipal elections because it was not possible to "serve two flags" at the same time.[2] The king's wishes were the subject of sermons in all of the mosques because he was, according to Islamic tradition, the "Commander of the Faithful." The imams discouraged their followers from voting because it was seen as a step in the wrong direction—a step away from Islam and Morocco.

Loyalty was an issue. The Dutch political leadership was concerned with Muslim immigrants who remained more loyal to the king of Morocco than to their country of residence. The king was concerned about losing his citizens and the income they generated each year for his country's economy. The imams represented the front line of the loyalty battle. In the Moroccan community, for example, they represented a direct link to the Commander of the Faithful, King Hassan II, who was believed to be a descendent of the Prophet Muhammad. By the mid-1980s, imams had moved from relatively quiet and passive positions to become more visible and outspoken. The secular Muslims who had so dominated the scene throughout the 1970s and early 1980s receded into the background, as everyone had come to realize that the power to influence the opinions of the Muslim immigrant community came from the mosques and consequently through Islamic religious leaders.

By the mid-1980s, the field of competition among the imams widened to include Arabic-speaking imams from a number of countries, ranging from Sudan to Egypt. Also available for the slaking of religious thirst were radio broadcasts, audiocassettes, and books by imams in Saudi Arabia and the Gulf countries that provided fodder for sermons and that were also sold in the mosques in Europe. In the 1970s, the Dutch introduced radio programming in minority languages (Arabic and Turkish) for secular immigrants to discuss issues on radio talk shows, but religious spokespersons were not involved. By the mid-1980s, however, the Dutch launched Muslim RTV (radio and television) for Muslim-centered programming featuring Moroccan, Turkish, and Surinamese Muslims and Islamic religious leaders who discussed and debated political and social issues. Because Muslim RTV was broadcast in three languages—Dutch, Arabic, and Turkish—if the discussion was in one language, the other two were subtitled. This brought Muslim topics a wider visibility among Dutch speakers, who gained knowledge of the positions taken on these issues by Arabic- and Turkish-speaking religious leaders. In short, it was a platform for the religion to attract adherents or criticism.

Muslim RTV was also a platform for religious viewpoints that were occasionally extreme. Weeks before Pim Fortuyn was shot dead by a Dutch animal rights activist just days prior to the May 2002 national election, at a time when Fortuyn and his newly formed LPF (Lijst or List Pim Fortuyn) were running high in the polls and constantly in the news, Muslim RTV began an evening program with a singing recitation of Sura 16 from the Koran and a sermon of jihad against nonbelievers. This spawned a major controversy in the larger society, as the Dutch press printed headlines about what Muslim RTV, subsidized by taxpayers of the state, was broadcasting.

The Rise of Islamic Leadership in Europe

In the two decades preceding the right to vote in municipal elections, from 1966 to 1986, Islamic religious leaders moved from the background to the forefront of public discussion, all the while retaining their "imported" status. By the 1990s, the competition intensified between imams in the cities and towns where Muslim populations were growing rapidly. Imams from different Arabic-speaking countries attempted to solidify and enlarge their communities, typically by lobbying for opportunities to build new mosques and establishing a kind of hierarchy among themselves. A competition of sorts for prestige and position in the country emerged and ensued over the course of the 1990s and continues today. By mid-2005, it intensified even further, with the field of competition reaching a global level: satellite broadcasts from Mecca and other locations in the Muslim world compete for the attention of the immigrant faithful who may choose to stay home and watch TV rather than venture out into what many Muslims now perceive as a dangerous and hostile environment in the Netherlands.

Fieldwork in Mosques

I conducted extensive fieldwork in the mosques of Amsterdam and visited other mosques in London, Paris, Lisbon, Madrid, Barcelona, Berlin, Bonn, Rome, Århus, and Copenhagen during the early to mid-1990s. I interviewed imams and observed them at work during their Friday sermons, which I taped or which were taped by colleagues with the consent of the imams. I also attended a number of sessions during the week, when the imam met with key members of his mosque for lessons and activity planning. I drew on these materials in this chapter to discuss the characteristics of the Islamic religious leaders in Amsterdam a decade ago. How did they come into their positions? How did they deal with one another? What did this mean for their publics?

Throughout Europe, the practice has been to import Islamic religious leadership rather than locally produce this leadership on European soil. The need to import imams first emerged in the 1960s, when Muslim guest workers left their families at home and migrated north to earn a living. Guest workers would bring money home on their annual visits, and it was at least several years before they were able to bring their families to live with them in Europe. Family reunions—the immigration of the worker's family into their new homeland—still occur today in many European counties, despite the tightening of immigration laws. Because there are few institutions in Europe to educate Islamic preachers, new imams are often imported. Another route taken by some notable second-generation Muslims has been to go abroad for religious training and to return as an imam. Imported legally and illegally, imams with little or no formal religious education but with a thorough indoctrination into the needs of the Umma—the transnational Islamic identity—have been serving the guest workers since the 1960s.

Competition in the Religious Field

The 1992 construction and opening in Amsterdam of a prestigious Moroccan mosque is an excellent example with which to understand the competition between imams and between the different Islamic traditions. According to the precise schedule of such an event, the doors of the mosque were opened to the residents of the district before nine o'clock on a sunny, fall Monday morning, and dozens of non-Muslims were allowed to enter. The red carpet covering the entire floor of the mosque was covered by a sheet of white plastic so that non-Muslims could come to this sacred place with their shoes on. The Muslims left their shoes on the rack at the entrance, as they normally would, and the non-Muslims entered wearing their shoes. To the best of my knowledge, this was the first time in the Netherlands that visitors were permitted to enter wearing their shoes. It demonstrated openness in the attitude of the imam of that mosque.

How could the presence of non-Muslims in a sacred space be reconciled? The question is more complicated than one might think. This particular imam found a practical solution: a plastic sheet to keep the property of the sacred space protected from everything that is non-Islamic. Everywhere in the mosque, there were guides explaining in Dutch the function of this religious edifice. The imam was wearing the distinctive clothing of the ulama of Al Azhar, the most prestigious university for religious training in the Islamic world. The young imam, a second-generation migrant, had thought about every single detail of the visit of the non-Muslims. At precisely eleven o'clock, the city council alderman who represented the district where the mosque was located addressed the audience, accompanied by politicians from the other political parties and by a delegation from the Moroccan consulate. After this, the Moroccan consul read a speech stressing the efforts of the Moroccan migrants in building the mosque. Arabic refreshments, including mint tea and traditional almond-paste Moroccan cookies, were in generous supply.

The call to prayer ended the morning's activities for the non-Muslims in the audience. Immediately after their departure, a number of Muslims standing in all corners of the mosque rolled up the plastic and placed it outside. This symbolized the return of the mosque to the Muslims.

After the second prayer of the midday, a number of the guests, the imam's assistants (including many imams from other Dutch and European cities, as well as Islamic countries), civil servants representing Morocco, and religious personalities, including one from the Islamic Cultural Center of Brussels, all sat in a semicircle facing the audience. The young imam, facing the guests, began reciting the Koran in a traditionally Egyptian style—more classic and less emotive than the Saudi, or Mecca, style that was rapidly emerging as the most popular mode for imams. The reverential Egyptian tone was noticeably appreciated by everyone. He introduced all the personalities and the other imams who were going to address the audience that day. He left his special place, behind the microphones, to give the floor to the first speaker.

Those in the semicircle now moved back to sit with their backs against the wall, still facing the audience. The *minbar* [pulpit], the mobile steps on which the imam normally stands to speak, had been kept inside the closet today to give the imam's guests space to sit with their backs against the wall. Someone said to me, "In fact, we don't want to use the *minbar* on days other than Friday. The *minbar* symbolizes the Friday sermon, and today is not Friday."

This part of the day was reserved for the technicians of Islam who have the high religious authority to legitimate a sermon and face a new public. At 16:30—five and half hours after the call to prayer had heralded the departure of the non-Muslims from the mosque—the marathon of sermons and interventions by a number of imams from Holland and the religious personalities from abroad began. Members of the public could leave the mosque at any time during the sermons or go to the first floor for food, tea, cookies, and restrooms.

I will limit myself here to discussing only the sermons and not the prayers that continued for hours. At 16:48, Imam A from Brussels proposes a lecture of the Hadid of the Prophet: "I marry women, I say my prayers, I fast...." He invites the Muslims to write down any questions they might have. For many, this was not possible because they are illiterate.

The young imam of the mosque intervened and said, "At 18:00 I will give the floor to Imam X for half an hour, then we will have a break, and then continue the two last prayers of the day. We thank the *djma'a* [the administrative councils of the other mosques] who came from everywhere. You can go upstairs if you would like to have tea or eat something. The people who just came have to do two *rak'a* [kneeling bow with one's head to the floor] to salute the mosque."

At 16:55, Imam A from Brussels murmured something in the ear of the young imam, whose face displayed his concern about what was being said. The young imam then gave the floor to an Egyptian imam, one who is very contested and not accepted by the imams of Amsterdam because he had not had the profession before coming to Holland, and who is the disciple of Imam A from Brussels. They worked together for one month in Amsterdam. The Egyptian protégé seemed awkward and ill at ease, causing some embarrassment among those in attendance, and said, "It is difficult for somebody like me to take the floor after what I just heard. It is not modesty on my part. It is just the truth. I am not even an apprentice." During the Egyptian's brief intervention, the young imam disappeared from the room. Because he could not refuse the Brussels imam's request to give the floor to the Egyptian, he left the room to signify his dissatisfaction with the situation. The name of this Egyptian imam did not even figure on the short list of the young imam; this did not fit with the detailed plans for the day.

To show his modesty to the Moroccan audience, the Egyptian imam read some questions from the audience to the imam of Brussels. To an observer, it appeared that the two of them had their own talk show. It gave the Egyptian the opportunity to give the microphone back to the Brussels imam and thus avoid having to return it to the young imam, who was noticeably displeased with the situation. This was all in order to win the sympathy of the Moroccan audience. Some questions from the public were polemical and caused tension in the audience. One such question was about applying for Dutch citizenship. The imam of Brussels said very directly, "I do not advise you to do it. Do not do it." His statement was a fatwa. The audience gasped.

Someone stood up and shouted, "These are real problems. You have to offer solutions." In the heat of the moment and with the buzz of voices from the audience, the young imam went up to the Brussels imam and insisted that he give the microphone back.

The young imam attempted to calm things down without offending the imam or the audience. He said, "We are going to pray to Allah now, and time is short. What has been spoiled in decades cannot be repaired in days. Every fatwa has its part of the truth, especially when we cite the Haditz. I asked the audience to submit questions corresponding to the themes of the conference today. After dinner we will leave one another."

The most prominent imam of Holland, Imam S, was not on the list of speakers that day. Before every prayer, there must be a call to prayer. The people who make the call to prayer are the assistants to the imam, never the imam himself. But on this day, the most prominent imam in Holland—who was conspicuously absent from the list of speakers—made the call to prayer to show the audience that he was present but that he was not invited to speak. After this, he went and stood behind the young imam. It was a smart move for him to be heard during the prime time of the day, which is situated between the two last prayers of the day. The audience stood in rows behind the young imam, who said, "Straighten the rows. The straightness of the rows contributes to the perfection of the prayer."

At 18:30, after the prayer, when the young imam displayed his talent in his technique of praying as well as his choice and recitation of *surat*, he ceded the floor, in an extremely respectful way, to an old imam from Amsterdam with the words "sayyid el imam shaykh."

The old shaykh began, "Allah save us from Satan. In the name of Allah, the clement, the merciful, Louanges a Dieu, senior of the worlds. . . ." The old shaykh was seen by the entire community of imams and by the Moroccan Muslims in the country as a mystic alim and sharif. His discourse is simultaneously a compliment to the community for building the mosque and a critique toward the community, which, in his view, was starting to move away from Allah.

At 18.55, Imam S, who was not invited to speak, graciously helped the shaykh leave his seat, which allowed him to grab the microphone before the last sermon of the day. Imam S then spoke for half an hour. The people responsible for the day's organization were visibly irritated. But the audience laughed and enjoyed his humorous style and critique of the organization of the day. He had obtained the highest visibility that day. He began his discourse in this way: "I salute you with the words of Islam. . . . I want to start with a hadith and a verse of the Koran. I feel that Allah opens for me the doors of speech and knowledge. This is the Baraka [blessing] of Allah."

This opening ceremony at a new and prominent mosque helps us understand the competition for legitimacy that always exists between imams and, at the same time, shows us the laws of the functioning of a mosque's space. According to the theory of Clifford Geertz, this microexample can help us draw important conclusions.[3] In fact, we can explain through this example the hierarchy between the owners of different types of religious capital and the way authority is constructed within a determined space: the mosque.

Principles of Hierarchy

We find ourselves here with two different principles of hierarchy: one external and the other internal. Both are interdependent, and the external is subordinate to the internal. These two principles determine the degree of autonomy in the production of religious goods. The principle of external hierarchy is the success of the imam in the eyes of the public, success that can be measured by number of followers, which implies an uncontested recognition of the religious capital of the imam, including the physical portrait, his social notoriety, the capital of exemplarity, and sainthood. These things contribute to an imam getting his message disseminated. The clothes, the voice, the delivery of the sermon—all play a role here.

The principle of internal hierarchy is the "degree of specific consecration" within the restrained space of the imams. The society of the imams acknowledges (or not) the legitimacy of the religious capital of a colleague. This religious capital may be accumulated and acknowledged by its long history or heritage, such as degrees from Islamic universities or familial affiliations; for example, an imam's family may claim to be of *shorfa* descent—descended from the Prophet. In other words, this refers to the respect for peer review.

In his study on the genesis of the literary field, Pierre Bourdieu explains that one's authority dictates whether one takes a stand and how.[4] This is true for the foreign powers that want to influence the religious field in the Netherlands, who want to achieve their goals through the mosque, and who take the specific forms of organization that are accepted in the religious and social field.

To understand the logic of this field, it is necessary to understand the positions of imams and to determine the principles of the objective.

Positions of Dependence

Among the prisoners of the mosque, we can distinguish two types of imprisonment: one to the mosque and its *djma'a* (council) and the other to the country of origin. The "prisoner" is constantly responsible for all the activities in the mosque. In fact, he lives in, above, or next door to the mosque. He is permanently fulfilling the function of the public servant whom the public claims. From the information I gathered, his situation is not different from that of many of his colleagues in the country. Having lived illegally or continuing to live without a legal status or proper papers is also an experience that the majority of the imams share or have shared at some point. At the beginning of almost every career, the imam is at the mercy of the council of the mosque.

This relationship with the council results from his lack of appropriate papers, and he relies on the council for his safe conduct. During an interview, one of the imams says, "Ah, I pray every day here from sunrise to sunset." This kind of answer makes clear that his social network is excruciatingly small. He says that he has no holidays and that he works the entire week, "from Monday to Monday," as he puts it. This condition of enclosure creates a feeling of reclusion, and he expresses it simply: "I can't move anywhere." This feeling can create a desperate situation, the feeling of what the imam calls "killing darkness." or enormous loneliness that tends to bring out a longing for his country of origin.

One said, "I prefer to go back, because here I have no life." These imams are relatively young, they have no wife, no families, and they are alone in a mosque, living illegally in a new country. This is not typical of imams in Islamic countries—imams there usually have a wife and a network—but these prisoners of the mosque experience a monastic existence. The imam who lives in these conditions lives permanently in the hope that it is only a transitory condition, that his time in this land of unbelievers, this "house of war," is only temporary, and he passes that feeling on to his congregation.

The prisoner, it is important to note, glorifies the king of Morocco and the royal family for pragmatic reasons, such as passport replacement from the Moroccan embassy.

Opponents of Morocco's government have compiled a blacklist of imams who are pro-Morocco, and they criticize them for working with the Moroccan regime. This only serves to stigmatize the imam who lives within the double enclosure of cultural isolation and legal isolation. Such blacklisting also fails to acknowledge that if the imam glorifies the king in his sermons and has good relations with the embassy of Morocco and the civil servants there, it does not automatically mean that he is a spy for the country, as critics allege.

Escape from the Mosque

For the dependent imam, a *khubziste* [bread] imam, the mosque represents the place and the tool for survival, and the sermon, in terms of spiritual investments, occupies a secondary place. The most important thing is the mosque. The imam is in an abnormal situation, and he makes every attempt to normalize his existence. In order to be "normal," he needs, in the eyes of the Dutch authorities, a legal passport. He therefore does not express criticism, either in private or in public, of the king of Morocco or the embassy and its civil servants because he needs to maintain good relations to have the possibility of getting a legal passport later. Those who criticize these imams for being hacks of the regime do not care to realize the more complex personal situation in which the *khubziste* imam finds himself, a personal situation of extreme vulnerability that requires daily diplomacy to guarantee his own personal safety.

The imam's oratory skills, the content of his sermons, and the image he creates of himself contribute to the second phase of his career by determining whether he will be able to obtain the legal status necessary to live in the country.

The most common route to legal status is to marry a woman who is legally living in the country. This path to legal status may be helped or hindered by the efforts of the council of the mosque. The mosque, as a physical place, represents a special opportunity in this regard because part of the mosque is reserved for women, and this secluded (usually curtained off) place has great sociological importance. As I have seen myself and as some imams have told me, it presents opportunities for an imam to meet a woman with the perspective of marriage in mind, and a woman who would present herself is usually already legally divorced or repudiated.

Many young, unmarried, and therefore celibate imams obtain legal status through marriage, and they meet their partner at the mosque. For example, one imam who had a minimum of institutional support made it very clear in a sermon one day that he had no papers. The sermon could be heard by the women behind the curtained-off secluded area for women, and within an hour afterward, he was presented with six individual offers to help him solve his problem. If a woman wants to approach an imam with such a proposal of interest, then she sends her child, a boy, a girl, or another family member to go to the imam's room and ask if he would be willing to meet with her to talk. If he agrees, then the imam and the woman meet briefly outside the mosque in the presence of others, usually her relatives, to discuss the possible joint venture, and if it is agreed, then the marriage usually takes place within a few weeks. If, on the other hand, the imam is appreciated by the local religious community, then the faithful will help him do whatever is necessary to become legal. For a very young and promising imam in one instance, this meant being paired off with the beautiful nineteen-year-old—and presumably virginal—daughter of a prominent member of the religious community.

It's significant that for the aspiring imam who wants a permanent legal status and a more independent status from the council, marriage can provide this independence regardless of the imam's relationship with the council. Marriage can offer freedom for the imam to move to another mosque, where he could have more influence and control over the council rather than feel that he is only there to carry out the wishes of the council. This can create conflict, however, with Dutch law, as well as tension within the immigrant community. One imam, for example, married a woman in Holland in order to obtain legal status to give him a better negotiating position with his council. Later, he moved to a different mosque entirely. No one was told that this was his second wife. His first wife was in Morocco, with their many children.

As these examples suggest, there is always a breaking point at which the prisoner imam marries, if possible. It is perhaps comparable in other professions to getting an outside offer in order to improve one's salary or working conditions. But in the case of the prisoner imam, it is far more significant because marriage gives him the opportunity to later pursue other career opportunities at other mosques while at the same time enhancing his negotiating position within his current mosque. Of course, there may also be love involved, but it is love of the kind found in the arranged marriage, which has a long and distinguished history in many countries and cultures. For the woman, it brings enormous status. By becoming the wife of the imam, a woman is automatically catapulted into an almost sacred status of reverence and respect. Imagine how life-changing this can be for a woman who was repudiated or divorced and is responsible as a single mother for her children. A woman in such circumstances might even think of herself as a prisoner of her situation, and marriage to the imam is a way for her to find a sort of freedom. So the instrumentalism is on both sides in instances where the benefits of marriage are great for both parties.

The experiences of three imams, Kacem, Hadou, and Semlal, illustrate how the imams become bound to the mosques and how their marriages may play a part in their indentured or free status.

Kacem, when not at the mosque, wears jeans and a corduroy blazer. In the mosque, he wears what he calls, with derision, "my working robe," his djellaba. He studied in the religious institute of Tetouan. Although this is not a particularly renowned institute, it distinguishes Kacem from the other two imams because he is the only one to have some formal religious training. He came to Holland in the early 1990s at the request of the council of the mosque where he works still. One of his cousins is a member of the council and presented him to the council. The council decided to marry Kacem to the daughter of the president of the council. The bride-price was fixed, and in the opinion of the one who paid it, "It was a big sum of money." He married her according to Moroccan tradition: after the wedding at the Moroccan embassy, the woman lived in the house of her father until the bride-price was paid entirely. Once all the money was paid, the marriage papers would be taken to the city authorities for certification so that the marriage would be accepted under Dutch law. But the imam later found himself in a financial quarrel with his father-in-law, the president of the council for the mosque, and was almost fired. To complicate matters, when his cousin, a member of the council, did not agree with the president's proposal to fire the imam, the president of the council retaliated by not submitting the marriage papers for certification, and that stopped the process of the imam's legalization.

By contrast, Imam Hadou was helped by his mosque's council to return to Morocco to apply for a legal visa and then come back to Holland with a bride. Hadou was not initially an illegal immigrant; he is, in fact, an excellent example of the transitional actor who came to Amsterdam on a tourist visa during a vacation and stayed after the visa expired because the council of the mosque liked him and wanted him to remain. So he eventually found himself without papers. But because the council of the mosque fully supported him, he was not a prisoner and lived rather openly and freely, although illegally, in the country. Ultimately, he had to flee Holland in a clandestine way to go to Morocco to obtain a legal visa from the Dutch consulate there, but because the council of the mosque wanted his services and liked his personality, they asked the Dutch immigration office to give him legal status. It worked. When he returned to Morocco to apply for the visa, he married a woman in Morocco, and he even brought her back with him legally to live in Amsterdam.

Semlal, the oldest of the three, also comes from a village in Morocco where there are many illiterates who have immigrated to Holland. When one of these immigrants returned to Morocco from Holland, he wore a suit with a posh pen proudly displayed in the outside front jacket pocket and carried an impressive briefcase, even though he could neither read nor write. "Why don't you come and work in Amsterdam?" he said to Semlal, and gave him the address of the head of the council of a mosque in Amsterdam. Semlal then wrote a letter and enclosed a photograph of himself to offer his unsolicited application.

Two years later, he received an answer. The letter said: "If you can come to Amsterdam, you will have opportunities." Three months later, a migrant from his village took him to Breda, and from there "a good Muslim" took him to Amsterdam. All this was done without papers, of course.

He says he will never forget the warm way in which he was received in the country. "The Netherlands is known as a state of rights, even in the most distant Moroccan villages without electricity." The rights of illegal immigrants to remain in the country motivated him to go there.

Another Kind of Prisoner

The difference between the position of the prisoner imam and the *fkih* imam is the difference between coercion and internalization. The prisoner is the product of coercion by imposed social conditions, often by the council of the mosque, and the *fkih* or village imam is the product of what Bourdieu calls a "habitus effect" (*effet d'habitus*).[5] The latter refers to when the imam is a victim of a particular lifestyle or tradition but without the legal status problems that plague the prisoner imam. The prisoner refers to a heterogeneous category of imams for which the habitus, the predispositions, and dispositions serve as catalysts to transition to other positions, to find a more independent way of living.

There is not a major difference between the prisoner and the village imams in the sense that they both have weak autonomy in dealing with the council of the mosque. The *fkih* is the authentic Moroccan imam we meet in small Moroccan villages, who teaches the Koran and Arabic in the village mosque, which also serves as a village school. We also meet this type of *fkih* in the old districts or poor neighborhoods of Moroccan cities, where they may no longer have their own mosque but still teach young children the Koran and Arabic in what in Europe might be known as child care centers. During the week, he wears a brown or gray djellaba; on Fridays, he wears a white djellaba. Only on Friday may he wear the *blgha*, the special slippers, everywhere. During the week, he uses normal shoes whenever he leaves the mosque. He is not interested in any social or political activities in Dutch society or in the society where he lives. He is interested only in the Koran, which he recites in a monotone, and his daily lessons stress rituality and moral and ethical problems. He prefers to keep his distance from the council of the mosque. In a routine way, he executes his work, prayers, reading the Koran, teaching, and the Friday sermons. In other words, he is a docile imam who is eager to have a life without problems and without confrontation, requiring only a salary in order to live and support his family. He does not want to know anything about the fluctuating budget of the mosque, and he tries to maintain a neutral position in any conflicts around him in the mosque or on the council of the mosque. The only thing he does is stimulate people to give gifts and money to the mosque to keep it functioning. He lives in conformity with what is expected from him. He is very sensitive to the social control of the council of the mosque, and he wants to keep the respect of the surroundings. His relationship with his employer, the council of the mosque, is like the relationship between the bus driver and the local transportation authority. He is required to make the requisite number of stops at specific times in an orderly manner. His Friday sermon is something he reads aloud, in an almost annoying monotone drone. One is reminded of the imams in Morocco who on Fridays simply read the sermons that are distributed by the Ministry of Religious Affairs. His linguistic competence in Arabic is adequate, but he may have a considerable amount of apprehension about his own performance. I came to the conclusion after many interviews with these imams that their insecurity while preaching stems from the fact that their mother tongue is Berber, not Arabic. During a number of meetings I organized with some of the imams, one of them did not even want to speak the Moroccan dialect during the conversations we were having; instead, he prepared all his questions in written classic Arabic, and he read them aloud. One of them said to me, "I prefer to hear people speaking Arabic. Me, I'm coming from the Rif, and I learned Arabic to earn my daily bread." The fact that he is Berber-speaking gives him a feeling of inferiority in comparison with other colleagues, but it's important to note that not all Berber imams feel this way. Acceptance of their language varies within the community.

In contrast to the prisoner of the mosque, the feeling of enclosure that the *fkih* or village imam has is one that he has accepted voluntarily. Two examples illustrate this. Tarik is an imam from a very large family, for whom he is solely responsible. He learned the Koran by heart in his village. He attended courses with an alim in the north of Morocco. He went back to his village as an imam *m'shart*—an imam who shares in the money collected from the congregation of the mosque. During the opening ceremony of a school in his village where he served as the village imam, he was presented with a life-changing opportunity. The governor requested Tarik to come to his office and asked him what he, the governor, could do to help him. The governor asked him if he wanted to be a cab driver or wanted permission to open a small business. A month later, the imam went to see the governor, and instead of asking for permission to run a taxi or a small business, which is what people normally ask for when they meet with the governor, he asked for help in obtaining a passport to immigrate to Europe. He first went to work in Belgium for three years. Then, after two years in the south of Holland, he came to Amsterdam in the early 1990s. He worked the whole day and part of the night in the mosque. He almost never left the building. He was enclosed in the mosque because he liked to be there.

Falah, another imam, worked first in Algeria, then the eastern part of Morocco, and finally migrated to Europe, first to Brussels and then to Amsterdam. He has family in France and hopes that one day they will come and stay with him in Holland. He is authentic, like the imam Tarik; they both wear the djellaba and the turban.

Positions of Independence

Imams with stable legal status have enormous liberty and experience considerable freedom vis-à-vis the council of the mosque and the country in which they live. Two substantial principles of positions of independence can be distinguished, along with a third one that is rather marginal. The two principles of positions are the entrepreneur imam and the revolutionary imam. The third, the freelance imam, is described as marginal because he not only is rare but also can move in and out of other positions.

The entrepreneur imam combines various perspectives and is a strategic person. He is ambitious and multifaceted. He is not only literate but also highly educated in comparison with other imams. He does not fear confrontation, and at the same time he can use consensus to achieve his goals. He is a technician of the ritual and of the religious cult—in Max Weber's terms, a technician of cult. He is a professional. The entrepreneur uses the theatrical model in his preparation of the sermon during the week. For example, he tries out his jokes and ironic statements on the small number of people who attend his lessons each day. During the week, he tries to develop themes and ways of making statements more effectively, and he rehearses them. By Friday, he is very well prepared and delivers the sermon without a script. His facial expressions are very well executed. His professionalism is also evident in the way he works on the job: he always takes Thursday off in order to be relaxed and prepared for his big sermon the next day. Although he may pray on Thursday, he does not work on that day. He has conquered the market of the faithful, and this can be seen by the fact that during the week he receives more gifts than any other imam. He once said, "I never buy meat. Last week the *hadj*, the butcher, gave me half of a veal calf." "You know," he chuckled, "*fukaha* [fkih plural] like money and gifts." When he began his career, he was in conflict with the council of the mosque. All the entrepreneur imams I studied had this initial conflict. He looks on the members of the council of the mosque with disdain and once said of them: "Illiterates and villagers, they can't by any means be the boss." In his view, the members of the council of the mosque must do two things: "dress well and listen to the orders of the imam." He knows that he is the only one who can mobilize the masses and ask them to pay the *shart*, which is the monthly fee to be paid to the mosque. The *shart* enlarges the mosque's budget substantially and helps make it possible for the mosque to purchase the homes around it so that the mosque can grow. It also helps to subsidize the other activities of the mosque. He is very active outside the mosque. He has one foot in the mosque and the other in the society in which he lives. He does pastoral work in prisons and hospitals, and he appears every Friday on radio programs. More than any of the other types of imams, the entrepreneur is interviewed in the news media.

Adil, Mehidi, Hachmi, and Fakhir are four entrepreneural imams. Three are from the Rif, and one is from the south of Morocco. Imam Adil comes from a Berber family. His father and brother have a considerable Koranic education. All the men in the family know the Koran by heart. They are a family of *tolba*, reciters of the Koran. From a very young age, Adil was prepared like his brothers to become a *fkih* and then to go work as an imam and religious teacher in a different village. In the meantime and because of an opportunity to go to Casablanca, the economic capital of Morocco where many of his fellow villagers had moved to form a new bourgeois community, he worked for a time at the best known business addresses in the city. He later studied at a religious institute in the south of the country. He then migrated to the north of Morocco, to a small village where he earned a good living of 3,000 dirhams a month in the 1980s by teaching children the Koran and serving as a village imam in the local mosque. It was a well-to-do village because most of the families there had a son or another relative living in Amsterdam. Through his fellow villagers, he was given a temporary job in Amsterdam at one of the mosques where the imam had become very ill.

Adil learned the Berber of the north, as well as Arabic. He constructed his network of friends in the Rif and also in Europe, especially in Amsterdam. Once in Amsterdam, the council of the mosque tried to impose on him a great number of rules. Because he had no legal status at that time, having come in on a tourist visa, he had to wait a long time to change his situation and endured a low salary, without any insurance. He used another tactic, marriage, to obtain his legal papers in order to distance himself from the council of the mosque so that he could operate freely and independently. Since his marriage, his star has begun to rise. With respect to traditional dress for imams, he could be considered a bit hip: he always wears a thin, white, woolen djellaba, made of a fine merino wool, and the traditional white cap.

Mehidi is a kind of neo-imam. He arrived in Amsterdam at the age of ten in the context of a family migration reunion. He learned the Koran by heart at the biggest mosque in Amsterdam. He went to Syria and Egypt, where he attended the famous Al Azhar in Cairo, because it allowed admittance to foreigners who had memorized the Koran. Mehidi worked for a long time as a freelancer in different mosques. He does not accept the strict regimen of the council of the mosque. He broke ground on the construction of the most beautiful mosque in Amsterdam and gave it the name Umma, after the transnational Islamic "nation." He is the only imam who has assistants who are paid according to Dutch norms with standard working conditions and benefits, including paid holidays. He wears clothing like that of a shaykh in Syria or Egypt.

Hachmi is one of the youngest imams in the country. He studied at one of the institutions of Sharia in Morocco, and he specializes in the recitation of the Koran. In the early 1990s, he migrated to Amsterdam, where he has more relatives than he has in Morocco. He believes his main task is to convince young Moroccans to detach from Morocco and build a life for themselves in Europe, while living in harmony with their parents and their religion. He wears European clothes and, only on Friday, he uses a *kamis* (a fashionable lightweight djellaba that one wears over contemporary clothes) with the traditional large cylindrical cap.

Fakhir arrived in Amsterdam in the 1970s. He was installed by the council of Mosque Z. After twelve years of work, he became ill and was officially deemed disabled under Dutch law, but he remains active, gives lessons, and from time to time delivers Friday sermons in the mosque. He does not conduct the daily prayers in the mosque. He comes from a well-known *shorfa* in the Moroccan community in Holland. He refuses television spots and never agrees to speak on radio. He often is asked to mediate conflicts within the Moroccan community. He is not seen as an imam but more as a shaykh imam. The title of shaykh is given to him by the public and the imams to distinguish him as special and exalted. As a shaykh, he is highly respected. He is invited to the openings of all the new mosques in the country, and all Moroccan imams pay homage to him. In his sermons, he tries to imitate the Egyptian shaykh, the rebel *kichk*, not in the content but in theatrical style. Imam Fakhir never uses any piece of paper and always wears authentic Moroccan djellabas.

The Revolutionary Imam

The revolutionary imam takes tendentious stands. His clothes distinguish him from all other imams, as does his performance. He can change the morphology of the mosque, by changing the way the *mihrab* [pedestal] is positioned by moving it away from the wall into the center of the mosque so he is surrounded by everyone, and he never uses a wooden *septre*. For him, the West is the very negation of Islam. He regularly invokes controversy in his sermons that can make it difficult for his listeners to operate as citizens in a non-Muslim country if they take him seriously. "Do we need to shake hands with Christians?" he once asked on a Friday. On another occasion, he claimed that "every child born to a non-Muslim woman is a bastard" and that only "Muslims and Arabs will prevail in the world." He is often not identified as a Moroccan but as a member of an Islamic movement, *jihad wa-takfir* [jihad and excommunication], a branch of the Muslim Brotherhood). In Holland, he is more often than not identified as an Egyptian or Libyan working for a Moroccan mosque. He has no theological training, and yet he is extremely confident in a way that some might describe as arrogant and pretentious.

The freelance imam is one who is not connected to any particular mosque. He has the luxury of not accepting the strict conditions of the council of the mosque. He negotiates his contract and does not work five days a week as an imam. He works only on Friday and not any of the other days. He can move from one mosque to another easily, and most of the time he has another job apart from his work in the mosque, such as consulting to prisons and/or hospitals on Islamic issues, which provides him a regular income and housing.

Merging the Space of Positions

Despite the similarities in the ritual of preparing the sermon, there are differences in the ways that imams practice their profession. One of the differences can be found in their skill in public speaking. One is an excellent orator capable of speaking effectively in public at any moment; another cannot speak in public without reading from a prepared text. The experienced speaker can entertain an audience for ninety minutes without interruption; another cannot speak for more than twenty minutes before both audience and speaker become tired. This is indicative of the capital of notoriety imams can acquire by being eloquent and less attached to written sermons. Mosque-goers mention those skills after the Friday congregational sermon.

Another source of variation is the autonomy of the imam in selecting his topics. One imam may be totally autonomous, but another may be totally dependent on the council of the mosque (*djma'a*). The latter may not select controversial topics and finds himself in a situation in which the council imposes on him the topics of his sermons. A third source of variation is the content of the sermon. There are imams who focus on dogma and morals and the legal and ritual obligations; others give priority to political topics and current affairs, mixed with doctrinal and moral teachings. A fourth source of variation is the complexity and richness of the literature on sermons, which is already abundant in the Islamic world. Certain sermons contain a large number of citations from the hadith, the Koran, known generalizations, and sometimes total reproductions of previously published sermons available in books. Other sermons are based on research, citations of books and journals, news broadcasts, and treatment of complex subjects in which a considerable amount of personal effort is required for preparation. Some sermons are rooted in ideologies of specific Islamic groups and take a clear stance on different kinds of behavior; other sermons try to avoid all controversies by focusing on safe topics such as miracles or mysteries of the prophet. Certain imams have very exact views on issues, and others are less categorical and give room for new interpretations. Because every subject lends itself to interpretation, almost all subjects are possible fodder for discussion and negotiation. These discussions reveal active and passive dimensions that form the basis of the variation in the opinions of imams.

Two aspects of the social trajectory are related to the oral performance capacity of the imams studied here. The first aspect concerns the imam's schooling and training, as well as his experience and his natural talents. The imams who have had religious training in a specialized institute and considerable experience feel at ease and confident in delivering a sermon without notes. The second aspect has to do with whether one belongs to an old Islamic family with a tradition of producing *tolba* or marabous, in which the father and other antecedents have presented the techniques of oral presentation to the imam from a very young age. We have an example of Imam Adil, who recites the sermon by heart: his body language is very impressive. He has a strong voice, and at the same time he is able to change the way he emotes from being tough and hard at one moment to being tender and sensitive, almost crying, at another. In his way of presenting the sermon, there are many elements of mime and spectacle. He uses classical Arabic in his sermons but includes some words from the Moroccan dialect to make certain points, and even some Dutch words concerning social security and welfare when relevant. He often emphasizes current topics.

Imam Mehidi has an impressive presence on the *minbar* [pulpit]. He tries to recite the Koran in the way of the famous Egyptian orator Sheik Abdel Basit abd Assamad, a Koran reciter whose voice has dominated streets and homes in the whole Islamic world.

Imam Hachimi's presentation is lively, and he can speak freely without notes. He uses classical Arabic in his sermons and his weekly lessons, and sometimes he adds a Moroccan dialect. The topics concern morals and rituals, with a slight preference for current affairs.

Imam Hadou is a mediocre speaker. His sermons are characterized by a rote way of reading a prepared text. He constantly uses classical Arabic in an inflexible way, seemingly unable to unchain himself from the written sermon that he reads in a monotonous way, which is sleep-inducing for many people in his audience. In his meetings with his followers during the week, he speaks Moroccan dialect and Berber from the Rif region. He remains stiff and still while speaking, with little body language, and he is a mediocre speaker of classical Arabic.

Imam Tarik also reads in a monotone, and his sermons are delivered in classical Arabic in a rote fashion. His mother tongue is Berber, and he is not confident while speaking in public in the Moroccan dialect. That is why he always reads from a prepared written text. Although he has a Berber audience, he speaks to them in classical Arabic because he and others like him believe that delivering sermons in any other language diminishes the majesty of Islam.

Imam Fallah, on the other hand, pronounces Arabic well but limits his topics to morals and rituals. Sometimes he imitates the famous blind Egyptian Shaykh Kichk, seeming agitated or alternately slow, emotionally manipulating his followers. Shaykh Kichk, who during his lifetime had, and still has, a worldwide audience because of the cassettes he produced, was, according to Gilles Kepel, a fervent critic of Islamic governance.[6] He was jailed for a long time in Egypt because of his stands and was well known before the ascension to prominence of the Ayatollah Khomeni, who destabilized the Shah's regime in Iran. Shaykh Kichk's cassettes had the greatest influence on North African imams, and consequently, he has many imitators among the imams of that region. In response to these cassettes, a number of Islamic governments began to use radio and television to counter the efforts of imams like Kichk. To paraphrase Kepel, Sheik Kichk had the characteristics of an Islamic Robin Hood, which has helped to preserve his popularity among imams like Fallah.[7]

Imam Moukhtar's sermons are very long and made up of many very sober and serious topics. His classical Arabic is full of grammatical mistakes, but his way of speaking is captivating.

Imam Smail does not know the Koran by heart, but he has a beautiful voice and an Egyptian accent that makes the council of the mosque happy. His performance is theatrical and uses a mixture of classical Arabic and Egyptian dialect.

In the freedom of the imam in selecting the contents of his sermons, we see a parallel with the freedom of the imam to function independently of the mosque. Sometimes the migration trajectory and the lack of permanent legal status make an imam very vulnerable to the scrutiny of the council of the mosque. For example, the prisoner of the mosque and the imam *fkih*, both hobbled by their dependent legal status, often speak about moral and ritual topics, with an emphasis on solidarity, but the revolutionary imams treat topics like the moral order and political order by adding religious and political ingredients. The imam entrepreneur finds the right combination by juggling different topics to appeal to a wide audience interest.

The complexity of the sermon is also related to the social trajectory of the imam. The level of education and a classical schooling in Arabic and exegeses are very important in utilizing the talents of the imam in the composition and performance of his sermon. Only four of the imams read Arabic newspapers regularly and have a personal library with new and different religious books; the others have old "yellow" Arabic books or older books donated by Gulf countries. These yellow books are known for their outdated contents, manuals of sermons, and old interpretations of the Koran.

Finally, the social trajectory of the imam is also related to his opinions. Every imam has been influenced by another imam at one time or another. There are many imam role models in the Islamic world. Every imam with whom I spoke described his past in terms of a special figure who influenced his life. The admiration of an icon or role model is part of the construction of the profession of being an imam. Take, for example, the *fkih*, who is the prototype of the docile Moroccan imam who aims for a special image and certain reputation. He behaves as a conformist with respect to the ideas of the dominant order. Even the imam who chooses to imitate Shaykh Kichk opts for identifying with him by imitating the way he addressed the public and dressed. Another indication of the significance of role models in the field of imams is the fact that many imams have distinct clothing and facial hair. If an imam does not have facial hair and is asked why, the response is always a reference to someone he admires and chooses to imitate. Identification and imitation are the key words in the professionalization of the imam.

This means that imams are aware of the impact of their voices, their body language, and their appearance; it is why they developed a range of techniques and clichés to enhance their performance. At the same time, we may ask ourselves why they need to hide behind a special image, like an actor wearing a mask.

Just as a musician would never play an instrument that is not properly tuned, the imam also wants to attune himself to his audience. He prepares himself to be on stage—to be on the *minbar*. He composes himself and his personality in order to appear strong, sentimental, or caring, and he bows or inclines before the words of Allah. This is what the audience expects and wants. While imams use a lot of Koranic metaphors and the sayings of the Prophet (the sunna), the imam himself becomes a metaphor because he wants to distinguish himself from the pedestrianism of the audience and create a distance between himself and his followers.

Imams with less religious capital generally have no formal theological training. They reproduce standard sermons from Islamic societies originally written and delivered by imams in Islamic countries. These sermons concentrate on rituals and the religious calendar. Imams with less religious capital largely focus on the religious activities within the mosque, such as daily prayers, weekly lessons and sermons, washing (ablution) rituals, and religious festivals. They are more dependent on the council of the mosque and participate less in the European society in which they live. Their contacts tend to be limited to their faithful followers. The two examples of revolutionary imams in this study can be classified as low in religious capital because they tend to follow these patterns of reproducing sermons from other transnational revolutionary preachers. Imams with more religious capital generally have formal theological training in the sense that they obtained training from an early age, either via the family or via a special institute. They are less dependent on the council of the mosque and take more opportunities to participate in other domains of the society in which they live, for example, by paying attention to current affairs in the news or doing volunteer work in hospitals or prisons and then integrating these experiences into their sermons. With one foot in the Dutch society and the other in the Moroccan migrant community, they have a market value outside the mosque to the larger religious community.

Imams with less religious capital, notoriety, and prestige have few financial resources. They have no family wealth and no accumulated savings. They are extremely dependent, therefore, on the council of the mosque for monthly payments, and this may be an amount that is below the official poverty level. For example, when an imam needs to have his legal residency permit extended, he must apply to the foreign police with appropriate documentation, including a letter from the council of the mosque that states that he is paid 1,600 guilders (about $800) per month, which is the official base rate for a low-income household. But in fact, he may be paid 750 guilders (less than $400) per month in cash by the council of the mosque because their budget is dependent on donations from followers. The imam with low religious capital will most often also live alone, in the mosque, and send part of his monthly salary abroad to his extended family. They often get around by bicycle if they leave their neighborhood at all.

Imams with more religious capital have more financial resources. They may have inherited family wealth in Morocco or accumulated savings. They are less dependent on the monthly salary paid to them by the council of the mosque, and they usually live outside the mosque. Some own their own homes and cars and even carry business cards. They sometimes receive large gifts of money or goods from their followers, such as groceries or lamb during special holidays. They rarely travel by bicycle and sometimes even have volunteers who chauffeur them around.

Imams with more religious and economic capital have more autonomy and more prestige, both within and outside their religious community. In Pierre Bourdieu's words, they have a "symbolic capital" that they harness, which protects them and gives them the aura of being beyond infallibility—it grants them immunity. In this study, the entrepreneurial imams and one of the freelance imams fell into this category.

The next category is imams with more economic capital but less religious capital. Entrepreneurial imams also fell close to the line here. In this study, the revolutionary imams fit solidly in the middle of this category. They had more economic capital because they were subsidized by foreign sources, but they had little religious capital, in other words, little or no formal theological training. They relied heavily on the standard sermons made by revolutionary imams elsewhere. A number of *fkih* or village imams also fit in here; they brought with them some savings from Morocco but had little formal theological training.

The next category is imams with low economic capital and low religious capital. In this study, one freelance imam was in this category, along with imams who were described as prisoners of the mosque. Also in this category were some of the *fkih* or village imams. Finally, there were imams with low economic capital and high religious capital. In this study, some *fkih* or village imams were in this category, along with one of the imams described as a prisoner of the mosque.

Conclusion

In the 1990s and prior to that decade, the profession of the imam in Europe was improvised, and it continues to be so to a great extent today. Put simply, one does not need to have formal theological training or any special characteristics to become an imam. One needs only to be identified as a candidate for an imam vacancy in a mosque and approved by the council of the mosque. One needs to have the right network of friends and family. I use the term *pseudo imams* to refer to those individuals who came to Europe for employment as manual laborers and ended up becoming imams instead.

Two properties based on their personal qualities or characteristics can be used to classify imams in the religious field. One is religious capital, and the other is economic capital. If one has high religious capital, for example, even if one begins in Europe as a prisoner of the mosque, one has the possibility of moving beyond this trapped status into a prestigious position. Economic capital is equally important. With more economic capital, an imam has room to negotiate for his salary and to leave his position for another mosque when he so decides. Both of these properties, religious capital and economic capital, are important for determining the imam's degree of autonomy from the council of the mosque.

Added to this are personal characteristics such as physical appearance, including the imam's wardrobe and the imam's public speaking abilities. With few exceptions, those imams with high religious and economic capital are also the more talented and experienced public speakers, often able to mesmerize an audience for an extended period of time—possibly because they are not shackled by the council. Speaking freely without notes, they use dramatic gestures, expressions, and body language to reinforce their rhetorical skills. They also appear to take more care with their personal appearance and make more statements with their way of dress.

In addition to all the personal characteristics mentioned here, the imam and his mosque operate within a certain social and economic context in which there are external factors over which they may have little or no control. What happens when the economic basis of the mosque changes in a decisive way, when a mosque moves from being a well-to-do organization with many followers and sufficient contributions to becoming a mosque with few followers and little funding coming in from the community or other sources? Such a major change in Tayob's South African examples, in which mosques moved from being well-off to being poor, revealed that the attitudes of the same imams and their followers also changed, as did the sermons.[8] During my fieldwork in Amsterdam in the early to mid-1990s, I found examples of mosques moving in both directions, from wealthier to poorer and from poorer to wealthier. The economic context in which the imam and the mosque operate is obviously important, but it is also likely to be more variable than the personal characteristics with which imams begin their professional journey in Europe.

Of the five types of imams (which are discussed further in the next chapter), the one that most invokes sympathy is the one I have called the prisoner of the mosque, who finds himself literally held hostage within the confines of his building because of his illegal status. He suffers daily from his marginalized situation and delivers sermons that are totally dependent for their texts, ideas, and approval on the council of the mosque. At the other extreme is one who may for many invoke feelings of repulsion or disgust, what I have called the revolutionary imam. He is dogmatically wedded to his beliefs, which are part of a larger worldview that is propagated by organized transnational Islamic movements. He delivers his strong opinions with a confidence and self-assurance that some would describe as pretentious.

The *fkih* or village imam may begin with more or less religious capital but almost always with little economic capital, and his poor economic status rarely changes. (The *fkih* is not to be confused with *faqih*, which refers to someone who is well versed in religious matters in a more scholarly sense. The *faqih* is someone who has formally studied the Koran. The *fkih*, by contrast, is a religious figure who conducts rituals—including reciting the Koran in cemeteries and presiding over births, weddings, and funerals—on only the most elementary level. His knowledge is rote rather than intellectual.) The freelance imams in this study, defined as those who were not contracted to one mosque and work in a mosque only part-time, were high in economic capital but may have been high or low in terms of religious capital. Their economic capital gave them a certain freedom that the *fkih* imams did not have.

Finally, I described imam entrepreneurs as those who began with high religious capital but who may have moved from low to high economic capital, based on their ability to adapt and change to the needs and interests of their clients. They are very market oriented. They aim to attract a larger following. By bringing more people into the mosque, they bring more money to the organization. They are clear examples of upward mobility, but they almost always begin with higher religious capital.

These imams are central to Islamization from below and above. The waves of Islamization—from the immigrants themselves and the shock of Western society that has galvanized them—combined with the official Islamization dictated by Islamic countries through their embassies and the more extreme imams and schools they sponsor, have put pressure on moderate imams. The inflammatory discourse against the secular West rose to unprecedented proportions with the increased visibility of radical imams who came mainly from the Middle East. The Islamization from below targeted mosques where a potential captive audience needed to hear a discourse that raised self-esteem and helped them feel they had a reason to remain isolated from the larger Western culture. But as we see in the following chapter's analysis of how Pim Fortuyn was catapulted to political power largely through his interaction with a notoriously orthodox imam, Khalil El-Moumni, the imams also provide an easily attacked effigy of Islam.

With the rise of Fortuyn came the externalization and media proliferation of the content of the imams' sermons. Their exposure in the public sphere led to more tension and separatism.

5

Pim Fortuyn versus Islam

Muslims, Gays, and the Media's Reliance on Conflict

Before Pim, long before Pim, vast tracts of time kinds of thoughts same family diverse doubts emotions, too, yes emotions, some with tears yes tears motions too and movements both parts and whole as when he sets out to seek out all of him sets out to seek out the true home.

—Samuel Beckett, *How It Is*, 103

Did I speak to Muslims before? I've even gone to bed with them, Mr. Imam. And there we had deep conversations. But I must confess I sit at the table, for the first time, with a real imam.

—Pim Fortuyn

In early 1997, the fax machine in my office in The Hague hummed out a missive from a columnist named Pim Fortuyn at the magazine *Elsevier*. He wanted to have lunch. He felt that my review of his book, *De borrelpraat van Pim Fortuyn* (*Café Talk with Pim Fortuyn*) was overly critical. I had written the review for *Liberaal Reveil* (*Liberal Awakening*) and remarked in it that Fortuyn was too dismissive of the role of Muslims in Dutch society.

We never had lunch—thanks to the intricacies of party politics—but in the years to come, I often wished that I had, because having a real café talk with Pim at that time might have told me much more about his views and motivations prior to his meteoric rise to power.

The victory of Lijst Pim Fortuyn (LPF) in mid-May 2002 set off the equivalent of an earthquake on the Netherlands' political landscape. The Purple Coalition, made up of the "red" PvdA (Labour) and the "blue" VVD (the free-market-liberal) and D66 (social Liberal) parties, that had ruled the country for two terms since 1994 was ousted. Fortuyn's LPF won 26 seats in the 150-seat Parliament, becoming the second largest party in the country and the first party ever to win an election with a dead leader. Had Fortuyn been alive and well, he may well have been the next prime minister.[1] The CDA (Christian Democratic Appeal), which had held control of the PM's position prior to 1994, became the largest party and once more stepped into the top job, forming an unlikely coalition with the LPF and the VVD. Labour retreated into the opposition after some LPF supporters alleged that the bullets that killed Fortuyn had, in essence, come from Labour's "church of the Left." Some believe this contributed to Labour's loss of more than half its seats in May 2002.

Because of his flamboyant, articulate, and authoritative way of communicating with the public, Pim Fortuyn has been compared posthumously with Mussolini, Austria's hard-right Haider, and even former New York City Mayor Rudy Giuliani—in addition to being called the "new Messiah" in the Dutch press.[2] Even during Fortuyn's lifetime, BBC star reporter John Simpson's interview with him in his Rotterdam home was brought to a flamboyant end when, with camera running, Pim ordered Simpson to leave after the journalist had politely asked a question that suggested a comparison between Pim and France's Jean-Marie Le Pen. Pim Fortuyn compared himself to Moses, who wanted to bring his people to the Promised Land after forty years in the desert.[3]

The media were instrumental in Pim Fortuyn's rise to national power, as I will show in the following pages. But at least as important are the ways in which the media have kept Pim Fortuyn's image and his key issues alive after his death.[4] The many compelling visuals of Pim also keep his image ever present.[5] On the cover of the weekly news magazine *HP De Tijd*, the Dutch equivalent of *Newsweek* or *Time*, the week of May 2, 2003, almost a year after his death, Pim's headless bronze saluting statue was pictured with the headline: "Fortuyn's Absence: Who Is Going to Take over the Torch? Plus the Cover-up after the Murder."

The statue was one of two that had been erected on the orders of wealthy estate agent and media entrepreneur Harry Mens, Pim's personal friend, who had given Pim his first television program and who was the last person to speak with him by phone before he was gunned down in the parking lot of the Dutch public service broadcasting offices in Hilversum after his participation in a radio talk show. The larger-than-life bronze was being transported by truck from Mens's tulip-field-encircled hometown in Lisse to Rotterdam, where Pim had lived, and the truckers had secured it to the truck bed in a standing position. When they came to a low bridge, the statue was accidentally beheaded. But it was done perfectly, with Pim's saluting right hand unharmed. To anyone aware of the phenomenon of Pim Fortuyn, the saluting hand brings to mind his "At Your Service" promise, which was probably the most widely circulated image of Pim's political career. Ironically, the statue's beheading in April 2003 occurred the same week that Saddam Hussein's larger-than-life statue in Baghdad was brought down, meaning that both visuals were featured prominently in the Dutch news.

In early May 2003, Pim Fortuyn's face appeared almost daily in national magazines and newspapers as the first anniversary of his death approached. Pim souvenirs were sold to commemorate the occasion of his death, including a CD-ROM of his life and politics, a small Pim bronze statue bearing his signature on a plaque, Pim cufflinks bearing his family crest, and even a flag in the red, white, and blue colors of the Dutch flag, with Pim's profile shining like the sun and the words "Let us be alert to protecting freedom of speech. 6 May, Day against Violence." The Dutch tulip growers named a new tulip after Pim Fortuyn, set to bloom in the coming years. Pim supporters around the country tattooed themselves with his name and other memorabilia. One year after his death, not only had Pim's pin-striped suits and wide collars with wide ties become the fashion of the day among the political elite and the nouveaux riches but also even bank clerks assisting customers in Amsterdam's ABN-AMRO sported the Pim-inspired combination as a company uniform.

It was once thought in the Dutch publishing industry that a picture of the queen would guarantee a boost in print media sales, rather like that produced by photos of Princess Di in the British press. But since Pim's arrival and departure from the Dutch political arena, it seems that his picture is guaranteed to sell even more newspapers and magazines. The press and political commentators predicted that the mass hysteria that swept the country in mourning during the week of May 6, 2002, would resurface one year later, and although it did not happen on the streets, it did reemerge in the press. The media were filled with images of Pim a year after his death.

On May 6, 2003, the anniversary of his assassination, public and commercial television channels carried more than one prime-time TV documentary. "The Messiah," on Nederland 1, the public service flagship channel, discussed the religious aspects of the emergence of the phenomenon Pim Fortuyn and reached a large audience. The documentary was in the Oliver Stone *JFK* movie style, based on interviews with people "from all walks of life" about where they were when they heard that Pim had been shot and how they felt. Another documentary, "The Night of Fortuyn" on public service channel Nederland 2, focused on the night he was voted out of one party (Leefbaar Nederland, LN), which led him to form his own LPF; it included never-before-seen amateur video (the so-called lost tapes) of Fortuyn speaking at the LN board meeting and the controversial and secret content of his and his colleagues' words, more about which will be said later.

The flagship commercial channel, RTL4, had two prime-time programs on Fortuyn, one called "Typical Fortuyn," a documentary made by Peter van der Voorst, the reporter assigned to cover royal affairs for the program *RTL Boulevard*, and the other the country's most popular current affairs talk show, *Barend en Van Dorp*, which featured guests talking about Pim. On the other commercial channel, SBS6, "The Murder of Pim Fortuyn" interviewed many individuals, experts, and family members about that sad day. Every newspaper and magazine carried a picture of Pim and one or more articles about him. The newspapers' magazine inserts were largely devoted to Fortuyn. "Fortuyn's Security: A Bloody Shame" was the headline on a story about how the country's security service had failed to provide him with bodyguards when his life had been threatened during the campaign and the postelection continued cover-up in the investigation of his death.[6] Parliament, the Cabinet, and the former minister of interior all stood accused by the press of having left Fortuyn open to being gunned down. Although most Dutch know that Fortuyn was killed by a white Dutchman, an animal rights activist, many people outside the country may continue to believe the rumor the press circulated immediately after the killing, which was that a Muslim immigrant was probably responsible.[7]

The Media and Neopopulism

A recent comparative study of neopopulism in its variety of forms in societies around the world shows how the media is instrumental in the rise and fall of populist parties and leaders.[8] In Austria, for example, scholars have established a link between the type of newspaper one reads exclusively and support for populists such as Jorg Haider.[9] Mazzoleni, Stewart, and Horsfield identify three phases in neopopulist movements and their relationship with the media: the first phase is known as the insurgent phase, the second is the establishment phase, and the third is the decline phase.

The first phase is characterized by "intense media attention to the newly born political force."[10] The second phase occurs when the movement achieves "public legitimacy" and "has become a more durable feature of the national political scene." In this phase, the neopopulist leaders "find it more difficult to maintain the levels of attention of the news media." The second phase may be "simultaneous with the fading of the neo-populist party or movement from the media scene." The decline phase does not apply to all movements, and some continue to thrive, such as the National Front in France.[11]

Some researchers have also found a connection between support for the far right and one's daily news diet, which in Belgium has been linked to one particular item on the menu: crime news.[12] Commercial news programs tend to focus on sensationalistic topics such as crime, which is also a major issue used by the nationalist Flemish Belgian Vlaams Blok in elections. The party and the public also make the link between immigrants and crime, and sometimes the media also do this explicitly.

Media Framing and Europe's Imagined Muslim Community

Much of the sociological research on how the media present certain topics has focused on the resonance of frames and mobilization.[13] Framing—how, and in what context, topics are presented—is intended to help news audiences categorize and interpret issues and problems. Research in the United States has pointed out the racial subtext used in framing crime reports and the ways African Americans are projected in the press, but less is known about the characteristics of the coverage of ethnic groups in European countries in the various European national media.[14] Brubaker offers a theoretical discussion of ethnic framing in Europe. He argues that the use of "ethnicised ways of seeing" produce "ethnically-oriented frames" (that include systems of classification and categorization, both formally and informally), which lead to the public having a "taken for granted background knowledge" embedded somehow in "institutionalised routines and practices" offering a prefabricated understanding and interpretation of people and places.[15]

William Gamson's work was among the first to unite framing approaches with ethnicity.[16] According to Bob Entman and Andrew Rojecki's recent United States–based study of the black image in the white mind:

> The deeper connotations of the conflict exaggerating, simplistic coverage of affirmative action told audiences that blacks and whites may hold fundamentally incompatible values and interests, sharing only a tenuous cultural bond. Such material can support the idea that racial boundaries and distinctions are inherently meaningful as it imagines a community in which blacks are the outsiders and whites are the authentic members. Although the research shows considerable overlap in values held by both groups, media have pounded in

the lesson of fundamental difference, bolstering the argument that racial identity determines and distinguishes blacks' political behaviour, interests and values from those of whites. When out-group members seem to possess fundamentally different traits, it becomes difficult for in-group to trust and empathize with them. And that feeds a downward spiral: members of the out-group recognize the dominant group's distrust and the media's signals of exclusion; the out-group's own sense of trust and goodwill erodes, their suspicion and resentment mount. Such conditions make for hostile communication in public spaces—which further feeds each side's negative emotions.[17]

The routine practices of news making in a number of European countries, in combination with key events such as 9/11 and its aftermath, have led to the construction of an imagined Muslim community, a kind of imagined Muslim nationhood that emphasizes transnational bonds through various diaspora. Within the Netherlands, what in the past were considered to be different ethnic groups of immigrants or asylum seekers (Turks, Moroccans, and Surinamese are the largest, and Somalis, Pakistanis, Iraqis, Iranians, and others are fewer in number) have come to be seen as an imagined community in Benedict Anderson's sense of the term.[18]

In his book *Distinction*, Bourdieu describes an interactive process that occurs when groups are identified in terms of one key property, such as their Muslimness or their Europeanness.[19] Stigmatization occurs when one group internalizes a devalued image of their group in the society. Mobilization occurs when they create and reshape a new and stronger public identity as a way of diminishing the burden of this stigma. The stigmatized identity, one that might, under certain circumstances, make something as seemingly innocuous as couscous into a sort of ethnic badge, brings one closer to mobilizing around a label. Both positive and negative perceptions of what the Muslim identity means shape its understanding in contemporary Europe. For those who have little in the way of political affiliations or awareness, a "sudden mobilization" around an issue may be short-lived[20] but lead to long-term developments for the group in the society. Bourdieu's discussion of stigmatization and mobilization provides insight into the more recent research on "contentious politics"[21] and is of central importance in the context of immigration in Europe.

For example, in the early to mid-1990s, the problem of petty theft in the country was a very real one, and accounts in the press often attributed it to young men of Moroccan and Afro-Caribbean (Antillean) descent. If Entman and Rojecki were to conduct a similar study in Holland over the 1980s and

1990s, they would probably come to the conclusion that the Dutch media have racialized the crime problem. But the Dutch speak instead of "an American obsession with black and white."[22] The issue of race is generally not considered to be important in Holland, and the focus is instead on Dutch norms and values, language, and assimilation.

Islam came to be an issue in the news in the country in the early 1990s, and only later were connections made between those who were ethnically different from the Dutch and the non-Western religion as sources of conflict in the society. Islam was initially viewed as a potential enrichment of Dutch multicultural society, because as a religion in Holland, alongside other religions, it was a positive channel or pillar through which individuals become full participants in civil society. The first Islamic schools in the late 1980s were welcomed and took their place alongside Protestant and Catholic schools. The problems arose when the number of Islamic schools increased in response to Muslim parents' concerns about poor-quality public education in inner cities and the corresponding development of what the Dutch call "black schools," which are those that predominantly cater to immigrant children of color, and "white flight" from the inner-city areas in which immigrants lived. Islamic schools and segregated communities became something of an issue in the 1994 Dutch national election, so the issue was already present when Pim Fortuyn began to focus on political power.

Islam and the Media

Sniderman and his colleagues make no mention of the media in *The Outsider*, although they do make a number of comments that lead one to think about the media's contribution to the process by which citizens form opinions about immigrants.[23] They say, for example, that the general level of prejudice in a society may rise, fall, or change with the times, and they link this to external factors such as the "shock" of a large influx of immigrants or, to take another example, an economic downturn. They do not discuss, however, that the media and the views depicted by journalists and put forth by political elites in the public space may be an instrumental source for shaping public opinion about the extent of the shock, nor do they mention that the changing context of the news business in Europe may be contributing to more sensationalistic news stories that can directly or indirectly result in stigmatization and mobilization.

Islam itself satisfies important criteria for getting into the news in Western countries. It is rich in the characteristics that determine "newsworthiness": timeliness, human interest, conflict, proximity, and—depending on who is speaking out about it—prominence.

As a topic in European news outlets, it tends to be inherently conflict-ridden.[24] It is a topic that can often induce emotional responses, which have been found to be advantageous to program makers who want to retain audiences.[25] Even descriptive reporting about Islamic holidays and accompanying rituals, such as the slaughtering of sheep in the traditional style for human interest stories, has been the focus of what could be described as sensational reporting on a fairly neutral topic. Reporting the large number of sheep slaughtered in one day by the Muslims in the country, which is common in French, Belgian, and Dutch news when special abattoirs are set up for the religious feasts, can trigger a range of reactions from non-Mulsim audiences. Brigitte Bardot, the famous French actress and animal rights activist, has been the subject of much reporting on these occasions in the European media. She is, in fact, simply describing what is happening when she says "Muslim slaughterers" (*bouchers* in French); however, her role in the story lends it a prominence that increases its news value. She, in effect, is a magnet for public attention to a topic that already has some news value in terms of timeliness, proximity, and human interest. Throw in Bardot, and the values of prominence and conflict are added—satisfying all five criteria for newsworthiness and virtually ensuring placement on the front page or at least on the front of a section of the newspaper. For those unaccustomed to the (sometimes gruesome) visuals of lambs' throats being cut, such a report can be a highly charged viewing experience, and the feedback to such stories creates another layer of conflict and perpetuates the topic in the news cycle.

Islamic religious practices and a European society's social norms may conflict in ways that have not been the subject of much discussion in the public space—that is, until journalists bring the topic into the news. During the Muslim month of Ramadan, if a Frenchman leaves a bar and hails a taxi, for example, the Muslim driver may decide not to take him if he smells alcohol. This may be just an occasional incident, but once reported in the news, it may become perceived as the tip of the iceberg. Inevitably, the public begins to see similarities in other everyday transactions. It is not only issues of conflict, however, but also the novelty of Islamic religious practices that can interest reporters. The ritual of ablution (washing one's hands, face, and feet before praying), for example, attracted the cameras when Muslims demonstrating in front of the French Embassy in The Hague on a cold day in the late 1980s used snow instead of water. On some Fridays in the early 1990s, when religious Muslims wanted to get to Amsterdam's largest mosque located on the Amstel River during a time when the key bridge there was closed for construction, the cameras captured some unusual pictures. They were unusual because, if they had been cropped closely, viewers might think that they were looking at a picture of an Asian society rather than a European one. On a bright and sunny day, gender-segregated crowds of Muslims in religious white were standing in a flat-topped ferryboat that was taking them and some of their bicycles from one side of the Amstel River to the other. All were looking toward the large door at the entrance of the mosque.

In *The Sociology of News*, Michael Schudson discusses the processes by which the news is manufactured.[26] He points out that journalists not only construct reality but also create it, albeit with constraints. He notes: "Journalists normally work with materials that real people and real events provide. But by selecting, highlighting, framing, shading, and shaping in reportage, they create an impression that real people—readers and viewers—then take to be real and to which they respond in their lives."[27]

Schudson calls attention to two "master trends—commercialization and professionalization" that have "deeply affected the American experience of news."[28] Although he focuses largely on the American example, the trends he describes are also found in contemporary Europe, particularly within the last two decades as the national media markets once dominated by public service television became liberalized, and a number of private channels were introduced. The consequences of this for European democracies and for citizens' views about political parties and institutions and the key issues of the day remain a matter of much debate and interesting scholarly research.[29]

The professionalization of the news is characterized by reporters offering their perspectives as experts in their own stories and news programs and, if resources permit, doing more reporting of the kind that can be described as "newsmaking"—the kind of reporting that begins a domino effect of news stories throughout the community.[30] Islam and Islamic traditions in Europe became the basis for "newsmaking" stories well before 9/11.

News about Islam in Europe may also contribute to the construction of what Benedict Anderson calls an "imagined community."[31] Imagined communities refer to those mental constructions by which people orient and identify themselves. News about Islam in Europe may contribute to non-Muslim public perceptions that there is one monolithic Muslim community in their country, in Europe, or the world. It may also contribute to the thinking of European Muslims of different ethnic, national, and sectarian origins to foster the idea that they are indeed a larger transnational community. The preponderance of satellite dishes in predominantly Muslim neighborhoods in many European cities suggests that the availability of channels from Muslim countries may also contribute to the construction of these imagined communities. Al-Jazeera is only one example of a television channel that prides itself in offering "The Opinion and the Other Opinion."[32] This key phrase in their corporate image emphasizes not only the importance of conflict in the news but also the position of Islam as a focal point of debate between and within societies, and even within Islamic societies.

The research that I have discussed so far stems from the social and behavioral sciences. There is also a considerable array of research in the humanities, specifically in the fields of philosophy, religion and theology, comparative literature and language, cultural studies, and critical studies. Some of these focus on the ways in which religion has become "media-tized," which refers to the opening of a field of "negotiation" between private and public spheres.[33] According to the Dutch philosopher and professor of religious studies Hent de Vries, "the relationship between religion and media sheds light on the question of how cultural identity and difference are constituted, as well as on how they relate to the aims of sociopolitical integration. Religion, thus interpreted, forms the condition of possibility and impossibility for the political."[34]

The work of Edward Said is perhaps the best known in the field of comparative literature focusing on the stigmatization of the "oriental other." In *Orientalism*, he argues forcefully that Western journalism and literature stereotype and stigmatize Arab countries and Muslim societies.[35] In *Covering Islam*, he also criticizes the reporting on Islam in the Western news media for its stigmatizing characteristics.[36]

Key Question

What role did the media play in Pim Fortuyn's rise to power? I argue that various media (magazines, newspapers, broadcasting, and book publishers) proactively contributed to establishing Pim as a brand name in advance of his ascent to political power, so that he already had a sympathetic audience among opinion leaders, as well as the general public, when he became a candidate officially in early 2002. Routine reporting of local events in 2000 and early 2001 and world events from September 11, 2001, along with proactive newsmaking activities by key Dutch television programs in the spring and summer of 2001, provided visibility for a key issue, Islam, that fueled Pim's political success. Most of the Dutch media regularly framed Islam and Muslims as a problem in Dutch society, categorizing Muslims and especially Moroccans as a "lesser breed" (the Dutch word is *tuig*) and reinforcing the major theme of Fortuyn's 1997 book, *Against the Islamization of the Netherlands*. The substantive content of Pim's most important message (which was an anti-immigrant and anti-Islam message) resonated well with the public and was the basis for the LPF's electoral support in 2002. Pim's personal qualities (such as his way of speaking and dressing and his homosexuality) were also considered extremely newsworthy, were well received in the popular culture in the run-up to the election, and continued to be newsworthy even after his assassination. Here I draw on my qualitative analysis of news coverage during this period, interviews with political elites and journalists, and my observations of political developments over the past decade.

The Role of News, Newsmaking, and World Events
in Pim's Success

In the period between 2000 and mid-2001, a number of events put the Muslim community in general and the Moroccan Muslim community in particular in the news in a negative way in the Netherlands. Without going into the details of these here, let me relay some idea of the nature of each event by describing each with a short headline:

> The Censorship of the *Aicha* Play in Rotterdam
> The Expulsion of the Libyan Imam from a Moroccan Mosque in Utrecht
> The Zwolle Courtroom Assistant Who Insisted on Wearing a Headscarf
> The Moroccan Boys in Amsterdam Who Pounced on Bikini-Clad Dutch Girls in the City's Swimming Pools

There was also a confidential draft policy document circulated in The Hague that had been written by a concerned civil servant about Islam as a security issue in Europe. The document claimed that every mosque is a potential danger and called for the Dutch secret service to monitor mosques.

On May 3, 2001, Rotterdam Imam El-Moumni, from the largest mosque in that city, made an impromptu statement on *Nova*, the major late-evening current affairs program (the Dutch equivalent to Britain's *Newsnight* or Germany's *Tagesthemen*). El-Moumni had agreed to be interviewed on tape days before the program because the program's producers were planning to do a story on the problem of crime perpetrated by Moroccan teenage boys. Moroccan boys had been the subject of more than a little attention in the press as troublemakers because they had been stealing and pickpocketing, pouncing on bikini-clad girls in swimming pools, and even beating up some homosexual schoolteachers. The imam was reluctant to be interviewed, as he had never before been interviewed by the Dutch news media, and he did not speak Dutch. But after encouragement from the board of governors of his mosque, he agreed to be interviewed, with the understanding that he would see the tape and approve it before broadcast.[37] That was not the way it turned out, however.

The interviewing journalist asked a simple question: "What do Muslims think about homosexuality?" The imam's answer was simple, too. "It is a sickness," he said. The reporter then asked, "What do you think about gay marriage?" The imam replied, "If men continue to marry men, and women marry women, then Dutch society will disappear."

One of *Nova*'s major aims is to be newsmaking, to be quoted in other media, and to bring forth topics that rock the nation's political agenda. This unequivocal response was a newsmaker for *Nova*. The program had an exclusive interview with the imam. Three days before the program was aired, *Nova* issued an embargoed press release that found its way to a number of gay organizations.[38] The press release indicated that these controversial statements could be seen on the upcoming Friday evening program. The embargoed press release was widely circulated, and it primed other media and social groups to focus on the story that aired on May 3.

This is a highly contested issue involving two contested minority groups that have experienced years of discrimination in a country built on "minorities."[39] Islam and homosexuality have been a continuing news story that involves big names, celebrities, and political personalities, including the prime minister, the minister of integration and major cities, and members of the national parliament. One gay member of parliament from the Labour Party immediately called for the imam's expulsion. A well-known gay soccer referee said he would sue the imam because he was so deeply offended. At the same time, the Turkish, Surinamese, Moroccan, and Pakistani imams from the largest cities in the country declared their support for Imam El-Moumni and declared publicly that they, too, believed what he said.

The May 3 report on *Nova* had a snowball effect, and soon all the media from the right to the left were discussing this issue and its various digressions. Since El-Moumni's statement, the topic was in the news almost every day in one form or another, even into late June and early July. It was watercooler and cafeteria fodder for more than a month in the Dutch Parliament. In fact, one government minister came to me to say, "Why do the Moroccans have so many problems? We have good Moroccans like you; why aren't they all like you?" Even the so-called good Moroccans became stigmatized. The story and its direct consequences appeared to have peaked as a news item on May 30, at which point a number of stories began to emerge on the negative aspects of the Moroccan community in the country. As Imam El-Moumni is a Moroccan, this community became "inferiorated."

Many people said that the Moroccans should feel ashamed, that they were in the Dutch society and they had all the opportunities to live and work there and to live off the benefits of the Dutch welfare state; therefore, they should respect Dutch values. News coverage suggested that Christians in the country had never uttered a word against homosexuality and that this type of speech was coming solely from the Muslim community, but a look back over the previous few years shows that was not the case. Leen van Dijke is the leader of the RPF political party, the Protestant party that is now a member of the Christian Coalition of extremely religious parties. They begin all party meetings with a reading from the Bible. In 2000, Van Dijke was fined 300 guilders (about $120) by a Dutch court and required to apologize for publicly saying that homosexuals are comparable to thieves. Ten years earlier, Catholic Monsignor Simonis from Brabant also spoke out against homosexuals in a discriminatory way. There are many other examples of religious people who have said these sorts of things, as we know from reading the novels of Gerard Reve, an award-winning Dutch author who describes himself as a homosexual and a good Christian and whose writing has been very critical of these and other religious preachers. But none of these public statements was followed by the storm of publicity, the calls for expulsion, or the fears for national security that emerged in the pre-9/11 case of Imam El-Moumni and the Islamic community. An interview with a Dutch BVD (CIA) officer on the top Sunday TV current affairs program *Buitenhof*, on the first Sunday after May 3, 2001, revealed that the Dutch secret service was already planning to put undercover agents in some of the mosques.

Conflict in the News: Two Normative Regimes

There appear to be two normative regimes in confrontation here. One normative regime disapproves of the conduct of gays. The other disapproves of the conduct of Muslims. The tension between the two regimes is high because freedom of speech and freedom of belief are at stake for both. The Muslims believe they have a right to speak what they understand to be the word of God. The homosexuals, who are living in the only country in the world where they have achieved the full range of major civic, social, and cultural rights, such as legally recognized marriage and adoption, find the Muslims' discriminatory statements to be a form of hate speech. Such hate speech, in their view, calls for action in the form of lawsuits, and a number of individuals have filed suit. These are inevitable frictions between these two normative regimes in what is arguably the most sexually liberal city in the world. There has been a long struggle for freedom in the Dutch public sphere,[40] but Holland nevertheless retains its "high moral judgment,"[41] and in the Dutch case, high morals are quite different from high morals in Italy, France, and many other countries. This was the climate in the summer of 2001, just months before 9/11. This may help to explain why, after 9/11, the Netherlands had the highest rates of reported attacks on mosques and on Muslims of any country in Europe.

The confrontation itself between these two normative regimes was very real. It more than satisfied the news media's interest in reporting conflict. It also had all the ingredients of a good story: important people, important issues, and contested views on sex, sexuality, race, and religion. This conflict between Muslims and homosexuals—and the sensational way it was reported in the Dutch news media—was the precursor to the success of Pim Fortuyn's anti-Islamization message.

The initiation of this conflict by *Nova* (on the public channel Nederland 3) stemmed from the program's need to be more of a newsmaker in a highly competitive news market since the arrival of commercial television's popular political current affairs program, *Barend en Van Dorp* (on RTL4), had affected its ratings. This story was just the beginning of the focus on Islam that the program adopted in its effort to revamp and reorganize internally so that externally it would be viewed as the most important elite news program. Felix Rottenberg, a former *Nova* anchor, claimed that the program aimed to be like BBC's *Newsnight*, but most would agree that despite various reorganizations, new faces, and newsmaking stories, it still hasn't reached that goal.[42]

How the Media Established Pim as a Brand Name

The news media were not only instrumental in focusing on one of the main issues that propelled Pim to the forefront of Dutch politics. The media and publishing industry also brought Pim opportunities to reach the public. In the late 1980s and during the 1990s, Fortuyn was asked to contribute columns regularly to *Elsevier*, a major news magazine on the right that is the Dutch equivalent of Germany's *Stern*. In 1989, he wrote that he wanted to become prime minister. During the eight years of the Purple Coalition from 1994, Fortuyn heavily criticized how the government was handling the problems of immigration, crime, health care, education, and public transport. He was also outspokenly critical of the country's established political elite. He said he did not want to be the leader of an established political party and instead proposed to run the country in close alliance with business.

In the mid-1990s, he began to appear regularly on television. Fortuyn was given a spot on the Sunday program called *Business Class*. The program was on a private channel, RTL5, and was paid for by his wealthy friend Harry Mens, who with his daughter hosted the program. The midmorning program competed with the public service channel's main Sunday morning talk show *Buitenhof*, in which high politics was the order of the day. In *Business Class*, politics was served up in another fashion. The hosts and guests moved around a set that included a kitchen, dining room table, and living room chairs. A chef cooked during the program and presented dishes for tasting, along with special wines, as if one were flying business class. "Professor Fortuyn," informally "Pim," was interviewed by Harry Mens each week about the issues of the day.

Fortuyn further established his name in intellectual and political circles by publishing a number of controversial books for the Dutch market. In 1992, he wrote *To the Dutch People*,[43] and in 1994 he published *The Business Cabinet of Fortuyn*,[44] in which he described himself as a panther waiting to pounce on the right moment to achieve political power. In 1997, he published his best known book to date, *Against the Islamization of the Netherlands*,[45] which was republished in 2002 in advance of the May elections.

In March 2002, he published his last book, his personal manifesto and the equivalent of the LPF's manifesto. The book was called *The Disastrous Eight Years of the Purple Coalition*.[46] The subheadings were many: "The Waitlists in the Health Care Industry," "The Problems in Relation to Security," "The Untrustworthy Open Government," "The Worried State of Education," "A Merciless Analysis of the Collective Sector and a Powerful Program of Solutions."

After having been first friend and then foe of most of the established political parties over the previous two decades, in November 2001, he was elected leader of the newly formed party Leefbaar Nederland (LN). At his acceptance speech, he concluded by stepping away from the podium, smiling, and saluting the audience with the words "At your service." This unforgettable visual was the beginning of a new political order in the country. His criticisms of the establishment came against the backdrop of corruption scandals in the construction industry and the fraudulent use of monies from the European Social Fund, which had been the subject of political debate for some months and had hit the Labour Party in particular. In January 2002, one newspaper headlined a quote from the Labour leader saying, "The press makes Leefbaar Nederland popular."[47]

Islam as the Issue, Dutch Moroccans and Turks as the Focus

An interview with Pim published in the *Volkskrant* on February 9, 2002, propelled him into a situation in which he could form his own political party. It is still a matter of dispute between Pim's supporters and the newspaper about whether Pim actually said what he was quoted as having said or whether he was quoted out of context. The headline was: "Fortuyn says: 'Borders closed to Islamites.'" (The Dutch term *Islamieten*, which carries a pejorative meaning in Dutch, was used rather than the term for Muslims, which is why I translate it as "Islamites.") The article quoted him as saying the antidiscrimination clause in Article 1 of the Dutch Constitution should be abolished (with respect to Islam because the religion discriminated against homosexuals and women). This led to an outcry among political leaders and politicians from the established parties, and even those on the board of Pim's party Leefbaar Nederland were very distraught. Within days, the national board of the national LN ousted him from the leadership of the party. Just as quickly, Pim formed his own party, the LPF.

Table 5.1 displays the number of times certain key words were used in the leading Dutch newspapers between 1997 and 2002. It shows that *Islam* and *integration*, together, were more visible in the news in 1997, the year Pim's anti-Islam book was published, and then the combination declined in 1998 and 1999. The various issues mentioned in the period prior to El-Moumni appeared more often in the news in 2000, which led to the words *Islam* and *integration* being featured more often in the news, and this number nearly doubled in 2001, with the El-Moumni statement in June and the 9/11 terrorist attacks in September and their aftermath. In 2002, Pim Fortuyn had risen to prominence in the national political scene and was actively campaigning, which meant that the number of references to *Islam* and *integration* nearly doubled again.

At the same time, Moroccan Muslims were increasingly visible in the Dutch news media, and these stories were largely domestic in focus and negative in tone.[48] Turks, as another minority Muslim community in the country, were also highly visible in the news, often with negative connotations, but a large portion of these stories concerned Turkey's possible entry into the

TABLE 5.1. Keywords in Five Major Dutch Newspapers 1997–2002

Keywords	1997	1998	1999	2000	2001	2002*
Islam and Integration	105	74	51	125	213	517
Islamization	163	49	29	20	41	67
Moroccans	464	674	707	855	866	1197
Turks	1326	968	1482	1389	1062	1393
Turks and Europe	(821)	(572)	(863)	(791)	(746)	(1022)

Sources: Volkskrant, NRC, Trouw, Algemeen Dagblad, Het Parool.
*This is actually the twelve months prior to May 2003.

European Union. Turks as Muslims in Holland were therefore not the focus of as much negative news as Moroccan Muslims.

The atmosphere in Holland, one year after Pim's death, could be described as a collective effort to explain Pim as a misunderstood man, a phenomenon that was not like the far right and that cannot be explained in terms of xenophobia or other far right issues. This appears to be the common line taken by a number of prominent political commentators and social scientists, including those on the left who, in hindsight, talk favorably in terms of the "aesthetic contribution" of Pim to Dutch politics and who also describe populism as "not always bad."[49] But just as the news media then appeared to emphasize a perspective on Pim that fits nicely with the Dutch reputation of openness and tolerance, the news media also brought to light, through the airing of an amateur video in the Nederland 2 documentary "The Night of Fortuyn," what Pim and his political supporters actually said about ethnic minorities in the country. In a closed meeting of the board of LN, on the night that Pim was ousted from that party, he said: "We have a Fifth Column of people in this country who want to bring it to destruction. . . . I stand for this country." Those present said: "We agree with you. It makes sense when you say it like that." One party member was seen crying and saying: "We love you, but some things we just cannot say."[50]

There are two views in the country on what has come out of the emphasis in Holland on Islam and Fortuyn in the news media. One view is that this was a healthy response to years of politically correct silence on an issue that was bothering many of the Dutch people and most of the country's political elite. Pim's openness and frankness on the subject, letting out his own views on the religion and its consequences for others in Dutch society, is seen in a positive light, even by those on the left who may not be sympathetic to Fortuyn or the LPF. An opposing view is that Holland was not politically correct in the first place, since prominent individuals and politicians in the past decade have also emphasized the issue of Islam and integration. They include the VVD's former leader and Euro commissioner, Frits Bolkestein, who spoke out against Islamic schools in the 1994 and 1998 elections (although it is worth mentioning that the Liberal "pillar" does not support religious schools[51] of any sort, despite Holland's constitutional protection of such schools). Another is Paul Scheffer, a prominent intellectual, columnist, and ex-Labour (PvdA) Party member, who introduced the topic in a controversial article in the *NRC* in 2000 called "The Multicultural Drama." The difference between Pim Fortuyn's message and those of Bolkestein and Scheffer is that Pim was more direct, negative, and authoritarian. He did not call for a dialogue or highlight positive examples, whereas the others did.

The Media and the Personalization of Politics

Pim Fortuyn's 1997 book, *Against the Islamization of the Netherlands*, led not only to Islam becoming an increasingly visible and important issue in Dutch society but also to increased visibility for Pim Fortuyn himself. He formed his own party in his own image at a time when Dutch politics had never been more personalized in the Dutch media.[52] This was the first time a major movement had been named after an individual. He floated the name of his party even before he formed it, and the published opinion polls reported back that this LPF would attract a not inconsiderable amount of support among the public. The news media did his political research for him. On February 21, 2002, *Trouw* headlined: "List Pim Fortuyn bypasses Leefbaar Nederland [Livable Netherlands]." This was weeks before LPF was even formed, when Fortuyn was still a member of LN and before LN ousted him in response to his anti-Muslim remarks, as well as his campaign to abolish Article 1 of the constitution, which protects religious minorities.

On March 2, 2002, shortly before the city council elections across the country, Prime Minister Kok was quoted in *Algemeen Dagblad*, a major newspaper, as saying, "Fortuyn is asocial." On March 6, the day of the elections, while he continued to be the head of Livable Netherlands in Rotterdam, Fortuyn and the local LN party grew from 0 to 17 seats, approaching a majority. This propelled Fortuyn into real elected political power and into the position of being the hero of Rotterdam. He became the leader of the Rotterdam City Council. Rotterdam, the second largest city in the country, rivals Amsterdam in terms of business and economic power. There is a Dutch maxim that says: "We make our money in Rotterdam and we spend it in Amsterdam."

That same evening, on March 6, Fortuyn was invited by public service broadcasters to discuss the results of the municipal elections on a late-night talk show with other national party leaders. This invitation and his appearance alongside other national political leaders were as unusual as his victory earlier that day. Paul Witteman, one of the most important political reporters in the country, hosted the talk show, where Fortuyn's superior debating skills were established on a national stage. He came across more effectively than anyone else on the show, including the interviewer. The next day, the evening newspaper *NRC* reported that VVD and PvdA leaders were under fire after their poor performance in the previous evening's debate.

Many political pollsters and political commentators in the press talked about Fortuyn as the next big thing in Dutch politics. Their comments reinforced the visuals of Pim: Pim going to and from television studios, Pim seated in the back of his chauffeur-driven Jag with his two cocker spaniels, Pim smiling and smoking a cigar, Pim often waving and saying, "I will be the prime minister of this country!"

On March 12, 2002, at the official launch of his book *The Disastrous Eight Years of the Purple Coalition* on live TV, Fortuyn was hit with a pie and then with tomatoes. As he wiped the pie cream from his eyebrows, people began to ask who was in charge of his security. As he walked to his car afterward, journalists asked him what he would do about the stains on his suit. Unflappable as ever, he replied that he had dozens in his closet, and it would not slow him down. Politics in the consensus democracy had never been so exciting.

Pim himself was the focus of the news for the first three weeks of March 2002. His candidate list for the LPF was not presented until March 21, 2002. The next day, *Trouw* called him "the magician." Two days later, on March 23, 2002, he participated in a debate with party leaders at Erasmus University, where the Green Party leader Paul Rosenmöller launched a personal verbal attack on Fortuyn.[53] Rosenmöller ended the onslaught with an outstretched hand for Pim to shake, but it was not accepted. Political commentators in the press in the days that followed described this as Fortuyn's "first loss."

One study on the 2002 campaign shows that television news coverage of the parties was highly personalized, and the LPF coverage focused heavily on the party's leader.[54] The same study showed that the media effects on the vote were strongest among those with low levels of political knowledge who watched a great deal of television news. The authors concluded that the LPF benefited most from the media effects of the campaign. Two other studies looked at why people voted for the LPF without taking into account any focus on the news media. One study found that of the two messages of Pim Fortuyn and his self-named party, LPF—the antiestablishment message and the anti-immigrant message—only the latter formed the basis of the vote for the party.[55] From this, we can assume that the continued emphasis on Islam in the news, particularly since the 1997 publication of Pim Fortuyn's book against Islam in Holland, contributed to his rise to power.

Conclusions

The political life of Pim Fortuyn and his LPF is a good example of two of the three media phases in the life of neopopulist parties: the first phase being the insurgent phase; the second, the establishment phase; and the third, the decline phase. Fortuyn did not experience the third phase, probably because of his assassination early in his political career. Fortuyn, like the neopopulist leaders described by Mazzoleni and colleagues,[56] was a charismatic leader who staged events that appealed to the news media, engaged in verbal extremism, and bluntly attacked established parties and government policies. During the first phase, research on campaign news suggests that the Dutch media were instrumental in bringing the LPF to power. The media did so by following the negative agenda about the incumbent coalition, which was Pim Fortuyn's agenda, and by focusing on immigrants and Islam, which was also to the advantage of LPF. Research also shows that those who voted for the LPF in the national May 2002 elections had become more cynical over the course of the campaign, an aspect that may have long-term consequences for political participation[57] and that may have been evidenced in Geert Wilders's emergence (see chapter 7).

According to a study of the role of the media in the Dutch 2002 parliamentary election by Jan Kleinnijenhuis, Dirk Oegema, Jan de Ridder, Anita van Hoof, and Rens Vliegenthart, the impartial news media became partial, and this contributed directly to the support for the LPF in May 2002. They concluded that to stress the disasters of the Purple Coalition in the news and to make right-wing topics and the problems surrounding asylum seekers central could create the basis for a political earthquake. The other question is whether the media itself may have created discontent and cynicism that favored Fortuyn's campaign. The media did not ask itself this question, perhaps because Fortuyn brought the journalists an exciting topic in a society that shows characteristics of a hyperventilating democracy: in the midst of the frenzy, voters, politicians, and media seemed grasping and superficial.[58]

The May 2002 elections signaled the beginning of the second phase in the life of the LPF. At that point, the party became a more durable feature of political life, having won 26 seats in a 150-seat parliament, and became a member of the governing coalition. During this phase, the media continued to closely follow the activities of the LPF politicians in the coalition negotiations over the summer and of the LPF ministers and the parliamentary fraction in the fall.

The news program *Nova* kept Fortuyn's key issue of Islam prominent in the news even after his murder on May 6, 2002. In the May 2002 election, his party scored a posthumous triumph for him by earning the second largest cache of votes, which allowed LPF a prominent place in the coalition government. The media kept the nearly canonized Fortuyn's views on Islam at the forefront of the political debate in June 2002 by airing two controversial investigative reports about what imams in Dutch mosques were saying in their sermons.[59]

The third phase takes a different form in the Netherlands. It was not a clear-cut decline, as such, because of Fortuyn's killing. Instead, the assassination of Pim Fortuyn was effectively the assassination of the party List Pim Fortuyn. Although LPF won twenty-six seats in Parliament about two weeks after

Fortuyn's assassination, it was the beginning of the end of his party. Internal strife over what was or was not his ideological legacy effectively destroyed the party within six months of the election. LPF has, for all intents and purposes, been dissolved. It now has no seats in the national parliament. However, this does not matter much because the immigration-integration and anti-Islam stands of the LPF were adopted by almost all of the other parties on the left and right of the Dutch political spectrum in the January 2003 election campaign. In this sense, the neopopulist movement lives on in the heart of the other major political parties in the country.

What is left of the political earthquake that shook the country in May 2002 with the LPF's win of twenty-six seats in Parliament? The January 2003 elections produced a result that may have caused Pim to turn over in his grave (which, rather ironically, is not in the Netherlands, but Italy): the LPF fraction was reduced to a mere handful of seats, and Pim's archrival, the Labour Party (PvdA), gained many seats with a new young leader elected after Labour's May 2002 fiasco. Labour's Wouter Bos called himself the "Pim of the Left." As the LPF leader Mat Herben said during the January 2003 elections, Labour and the other parties did well because they took over all of the most popular aspects of the LPF's policies, particularly those on immigration, integration, and Islam. As the televised debates between the party leaders revealed, there was little or no disagreement on these issues. Even the extreme left Socialist Party leader found himself agreeing with the extreme right LPF leader on the policy of raising the legal age at which Dutch citizens of Turkish or Moroccan origin are allowed to bring a foreign spouse into the country to twenty-four.

Fortuynism without Fortuyn

The legacy of Pim Fortuyn is what many have described as "the end of political correctness" in the consensus democracy, where, it is now said, that for decades politicians and the public had been afraid to speak their minds about the country's problems of immigrants and their lack of integration. The most striking example of this silence is the plight of the much beloved and respected former Labour Prime Minister Wim Kok. Kok was seen as being above party politics. He was thought of as the embodiment of political correctness; what was appropriate or not appropriate was defined by his genteel actions and words. Only after a report made the matter public did Kok and his government take responsibility for the massacre of Muslim men and boys who were guarded by Dutch troops, part of a United Nations peacekeeping force in Srebrenica, during the Bosnian conflict of the early 1990s. Kok resigned shortly thereafter in April 2002.

On May 2, 2003, almost a year after Pim's death, Kok said that Labour lost the 2002 parliamentary election because they had been too politically correct to address the very important problem of immigration and integration, and he credited Fortuyn with bringing to an end that politically correct era in Dutch politics.[60] Kok is not the only politician who saw the bright side of the end of political correctness in Holland. Many journalists were also pleased to be able to speak openly regarding their concerns about the perceived visibility of immigrants and Islam in the public space.

On the first anniversary of Fortuyn's death, the news media were nearly unanimous in stating that anyone who attempts to fill the void left by Fortuyn will need to address the issue of Islam in the Netherlands. The media framed Islam as a problem for Dutch society in the example of the El-Moumni statement in spring 2001, but the continued emphasis on the religion in the Dutch press is now often driven by political elites from the various parties, as well as by the news media themselves. Islam is framed as a contested issue in Dutch society rather than as merely one religion among others. The consequences for political mobilization among Holland's ethnic minorities will remain a vital question in the country's political discourse.

6

The Public Intellectual versus Islam

A Year of Sex and Rhetoric

If you want to work on a better image [for Islam], it doesn't work, because all you need is another September 11th or Pim Fortuyn and then the image is bad again.
—Dyab Abou Jahjah

Having lost the May 2002 election, along with eighty-three of my fellow members of Parliament, I was once more just a citizen rather than a representative of citizens, but even as such, the paroxysms of anguish running through my country shook me. The anti-Muslim fervor that had rolled like a flood over the dykes, overturning Parliament, tore away the façade of social progressivism and soaked into the day's newspapers.

In December of that year, just before the Netherlands' January 2003 election campaign, a Moroccan Muslim schoolteacher was murdered by his neighbor, a European Flemish man in Antwerp, Belgium, a twenty-minute drive from the Dutch border. While others described the murderer as mentally ill, many Moroccans and Muslims in Antwerp claimed that he was a racist and that racism had prompted the killing. When they protested in the public market square in Antwerp to raise awareness of such racism, the police came and arrested some of them. According to Dutch Radio One, these arrests triggered the riots that followed. Then, in response to the riots, Belgian Prime Minister Guy Verhofstadt called for the arrest of Dyab Abou Jahjah, the leader of the Flemish AEL (Arab European

League). The PM accused Abou Jahjah of being involved with Hezbollah in Lebanon and suggested that he and his foreign connections were the cause of the riots in Antwerp. Belgium as early as the 1970s had instituted classes in Islam in its public schools. The government hired Moroccan and Turkish teachers to lead the classes, thus creating its own version of official Islam. Now, Abu Jahjah, described by the media as a radical with ties to Hezbollah, emerged as the representative of unofficial Islam. The tug-of-war that resulted illustrates the third part of the trifecta of coercion—the pressure felt by Muslims and their communities when official Islam conflicts with radical unofficial Islam.

The Belgian chain of events had begun thirty-six years earlier in southern Lebanon, with the birth of Abou Jahjah in 1966. The grandson of Palestinians—a connection that he would often mention later in life—he was born in a village that was occupied by Israel until 2000. He sought asylum in Belgium in 1991 and settled in Antwerp, forming the AEL nine years later. After he was arrested on the prime minister's orders and held in the Antwerp municipal jail for several days, the local court ordered his release on the grounds that there was no evidence that Abou Jahjah, with or without the help of any foreign entity, had been involved in the Antwerp riots.

The Dutch media were consumed with the saga in Antwerp on the eve of yet another national election campaign. The Dutch had just come through a regularly scheduled parliamentary election in May 2002, but the government coalition could not be maintained so a second national election was called for January 2003. The Dutch media's obsession with Abou Jahjah was a product of proximity and anxiety: just across the border, this charismatic Western-educated academic who was fluent in French, Flemish, Arabic, and English was calling for the unity of Muslims not only in Belgium and the Netherlands but also throughout Europe. The swirl of publicity surrounding the murder moved Abou Jahjah to call for the creation of a branch of his AEL in the Netherlands, and almost immediately, fifty prospective members in Holland contacted him via his AEL Web site. As of March 7, 2003, less than four months after the murder in Antwerp that had prompted his call for Muslim unity, his Dutch AEL branch had more than five hundred paying members.[1] On the first day of the opening conference of the Dutch AEL, according to the center-left newspaper *NRC Handelsblad*, members of the public were required to pay 50 euros to attend, and members of the press working for a media outlet that had given negative publicity to Abou Jahjah were charged 5,000 euros to get in. In the first week of March, Abou Jahjah was interviewed in one or another Dutch media outlet every day. When asked by a Radio One interviewer: "Where do you get your funding? Are foreign countries funding the AEL?" He laughed and replied: "Our paying members supply our funding, and those who attend our public meetings."

Abou Jahjah is compared with far right leaders in Belgium and Holland. In Belgium, Abou Jahjah is described as the Muslim Filip Dewinter (leader of the far right Vlaams Blok). In the Netherlands, they call him "the Arab Pim," a reference to the charismatic Pim Fortuyn.[2] Abou Jahjah uses his personal charm to mobilize the dissatisfied. Because he doesn't entirely trust the people he is working with, he attends almost all public events and releases all public statements himself rather than delegating authority, which, according to one reporter, are both qualities that Pim Fortuyn displayed: magnetism and paranoia.[3]

Abou Jahjah describes himself as the Arab Malcolm X. He wears only black and surrounds himself with bodyguards because he claims his life is in danger. During an interview with him on *Nova*, the popular Dutch public broadcasting current affairs program, journalist Felix Rottenberg[4] showed a film clip that Abou Jahjah said had special meaning for him and asked him to explain why. The clip showed Malcolm X saying: "We love those who love us and we hate those who hate us."[5] Abou Jahjah explained that as citizens, not guests, of the Netherlands, Muslims have the same rights as other citizens and deserve the same respect. In a subsequent radio interview, he criticized the first generation of Muslims in the country for maintaining a "guest worker's mentality," which he said ultimately leads to accepting the Vlaams Blok party's belief that Muslim immigrants should be thankful to be in Europe and, in short, "if you don't like it here, then you can go back to your own country." When he compared Belgium and the Netherlands, he concluded: "It may be better in some respects in Holland from a social economic perspective, but in Belgium there is less criminalization of Islam."[6]

One Dutch radio interviewer said to him: "You make me fearful when I see you surrounded by people wearing black, it gives me an uncomfortable feeling." Abou Jahjah replied: "You Dutch are very fearful people. Trust yourself, and have a discussion with me, and everything will be OK. When I ask for Islamic holidays to be recognized, I don't want to drop Sinterklaas,[7] I just want to give you Dutch an extra holiday." He is often asked why the AEL is not called the BEL, because there are more Berbers than Arabs in the Netherlands. The distinction is significant. The Berbers are not, in fact, Arabs, but instead Morocco's indigenous people and, as such, have inhabited a place of minority in Morocco for centuries, with all the prejudice such a role entails. Abou Jahjah, who is Lebanese and therefore disconnected from the Berber cause, typically responds to such remarks with "I'm a Muslim and Arabic is the language of the Koran. This means every Muslim has to identify with AEL."[8] Part of his political agenda is to have the Arabic language recognized as an official minority language in EU countries, starting with Belgium and the Netherlands. What results from such recognition are state subsidies for teaching the language and for building a state-sponsored infrastructure for the cultural aspects of the language. For example, Belgium now recognizes French, Flemish, and German as official languages, and each language community has its own legislative body.

One of Abou Jahjah's main objectives is to improve the rights and future prospects of young Muslims who, in his view, are demonized by the European society. In his words: "In Europe, the *allochtonen* form the most stepped on part of the society,"[9] which is to say, in his view, that they allow themselves to be walked over in exchange for being identified as "good" or "civilized" Arabs. He speaks out against those he describes as the ethnic or *allochtoon* establishment: "We came with a movement which will break their status quo and we will of course clash with those who have interests in maintaining the current system. These are the federations, subsidized *allochtonen* associations, *allochtonen* politicians, the Muslim executives. Their power bases will crumble because of the growth of AEL."

An equally important objective, in his view, is to destigmatize Islam in the Flemish- and Dutch-speaking countries and eventually in all of Europe. In interviews, he has explained that during his first five years in Europe, he had told himself that the discrimination he experienced in his daily life was the result of his being a newcomer without the right papers, someone who did not speak the language well. But once he learned to speak Flemish and Dutch fluently, and when he had obtained educational credentials by completing his university degree in political science at the University of Antwerp, he came to realize that the discrimination he experienced did not diminish. In 2003, he said Muslims and immigrants in Belgium are really second-class citizens and the extreme-right Vlaams Blok has infiltrated the police, who harass Muslims without cause.[10] His Belgian AEL has some two-thousand dues-paying members.

He also has affiliations with groups in France and the United Kingdom, as well as in Egypt and Lebanon.[11] He supports a certain level of autonomy for Berber regions in Arabic countries, to give them minority status, but he believes this is a struggle within the Arab countries themselves and his work is only to assist in that struggle because his main focus is in Europe. That said, he does address the issue of a Palestinian state: "I am a nationalist because my nation is not liberated but when my country becomes liberated I will no longer be nationalist. It has nothing to do with ideology. It has to do with the position you take in a struggle for independence. As long as my nation is not liberated, I have to be a nationalist."[12] He believes a Palestinian-Arab democratic state is the only solution to the Israeli-Palestinian problems.

Even after the January 2003 national elections, the development of the Dutch branch of the Flemish AEL remained a prevalent topic for the media in the Netherlands. Abou Jahjah began a Dutch public speaking tour and neighborhood visits in early March 2003, starting with the city of Amsterdam. Dutch Protestant broadcasting (Evangelische Omroep) described his arrival as if a foreign aggressor had crossed the border, saying: "Abou Jahjah set foot on Dutch soil." Well-known reporter Paul Brill characterized the Muslim community's reaction like this: "You might think that we are talking about a prophet arriving in a Jahjah-mobile or even walking across the water (the Schelde) between Belgium and our country."[13]

The AEL Web site announced his speaking tour of the country for the week of March 2, calling for Muslims and young people to come hear him and learn about AEL's plans. The AEL agenda was also published on the Web site, where a bulletin announced: "The young people from CIDI (the Center for Information Documentation Israel) called for a demonstration against the leader of AEL, our brother Diab Abou Jahjah. This will happen during his visit to the University of Amsterdam tomorrow morning Friday, 7 March 2003. AEL's interim board asks everyone to be calm and behave in a dignified manner. Brothers are asked not to respond to any provocations from CIDI or anyone, even the police."[14]

Dozens of young people from Jewish organizations did indeed demonstrate against what they called "Abou Jahjah's hate campaign" at the University of Amsterdam when he spoke to the law faculty. He received Category I protection from the police, the level of protection that is usually afforded only the queen or diplomats. Helicopters advance-filmed the area, plainclothes security officers were everywhere, and Abou Jahjah wore a bulletproof vest and was transported in a bulletproof vehicle. He said: "There are forces who want to shut my mouth. There are people who want to eliminate the debate." Asked "What would happen if they kill you?" he replied, "Then I'm a *Shaheed* [a martyr]," which brought much applause.

Asked if he was an anti-Semite, his response became a headline in the nation's most popular newspaper, *De Telegraaf*, the following day: "Abou Jahjah says that hating Muslims is the same as hating Jews." According to Abou Jahjah, "If you replace the word Muslim with the word Jew in the Dutch media, you get the discourse of Hitler.... Muslims need to organize themselves as a popular movement.... We [AEL] are born from an ideology, just like the LPF [the Lijst Pym Fortuyn]." He also criticized Ayaan Hirsi Ali, the VVD MP elected in January 2003, for describing herself as "anti-Islamite," and he said this is the same as being an anti-Semite. He said he believes that Muslims should speak Dutch and be citizens of the country, but he also argued that forcing people to assimilate to the Dutch culture is racist: "If your target is to assimilate me, then you want me to disappear, you want to destroy me."[15] He spoke the same evening to a full house at Amsterdam's De Balie, and the next day, he visited one of Amsterdam's poorest and most migrant-dominated neighborhoods, the renowned Bos en Lommer, an area with Moroccan and Turkish supermarkets, schools, and mosques. Nearly two-thirds of Bos en Lommer's population is Muslim, mainly Moroccans and Turks, and the white Dutch in the neighborhood describe themselves as the minority.

Abou Jahjah argues that the high unemployment among Muslim immigrants and especially among young male Moroccans is a product of exclusion and discrimination. He highlights police harassment as a special problem for young Muslim men and women. He points out that, formally, everyone has the same rights in Holland but, in reality, Muslims are second-class citizens.

In a March 2003 profile article in *Trouw* titled "Abou Jahjah Has an Answer to Everything," a twenty-five-year-old Moroccan man in Amsterdam named Said Chabbi said: "There is polarization. The VVD says that Holland is full and that in the past it was taboo to say it. It [hearing Abou Jahjah speak] makes me think of becoming a member of the AEL. I was thinking that maybe AEL is radical, but it is not." Hakima es Sannouni, a twenty-year-old Moroccan woman, said: "It is a pity that the Dutch think Abou Jahjah is a danger. He wants the best for us all, *allochtoon en autochtoon* [non-Dutch and Dutch]." *Trouw* reported that in one of his speeches about Islam in Tilburg in early March, Abou Jahjah said: "Islam gives room for people to live together, but Islam is also a religion of dignity. If you hit a Muslim, he will not turn the other cheek, he will hit you back." This brought much applause. "Nobody needs to be afraid of a good Muslim, because it is forbidden to be an aggressor. Do you know who is afraid of Muslims? People who are themselves aggressors, because they know Islam is going to resist them." This brought even more applause. On the topic of the media he said, "If you want to work on a better image [for Islam], it doesn't work, because all you need is another September 11th or Pim Fortuyn and then the image is bad again." His message, the words of a Western-educated Muslim, resonated with a broad swath of people, but it was aimed at one group in particular: young Muslims. Naima el Maslouhi, his twenty-year-old public relations staffer, said "We are interested only in our target group, our people." The reporter elaborated that AEL therefore doesn't care about the media.[16]

Shortly after the Iraq War began in March 2003, a small, inexpensive paperback, *Resist! Much More Than a Culture Shock*, took a prominent place in Belgian and Dutch bookstores catering to both the mass market and the intellectual elite. Its cover showed a photo of Abou Jahjah and his coauthor, a Moroccan-Belgian woman lawyer named Zohra Othman holding a poster bearing the colors of the Palestinian flag with the Dutch and English words *Verzet* and *Resist*. The book includes all of Abou Jahjah's and AEL's stands, which are one and the same. On the topic of the Iraq War, he wrote: "We cannot just be content to be against the war. But we have to have resistance against the war. We want the Americans to be sent home from Iraq in body bags. We are very open about this."[17]

Having embraced the doctrine and the story of Malcolm X, Abou Jahjah sees the American government within the pre-1970s context, a context that requires one to view the U.S. government as partial to the white majority to the detriment of other races, a situation that Abou Jahjah and others have compared with the inequality that exists between the white European population and the North African migrant community. His remarks regarding American soldiers, however, did not take into account that many of those soldiers are themselves both black and Muslim, but his oversight may have been intentional: his goal was to appeal not to American Muslims but instead to the young Muslims in Europe who formed his constituency. The fact that some of his ideological casualties—those Americans in body bags—shared his faith, was immaterial to him. His appeal to young Muslims in Europe is based in part on his seemingly edgy persona—he admits to having cooperated previously with Hezbollah but says that he has never been a member of the radical Islamic group,[18] one that is described as a terrorist organization in most Western countries. He believes that the path for change in Europe is not through the ballot box and has said, "We don't have the illusion that we will change things through elections."[19] He wants AEL to remain a popular movement (*volksbeweging*): "If you struggle when you are being stepped on, you have to do it as a people's struggle. If the struggle becomes institutionalized and structured, then it is broken."[20]

Paving the Way for Abou Jahjah in the Netherlands

What has become known as the *kut Marokkanen* incident (*kut* translates as "cunt") occurred about a year before Abou Jahjah's press tour, during the March 2002 Amsterdam City Council election campaign. It became a major focus of the Dutch press and helped set the stage for Abou Jahjah's popularity.

Labour Party MP Rob Oudkerk, who was being considered for a post as a city alderman, initially said, "*kut Marokkanen*" to Job Cohen, fellow Labour Party member and mayor of the city of Amsterdam, at a neighborhood visit on the eve of the city council election in March 2002. Not realizing that the news cameras were still rolling, Mayor Cohen asked Oudkerk if he thought Pim

Fortuyn would get much support there. Oudkerk said, "yes" but added, "We also have *kut Marokkanen*" or, to translate, "these Moroccan cunts," which referred not only to women but also to Moroccan people in general. A camera from the popular current affairs TV program *2Vandaag* picked this up, and it was broadcast news and in the press for weeks. A Moroccan man from the city of Zeist was so upset that he went to the police to file suit, claiming under Dutch law that his group had been particularly offended. It is a crime in the country to make a statement that is aimed at offending one particular group.

The Labour Party in Amsterdam, as well as Oudkerk himself, apologized. Oudkerk was not prosecuted.[21] It was a particularly troublesome occasion for him, because he is Jewish and had himself been the target of unkind words and discrimination.

Several months after the incident, however, the words *kut Marokkanen* returned to the air. In September 2002, a young Moroccan rapper released a record by the same name and wore a T-shirt bearing those words. Both were an instant success, and the song became the number one hit for a time on Dutch MTV. The rap by Raymzter is political, historical in its reference points, and poetic in style:

> So I mean it when I rap, and it's that thing.
> That way I win, like Abdel Krim, in 1921.
> Surrendering is for the weak...
> Unjust, they hate us and they fear us. The newspaper plays with it, TV does even more.
> ...Raymzter is a poet who can really talk well. Just like the
> Prophet Muhammad that you need to know.[22]

Interpreting the Raymzter

Before turning to its place in the larger public space and the importance of this song in the political arena, I want to provide some explanation of what lies behind the lyrics. The song begins with "They want to make us 'black.'" In Dutch, it simply means to badmouth someone. But it can also be understood as a reference to Zwarte Piet or "Black Pete," the Black Moor elflike creature who accompanies Sinterklaas (Saint Nicholas, who looks a bit like Santa Claus) ashore—the Dutch Santa travels by boat—in the story celebrating the Dutch national holiday of December 5, Sinterklaas Day. The celebration is often enacted on the holiday itself with white Dutchmen sporting blackface (Little Black Sambo style), and major stores across the country feature Black Pete in larger-than-life window displays.[23] From a traditional Dutch perspective, there are no negative racial overtones in these characters. From another perspective, however, Sinterklaas is the white man, and the Black Pete characters are guest workers under his control. Raymzter says, "It's time that this has to change, don't you get it?" He tells us that "we" don't want to tolerate this subordinate or stigmatized position any longer.

As a rapper, he "wins" because he says what he believes and his message is inspired by his hero "Abdel Krim in 1921," who brought suffering to the Spanish troops occupying the northern mountainous Rif region of Morocco. Krim wanted to make the Rif region independent from the central Moroccan state, he did not want to deal with the central government of Morocco or with the occupying Spaniards, and he brought pride to the Rif people. Rather than surrender, he chose to live in exile in Cairo with his family. "Surrendering is for the weak," says the rapper, who implicitly compares living in the Netherlands with living in exile. And like Abdel Krim, the rapper wants to make this exiled place his home: "Even though it was years ago, history repeats itself, and we saw it again and again."

When the Twin Towers fell on 9/11, Dutch news cameras captured young Moroccan people dancing and celebrating at a party in the small town of Ede, near Utrecht. These dancing visuals were broadcast throughout the world on CNN International and across the Netherlands on many channels. The pictures of young Moroccans in Holland celebrating 9/11 shocked many viewers. The rapper says that many of "you"—the Arabic and Muslim community—in the audience were "happy" until they saw "partying Moroccans in Ede" broadcast internationally. He criticized the media and the audience for being too quick to "react without reason" because the party that was captured on film was, in fact, a birthday party that had nothing to do with the events on 9/11. He implies that the media are not accurate and says, "Now it's time to pay attention to real problems, described mathematically"—in other words, described accurately—to say something accurate about "what conditions Moroccans live under here."

He attacks the media especially for playing up "unjust" perspectives: "Unjust, they hate us and they fear us. The newspaper plays with it. TV does even more." But he expresses even more astonishment that "you," the audience, which also includes Moroccans themselves, take part in it: "But that you also are part of it astonishes me more." He implicitly refers to a vicious circle between the media and their audiences. But he is determined to break the circle: "I am fully focused, and once I start no one must stop me because I can't control myself."

He is constantly stigmatized. "What I say sounds maybe simple, but they look at me as if I flew into the Twin Towers." And then he tells the history of the "*kut Marokkaan*": "We came as guest workers. On the low down we passed the hash around." The Rif is the one of the world's largest producers of hashish. The European Union sends money to Morocco to pay farmers to stop producing it, but in the Dutch coffee shops where hashish is sold legally, Moroccan hashish is considered to be the best. It means that in a hidden way, "on the low down," some people from the Rif are illegally bringing it into the country without being caught, so that it can be sold legally. In the past, the rapper says, because of this drug trafficking, "I know what they called me"; in other words, he knows that they looked down on Moroccans but their attitude was more of a quiet murmuring. Now, however, it is loud and nasty: "I was little, and then *"kut Marokkaan"* this is what they said." Although the offensive term had been muttered in the past, the use of the term by a politician led to it being broadcast loudly, and now the rapper is feeling the harshness of this volume.

His refrain includes a reference to the fact that the Arab culture founded math and physics. He is angry about the constant commenting that Moroccans do not work: "The founders of physics and mathematics, who says that Moroccans cannot work?" He talks about "prejudice" which he hears "a lot." He says he is "a poet who can really talk well, just like the Prophet Mohammed." He implies that you, the audience, need to know the Prophet, too: "That you need to know." He wants to be heard and respected as a human being, and his exiled existence leads him to ask who he is: "You heard me surely. I am breaking through. I don't expect that you know who I am. Shit, I am a human being. God who am I? I'm as Moroccan as I'm Dutch." He shows how the Moroccans have much in common with the Dutch, they both "eat cauliflower" and sell hash. And, like the Dutch, he likes "cash."

Imam El-Moumni, as Raymzter reminds us, made inflammatory statements regarding homosexuals in May 2001. The rapper, singing in September 2002, says that what is now being said about Moroccans in the media is harsher than what El-Moumni said: "Words fall harder than the ones of El-Moumni." The rapper accuses the Dutch of focusing on superficial stereotypes and negative anecdotes because going deeper might reveal that the image is a false one, and that wouldn't sit well in the minds of many Dutch, who, in the rapper's words, "want nothing else than for me to get out." He tells us that he doesn't even speak Arabic, but at least the rhythm of his music makes it appear as if he does and that is an inspiration for young Moroccans: "it's magic. You hear the work shining as a star because you are part of this cultural heritage."

He tells us what it's like now to be a young Moroccan man on the streets in the country: "Shit, it ruins my day if I walk alongside a woman who pulls her bag closer to her." He tells us how he and his generation are different from their parents: "My father had it worse. He was a Berber, a guest from the mountains. But I'm born here and you can hear it on me." He speaks of the racism he faces here: "You give me dirty looks behind my back, and act sincere to my face. My sincere words hurt your ears." He warns that the Dutch mentality, or tendency to categorize Moroccans, is going to bring an end to the civil society as we know it: "With this mentality, the world is going to be lost. . . . I mean in every boat come some rats. . . . I saw no single person trying to make Moroccans look better. You prefer them to arrest us. So I came here, ladies and gentlemen, to teach you not everybody should be seen as the same." He tells us that there are some bad people everywhere, also in the boats that bring the immigrants. He then says the Dutch words *"over één kam te scheren,"* which translated literally means "one comb to shear," referring to the shearing of the sheep's coat of wool that requires only one kind of shear for many kinds of sheep. It means, one size fits all, or they are all alike. The rapper thinks that this describes the way the Dutch think about Moroccans.

It is ironic that Raymzter falls prey to his own criticism of the Dutch. His last words also implicitly describe the Dutch as having one view, yet he is criticizing the Dutch for having one view about the Moroccans. This kind of group thinking and identification, magnified by the media and popular culture, is part of what his song is about, part of the stigmatization and mobilization processes going on in the country in the months before Abou Jahjah arrived.

The Media-Initiated Action/Reaction

"*Kut Marokkaan*" was such a hit that the mainstream political talk shows soon became interested. When his song was released in September 2002, Raymzter was invited to appear on one of the Netherlands' most popular shows, *Barend en Van Dorp*, to perform the song and then sit around the table to discuss the issues it raised with journalists and two politicians, one of whom was Oudkerk, who sat across from the young rapper and immediately apologized to him. The rapper thanked Oudkerk for coining the term that made the Raymzter famous, and almost everyone laughed. The other politician present, however, was less pleased with the situation and appeared annoyed by the young man and his music. Winny de Jong was an MP who, with no prior political experience, had been ushered into Parliament in May 2002 as part of the new LPF fraction. Later, in October 2002, she played a major role in the downfall of the CDA-LPF-VVD coalition government because of her personal disagreements with others in her fraction. She left the LPF by November and formed her own two-person fraction in the Parliament after her colleague—and only fellow fraction member—punched a cameraman, a scene that was widely broadcast in the news. She is perhaps best known for baring almost all in a major news magazine,

Panorama, in the final days of the January 2003 election campaign, but her topless photo failed to win her enough votes to return her to Parliament. It was just four months prior to this political pictorial that she appeared on *Barend en Van Dorp*. Following Raymzter's performance of *"Kut Marokkanen,"* she turned to the rapper and asked, "Why did you wait so long to come out with this number? You just did it for the money." The Raymzter replied, "I'm an entrepreneur. I took advantage of the opportunity." Everyone but de Jong laughed—the LPF fraction, of which she was a part, was made up almost entirely of entrepreneurs.

A Renegade Muslim Leaves Dutch Socialism for Dutch Liberalism

On September 18, 2002, shortly after Raymzter's appearance on *Barend en Van Dorp*, the Dutch police were called to protect the empty house of Ayaan Hirsi Ali, a thirty-something Somali-born refugee who took a degree in political science at Leiden University and was employed by the Dutch Labour Party's think tank. She had left her home in Leiden because she was afraid of extremist Muslims who had threatened her life in response to her statements about the situation of women in Islam on the talk show *Barend en Van Dorp* the day before. She had said: "Everywhere where Islam has a majority, women have to be covered or hidden." She said she was fighting for the right of Muslim girls and women to have sexual freedom, their own income, and the right to decide their own futures. She had made many such statements prior to this, but by mid-September 2002, she felt she had to flee the country because of the threats on her life. Already in June 2002, well-known Dutch columnist John Jansen van Galen had written an article headlined *"Marokkaanse billenknijpertjes"* [Moroccan butt pinchers], in which he featured Hirsi Ali's remarks: "As Fortuyn, she has sharply defined the debate. . . . She mentions the bad behavior [of Moroccan boys towards girls] in discos and swimming pools. The upbringing of these boys from Islamic countries ('I come from a country like that, I know that') leads them to think that they 'can pinch the girls on their butts.' The Dutch have to learn to be hard on these boys . . . and migrants have to learn that the Netherlands has other rules. . . . Hirsi is less easy to demonize than Fortuyn."[24]

Hirsi Ali had become famous in the country after the May 2002 national election because she publicly told the story of being forcibly circumcised at age five in Somalia with the involvement and consent of her parents. At age twenty-two, she said, after her father tried to marry her off to a distant cousin whom she had never met, she fled Somalia and became a political refugee in the Netherlands. Once she learned the Dutch language, she worked as an interpreter for Dutch social services dealing with immigrants and discovered "suffering on a terrible scale" among Muslim women and children in the country. She discovered sexual abuse in Muslim families, incest, beatings and abortions, and girls committing suicide. All of this was surrounded by silence, she said, because social workers in the Netherlands are sworn to secrecy.[25] Her outspokenness captured attention around the world, and even Salman Rushdie wrote about her: "Let us not forget the horrifying story of the Dutch Muslim woman, Ayaan Hirsi Ali who has had to leave the Netherlands because she said that Muslim men oppressed Muslim women, a vile idea for the expression of which outraged Muslim men have issued death threats against her."[26]

The horrific details of her childhood story of female circumcision, and the similar stories she told about other women and girls in Somalia, became major news in the press and on television over the summer of 2002, months before Raymzter's rap plea for better understanding of Muslims hit the airways.[27] In some of her television interviews, she cried as she recounted what she and other girls had to endure. Her personal story came out shortly after *Nova* had aired an investigative exposé asserting that imams in some mosques in Holland were saying that Muslim men should dominate disobedient Muslim women. With the *Nova* expose and Hirsi Ali's personal story in June 2002, the rights of Muslim women had suddenly become the subject of almost daily *borrel'* [pub and café] conversations.

In August 2002, Hirsi Ali published her first book *De zoontjesfabriek* (*The Sons Factory: About Women, Islam and Integration*).[28] In it, she tells the story of her grandmother, who had nine daughters and one son. The grandmother was fond of saying "we have only one child." When Hirsi Ali and her sister asked, "And what about us?" the grandmother replied, "You two will give us sons." She wrote about the "imprisoned women of Islam," whose prison was their home and whose main task in life was to produce and cater to boys and men. "For women there are in Paradise only dates and grapes, and nothing more," she said. Less than a month after her book came out, in September 2002, because of the threats on her life, the Dutch government paid for her refuge in the United States, where she hid among the Somali community in California. She returned to the Netherlands a month later, in October, surrounded by an entourage of bodyguards amid the public announcement that she would be switching her political allegiance from the Labour Party to the Liberal Party, VVD. She claimed the Labour Party had been "hijacked by Muslims and multicultis" and complained of their "soft" approach to integration issues and their lack of attention to the liberation of Muslim women. In her view, the Dutch social services system and the Dutch policies on integration left Muslim women alone and vulnerable in their homes.

However, the facts of her personal story were contested by members of the Somali community in the Netherlands, and in October 2002, the investigative news magazine *Vrij Nederland* devoted a major article to questioning the validity of her story, an article for which the magazine later had to officially apologize after being attacked by well-known Dutch intellectuals and journalists such as Emma Brunt for not helping in the struggle to emancipate Muslim women.[29]

Hirsi Ali has continued to stand by the beliefs she stated at that time, that Labour's support for Islamic schools and associations backfired and the result is segregation and misery for Muslim women. She believes Dutch law should be used to prosecute Muslim men for domestic violence against their wives and daughters, that immigrants should stop being taught in their own language for the few hours a week that is required in Islamic schools, and that the state should stop paying for hundreds of Islamic clubs that she describes as "run by deeply conservative men and perpetuate the segregation of women."[30]

Generational Change at the Top

In response to their major defeat at the polls in the May 2002 national election, by November 2002, the Labour Party elected a new leader, Wouter Bos, who had entered Parliament just four years before. The Green Left also elected a new leader in the aftermath of May 2002, Femke Halsema, a Dutch thirty-something woman who had also only served as a member of Parliament since 1998 before becoming the Green Left leader. Born in 1966, her choice to lead the party rather than have a baby was the talk of the day among a roundtable of journalists on Radio One. These two young political leaders, Bos and Halsema, represented a major generational shift in the public faces of their parties.

The VVD leader Hans Dijkstal also stepped down. He was replaced by Gerrit Zalm, the two-term minister of finance during the Purple Coalition, who had been responsible for one of the most successful economies the country had experienced. Creator of what became known as the Zalm-norm, he advocated not spending more than what was taken in and reinvesting at times of budget surplus.

In the smaller parties, there was also change at the top. Leefbar Nederland (LN), the party that made Pim Fortuyn its leader in early 2002, elected Haitska van der Linde, a twenty-two-year-old woman who had battled for the post against the infamous Dutch motivational speaker and celebrity Emile Ratelband. Winny de Jong, who had left the LPF and formed her own party called Conservatieven.nl, of which she appointed herself leader, selected as her running mate a man from Rotterdam who was seen as far right. And the conservatieve Christen Unie (CU) also elected a new leader, Andre Rouvoet.

The Socialist Party, SP, which is the former Communist Party, was conservative by comparison because it continued to be led by the same leader, Jan Marijnissen. Popular, working class, and known for his dynamic way of speaking, Marijnissen had led his party to a successful outcome in May 2002 by continuing to campaign on his slogan *"stem tegen"* [vote against]—running against the establishment. His party nearly doubled in size in the 150-seat Parliament, from 5 to 9 seats in May 2002. When the majority of the country shifted right (CDA and VVD) or even extreme-right (LPF), the SP, an extreme left party also known for its anti-immigrant stands, reaped some benefits. After the death of Fortuyn, and in the period leading up to the election of Wouter Bos as the leader of the Labour Party in November 2002, Marijnissen's popularity in public opinion polls continued to climb, and some thought his SP might achieve an unprecedented fifteen to twenty seats in the next elections. He promoted his book *New Optimism*, published only twelve days before the January 2003 election, with the slogan *"Tegen Paars en Pimpelpaars"* [Against the Purple Coalition and the Pim Violet Coalition], in which he criticized neo-Liberalism, the Purple Coalition, and the Pim Coalition.

Containing Islam: All Parties Agree in 2003

Setting aside the generational change, the parade of new faces at the top, and the brushed-up wardrobes (or no wardrobe, if we think of Winny de Jong), the most striking difference between the May 2002 and January 2003 elections was the change in the range of elite political opinion on Islam, integration, and immigration. Just eight months after Pim Fortuyn's death, after a campaign in which he and his LPF had made Islam the defining issue and pitted this view against the multicultural policies of the Dutch pillar system represented by Labour in the Purple Coalition government, by January 2003 little or no difference could be found among most of the political parties on these questions. And that was where most people obtained their information about where the parties stood on the issues. With the exception of Green Left leader Femke Halsema, who spoke out in favor of keeping all the political asylum seekers who were already in the country, all of the other main parties and their leaders had for the most part adopted the LPF's positions on these and related questions.

One of the extraordinary moments of the 2003 campaign was the party leaders' debate in which the topics of integration and immigration were discussed by first pairing off the extreme-left SP leader Jan Marijnissen against the extreme-right LPF leader Mat Herben. The Dutch would not wish to describe either party as extreme, but I do here to illustrate the parameters of the debate. An excerpt from this debate illustrates the profound effect of Pim Fortuyn on Dutch politics: the common perspective shared by two leaders, one on the left and one on the right.

The televised debate between a number of party leaders took place on January 8, 2003, at the Aula of Erasmus University. It was moderated by two journalists and had six segments. The first was about the economy and jobs, the second segment was about integration and immigration. A short film was used to introduce the topic, and then the debate began. There was little in the way of differences among the main parties on these topics with respect to positions on specific policy outcomes. Only the Green Left leader occasionally positioned herself and her party against the others by sometimes taking a more proimmigrant stand. The leaders on the LPF and the SP agreed, for example, on the policy of raising the minimum required age from twenty-one to twenty-four years old for young people of Turkish or Moroccan origin, who are Dutch citizens, to be able to marry someone from outside Europe—a measure designed to prevent what would be called "green card marriages" in the United States. Here is the segment from the January 8 debate on this point:

> JOURNALIST: Let me talk about another category of people. Can a Turkish or Moroccan man bring his bride from Turkey or Morocco?
>
> HERBEN [LPF]: It is now possible to do that when the man is 21, but the LPF wants to make that 24 years old. It is the Danish model. Denmark is an enlightened example in Europe. They have the 24-year-old age limit. In our strategic accord, I think 21 years old is too easy. I think family reunion at the age of 24 is not abnormal.
>
> MARIJNISSEN [SP]: I was 24 when I got married. [laughter]
>
> HERBEN [LPF]: 24 years old, it's a good proposal.
>
> MARIJNISSEN [SP]: If it doesn't get higher. . . .

And later, on the topic of citizenship (*inburgeringscursus*) for immigrants, the two leaders also agreed:

> HERBEN [LPF]: . . . One of the most important points is that you have to start with the spiritual leaders. He [Mr. Nawijn, Minister of Integration] started citizenship (*inburgering*) courses for them, I mean the imams. We want them to learn Dutch.
>
> MARIJNISSEN [SP]: We don't need the LPF for that (laughing). All the parties agree on this point.

Although the short film at the outset of the debate was about women who want to wear the scarf, and included visuals of women wearing scarves, the scarf itself was not a point of discussion in the debate. Instead, the discussion focused on the chador and the burka, the rarely worn long robe in combination with a veil, covering the woman's entire body. This became a point of discussion for all the party leaders. The discussion moved from what women should wear to what should be done to those who do not integrate:

JOURNALIST 2:   We are going to talk more about integration. Mr. Bos, the burka and the chador, this large robe covering the entire body, are they bad for integration?

BOS [PvdA/Labor]:   Yes.

JOURNALIST 2:   And what about Mrs. Femke Halsema [Green Left leader]?

HALSMA [GL]:   It is very bad for the emancipation of women. The Netherlands is a free country. Women had to fight for their freedom. We are proud of it. I don't want women to be blindfolded on the streets, unidentifiable.

ZALM [VVD]:   My answer is with my entire being [*volmondig*]: I'm against it. You can't give lessons in the classroom when you have people wearing that. If they continue like that in the Netherlands they will never find a job.

BALKENENDE [CDA/current Prime Minister]:   It is about communication. This kind of clothing doesn't make it easy to talk to each other. It is not good.

JOURNALIST 1:   Where does the state's authority stop? How far can you go? Are you talking only about newcomers or also about people (*allochtonen*) who are living here for years? Do you want to force them also?

BOS [PvdA/Labour]:   We have to question all the possibilities that the Dutch society gave them or can give them in order to learn the language and *in te burgeren* [become citizens]. If they don't do that, then the government has to question their responsibility [to integrate].

JOURNALIST 2:   If not?

BOS [PvdA/Labour]:   Then you have to have sanctions. There are many possibilities. People who come here on their own free will, and have all the possibilities for *inburgering*, and they don't do it, the ultimate sanction is to take away their permanent residence permit.

JOURNALIST 2:   Do you agree, Ms. Halsema?

HALSEMA [GL]:   No. Permanent residence cannot be a subject here. We are talking about integration and not about reducing the number of legal immigrants who live here.

JOURNALIST 2:   And people who cannot integrate, can they stay here in the Netherlands?

HALSEMA [GL]:   Well, financial sanctions are possible. If you give people the same rights as we have in the Netherlands, which is the right thing to do, but you cannot blackmail them with expelling them from the country [if they don't speak Dutch]. You have to be accountable. You can't expel political asylum seekers.

BOS [PvdA]:   Be careful. I'm not talking here about political asylum seekers. I'm talking specifically about those who came here out of their own free will. I refer to people who came here through the family reunion program and I am not talking about political asylum seekers, they have to integrate, I cannot accept that.

This was followed by another leaders' debate, but on radio instead of television, on January 12, 2003, in which integration followed the topic of Dutch policy on "toleration" of drugs. It's useful to look at this brief segment to see where the party leaders stood on *gedogen* [toleration], in other words, the practice of closing one's eyes on the implementation of the law, such as the toleration of pimps who are not legal within the legalized industry of prostitution.

BALKENENDE (CDA/Prime Minister):   Toleration is very bad for norms and values. In Holland, everything is possible. We are now synonymous with NL for No Limits. We are too soft. We are the biggest producer of ecstasy in the world and at the same time we help to control the quality of the drugs in house parties.

HALSEMA (GL):   I think that the government first has to respect its own rules. I'm proeuthanasia and I don't want the CDA now in government to revoke it and then close their eyes to the fact that it will continue to be practiced. This is bad for democracy.

MARIJNISSEN (SP):   Norms have to be implemented and respected, otherwise they are going to erode. You cannot just have a policy of letting it happen.

BOS (PvdA/Labour):   The Netherlands plays a big role in producing ecstasy in the world but the point about house parties is that parents are afraid that children will die using bad drugs which is why they have to be assisted to check the quality of the drugs available.

This brief exchange of views provides insight into the unusual ways in which toleration operates in social life in the Netherlands, which is perhaps the only country in the world where local organizations go to teenagers' house parties to check that the drugs being used, such as ecstasy, are of a certain degree of purity so as to minimize the risk of death. Abou Jahjah has made the point that he wants to stop the sale of drugs in "coffee shops," as well as this kind of civic involvement in the use of drugs at house parties, should he ever be in power. Ironically, this puts him in the same camp as Dutch Prime Minister Jan Peter Balkenende, whose party is the Christian Democratic Alliance (CDA), and U.S. President George W. Bush, whose administration criticized Dutch drug policy.

Drugs are not in Islamic schools, however, which are far less likely to be tolerated by the main political parties nowadays. The topic of Islamic schools was introduced into the debate when the panelists were asked to discuss the belief that "The Netherlands is full."

> JOURNALIST: We are going to talk today about education and integration. Is it easier if everyone speaks Dutch? What do you think about forced integration [busing] to solve the problem of having "black schools" [schools where the predominant concentration is migrant children]? Why not require Christian schools to accept Islamic and migrant children and to forbid the existence of Islamic schools? In that case, do we need to forbid Christian schools too? The thesis is: Special education [that is, education based on religion or ideology] is a barrier to integration. [author's translation/comments]

The issue of Islamic schools brings with it three complicated aspects: one is the existence of other religious schools in the country and that if some religions have their own schools. why not all religions, given that the Dutch constitution permits this? The second complicated aspect is that an investigation by the Dutch BVD (which is like the FBI in the United States) found that the teaching in some of the thirty-five Islamic schools in the country was a problem. Specifically, some schools were found to be circulating anti-Western material in their religious courses, and students were being taught that Islamic values were fundamentally different than Western values in those religious courses. While Islamic schools, like Dutch confessional and public schools, are regularly inspected by the state for compliance with curriculum norms, religious instruction has never been the focus of an inspection because of the separation between church and state in the constitution. The BVD's report led to a proposal to have an additional inspection for Islamic schools to identify what was being taught in religious courses alone. Part of the debate concerns whether such an inspection should be executed in religious courses in other confessional (Catholic, Protestant, Jewish, and Hindu) schools. Finally, the third important complicating aspect of the discussion of Islamic schools concerns what the French call *banlieusisation*, the segregation of communities. Part of the response of Muslim parents to the poor public schools in their segregated communities, and to the fact that many have found it difficult to get their children admitted to the more affluent confessional schools in the area, is to start their own Islamic school. The issue of busing therefore becomes linked to the issue of Islamic schools, because with busing, perhaps there would be no need for Islamic schools—underprivileged children could attend better schools outside their neighborhoods. Busing would have an impact only on public schools and would not affect students whose parents pay for them to attend confessional schools or other private schools. The debate shows how the left and right find many points of agreement; despite some differences in the reasoning, they end up in the same policy camp. No one suggested abolishing the right to have confessional schools, so no one argued that Islamic schools should be forbidden. Most believed that busing among public schools would help to reduce the need for Islamic schools or, as they are more commonly called, "black schools," and Islamic schools should be subject to special inspections, though some of those on the left believe this should be extended to all confessional schools.

Change Course Mobilization in the 2003 Campaign

Just days before the vote, on January 16, 2003, a group of fifty leading Moroccans, including a number of journalists, writers, students, intellectuals, businesspeople, and some politicians, published what became known as the Change Course Petition in the *Volkskrant*. They also arranged meetings with Amsterdam's mayor and members of Parliament in Den Haag to present the petition and emphasize their concerns. They complained that there was not a day when they did not read something bad about Moroccans in the Dutch newspapers. The petition began:

> This message to you is because we feel so bad and have an intense desire to break the negative spiral. We meet in Holland people who

are born here who feel at home here. There is a movement backwards, trying not to have discussions in a time when open and frank dialogue is crucial. Even youth who are strongly engaged in the society have doubts about the extent to which this situation can continue. For too long, Dutch Moroccans have been painted in a corner. Collectively blamed. . . .[31]

Despite this effort to change course, the last leaders' debate on television, a few days later on January 21, also included a discussion about integration. In advance of the event, most newspapers predicted that immigration and especially integration would be a key focus in that debate. And there were no major differences between the leaders on most key points of policy.

The Changing Electoral Landscape with a Common Anti-Islam Terrain

Mat Herben, the LPF leader, was known to have remarked that the legacy of Pim Fortuyn is evident in 2003 because all the Dutch political parties agreed on the main points of policy on issues of immigration and integration. This was illustrated in the discussion of the points of agreement in the various leaders' debates. Although most would reject the idea that they appear to be the heirs of Pim Fortuyn, and this would be especially insulting to the PvdA, the Labour Party, the results of the 2003 election show that by taking the same stands on these issues as the LPF, the Labour Party improved its position considerably. Labour went from 23 seats in May 2002 to 42 seats in January 2003. The CDA remained the largest party, but with only 2 more seats (44) than Labour. This left the right-leaning CDA leader, Prime Minister Balkenende, in a difficult position for embarking on discussions to reach a coalition agreement.

The press summed up the situation like this:

The current dominant position of the CDA and PvdA is built upon shifting sand. The voter is shifting, jumping from one party to another party, but is seeking, paradoxically enough, more cohesion in the society. Whereas the LPF was the big winner in May 2002 and the PvdA the big losers, this week the roles were reversed. This means that the spectacular election result in May 2002 will have to be seen as a short interlude and that we have returned to the ancien regime, the Purple Coalition.[32]

The "Perverse Tyrant," the "rage" [*razernij*], and the "Unveiled Women"

Between November 2002 and Election Day, January 22, 2003, there was rarely a day when Hirsi Ali or one of her topics was not in Dutch news, in the press, radio, and television. This prominence continued after the elections, when she wrote an article in *Trouw* on January 25, 2003, in which she described the Prophet Muhammad as a "perverse tyrant." This became front-page news that day in *Trouw* and later in all other Dutch media, and it extended into the Arabic media, which had already made her the subject of regular reporting. Four ambassadors representing fifty-six Muslim countries from the Organization of the Islamic Conference (OIC) later met with the VVD leader, Gerrit Zalm, to ask him to ask her to publicly apologize for her statements about Muhammad. On February 26, Zalm's office instead published a report of this meeting on his Web site, which led to its wide coverage in the broadcast and print media. When asked by journalists, he said that "Hirsi Ali is free to speak as she wants because the VVD is not a religious party." His defense of Hirsi Ali was the subject of much criticism from Dutch intellectuals, who said he should have emphasized the fact that the ambassadors were coming from nondemocratic countries. *Trouw*'s front page also criticized Zalm for not using stronger terms to tell the "homosexual-hating" ambassadors that the Netherlands is a democracy. An editorial stated: "Hirsi Ali deserves a better defense."[33] Bart Tromp, the intellectual socialist ideologue of the Labour Party, wrote in *Het Parool* that these Muslim ambassadors were like "Islamic rabid dogs" [*razernij*] in their angry call for Hirsi Ali to stop speaking about Muhammad. Hirsi Ali then said publicly that she was "sad" to see the press so critical of her party leader, because Zalm "has done so much."

In time for Women's Day on March 8, 2003, Hirsi Ali came out with her version of Martin Luther King Jr.'s "I Have a Dream" speech. She said:

> I have a dream. It is 8 March, International Women's Day. Crowds of veiled women are streaming into the Dam Square in Amsterdam. Then Mayor Cohen rings the bell. All these women immediately and at the same time, together, remove their veils. . . .. A Dutch man who beats his wife will be censured but a Muslim man will be respected for giving her a "corrective slap." . . . How can it be that so many young Muslim women suddenly wear a scarf? This wasn't the case some years ago. It's a symbol of segregation. They want to say "We are different." But I prefer to talk about what binds us. It's time for a third feminist wave, let's start with it today.[34]

March 8, 2003, was also the occasion for Adelheid Rosen, a Dutch actress and writer, to perform her play *Veiled Monologues* in Amsterdam's Balie. The title may sound innocuous to some, but interested observers who connected the dots realized that exactly a year after Rob Oudkerk came out with *"kut Marokkanen,"* this Dutch woman playwright came out with her Muslim twist on a previous year's hit in Dutch theater called *Vagina Monologen*, which itself had been adapted from a hit feminist Broadway play, *The Vagina Monologues*.[35]

There was yet another Islamic sexual taboo to be explored in the 2003 Dutch Book Week in Amsterdam. This annual event is the place where all Dutch writers come together to discuss the best books of the year, and one author each year is asked to write a short novel that is printed in a limited edition and handed out to all who attend opening night. In 2000, this honor was given to Salman Rushdie. In March 2003, the sixty-eighth Dutch Book Week, Dutch writer Ronald Giphart presented a short novel about death called *Gala*, in which he ironically jokes about *neuken*, *pijpen*, and *slikken*, the lewd Dutch words for the sex act, oral sex, and swallowing. The Dutch Union against Swearing, a religious organization, criticized him for the way in which he often wrote about sex in reference to God. One scene in particular was especially written for the times: a beautiful, intellectually sophisticated, Muslim Moroccan poet felt belittled by the constant praise she received for speaking faultless Dutch and did not want to be the *allochtoon*. Her thoughts are instead about wanting to write a book of poetry on these topics: "Ik krijg een natte kut van Allah . . . Masturberen met mijn spleet naar het Oosten."[36] This translates as: "I get a wet cunt from Allah. I masturbate with my vagina (crack) toward the East." The scene was not entirely from Giphart's imagination: a year earlier, in April 2002, a young second-generation Moroccan Muslim woman writer, Naima El Bezaz, published her Dutch book called *De Minnares van de Duivel* [*The Mistress of the Devil*]. In it, she describes the lives of Islamic women in Morocco and virginity cults in Islamic countries, in which the focus of the wedding night is on the blood-stained sheets. The climax of the book for many who reviewed it was the female orgasm scene during the prayer, which even became sermon fodder for an Amsterdam imam who "had heard about it, but hadn't read it."

The coming out of the Muslim female's orgasm in a work of Dutch fiction was followed in early November 2002 by a book about the lives of twenty-four Muslim homosexuals in the Netherlands, *Mijn geloof, mijn geluk* [*My Faith, My Happiness*].[37] The book was written by two Muslim men who had interviewed twenty-four young gay Muslim men. According to Hannah Belliot, the first Surinamese alderwoman of culture in Amsterdam, the interviews in this book opened a public discussion about living together in one society and about acceptance.[38] But for Muslims in the Netherlands, the year of sex and Islam was tense and sometimes humiliating, as if the Dutch wanted to needle those who subscribed to a culture that treated sex in much more covert and nuanced ways than their own.

Perhaps because of this overriding sentiment, seemingly enlightening messages intended for a Muslim target audience missed their mark. Hirsi Ali's stated mission of liberating Muslim women was not publicly endorsed by Muslim women in the Netherlands or Belgium, and a number of modern (unveiled) leading Muslim and non-Muslim women instead were featured on television in debate with Hirsi Ali. One such woman was Turkish Labour MP Nabahat Albayrak, who criticized Hirsi Ali for using the same sorts of populist appeals as Pim Fortuyn and for furthering the stigmatization of Muslims in the country.

Muslim Responses to Abou Jahjah

Although Hirsi Ali speaks about the liberation of Muslim women, it is Abou Jahjah who actually has young Muslim women in his audiences, both the veiled and the unveiled. Abou Jahjah was the topic of discussion in an Arabic program on Migrant Television in the Netherlands (MTNL) on March 13, 2003. A Moroccan imam from Amsterdam said: "If Abou Jahjah was a Moroccan, no one would follow him because there is no unity between Moroccans and we don't trust each other." Mustapha Arab, the presenter, a Moroccan Berber himself, countered:

> There is a major Shia movement now in this country and Europe to get the new generation, and they take different faces to make the Sunnis into Shias . . . the second and third generations born here are not interested in MTNL Arabic or Berber programs, they are interested in Dutch and Abou Jahjah gives them what they want. There is a tension between being Berber, Arab and Dutch and in the end the Dutch language will prevail because it becomes the spokesman of the identity.

There is a clear generational difference in Muslim responses to Abou Jahjah, based on my discussions with Dutch Muslims from the first and second generations. The older first-generation guest workers want to have nothing to do with him. They see him as a foreigner—he is not Moroccan or Turkish—who is unnecessarily radicalizing the young people. They want only that their children find good jobs, maintain strong links with their extended families in Morocco, and send money home. The second generation, however, born and educated in the country, find Abou Jahjah's message about racism especially appealing. Although the journalists I cited earlier tend to publish interviews with young Muslims in his audiences who say that his message is not extreme or dangerous, I found in my conversations with young people who attended the same rallies in Tilburg and Amsterdam that several were concerned about his political extremism. One specifically mentioned her concern about his stands on the position of women, given his strong support for the sharia, and she questioned the value of his strong stand on Palestine, pointing out that it might bring Moroccan communities in Europe into conflict with Jewish communities. Another youth, who studied econometrics, expressed concern that Abou Jahjah's ideas could have a negative impact on business, especially the Moroccan and Muslim business communities.[39] The picture I have of younger Muslims' reactions to Abou Jahjah is therefore different from the portrait painted by the Dutch press. Clearly, there is a range of opinions on Abou Jahjah among the second generation, but no one doubts his popularity. One Moroccan journalist for a leading Dutch newspaper told me that Abou Jahjah's extremism is needed "to counter the extremism in the Dutch media."[40] She was referring to the stigmatization of the Moroccans in the country.

In response to Flemish nationalism, Abou Jahjah offers appeals based on ethnic class struggle combined with political Islam. He has a political project and uses Islam as a political strategy to mobilize support among his target audiences. He counterattacks Flemish nationalism with Arab nationalism dressed as Islam. In the Belgian context, the far right Vlaams Blok, the Flemish nationalists, are separatists within the nation who argue that the poor French-speaking part of the country is costing them too much money. They are linguistic nationalists who take strong anti-immigrant stands at Belgian elections. They refer to the Moroccans as *Makak*, which is a Dutch word for "white ape" (connoting "macaque"), and the neighborhood called Borgurhout near Antwerp they refer to as Borgorokko, to mark it as a Moroccan ghetto. The other political parties in the country have stayed away from the Vlaams Blok, keeping them in a so-called cordon sanitaire, and no party is willing to cooperate with them at any level of government, local, regional, or national.

It's that kind of conflict-laden atmosphere that concerns the Dutch, who are accustomed to consensus and resolution of differences through discussion and debate. Vlaams Blok gained an unprecedented one-third of the vote in the local elections in Antwerp in 1991, and this is explained by Abou Jahjah as the result of how the Gulf War led Moroccans in Belgium to be seen as a fifth column, which contributed to further polarization in that country. Two years later in Antwerp, after a mosque and Arab tearoom were burned by far right extremists, masked Arab young men destroyed several cafés that were known to be far right hangouts. Abou Jahjah is known for having said "the ghetto is our strongest card"; he believes the Dutch system of pillarization helps to ghettoize the Muslim community, and ghettoization makes his access to his target audience easier.

According to a representative of KMAN, a key Moroccan organization in the Netherlands (see chapter 2), the "success" of Abou Jahjah is due to a Dutch media frenzy. It is further evidence of the Dutch media's disrespect for the local Moroccan population and their inability to distinguish one part of the Muslim population from another, in his view: "He is not Dutch and he is not Moroccan, and what he is saying has the effect of further stigmatizing the Moroccans in the Dutch media."[41] Abou Jahjah's response to criticisms such as these is that he does not trust statements from any organization that is subsidized by the Dutch or the Belgian state, because "you cannot bite the hand that feeds you." His strong feelings on this point led him to refuse to accept an invitation to become a member of (Flemish) Parliament for the Belgian Socialist Party (PvdA) in the past, because he found that they would not accept his viewpoints, and he did not want to be "used" as what he would describe as an example of cultural incorporation.[42] A political scientist from the University of Antwerp, Stefaan Walgrave, said the Dutch media frenzy was responsible for making more of Abou Jahjah in Holland than he actually is in his home city of Antwerp, where he has a lot of support among members of the Muslim community.[43]

By April 2003, the AEL had selected its new leader in the Netherlands: twenty-six-year-old Mohammed Cheppih. He is a Dutch citizen, born to first-generation Moroccan immigrants, and he speaks the Dutch language eloquently. He spent several years in Saudi Arabia, where he studied Islamic law at the University of Medina. He lives in the southern part of the country, in Eindhoven, where he works as a freelance imam in various mosques. He is also president of the Dutch branch of the Muslim World League (MWL), which is described in the press as a Saudi-sponsored organization aimed at spreading the faith. Like most in the MWL, he does not believe in saying that bin Laden is responsible for 9/11 because "one is innocent until proven guilty."[44] A member of the AEL said the organization needed an imam as leader "because of the Islamophobia in the Netherlands." Cheppih said, "They think I am a dangerous fundamentalist ... one wants to hear only that Islam is wrong."[45] According to the BVD (the Dutch FBI), he has provided legal assistance to twelve Muslims accused of terrorism in the Netherlands, and he also helped the Kurdish leader Mullah Krekar, the leader of the Islamic organization Ansar al Islam, to find legal representation in the Netherlands. Krekar is accused by the United States of having links to al-Qaeda. Cheppih explains that as the president of the MWL, it is his job to provide legal assistance to Muslims whenever he can. Like Abou

Jahjah, he also makes public statements regarding his stand on the Israeli-Palestinian conflict: "We are not against Jews, we are against Zionists." By June 2003, Cheppih had stepped down as leader of the Dutch AEL, and Abou Jahjah took over as leader in both Belgium and the Netherlands.[46]

In May 2003, Belgian national elections resulted in more than one-third of the votes in the city of Antwerp being cast for the nationalist, strongly anti-immigrant Vlaams Blok, and less than 2 percent voted for Abou Jahjah's party, Resist.

The years 2002 and 2003 were pivotal in bringing fear of Islam to the forefront of the Dutch media, and heroes such as Hirsi Ali and Abou Jahjah to speak on opposite sides of the debate, with the former framing the issue as gender and the latter framing the issue as race discrimination.

The Islamization of Citizenship

Across the border, a deep divide in Dutch society had been spreading since the early 1990s. In March 1992, public opinion polls showed that a large majority of Dutch believed that there were too many immigrants in the country and that politicians should take action to reduce immigration in the future.[47] That same year, Liberal Party (VVD) leader Frits Bolkestein publicly asked Muslim parents not to send their children to Islamic schools because, he said, it would only further segregation.[48] In the 1994 parliamentary elections, Bolkestein and his party focused on the Muslim immigration issue with three points in their manifesto: Reduce Immigration, Enhance Integration, Fight Discrimination.[49] The VVD was rewarded with a major increase in its number of parliamentary seats, from 22 to 31 seats in 1994. The parliamentary size of the VVD went up to 38 seats in the 1998 election. During that campaign, Bolkestein called for the deportation of illegal immigrants, which was perceived by many as a politically incorrect statement, and many of the other parties criticized the VVD's policy on this point.

During the first four years of the Purple Coalition, 1994–1998, the Labour Party ran the country with Prime Minister Wim Kok. The VVD was the second largest party and included Minister of Finance Gerrit Zalm. The Social Liberal D66 was the third party in the coalition and included Minister of Foreign Affairs Hans van Mierlo. During this coalition government, there were frequent public exchanges between leading people in the governing parties over integration of minorities and, in particular, Islamic minorities. Despite public conflicts between the coalition partners, major legislation curbing welfare, designed to make life more difficult for illegal immigrants, was passed. In the

1998 term, laws were passed to toughen existing legislation so that economic immigrants would be dissuaded from attempting to enter the country and only real political asylum seekers could be taken in.

After the 1998 elections, the style of parliamentary political debate changed. In the first term, there had been small but theatrical and sometimes highly visible confrontations among the coalition partners, which made it difficult for the opposition to get its message across because it was more of a bystander as the news focused on the conflicts within the governing coalition. When Bolkestein, Van Mierlo, and Labour parliamentary leader Jacques Wallage left the stage after the 1998 elections and three new parliamentary leaders stepped forward to take charge of their parties, the style of debate became comparatively quiet and more technocratic. Described in the press as the Purple Regents or as dealmakers who shunned public debate, preferring instead to find agreement behind the closed doors of the prime minister's office, there was little excitement left in the parliamentary debating chamber.

Three years into the quiet reign of the Purple Regents, Rotterdam Imam El-Moumni spoke in what he thought was an off-the-record moment in an interview about reducing crime among Moroccan youth in the country. He was asked, in conclusion, what he thought of gay marriage, and to paraphrase his off-the-record reply, he said, "If men continue to marry men and women continue to marry women, it is the end of Dutch society." His remarks were broadcast around the country in a special news program on May 3, 2001, and this brought the issues of immigration, integration, and Islam together at the forefront of the political arena more profoundly than when Pim Fortuyn's anti-Islam book had been published in 1997. Minister of Integration and Cities Roger van Boxtel immediately met with Imam El-Moumni to discuss the limits of free speech in the country. The minister was promptly criticized by politicians and the press for holding such meeting because, they argued, such recognition gave too much importance to the imam. The "inferiority" of Islam, its "backward" perspectives, and the "superiority" of the West was the predominant view in the Dutch media in June 2001. In the two months prior to 9/11, there was hardly a day when Islam, integration, or problems with certain immigrant groups in the society were not mentioned in one or another news outlet. This was the background for the emergence of Pim Fortuyn in late 2001 and early 2002, when he won on an anti-Islam and anti-immigrant ticket in the Rotterdam City Council elections.

In moving from Pim to Abou Jahjah, the public space in the Netherlands was primarily split by the Dutch community and the Muslim community, in which the Moroccan Muslims were a major part. The two communities came to be seen as increasingly distinct and opposite one another. The Changing

Course petition discussed earlier in this chapter showed that there was a consensus among many of the elite about the bias against Moroccans and Muslims in the Dutch news media, a bias about which even many journalists complained.

The Islamization of citizenship is the consequence of this growing divide between "us" and "them." The modern-day legend of *hidjra* shows how, in the early 1990s, imams inside the Moroccan mosques in Amsterdam told their faithful not to become Dutch but to remain Moroccan because, according to the imams, a change in nationality was an irreversible and profound step away from the Islamic faith. A decade later, with the second generation now old enough to become imams themselves, we see that this earlier perspective against taking Dutch nationality no longer predominates. Instead, there appear to be religious and legal reasons to give full endorsement to acquiring Dutch nationality, which can then be used by a "good Muslim" to further spread the faith.

In the early 1990s, imams remained largely within the mosques, but a decade later, they were just as often to be found outside the mosques. The movement of imams and Islamic religious leadership from inside to outside the mosques in the Netherlands was assisted by events in neighboring Belgium, where Abou Jahjah launched the AEL and proudly brought it across the border. The Dutch AEL sent a major message in mid-2003 by finding a new leader, a Dutch citizen and fluent Dutch-speaker, Imam Mohammed Cheppih, a second-generation son of Moroccan immigrants from the Rif who went to Saudi Arabia for his religious training. From a religious perspective, Cheppih was more radical than Abou Jahjah, who is seen by many Muslims as a Shia and not a Sunni like Cheppih.

In the environment of the stigmatized Muslim community, Abou Jahjah found fertile ground for maximizing his visibility in a media world hostile to his message, an environment he chose to ignore while continuing to speak directly to his target audience, young Muslims. He spoke openly, paying no attention to taboos. Like Pim Fortuyn, who had also found himself in a hostile media environment after he was ousted by Leefbar Nederland and before he started the LPF, Abou Jahjah became well known because of the hyped and fear-filled reporting in the Dutch press,[50] and the nervous reactions of the Dutch political parties like the CDA in early 2003, which wanted to forbid the AEL from entering the country, only succeeded in catapulting him to fame. As part of a new form of politicized ethnic and religious leadership outside the mosque, Abou Jahjah takes public stands on contested issues. But his rhetoric may seem more palatable to a broader audience because he can often include moderate appeals. For example, Abou Jahjah spoke about being a Muslim democrat, a fairly inoffensive and even appealing concept. His call for the inclusion of Islamic values in European citizenship by adding Islamic holidays to national calendars was more contested, as was his plea to recognize Arabic as Europe's second language.

In moving from Pim to Abou Jahjah, politics continued to be appropriated by popular culture with Raymzter's hit song "*kut Marokkaan.*" The shift to a more personalized and popular form of politics has been the subject of research in many democracies, and Liesbet van Zoonen has shown how this has occurred in the Netherlands.[51] Individuals and their personal stories have become the focus for public empathy and public understanding of political issues.

This personalization means that in understanding political issues, individuals also focus more on personal experiences: Pim Fortuyn expressed to his friends that his dislike of Islam was because the religion dislikes homosexuals; Hirsi Ali told her own story and then related it to the stories of Muslim women and children taking refuge in Dutch public shelters; Abou Jahjah explained his controversial stands by telling stories about his life experiences. Fortuyn mobilized the Dutch white voters who were anti-immigrant,[52] Ali mobilized Dutch feminists and Dutch left-wing intellectuals,[53] and Jahjah mobilized some of the younger members of the Muslim communities.[54]

In the 1994 elections, the Green Party and the VVD each had a Dutch immigrant from Morocco elected to the Dutch Parliament. I was one of those elected, and this also occurred in the Labour Party a year later. We three MPs in different parties gave the appearance of some integration, in elite circles at least. This may have also marked the beginning of a revolving-door phenomenon for the ethnic or *allochtone* MPs (in comparison with the Dutch or *autochtone* MPs), as the two elected in 1994 found themselves off their party lists by late 2002 to make room for "new" Muslim or ethnic faces.[55] At the same time, ethnic politics outside the political establishment emerged, with Abou Jahjah and the shift of Islam from inside to outside the mosque, clearly indicating that Parliament, or public office for that matter, needn't be the path for establishing power.

Pim Fortuyn had two main messages. One was antiestablishment, basically "get rid of the old coalition." The other was anti-immigrant. As I mentioned in the previous chapter, research on LPF voters has shown that the anti-immigrant message resonated most with them, and they voted for the LPF because of these policies. But voters for the LPF also became more cynical over the course of the 2002 election campaign. Pim did not feed on their cynicism; instead, he induced it.[56]

Abou Jahjah's message is similarly antiestablishment and aimed at Muslims who have taken positions in the political establishment. In his view, they should remain silent or be active in the AEL, but to participate in the established political parties is wrong. He is inspired by Islamic values to be more devoted to political struggle, to end discrimination, racism, and Islamophobia. He is pro-Islam and represents a major shift in Europe to the beginnings of a serious form of ethnic politics that has the color of transnational political Islam and uses the symbolism of Islam in the way that a certain more aggressive—and, even in a few instances, violent—faction of the American civil rights movement used the fist of the Black Panthers to evoke a sense of power.

He links the issue of European citizenship to the aims of a larger global Islam. He explains to the idealists in the second generation that "we" are not like our parents and that we should be active and not passive as they were. Even though he calls for Arabic as a language to be recognized in Europe, his public speeches are almost always in Dutch. He speaks to young audiences who have been raised on the Dutch language. Their parents watch Arabic television, and they watch Dutch television. Abou Jahjah uses Dutch to speak for an Arabic culture. He translates all the Arabic symbols into Dutch, and by talking about citizenship, he Islamizes citizenship. But without the intense publicity given to Abou Jahjah in the Dutch press in early 2003, and earlier in the Flemish media in Belgium, he would not have become such an icon for so many young people.

In spring 2003, in the center of Amsterdam, at the square called Spui, the Atheneum Bookstore's central interior display reflected the transnational nature of the contested issues in this small country and in the enlarging Europe a month after the Iraq War began. On two adjoining tables, there were the covers of some twenty books. On the first, the faces of George W. Bush and Saddam Hussein appeared the largest, yet the corner of the display featured an eye-catching slim green book titled *Resist!* with the smiling Arab face of Dyab Abou Jahjah on the cover. On the second table, the Somalian face of Ayaan Hirsi Ali beamed from her book, *De Zoontjesfabriek*, next to an unauthorized biography of members of the parliamentary LPF (titled *Pimmels*[57]) that flashed the Dutch smile of leader Mat Herben, surrounded by men wearing the same bold Pim-striped ties. Amid these was a newer release, *The Dark Heart of Italy*, that showed a happy Italian Prime Minister Berlusconi standing, with his arms outstretched, above crowds of flag-waving Forza Italia supporters. The books not covered with famous smiling faces showed bolded words in their titles such as *Saddam*, *Islam*, or *America*.[58] The players in the process from Pim to Abou Jahjah included the international, the national, and the local.

As of May 2003, nearly a year after Pim's death and four months after the second national parliamentary elections in twelve months, efforts to form a new government coalition were still unsuccessful. Those who benefited from the chaos that ensued were already smiling on the covers on display at the Atheneum Bookstore.

7

Riding Pim's Wave

Islam, Women, the Sacred, and the Naked

For he who desires to help others by word or deed to enjoy the highest good along with him, will strive above all to win their love, but not to evoke their admiration so that some system of philosophy may be named after him, nor to afford any cause whatsoever for envy.
—Baruch de Spinoza, *The Ethics*

Before Hirsi Ali rose to international prominence via the 2002 election, when she was still a rank-and-file member of the Labour Party, I wrote of her in the magazine *Vrij Nederland*: "You are a pearl of our society and I will protect you as a sister [from the Muslim extremists]." I had written the article supporting her and defending her right to free speech.[1] At that time, she was not yet a member of Parliament, nor was she, as yet, a member of my political party, the VVD, (the Volkspartij voor Vrijheid and Democratie, "the people's party for freedom and democracy"). I met with her only twice, once in 2003, during a dinner discussion at the residence of the French ambassador shortly after she'd been sworn into Parliament. The second time was at a party convention. In general, Hirsi Ali has avoided close association with politicians of all stripes who originally hail from any country in Africa.

About four years later, on the weekend of March 10, 2007, the *Wall Street Journal*, one of the world's most respected newspapers, devoted the entirety of the top half of one of its two opinion pages to a flattering feature profile of Ayaan Hirsi Ali. A classic *WSJ* watercolor-style black-and-white illustration of Hirsi Ali took up nearly a third of the space allotted to the article. It showed an attractive woman with her hair demurely pulled back, pearl earrings dangling above a fur collar, and lips glistening with gloss reflecting perfect white teeth. The article, penned by Joseph Rago and titled "Free Radical," displayed a pullquote—a sentence plucked from the story to highlight its contents—that read "A child of Islam— and one of its fiercest critics too." Rago wrote about how Dutch Minister of Integration and Minorities Rita Verdonk had revoked Hirsi Ali's citizenship because of what Rago called "misstatements made on her asylum application." He then explained that the ensuing controversy resulted in the collapse of the Netherlands' coalition government and that "Ms. Hirsi Ali has since decamped for America—in effect a political refugee from Western Europe—to take up a position with the American Enterprise Institute."

She later left the institute to return to the Netherlands before being stripped of her special security detail, an event that then prompted her to return to the United States. Since 2007, her transatlantic treks have been her only newsworthy activities.

Hirsi Ali is known for her harsh critique of Islam and the Prophet Muhammad, which has been widely reported in the Dutch broadcast and print media in recent years.

While Hirsi Ali is recognized for having left Islam and for challenging the faith from the position of being in it and outside it, she has also had a more controversial effect on the Dutch political structure and the media elite. In successfully promoting her own critique of Islam, Hirsi Ali ended the top-down model of political communication that existed within her party, the VVD, which, in terms of communicating with the public, at least, exemplifies other Dutch parties in the Parliament. She single-handedly dealt a heavy blow to the mechanism of party discipline, in Dutch known as *"fractiediscipline."*

At the same time, Hirsi Ali, by being the subject of so much favorable media coverage in outlets that span the spectrum from left to right, has repositioned Dutch news coverage of politics. If the media in Holland was ever seen as occupying the watchdog role that is common in the literature on Anglo-American political systems, which suggests an impartial but also investigative and often critical role for journalists, that role was largely abandoned in the coverage of Hirsi Ali. And if the Dutch media system is described as a partisan one, Hirsi Ali turned that image on its head because her appeal spread beyond party boundaries. Major media outlets, well-known political commentators, columnists, and widely respected journalists have praised her for her outspoken views on Islam and for her unceasing efforts to push to the forefront of the political debate her concerns about the plight of Muslim women.

The Dutch print media, as well as Dutch public and commercial broadcasters, have openly admired her. *Elsevier*, the popular conservative economic news magazine with a well-educated and affluent readership, named her Nederlander van het Jaar [Netherlander of the Year]. And it was a popular summer television talk show known for its progressive-left leanings that chose to air her short film *Submission* in August 2004, setting off a domino effect that would end in a murder. The controversial film was produced by the flame-throwing filmmaker Theo van Gogh (great-nephew of the famous nineteenth-century artist Vincent van Gogh). Three months later, Van Gogh would pay for the film with his life. On the morning of November 2, 2004, he was gunned down and stabbed as he rode his bicycle to work. The murderer was a Dutch citizen of Moroccan descent, an extremist Muslim named Mohammad Bouyeri. After the murder, incidents against Muslims and Muslim schools and mosques were reported in unprecedented numbers. There followed retaliatory acts against some churches and synagogues. Dutch Prime Minister Balkenende made headline news across the country when he said in a major interview that "we are on the verge of a civil war."

After gunning down Van Gogh, the murderer slit the filmmaker's throat and used the knife to pin a letter on his victim's chest in which he wrote that Hirsi Ali would be next. She immediately went into hiding and remained there for months, under guard by the Dutch military. Amid much speculation in the press about her future in national politics, she returned to her work in Parliament in February 2005 and held a press conference in which she announced: "Dames en Heren, ik ga door" [Ladies and Gentlemen, I will go on]. "Ik ga door" was the headline of stories in the main evening news and on the front pages of many of the major newspapers the next day. She said she would go on to make the next film, and the one after that, *Submission II* and *III*, and to write books and appear in the news. She would continue as a member of Parliament and put forth her agenda on the national stage.

The murder of Van Gogh brought Hirsi Ali's eleven-minute documentary *Submission* even more stature than it would have enjoyed otherwise and Hirsi Ali became a darling of the international news media. On April 3, 2005, the *New York Times Magazine*, widely read among America's educated classes, featured Hirsi Ali in an extensive and sympathetic article accompanied by eye-catching photos under the title "Daughter of Enlightenment."[2] And in April 2005, America's *Time* magazine named her one of the world's most important 100 people of the year. In May 2005, Britain's *Guardian* newspaper, which had published a compelling critique of *Submission* in mid-November 2004, decided to use the pages of its popular weekend magazine to feature Hirsi Ali in a becoming portrait, much like that printed months earlier in the *New York Times*

Magazine. In June 2005, newly appointed French Prime Minister Dominique de Villepin praised her for her courage while introducing her as the guest of honor at a convention of the UMP (Union pour un Mouvement Populaire), the new party gathering of the various right-wing sensitivities—Gaulists, liberals, and some centrists—created by President Chirac in 2002. Hirsi Ali had been invited by the party president and Minister of Interior Nicolas Sarkozy—France's future president—to speak on migration and Islam. French national press coverage of Hirsi Ali ranged from uncritical to admiring, and *Le Figaro* even described her to be as beautiful as Condoleezza Rice, even though Condi speaks French and Hirsi Ali does not—refraining from the usual critical position the French press takes on officials who don't speak *la belle langue*.

Back at home, the Dutch media found news in the news that Hirsi Ali was making abroad. International recognition appears to have been taken by the Dutch media as validation of its unfailing support for Hirsi Ali. Newspapers, magazines, TV, and radio programs spanning the spectrum from left to right, reporters and politicians, even those on the far left, took pride in the foreign press coverage of Hirsi Ali. The Netherlander of the Year had been the only Dutch person in *Time*'s 100 Most Important People in the World in 2004, and she was applauded by those on the left and the right for this accomplishment. The news quickly turned to speculation over whether she would leave Parliament for an international position because "she may be becoming too big for little Holland" as the newspaper *Trouw* wrote.[3] The EU commissioner for the internal market, Nelly Kroes, said that Hirsi Ali is "ready for the world satege [sic]." In short, there was a nationalist sense of pride in Hirsi Ali representing the Netherlands on the world stage. Dutch political and media elite commented on her in a way that is usually reserved for soccer stars. At the *Time* magazine dinner in New York, Dutch reporters filmed her entrance in a magnificent floor-length gown and described her performance there as "brilliant."

The End of Top-Down Political Communication in the Parliamentary Party System

Timing is everything, and Hirsi Ali's opportune moment in Dutch politics was the bloom on the mold of a decaying system.

Following the desperate situation after the May 2002 national election in which 84 of the 150 seats changed hands, the VVD, led by the defeated Hans Dijkstal, changed leaders, reassessed its position, and in reviewing the national scene, recognized Hirsi Ali as someone with a radical view and a tough perspective that could mean more attention and possibly more supporters for the party. Hirsi Ali, too, felt she could benefit from being in a party like the VVD, a party with liberal philosophical roots—economically liberal in the Adam Smith sense of the term—with a reverence for individualism based on a platform of lower taxes and freedom of speech, but actually falling far short of anything Margaret Thatcher did in the 1980s in Britain to roll back the state and diminish union power. On the role of the state in supporting a national health care system, providing college tuition, and subsidizing social housing and child care benefits, and as a full discussion partner with labor unions, the VVD is well to the left of the British Labour Party in its tenure under Tony Blair. A major item in the VVD's platform in the 1998 general election was "more day care centers for children" so that more women would have the freedom to work outside the home. Rejecting religion, the VVD is prochoice, pro–gay marriage and civil unions, and a member of the Liberal International, a worldwide federation for liberalism. The VVD offers liberalism with not only a continental European twist but also a particularly Dutch twist that is to the left of most of the EU on social issues, with the exception of its treatment of migration and Islamic religious schools, which the party was against. Hirsi Ali joined the party in fall 2002 and accepted an invitation to run for office from the new VVD leader, Gerrit Zalm, the former finance minister. It was Zalm who led the VVD into the January 2003 elections and into the CDA-VVD-D66 coalition government headed by Christian Democratic Alliance Prime Minister Jan Peter Balkenende.

As a new MP in January 2003, Hirsi Ali immediately requested that she be the spokesperson for the VVD on the issue of integration and migration. Portfolio topics are distributed by the party leadership on the basis of seniority and expertise, usually with only the most senior MPs getting their first choice. Jan Rijpstra, who had held the integration and migration portfolio since he had entered Parliament in 1994, expected to keep it. The portfolio holder is the first—and often the only—person designated by the party to speak in public on the issue. Thus began a weeks-long public wrestling match between Hirsi Ali and and Rijpstra, as well as with her party leader Jozias van Aartsen, who had stepped in to lead the VVD in Parliament when Zalm decided to return to the position of minister of finance, and with her colleagues in the party fraction who were astonished by her ability to challenge tradition and authority within the party.

The press reported on the arm wrestling as it played out, with unnamed sources spilling the beans on what normally would never reach the public: what is said inside the fraction meetings. She then decided to talk to the media herself, when asked about the situation, and promised to do the best she could to represent the people. Jozias Van Aartsen was quoted in the press as calling her a "Somalian fighter" as a way of good-heartedly admitting defeat, and he has since become her strongest advocate. By June 2, 2003,[4] just three months after she was sworn in as an MP, she had successfully challenged her party on the allocation of portfolios. She was reported to have "twisted the arm" of Van Aartsen.

Just before this big overt clash with her own fraction in Parliament, on April 12, 2003, she coauthored with Geert Wilders, then a fellow VVD MP responsible for the portfolio on foreign affairs, an article widely cited for its radical stance against Muslim immigration and Islam in Holland titled "Liberal Jihad," which was published in *NRC*, one of the elite national newspapers with an ecumenical perspective.

Wilders was a colleague of mine in Parliament, where I was a member from 1994 until 2002, and I considered him a friend. (I once lent him a cell phone for two weeks while he traveled on parliamentary business.) We had several discussions regarding Islam in the Netherlands. As Pim Fortuyn's career was advanced by lashing Muslims, Wilders suggested that our party, the VVD, write our own legislation on the threat of Islam. I offered that we, instead, write about the security issue presented by the isolation and alienation of Muslims in the Netherlands. He was not interested. He insisted, candidly, that the way to garner more voter support would be to focus on Islam itself as the threat.

By early 2004, Wilders, who got his start in national politics working as a staffer for the party, had formally left the VVD fraction to form his own independent group, consisting of only himself, in Parliament. He left because he believed that the VVD was too soft on the issue of Turkey entering the European Union, something he vehemently opposed.

Wilders, who had been an outspoken supporter of Hirsi Ali's critical comments on Islam, had also received death threats. Because of the threats, the two sat together in Parliament in a location that prevents visitors in the audience from having access to them, as a security measure for their protection. For many, this seating arrangement was a symbolic statement about Hirsi Ali's support for Wilders and his stand on Turkish membership in the EU. According to Hirsi Ali, Turkey's inclusion in the EU would mean "the end of Europe." Her party, however, felt differently. It had officially supported the government, a CDA-VVD-D66 coalition, whose prime minister held the rotating presidency of the European Union and therefore chaired the December 2004 Summit in Brussels in which it was decided to open membership negotiations with Turkey.

Traditionally, party members avoid such contradictions with their party's positions by adhering to a certain public statement procedure. An MP is expected to discuss ideas in the closed parliamentary party meetings with the party leader and press officer before talking to the press. This was not something that suited Hirsi Ali. She benefited from the legacy of Pim Fortuyn, the man who used press opportunities to make his own party's veterans look like awkward, frumpy fossils: Pim had forged a path whereby anyone could say anything they pleased regardless of the party agenda they had been elected to represent. The fraction discipline, he'd argued, was a major mechanism for reproducing the status quo and reducing the role of the MPs to little more than cogs in a voting machine. According to former VVD MP Clemens Cornielje, who was in charge of coordinating the relations between the party and the press, Hirsi Ali "went too far as an *alleenganger*," a sort of lone wolf—to the point "that every possible consensus with her own fraction was impossible."[5]

The Repositioning of Dutch Journalism vis-à-vis Dutch Politics

Aside from a tiny minority of columnists, the press embraced Hirsi Ali, regardless of whether what she was saying was accurate or merely inflammatory.[6] One explanation for the behavior of the press is that Islam is a contested issue, a status that ensures stories about it will be read or viewed, and an equally plausible explanation is that reporting on controversial personalities and their comments furthers the careers of the journalists who do so and the editors who assign them to do so. The political motivation of the party and the self-interest of Hirsi Ali, irrespective of genuine motivation to serve or to rescue, fed this media frenzy. But by gaining power through such a cocktail of the cult of personality and vivid comments, the media necessarily takes a less critical tone—it will not report negatively on the personality its readers or viewers so obviously admire, for to do so would be to bite the hand that feeds it. This alters the relationship between the politics and the press. The focus shifted from criticizing the government to criticizing other parts of the public: the Muslims. All this happened against the background of the rise of the far right in Europe and the Dutch media's discovery of the public appeal of political incorrectness—it appeared, at least, as if the whole country were using the press to release a tremendous amount of pent-up resentment.[7] Given these circumstances, the national fascination with the new "black and female Pim Fortuyn," an attractive, pro-Dutch figure who legitimizes Islam-bashing in the name of freedom of speech, was inevitable.[8]

Except for a few critics who have access to the media (and soften their criticism by saying that they don't question her good intentions but don't agree with her style and tone), the reaction of the media to Hirsi Ali has been a warm embrace.[9] The number of articles mentioning her between January 2001 and April 2006 is 4,686, a number that trumps most other politicians.[10]

Hirsi Ali didn't only alter the way her own party communicated internally but also altered the relationship between the press and politicians throughout Dutch political parties. The press usually takes a skeptical stance in dealing with politicians, but few questions were raised regarding how she characterized Muslims. In one of these rare instances, an interviewee[11] said, "She is baiting the Muslims all the time in the name of free speech, it's pathetic. It's unbelievable."

Rather than being seen as a rabble-rousing demagogue, however, Hirsi Ali has been called a hero and a freedom fighter. Hers, they say, is an amazing story, and this continued to be the predominant sentiment in the Netherlands even after *Zemla*, an investigative television show, revealed that much of the story she told the public wasn't true. Not even her name was real. She was born Hirsi Magan. No matter. Why let the facts get in the way of a good Horatio Alger myth? As far as the majority of the Dutch were concerned, she was a poor political-refugee-turned-Dutch-citizen who successfully integrated, became affluently and influentially employed, and even became Netherlander of the Year.

What mars this tale of a woman who overcomes adversity to set her sisters free is the fact that these seeming sisters felt more wounded than helped by her. As journalist and cultural critic Ian Buruma points out in his award-winning 2008 book, *Murder in Amsterdam: The Death of Theo van Gogh and the Limits of Tolerance*, the reaction to Hirsi Ali by what should have been her natural constituency was surprisingly unfriendly. He gives an account of Hirsi Ali's visit to a shelter used primarily by battered Muslim women as broadcast by a news program. The program's producers showed her film *Submission* to four women in the shelter, who then talked with Hirsi Ali.

"Their first reaction was defensive," Buruma writes. "How could Ayaan be so deliberately insulting, they asked. The naked women were a sign of disrespect. Ayaan was only 'using' the film they believed. She was only 'playing with Islam' to further her own ends. Working with a man like Theo van Gogh, they all agreed, was bound to cause offense." Hirsi Ali responded that it was her duty as a Muslim to criticize what was bad about Islam.

"One of the women agreed that women were oppressed, but this was because of culture and education, and had nothing to do with the Koran. Ayaan repeated that she had quoted from the sacred texts. But that's not the point cried the women: 'You're just insulting us. My faith is what strengthened me. That's how I came to realize that my situation at home was wrong.'" The women demanded that Hirsi Ali stop making such films. She said she would never stop, to which one of the women replied "'You must stop! If you can't see that you're hurting me, I can't continue this discussion!' Okay, said Ayaan, with a dismissive wave of her hand, 'so long then.'"

Buruma recalls Muslim feminists like the Turkish columnist Funda Mujde saying of Hirsi Ali's meetings with other Muslim feminists, "I sensed aggression, a hatred almost, for the kind of people she was trying to save."[12]

Her strongest supporters are powerful "white males" writes the Amsterdam anthropologist Annelies Moors.[13] Among them is Jonathan Israel, the brilliant, widely respected Spinoza scholar who has said that Hirsi Ali is the "heiress of Spinoza"—a particularly odd thing to say for someone who knows Spinoza's reasoning extremely well. Throughout Spinoza's works, despite considerable provocation from the religious establishment of his time, the most revered Dutch philosopher (of Portuguese Jewish extraction) does not advocate scuttling any religion. Instead, Spinoza advocates the dominance of reason, a situation that would seem to dissuade one from religious dogma. Unlike Hirsi Ali, Spinoza gives an alternative to religion—not in the Dutch society of his time, but in a new incarnation of that society nurtured on reason. Even more unlike Hirsi Ali, it is not religion that is the focus of Spinoza's extraordinary intellectual labors, but reason itself and how one might use it, rather than dogma, for guidance.

Given Hirsi Ali's antagonistic relationship with the people she claimed to want to help, one passage (No. 25) from part IV of Spinoza's *The Ethics* strikes a note of particular irony:

> For he who desires to help others by word or deed to enjoy the highest good along with him, will strive above all to win their love, but not to evoke their admiration so that some system of philosophy may be named after him, nor to afford any cause whatsoever for envy. Again in ordinary conversation he will beware of talking about the vices of mankind and will take care to speak only sparingly of human weakness, but will dwell on human virtue or power and the means to perfect it, so that men may thus endeavor as far as they can to live in accordance with reason's behest, not from fear or dislike, but motivated only by the emotion of pleasure.[14]

Giving an alternative to religious dogma was the point of Spinoza's endeavors as an intellectual. It is useful to ask: "What was the point of Hirsi Ali's endeavors?" Was it to gain support for herself or only to make the best possible use of the support handed to her? And why would very intelligent people and one of the world's most progressive populations hand her such unbridled support?

It may be that Hirsi Ali has a sociological corollary in the character Song in the Broadway play *M. Butterfly* by H. David Hwang. Just as the Western male protagonist, Gallimard, was spellbound by the stereotypical image of a fragile, shy, submissive Asian mistress—spellbound to the point that he could not perceive the truth that Song was, in fact, a male spy using him for political objectives, so, too, were the Dutch media and intelligentsia caught up in the Grace Jones–like image of a fierce yet beautiful African woman fighting for the freedom of Muslim women. (An illustration in the *New York Times Magazine* depicted a crouching African wildcat and a black girl—one turned the page to look directly in the eyes of Hirsi Ali's full-page headshot, in a disturbing montage of small vulnerable girls leaning on the shoulders of wild cats.) The actual fight fell by the wayside as the media and a chorus of intellectuals fell for the image they had helped to create.

Just as Gallimard needed a submissive to reassure him of his machismo and was willing to accept a lie in to preserve the illusion of his Western manliness, so, too, did Western male intellectuals with certain views on Islam need to be reassured that they were not xenophobic or racist in order to preserve their self-image as open-minded and enlightened, and for that reassurance, they were more than happy to accept the illusion of Hirsi Ali as champion of Muslim feminism. If an intelligent and articulate Muslim woman would make such eviscerating allegations, they reasoned, then surely they were no less tolerant for suggesting similar things. She became their justification for not challenging the denigration of all things Islamic and for saying things that would have been intolerable to reason before her emergence.

The Significance of Hirsi Ali's Activism

Beyond the words and the gestures, an analysis is needed to understand the significance of Hirsi Ali's activism.[15]

What are the cultural, historical, and political references of her activism in the field of Islam? What criteria commanded her choice? Why make a radical choice in public to leave the religion? What is the source of her sweeping condemnation of all religion?

In her last heavily televised appearance in the building of the Dutch Parliament in May 2006, she gave a tribal pedigree for herself:

> I'm Ayaan, the daughter of Hirsi, who is the son of Magan, the son of Isse, the son of Guleid, who was the son of Ali, who was the son of Wai'ays, who was the son of Muhammad of Ali, of Umar, from Osman, the son of Mahmud. I'm from that clan. My ancestor is Darod, who 800 years ago came from Arabia to Somalia and established the big tribe of Darod. I'm a Darod, a Macherten, an Osman

Mahmud, and a Magan. Last week there was some confusion about my name.

What's my name? Now you know my name.[16]

She studied political science at the prestigious University of Leyden. After working for some years in a Labour Party think tank and witnessing the success of a former colleague who left the same organization to become the leader of the Green left, she also departed, becoming a member of the VVD, the conservative free market party. In the wake of the emergence of Pim Fortuyn, she became a strong voice against the soft approach of Labour toward the issues surrounding Muslim immigration.

Just a week before the definitive vote on its final *lijst* [election ballot], VVD placed Hirsi Ali at number 16 on the ballot, an extraordinarily high placement for a newcomer. During the party convention following her nomination, where she was greeted like a celebrity and escorted by the party leader, she became a media icon. Reporters and columnists on the left and right were hanging on her words.

Her own history, as told by herself, came to haunt her and her party, leading to the fall of the cabinet and ending with a clash with her own party member and friend, Rita Verdonk, the minister of integration. Hirsi Ali had "lied" about her name, the arranged marriage, and the location of her escape—all things that had figured in her application for citizenship. Rita Verdonk stripped her of her Dutch citizenship after a heated parliamentary debate on the matter.

She had become a victim of the very policies she supported. The timing couldn't have been better for Verdonk, who was struggling for party leadership: stripping Hirsi Ali of her Dutch nationality was a way to present herself as tough and no-nonsense. The law, she said, applies to Hirsi Ali, too. The long debates in the parliament brought the cabinet Balkenende III to an end. It also ended Hirsi Ali's Dutch political career, but the American Enterprise Institute gave her a job. Again, the international media gave her so much attention that this small country became ashamed of its asocial behavior toward a fervent defender of the Dutch culture. It was not long before Hirsi Ali regained her citizenship and was allowed to keep the name Ali, instead of Magan.

Dutch Public Broadcasting's Role

Submission was launched on August 29, 2004, by the late-night intellectual TV program *Zomergasten* [*Summer Guests*]. The show's format required the host to ask guests to select movie clips that were significant to them, then show the clip, and then discuss it. Selecting one's own movie was highly unusual, but that is what Hirsi Ali did. She selected *Submission*. The program gave her the opportunity to reach a TV audience and explain the motives behind the movie. She explained why she decided to struggle against female genital mutilation and other forms of women's submission.[17] Of the five hundred e-mails she received after the program, only five were hate mail;[18] the rest were complimentary of her film and comments on the show. Some of the five emails included death threats, so she went into hiding for more than two months. She didn't resume her work in Parliament for several months after the murder of the film's producer Theo van Gogh.[19]

On *Zomergasten*, Hirsi Ali said she wanted to show the movie to women in Saudi Arabia and Iran. That's the audience she was targeting, she said: "That's why I made it in English." To clarify, the interviewer then asked her the question: "That's including the Dutch Muslim women?"

Her answer was "Yes. Including the Muslim woman. The veil is a symbol of that. Looking one day through that veil. What happens in there?"

Significantly, she had appeared on *Zomergasten* with novelist and publicist Joost Zwagerman, who would later pen an essay in the magazine *Vrij Nederland* attacking writer Geert Mak, one of the monuments of Dutch literature, because Mak wrote a pamphlet that was critical of Hirsi Ali and her supporters. In the pamphlet, Mak described how the drumbeat against Muslims was becoming a daily ritual that would have severe consequences on the social cohesion of a small country like the Netherlands. He compared Muslim-bashing in the Dutch press with Nazi propaganda against the Jews.

Why did she choose such a film as the vehicle for her platform? Paraphrasing Hirsi Ali, she wanted to place Muslim women in a dilemma; she wanted to push them to think through images and words. She wanted to reach men, too. She made the following plea: "Muslim women, Muslims, and the Muslim world, must be confronted with the holy texts, 'Beat your wife if she doesn't obey you.'" She said further that a majority of Muslim women around the world are beaten by men because of the Koran's contents.

The interviewer asked her if she missed God. She answered: "I don't miss God. God was for me fear and afterlife and an afterlife that is very promising for the women—grapes and dates. That I can buy at the market." At the end of the interview, she spoke about producing a series of *Submission* films. Shortly thereafter, she wrote in a letter responding to her critics, Muslim leaders and some Dutch writers, that Theo van Gogh, the director of *Submission*, was, in her eyes, "one of the soldiers of freedom of expression."[20]

Hirsi Ali's Audience

The people Hirsi Ali wanted to change or have an impact on felt totally alienated by the film, by Theo van Gogh's aggressive persona, by the slavish devotion of the media toward Hirsi Ali, and perhaps even by the very idea that absolutely anything can be said, even if it defaces the sacred. The famous Flemish writer Tom Lanoye wrote an open letter to Hirsi Ali, "War in Times of Peace," published in *Letters to Hirsi Ali*. He refers to the age-old Dutch-Belgian sensitivities by saying: "I'm only a Belgian, maybe I don't see right, but I think you never wanted to adjust to the Netherlands as you found it when you came as a migrant. On the contrary, as you became Dutch you wanted to radically change the Netherlands. . . . Then you protested vocally that the Netherlands has changed to something 'un-Dutch.'" Lanoye explains that not one single fan of Theo van Gogh and the columnist and philosophy professor Paul Cliteur, who has been a powerful voice in criticizing Islam in Europe and establishing the superiority of the Western values, actually believes Hirsi Ali. Lanoye wrote that he expected *Submission* to be misused to spread terrorist sentiments—defensiveness and alienation—to all Muslim families. He suggested that Islam is a kind of fixation for Hirsi Ali. "You came from a country with a civil war," he wrote to her, but by her *inburgering* [the process of becoming a burgher or citizen], according to Lanoye, she didn't lose the urge to make war. He argues that the group she wants to emancipate feels more victimized than respected. For him, that is a problem one might expect from a politician but not from a sincere filmmaker, and he wrote, "Your flaming hate, I don't understand."[21]

Bouchra Zouine, a Moroccan woman writer of second-generation immigrant descent, wrote that the only shared concern she has with Hirsi Ali is women's emancipation. She explains why her solidarity with Hirsi Ali doesn't go further than that: "In an interview in [the magazine] *HP de Tijd*, you called yourself a Somalian warlord who is declaring war against 'the Muslims.' . . .'" Zouine believes that warlords bring misery and unrest wherever they go. A much heard critique about Hirsi Ali is, according to Zouine, that she did nothing to help the women she promised to help before the election, that she did not keep her promise to make them less dependent on their husbands when it comes to their juridical status as aliens. They can be dumped any moment, without rights, in their home countries. Zouine states that women suffer from being "collateral damage" of the Dutch policy on migration and asylum. "You direct your arrows as warlord on the religious-cultural aspects of the different clans," Zouine says of Hirsi Ali, "but you know that the solution is in the struggle against social-economic deficit, poverty and illiteracy and financial dependence. As a Rotterdammer, I invite you for a dialogue and action, no words but deeds, hand in hand as old comrades!"[22]

The Turkish writer Ebru Umar asks Hirsi Ali if *Submission* is a dilemma for her own party. Umar asks if her stance in *Submission* is also an official stance of the party since everybody in the party supports her. He advises the party to finance *Submission II* in order to be more transparent about its position toward Muslims and implies that hating is a way to get a free ride on the taxpayer's tab. "We taxpayers have for many years paid for your safety [in paying for body guards]. What a pity that you let people you hate pay for you. I ask you, are we, the Dutch people [taxpayers], also able to hate?"[23] Naema Tahir, a human rights lawyer and activist, also wrote a letter to Hirsi Ali, explaining to her how difficult it is to write to her about freedom. "What can I tell you? A woman who is free and lives in a free society, about freedom?" Tahir tells her a story about a female activist in an Islamic country: Asma Jahangir in Pakistan. "She was like you and me, a daughter," who at the age of twenty chose to become an attorney in order to defend her father, who was jailed for political reasons. Jahangir succeeded in getting her father out of prison but then went on to use her talents against the domination of women, children, and voiceless people, as well as non-Muslim minorities. Tahir ends with a citation from Salman Rushdie, "In the name of God, open the universe a bit more."[24]

Hasna El Mouradi wrote: "When you want to fight against [domination of women] I encourage you. But when you attack Islam I turn around and leave you. . . . You hoped that *Submission I* could help you [in the emancipation of Muslim women] but you went too far."[25] The movie was understood as being a definitive exposé of how Islam aims for women's submission, a perception that triggered the Muslim hatred toward Hirsi Ali. The dominated women who suffer at home have absolutely nothing to gain from the movie, which gives them no hope. *Submission I* opened a new world for Islamophobes; it was a finger down the non-Muslim throat, forcing Westerners to vomit up everything Islamic as their enlightened minds reacted to the movie's images. Hirsi helped the wrong people. Because *Submission* created a gap between Muslims and non-Muslims, Hasna El Mouradi advised Hirsi Ali, who says she is going to work on *Submission II*, to win the hearts of the people she wants to help by depicting happy, successful Muslim women; otherwise, the movie is not going to achieve its objective.

When Vice Prime Minister Laurens Jan Brinkhorst saw the movie *Submission*, he didn't hide his fear of the consequences: "You know what happens when you light a cigarette in a munitions depot," he said, and continued, "Don't misunderstand me . . . this movie has nothing to do with freedom of expression."

He compared the movie to someone saying *rothoer* [dirty whore] to his neighbor.[26] The minister was criticized for his analogy of the munitions depot and the cigarettes: who, after all, is responsible for changing the public space to a munitions depot? It's not the "smoker," in this case Van Gogh, who used to call himself the "healthy smoker."[27] In this case, he meant Hirsi Ali. Many intellectuals, including Hirsi Ali's supporters, agree with writer, TV pundit, and intellectual Maarten van Rossum's statement that after the death of Theo van Gogh, "The Netherlands is not the Netherlands any more. The Netherlands is heading down the wrong path. The Netherlands has lost its innocence."[28] It would be interesting, says Van Rossum, to compare the debate in the Netherlands with that in Sweden. The media was linking the killing of Van Gogh to the killing of Pim as two political murders that could only happen in the Netherlands, forgetting that in Sweden a prime minister and a minister of foreign affairs were murdered.[29] (Prime Minister Olaf Palme was killed in Stockholm in 1986. No other evidence has come to light since the conviction of Christer Pettersson, a drug addict and dealer. Swedish Minister of Foreign Affairs Ylva Anna Maria Lindh was assassinated on September 11, 2003, by Mijailo Mijailović, born in Sweden to Serbian parents.) Van Rossum explains how the killing of Van Gogh was linked in a "suggestive way" to Muslim migrants in the Netherlands and that the discussion about Muslim migrants is getting "pretty grim," with phrases like "multicultural drama" popping up alongside statements about the failure of integration and, most of all, the way all of this has enhanced the grip of radical imams. It's almost an apocalyptic scenario, says van Rossum: "The discussion about the immigration problem has taken on a threatening tone when stating that a million Muslims live in the Netherlands. The suggestion is made that they form a kind of unity and always show solidarity with their faith-mates which is indigestible for the Dutch society."[30]

Van Rossum states that the Netherlands is not used to big social problems. After 1945, it had a smooth and successful development, and in the 1970s, people even said that the development of Dutch society had reached its limits, but now people argue that the Netherlands is confronting an unsolvable crisis.[31]

Understanding the Semiology of *Submission*: The Sacred and the Naked

Why are the majority of Muslims in the Netherlands outraged by the film *Submission*? What has not been said in all that has been written about *Submission* is that it takes on the sacred—women and the family, particularly women in the family of the Prophet Muhammad—in such a way as to make them, in the Muslim mind, into permissive women, or "whores."[32] The image of the naked Muslim women in the film brings the nudity of the red light district to mind.

The suggestion is intentional. There are three important things to remember about the choices involved in putting the movie together:

> The language of the movie is English, so it's intended to reach out to an international audience and not only Arabic- and-Dutch-speaking Muslims.
>
> The location of the movie, Islamistan, is a nongeographic location that transcends space so that it seems to permeate the public sphere of Europe.
>
> By giving all characters in the movie history- and religion-laden names, Hirsi Ali makes a direct attack on Islam rather than on the submission she associates with Islam. These are the names of the daughters and wives of the Prophet Muhammad: Amina (the mother of the prophet), Aicha (the very young wife of the Prophet, who married him when she was a child), Zainab (also his wife), and Fatima (his daughter).

Using the naked bodies of the women as slates for the calligraphy of sacred Islamic texts from the Koran simultaneously cheapens both the texts, by reducing them to tattoos of a particular culture, and the women, who become merely vehicles for the texts.

Many women and men have criticized the movie on the grounds that it had not really been made to emancipate women who might be battered at home.[33] English, after all, can be understood only by women who are educated and who are probably working. If it had been designed to emancipate the women in the Netherlands who are suffering in those types of circumstances, then the characters would have spoken the languages understood by the target groups: Turkish, Arabic, Berber, or Dutch. Instead, critics suggested that the film was made to get her message out to a hostile and elite audience, in English. Academic critics from the postcolonialist perspective have also suggested that the use of English alienates and orientalizes the subject.

The location of the movie is Islamistan, a fictitious country where the majority of people are Muslims and where the sharia, the Islamic law, is the established rule. But it clearly takes place in Europe, which makes every European law-abiding Muslim citizen a potential danger. The name Islamistan naturalizes the myth as reality.

Submission is full of signs and symbols that alter the very heart of the religious experience. Here is the synopsis and description of the eleven-minute movie: five women, Amina (talking to Allah), Aicha (in a fetal position after being lashed 100 times), Safiya (who experiences sleeping with her husband as rape), Zainab (severely bruised from a beating she received because she doesn't obey her husband), and Fatima (totally veiled, who endures incest). The five women in total submission are having a dialogue with God about the abuse and suffering caused by men through forced marriage, religious penal lashings because of "illegitimate" sexual relations, rape, domestic violence, and incest. Amina, the central personage, is facing a half circle of the other women who pray every day to Allah. But once, after reading the *fatiha*, the opening sura of the Koran, something magical and mysterious happens: they begin a conversation with Allah himself and have a kind of collective orgasm with God against a backdrop of oriental décor, music, and Koran recitation.

Submission of women is legitimized by the holy text. A woman covered in black rolls out a little carpet and starts to pray, and four nude women veiled in transparent négligés sitting in a half circle are covered in a calligraphy of Koranic texts that support the abuse and submission of women. On the back of Aicha, we can read the following sura: "The woman and the man guilty of adultery or fornication flog each other with a hundred stripes; let no compassion move you in their case, in a matter prescribed by God, if ye believe in God and the Last Day; and let a party of the believers witness their punishment" (Koran 21–23). Aicha met a handsome man, "Rahman," in the souk and fell in love with him. They "shared drinks and delicacies" and "made love in every secret meeting." Aicha and Rahman thought naïvely that Allah was on their side "until we were summoned to court and charged with fornication."

Aicha carries on her body her destiny and the inscription of the eternal suffering of Muslim women in her situation. For Hirsi Ali, these women are the prototypes of how most Muslim women experience their miserable lives. The outcry of Aicha is very powerful: "Oh Allah, how can I have faith in you? You who reduce my love to fornication? I lie here flogged, abused and shamed in your name. The verdict that killed my faith in love is in your holy book. Faith in you ... submission to you ... feels like ... is self-betrayal."

Safiya's scene, like the next three, is very short. We can summarize her soliloquy in the following sentences: "My wedding was more my family's celebration than mine. Once in my marital home, my husband approached me. Ever since, I recoil from his touch. I am repulsed by his smell, even if he has just had a bath. Yet, O Allah I obey his command. Sanctioned by your words."

Amina says every time she refuses to have intercourse, her husband quotes the following verse of the Koran: "They ask thee concerning women's courses. Say: they are a hurt and a pollution, so keep away from women in their courses, and do not approach them until they are clean. But when they have purified themselves, ye may approach them in manner, time or place ordained for you by God. For God loves those who turn to him constantly and he loves those who keep themselves pure and clean." Amina stretches the days of her periods in order to not have intercourse with her husband. Her last sentence is "My faith shall weaken."

Zainab, who is battered and bruised, ends her dialogue by saying, "I wonder how much longer I will submit."

The story of Fatima's rape by her uncle Hakim reflects the patriarchal relationships in Muslim families. Nobody in her family believes her story. When her mother tells her father what Fatima has told her, his answer is that nobody can question the honor of his brother. "Twice he unveiled me, ripped my inner garments and raped me," she says. Fatima feels "caged, like an animal waiting for slaughter." Her story ends with the same sentence as Zainab's: "I wonder how much longer I will be able to submit." Welts and bloody bruises are visible on their backs and bodies.

A Proven Formula

Submission certainly wasn't the last time that Westerners would be privy to a thorough trashing of Islam. In fact, it was such a smashing success in terms of the amount of publicity and, in turn, curiosity that it garnered that artists and filmmakers noted its formula. It's a fairly simple, three-part process:

1. TEAR THE KORAN NOT ONLY FROM ITS SPIRITUAL CONTEXT BUT ALSO FROM ITS HISTORICAL CONTEXT. Dragged from the mosque, it takes on a different hue, much as any other sacred text, associated with any religion, takes on an odd tone when thrown out of its community and into the public sphere. Removed from its sacred sphere, it can be made to serve any agenda, just as the Bible and the Talmud have been made to do. As Edward Said explained: ". . . Islamic doctrine can be seen as justifying capitalism, socialism, militancy as well as fatalism, ecumenism as well as exclusivism, we begin the tremendous lag between academic descriptions of Islam (that are inevitably caricatured in the media) and the particular realities to be found within the Islamic world. . . ."[34]

Christopher Rowland, a theologian at Oxford University, notes the same utility in the Bible. In a chapter titled "Radical Christian Writings" in the book *Faith-based Radicalism: Christianity, Islam and Judaism between Constructive Activism and Destructive Fanaticism*, Rowland explains that "Christian radicalism is rooted in the Bible. Both those committed to violence, and those who resorted to peaceful means to bring about change, have appealed to the Bible, albeit using different hermeneutical strategies."[35]

2. DESTROY THE IDEA OF THE MUSLIM INDIVIDUAL AND SUPPLANT IT WITH THE IDEA OF MUSLIMS AS A DANGEROUS GROUP. As Lamont points out in *The Dignity of Working Men: Morality and the Boundaries of Race, Class, and Immigration*, French colonial soldiers, missionaries, and farmers who occupied Algeria for more than a century viewed the North African male as someone who understand only force, "an innate criminal and an instinctive rapist." This image has remained within easy reach of Europeans and is now constantly accessed to support the current violent perception of Muslims.

3. PRESENT THE FOLLOWERS OF ISLAM AS INCOMPATIBLE WITH WESTERN SOCIETY. But be sure to include a loophole, most notably disavowal of the faith, as the only way to social salvation. As Sniderman notes in *The Outsider: Prejudice and Politics in Italy*, the social construction of the concept of the outsider[36] relies on stigmatizing immigrants as incapable of integrating. The concept harks back to Lamont's idea of "mental templates"—boxes in which immigrants are incarcerated and kept from participating in the surrounding society. Lamont presents the double-bind of being both an immigrant and a Muslim; the individual is deemed more acceptable upon shedding at least one of the labels, and being an immigrant, after all, is the more immovable condition.

All three elements of the formula were present, albeit unwittingly, in the cartoon published in 2005 by *Jyllands-Posten*, a newspaper in Denmark. The intent of the cartoonist, Kurt Westergaard, was to challenge the chilling effect of the Islamic threat to freedom of expression, and he did a masterful job of doing exactly that. The Danes, in essence, said: "In our culture, nothing is sacred. Everything is subject to ridicule." It was an entirely acceptable sentiment within the boundaries of a European society. However, in today's world, the Internet erases such boundaries.

For three months following the publication of the cartoons of the Prophet in *Jyllands-Posten*, there were no signs of massive protest on the Arab street. But once the Arab media, led by Al-Jazeera and Al Arabiya, mounted a media frenzy against Denmark, the message became a movement that went beyond the Arab street to enrage the entire Muslim world. Al-Jazeera, in particular, put the cartoons controversy high on the public agenda. The reporting aroused the Arab street and promoted the boycott of Danish products. It then became the most important issue on the agenda for discussion at meetings of the Arab League and the Conference of the Islamic States.[37]

Imam Abu Laban, who lives next door to the Danish historic site commemorating the Christian philosopher Søren Kierkegaard, did not read the sentiment in the same way as his neighbors. The cartoon, which showed an image of Muhammad wearing a turban made to look like a bomb with a lit fuse, struck him as sacrilegious. It defamed the Prophet, he charged, whose image should never be reproduced in any form, according to fundamentalist Muslim doctrine. His outrage spread from Denmark's small Muslim community of some 170,000 souls to more volatile enclaves of Islam. In Iran, in what was presented as an act of artistic parity, the government sponsored a cartoon contest ridiculing the Holocaust. In Syria, angry Muslims burned down the Danish embassy; throughout Europe, Muslims marched in protest on Danish embassies and boycotted Danish products. Dozens of people—most of them Muslims—were killed in Muslim protests against the cartoons in Afghanistan, Pakistan, Libya, and Nigeria; many more were injured.

But that wasn't the end of the controversy. In November 2007, the Danish security and intelligence agency uncovered a plot by militant Islamists to murder Westergaard. Five suspects were arrested in February 2008, and in response to the arrests and the public revelation of the plot, Danish newspapers reprinted the cartoon.

"We are doing this to document what is at stake in this case," editors at the Copenhagen paper *Berlingske Tidende* wrote, "and to unambiguously back and support the freedom of speech that we as a newspaper will always defend."

This time, the reaction was more measured.

"We are so unhappy about the cartoon being reprinted," Imam Mostafa Chendid, head of the Islamic Faith Community, which had led protests in 2006, told the German magazine *Der Spiegel* in February 2008. "[But] no blood was ever shed in Denmark because of this, and no blood will be shed. We are trying to calm people down, but let's see what happens. Let's open a dialogue."

The reprints did not garner as much coverage from Al-Jazeera and other Arab media because Imam Abu Laban, who championed the Islamic protest, had died a year prior to the reprints. There were also newer, more provocative subjects for the Arab media.

Strife in the European and Arab World

In early 2008, two years after the Muhammad cartoons were published, *Fitna*, the much-dreaded and anticipated film produced by Dutch parliamentarian Geert Wilders, was released via the Internet. In *Fitna*, Wilders intersperses footage of imams reading the Koran with scenes from famous terrorist acts, including the September 11 attacks. In the film, veiled Muslim women are shown in stunning contrast against the backdrop of secular Europe. He hijacks the Koran and presents Muslims as dangerous, making it clear that they can never fit in.

Fitna garnered intense media attention, especially in Europe, but theaters refused to show the film, and Wilders ran into difficulty finding a Web host for it. Pakistan banned YouTube, which eventually hosted it, for a day until YouTube dropped it. Dutch cartoonists and pundits ridiculed Wilders. However, the popular vote, his target audience, according to surveys, watched the film and found its premise plausible. The day after the film debuted on the Internet, the Dutch polling organization Peil found that nearly half of those who saw it, 49 percent, believed that it was accurate. As for Wilders, his popularity increased. According to a poll by the agency Maurice de Hond published in *NRC Handelsblad* on April 6, 2008, if Wilders had run for office the day after *Fitna* hit the Internet, his party would have garnered six more seats than it actually had during the previous election.

Jytte Klausen, in an opinion piece published in *Spiegel* on March 28, 2008, noted that Wilders followed the Danish playbook in releasing his film. However, Klausen more clearly illustrated the differences in how the two things were brought to public light than in how they were similar. This is important, because much of the criticism of all things "anti-Muslim" has rested on the canard that this—whatever "this" might be—is just more of the same. *Fitna* was not more of the Danish cartoons, not only in substance, of course, but also in spirit. For example, Klausen herself notes that "the newspaper's idea was to test whether Muslims were attempting to dictate to the general public what could or could not be said about Islam." This was not Wilders's intent. He already knew what the response would be to the release of *Fitna*; he had at least two prior and very vivid models of that response—the response to *Submission* and the response to the Danish cartoons themselves. There was no "test" where *Fitna* was concerned.

Klausen goes on to explain that in the case of the Danish cartoons, two-thirds of the members of the Danish caricaturists' association "didn't want to contribute anything at all, and among those who did, several made fun of the Danes for complaining about Muslims and others took shots at the *Jyllands-Posten* editors. Many didn't bother to portray the Prophet at all." In contrast, *Fitna*'s creation was no such composite. There was no introspective debate within Wilders's party. While the Danes may have questioned and needled the whole oeuvre of cartooning under the folds of Westergaard's bomb-turban, Wilders, at least, seemed sure of what he was doing, and there was no humor to it.

Further, Klausen states: "*Jyllands-Posten* was targeting a group of Danish imams who had complained about the press, and the paper never intended for the cartoons to travel the world." Wilders, for his part, certainly did intend for *Fitna* to travel the world. He sought and received coverage throughout Europe and in the United States prior to the release of *Fitna*. He was a guest on both CNN International and Al Jazeera prior to the release, so there is no question that not only did he intend the world to see his film but also he specifically intended the Muslim world to see his film.

Klausen points to Egypt's government as the culprit in using the cartoons to inflame tensions between Europeans and Muslim immigrants. "Nothing happened until the Egyptian government—upset that Copenhagen had not responded to Cairo's diplomatic requests that it address the problem of growing Islamophobia in Denmark—took action by stirring up the religious authorities and considering a boycott of Danish products that the scandal gained steam," she writes. But *Fitna* came to light only through the efforts of Wilders, not because any outside government needed it to further an agenda.

(The two, however, do have something in common, much to the chagrin of Westergaard: an interest in cartoons depicting bomblike turbans. In March 2008, the Danish branch of Wilders's "Stop the Islamization of Europe" movement was enjoined to cease using Westergaard's cartoon. Westergaard later won his copyright infringement case.)

On July 1, 2008, according to a Reuters report, judicial sources said a Jordanian prosecutor charged Wilders with blasphemy and contempt of Muslims for making an anti-Koran film and ordered him to stand trial in the kingdom.

In Riyadh, the Organization of the Islamic Conference (OIC), a league of fifty-six Muslim nations, said it was "deeply annoyed" after Dutch prosecutors said on Monday they would not take action against Wilders as he was protected by the right to free speech. "The decision . . . encourages and supports the irresponsible defamatory style followed by some media outlets and instigates feelings of hatred, animosity and antipathy towards Muslims," the Saudi Arabia–based OIC said in a statement.

For his part, Wilders told *Washington Times* columnist Diana West on July 5, 2008, "I'm not saying that every Muslim in the Netherlands is a criminal or a terrorist. We know the majority is not. Still," he continued, "there is good reason to stop the immigration, because the more we have an influx of Muslims in the Netherlands, the strength of the (Islamic) culture will grow, and the change of our societies will increase." He sees his efforts as "a fight against an ideology that I believe at the end of the day will kill our freedom, kill our societies and change everything we stand for."

Who made Wilders so famous? According to Otto Scholten and colleagues, "For four months, the attention of the Dutch newspapers was seized by a movie no one had seen. The movie in question was *Fitna*, a political pamphlet by Dutch right-wing politician and Islam critic Geert Wilders. His aim was to visualize the 'threat' of Islam, which, he claims, originates from the 'rancorous' and 'violent' texts within parts of the Koran."

> In the period between the announcement in November 2007 and March 27, 2008, the day Wilders made *Fitna* available on the Internet, the case evolved into a remarkable media event.... The movie would appear on television in January, Wilders stated. Ultimately, this wasn't the case and the politician repeatedly postponed the "launch" of *Fitna*. However, somehow the attention didn't fade away. From then on, Wilders, *Fitna*, and Islam became the subject of a fierce, highly negative debate in Dutch society and—given the democratic function of journalism—in the news media.[38]

In a opinion piece published in the *New York Times* on January 29, 2009, Ian Buruma wrote, "If it were not for his hatred of Islam, Geert Wilders would have remained a provincial Dutch parliamentarian of little note. He is now world-famous, mainly for wanting the Koran to be banned in his country, 'like *Mein Kampf* is banned,' and for making a crude short film that depicted Islam as a terrorist faith—or, as he puts it, 'that sick ideology of Allah and Muhammad.'"

The Mother of Invention

Neither the Danish cartoons nor Wilder's *Fitna* would have been possible without the precedent of *Submission*. The response to it had raised the provocative specter of what could be made of the Western free press among Islamic fundamentalists. As a child won't stop touching the place from which a tooth has fallen, Europe simply couldn't leave the topic of the free press and Islam alone.

But even before there was *Submission*, there was Hirsi Ali, and she was shaped by Dutch socialism. Her political positions are based on two assumptions: first, that religion is irrelevant and has no function anymore in the Dutch society and, second, that the Dutch society where she lives is actually the best model of all modern societies.

Ruud Koopmans and Rens Vliegenthart did a study on the "limited" political influence of Hirsi Ali after she resigned from Parliament and the subsequent fall of the Dutch Cabinet Balkenende III.[39] They suggest that everything she said became a hyped topic of controversy, even her life history. She was the media's most frequently cited member of Parliament.

Koopmans and Vliegenthart say "she was the media darling of the Netherlands" and "her world fame is based on only some political statements." Koopmans and Vliegenthart retrace her big moments during her political trajectory as follows:

In 2002, she made her first political statement, saying that she decided to become an atheist while still working for the Social Democrats' think tank.

She received death threats when she criticized Islam. She emerged fully in the news and made headlines.

She was put high on the election ballot of the Conservative Liberal party VVD shortly before the January 2003 elections.

She became a member of Parliament.

In January 2003, after being elected, she called the Prophet Muhammad a pervert.

At the end of 2003 and the beginning of 2004, she wanted to stop the creation of Islamic schools. She criticized the minister of development and other members of the cabinet for not taking hard stands.

In August 2004, she presented her movie, *Submission*, on public TV.

On November 2, 2004, Theo van Gogh, the director of *Submission*, was murdered, and a long period of publicity followed. (Koopmans and Vliegenthart stress that her security situation was the main issue of public and political debate after the killing of Van Gogh.)

In February 2006, during the Danish Muhammad cartoons controversy, she criticized the Dutch prime minister and defended the cartoonists' right to offend.

The media and political establishment, heeding Hirsi Ali's commentary, played an important role in making people believe that female genital mutilation is an Islamic habit. Moroccan and Turkish women and girls, who constitute the majority of migrants in the Netherlands, were horrified at the ease with which the public accepted Hirsi Ali's version of the facts, because female genital mutilation is not something that occurs in their countries. The comparison between Somalia, her country of origin—and the country of origin for only a very tiny minority of immigrants in the Netherlands—and Turkey or Morocco is a stretch, not only ideologically and geographically but also because the latter two states are not failed states twitching in the death throes of political turmoil and anarchy. The media created ways to use a certain person to frame the issue of Islam and to simultaneously justify that unfair framing. In the same way that it is almost universally taboo to criticize those who have lost family members to a war or political coup or even a random crime, it is equally anathema in most societies to criticize a woman who has suffered genital mutilation and death threats. She was the perfect shield for media that might otherwise have had to answer for lopsided reportage on Islam.

Criticism in the hands of historians, social scientists, theologians, and other scholars is vital in providing a measured analysis of why and how societal change must occur. Criticism by a politician, however, functions as a clarion call to change policy and can function as an alarm that sends the affected parties into panic and defensiveness.

There were critical voices from within Islam, including Irshad Nanji, a Muslim lesbian who took a courageous stance, calling herself "a Muslim Refusnik. That doesn't mean I refuse to be a Muslim. It simply means I refuse to join an army of automatons in the name of Allah."[40] She goes on: "I'm asking questions from which we can no longer hide. Why are all Muslims being held hostage by what's happening between Palestinians and Israelis? What's with the stubborn speech of anti-Semitism in Islam? Who is the real colonizer of Muslims—America or Arabia? Why are we squandering the talents of women, fully half of god's creation? How can we be sure that homosexuals deserve ostracism—or death—when the Koran states that every thing that God made is 'excellent'? Of course the Koran states more than that, but what's our excuse for reading the Koran literally when it's so contradictory and ambiguous?"[41]

Other voices who expressed criticism from a more academic tradition when Islam was not as globally contested as it is now include Fatima Mernissi[42] in Morocco and Nawal Sadawi in Egypt, who have been fighting hegemonic masculine domination within Islam and from Islamic societies. Nawal Sadawi's most popular statement was "we need to free Allah from the text."[43] They fought against the cult of virginity in Islam and for the emancipation of women in patriarchal Islamic societies. Mernissi wanted to liberate Muslim men and women from the idea that women need to be virgins before marriage. Thousands of Muslim women in Europe and in the Islamic world undergo hymen reconstruction before marriage to please the ego of the groom and respect the tradition of virginity. There are many who challenge and critique the Islamic traditions and want to break the dogmatic closure of Islam. Many women and men in the Islamic world are part of a feminist critical tradition within Muslim societies[44] that has been around since the 1950s and 1960s in North Africa, when France withdrew as a colonial power, and even longer in Lebanon, Jordan, Egypt, Syria, India, Malaysia, and Indonesia. The feminist critical tradition, struggling for gender equity and emancipation, can be seen in publications by women authors and intellectuals in these Muslim societies. But this critical tradition has been less visible in the global public sphere and in the West, despite the new media revolution that in theory would have made it more accessible to global audiences. Muslim migration to Europe, Canada, and the United States was primarily responsible for bringing forth in the Western media a critical perspective on Islam from Muslim women.

In his brilliant book *Le Monde des Femmes*,[45] French sociologist Alain Touraine explains how Europe is just now understanding the revolution brought by feminist theorists in the United States and how Europe has to rethink its models of emancipation. He explains that women are the engine of their own transformation in society, and he asks if Muslim women in European societies form a nucleus of resistance to the ambitions of feminism.[46] In his well-documented fieldwork, Touraine said he couldn't find any Muslim women living in France who would adhere to Islam unconditionally against the doctrine of the West. He explains that the majority of Muslim women defend their own emancipation in their own way. No single woman of Islamic descent in France who was part of Touraine's study made reference to a "conflict" or a clash of civilizations, as Samuel Huntington's thesis would suggest. Huntington's thesis would "crash these women situated at the most violent location where the civilizations clash: the feminine condition itself." Touraine argues that the position of Muslim women in Europe occupies a double ambiguity: they are attached to Islam and yet reject any boundaries between them and the upward mobility that modern society requires.

He says, "They don't choose the future against the past, nor the past against the future. Everything for them is present: the love of parents, the refusal of arranged marriage and control of virginity, affection to France and specially its freedom of expression and denunciation of discrimination."[47] So, "these Muslim women are, in effect, entirely mobilized by struggle for emancipation."[48]

The struggle of Muslim women for the citizenship of their children in every single European country and against the laws of divorce in their own Islamic countries of origin is memorable. In many Islamic countries, a divorce by a tribunal in a European country is often not accepted, and even if the woman remarries somebody else in Europe, her marriage gets annulled by the courts in her country of origin. The pressure of thousands of Muslim women is obliging the EU government to reject any laws that don't respect fundamental human rights as stated in the European Charter of Human Rights. This is a significant slap in the face to all countries that use elements of sharia law in personal and family matters.

The critical perspective on Islam that has been visible in the Western media is, in some broad ways, similar to what is found in Muslim societies. To the extent that the focus is on gender equity and emancipation, there are broad similarities. In many Muslim societies, however, gender equity and emancipation require steps that were long ago taken in Western countries. In many Muslim societies, for example, women have demonstrated on the streets in recent years in the struggle for equal rights in marriage, in inheritance, and in divorce laws, and although the situation is still problematic, women have achieved many goals in Morocco, Tunisia, Algeria, Jordan, Egypt, Syria, Lebanon, and India with support from key leaders in these societies. According to Ronald Inglehart and Pippa Norris, it is "eros" rather than "demos" that is the main point of contention between Islamic and Western societies.[49] Publics in Islamic countries, for example, are supportive of democratization, but they remain quite conservative regarding gender equality. The subordinate position of women is more reinforced by traditional religious values and laws in Islamic countries than in advanced democracies. The question that has to be asked is if democracy is not the issue, is it possible that acculturation of Muslims in Europe will bring change to their "backward" attitudes toward women?

Based on their analysis of World Values Survey data from seventy-five countries between 1981 and 2001, Inglehart and Norris conclude:

> There is a persistent gap in support for gender equality and sexual liberation between the West (which proves most liberal), Islamic societies (which prove most traditional), and all other societies (which are in the middle). Moreover, even more importantly . . . the gap has steadily widened across all indicators as the younger generations in Islamic societies remain as traditional as their parents and grandparents. The trends suggest that Islamic societies have not experienced a backlash against liberal Western sexual mores among the younger generations, as some popular accounts assume, but rather that young Muslims remain unchanged despite the transformation of lifestyles and beliefs experienced among their peers living in post-industrial societies. . . . [T]hese predominant beliefs and values matter, not just for cultural attitudes, but also for the actual conditions of men and women's lives.[50]

There are two ways to approach Islam: from within or from outside. All these women have done it from within, and they still do in it from within. Like gay Christians, they want the church to hear them. They are still operating within a dogmatic closure in the absence of a secular public space in their countries of origin. Hirsi Ali offers the critique of someone with a particular background who rejected the faith. To back up this argument, we must read advice from the Pakistani-British writer Irshad Nanji to "stick to Allah"[51] if one wants to reform religion and advance the feminist cause.

The conclusion drawn by Hirsi Ali's movie is that the Koran is the source of submission and the perpetuation of the condition of woman as an abused subaltern to the man. The plea of Ayaan Hirsi Ali is simple: the Koran is a dangerous text. She got support from many columnists, who cited verses of the Koran and adopted new interpretations of them. This rush to interpret the Koran in the public sphere as Hirsi Ali did—not only in the movie *Submission* but also prior to that, by reading the Koran on public TV and explaining its dangers or explaining on camera to pupils in Islamic schools that God doesn't exist—is frequently done. This shows how, in the name of secularism, columnists and politicians are theologizing the public sphere. This theologization of the public sphere undermines the very essence of secular politics, turns politicians and columnists into new interpreters of the Koran, and therefore puts them in a competitive position with imams. No wander imams and religious leaders respond by doing the same: theologizing the political. This leads to a vicious circle instead of a virtuous one. This trend of making statements theologizing the public sphere continues in the Netherlands with Geert Wilders, with whom she wrote "Time for liberal jihad." In February 2007, Wilders said, "If the Muslims want to stay in this country, half of the pages of the Koran have to be thrown away." He added that "Muhammad was a radical."[52] This caused outrage in the Saudi circle in The Hague. The Saudi embassy registered a complaint with the Dutch government. If Hirsi Ali succeeded in mobilizing intellectuals and part of the country's political elite, she alienated the most secular as well as the most religious citizens of Islamic descent.

The legendary Dutch historian and writer Geert Mak wrote the following:

> Hirsi Ali has stressed many times that it's not her intention to suggest that all Muslims beat their wives. Still, that's the message of her short film. The abuse of women in every scene is coupled with the Koran and "the rights" and "duties" of Muslim men that stem from it. Without that, the filmmakers were aware of what they were doing, they used, for example, the same schema that Joseph Goebbels used in 1940 in his movie *Der Ewige Jude*, displaying repulsive images of Judaism and in addition to that, as in this case—citations of the Talmud. With excessive examples of some people, all the followers of religion can be stigmatized.[53]

Or as Spinoza put it in *The Ethics*, part III, proposition 46 (which he had already proven in proposition 16), "If anyone is affected by pleasure or pain by someone of a class or nation different from his own and the pleasure or pain is accompanied by the idea of that person as its cause, under the general category of that class or nation, he will love or hate not only him but all of that same class or nation."[54]

The Helsinki Report[55] states that there is growing tendency in the Western media since September 11 to portray Muslims in a negative way. This tendency is exemplified in the way that the media focus primarily on sensational events. The conclusion of the report, based on a Europe-wide survey, states that coverage contributed to popular perceptions of Muslims as "alien," "dangerous," and an "enemy from within," a "fifth column" often distinguished as "them" in comparison with "us."

Though Hirsi Ali has "decamped," as the *Wall Street Journal* reported, to Washington D.C., the Islam-bashing she set in motion has continued through the parliamentary work of a far right party that sought to hinder two Muslim ministers, a Turkish female MP and a Moroccan alderman from Amsterdam, from becoming the first Muslims to have seats in the Dutch cabinet. The two ministers survived the motion of disapproval from the far right.

European societies have begun to realize that the economic, linguistic, and cultural integration of migrants is not enough and that focusing on the integration of their religion and its emancipation is equally important to create loyalty and a feeling of belonging to the host country. This means that Europeans are beginning to understand that you can't focus on only one aspect of the identity of the migrant; all aspects have to be taken into consideration. The media play a key role in this and would do well, for the sake of accuracy and balance, to consider how the prevalent lens of secularism in the media distorts the condition of faithfulness.

Veteran American journalist Robert D. Kaplan, writing of Carl von Clausewitz, notes: "The suicide bomber is the distilled essence of jihad, the result of an age when electronic media provides an unprecedented platform for exhibitionism. Clausewitz's rules of war do not apply here, for he could not have conceived of the modern media, whose members tend to be avowedly secular as suicide bombers are devout."[56]

Muslims in general, on the other hand, have to know that secularism in public policy guarantees the freedom of religious practice in a non-Islamic society, and it's in their own interest to adopt it, even if some Muslims consider secularism as the extreme side of Christianity. Paraphrasing Bernard Lewis: "Muslims may perhaps have caught a Christian disease and might therefore consider a Christian remedy."[57]

Appendix

TABLE 7.1. Number of Articles about Hirsi Ali in Major Newspapers

| | July 2002–June 2004 | | July–Dec. 2004 | | Jan.–June 2005 | | July 2002–June 2005 | |
	Articles	%	Articles	%	Articles	%	Total	%
Australia	0	0.0%	16	21.9%	3	9.7%	19	15.4%
Canada	2	10.5%	4	5.5%	1	3.2%	7	5.7%
Ireland	0	0.0%	3	4.1%	1	3.2%	4	3.3%
Israel	1	5.3%	1	1.4%	0	0.0%	2	1.6%
Singapore	0	0.0%	0	0.0%	1	3.2%	1	0.8%
UK	11	57.9%	34	46.6%	12	38.7%	57	46.3%
US	5	26.3%	15	20.5%	13	41.9%	33	26.8%
Total	19	100%	73	100%	31	100%	123	100%

Source: LexisNexis, General News, Major Papers. The number of newspapers searched: 50

Conclusion

The Vanishing Muslim Individual

No one can be in doubt that individuals form a society or that each society is a society of individuals.
—Norbert Elias

You can't ask people to give up their religion; that would be absurd. Religions may be illusions, but these are important and profound illusions. And they will modify as they come into contact with other ideas. This is what an effective multiculturalism is: not a superficial exchange of festivals and food, but a robust and committed exchange of ideas—a conflict that is worth enduring, rather than a war.
—Hanif Kureishi

In early February 2009, police in Orchard Park, New York, began investigating the beheading of Aasiya Z. Hassan, age thirty-seven, the wife of a prominent local Muslim who had launched a television channel aimed at dismantling Muslim stereotypes. "Every day on television we are barraged by stories of a 'Muslim extremist, militant, terrorist, or insurgent. But the stories that are missing are the countless stories of Muslim tolerance, progress, diversity, service and excellence that Bridges TV hopes to tell," Muzzammil Hassan said in a press release issued on the eve of the station's launch in 2004.

Yet, Hassan himself, as of this writing, was the lead suspect in his wife's killing, a slaying believed by some to be an "honor killing," an aspect of fundamentalist Islam that has fed into Muslim stereotypes enormously. The couple had a history of domestic abuse. His wife had filed for divorce, and he had been served the papers shortly before the beheading.

Mark Steyn, a writer who has often called into question the violent aspects of fundamentalist Islam, seized on the event in a February 14 column titled "Headless Body in Gutless Press," for the *National Review*, one of America's most respected conservative media outlets. He wrote:

> Just asking, but are beheadings common in western New York? I used to spend a lot of time in that neck of the woods and I don't remember decapitation as a routine form of murder. Yet the killing of Aasiya Hassan seems to have elicited a very muted response.
>
> When poor Mrs. Hassan's husband launched his TV network to counter negative stereotypes of Muslims, he had no difficulty generating column inches, as far afield as The Columbus Dispatch, The Detroit Free Press, The San Jose Mercury News, Variety, NBC News, the Voice of America, and the Canadian Press. The Rochester Democrat & Chronicle put the couple on the front page under the headline "Infant TV Network Unveils the Face of Muslim News."
>
> But, when Muzzammil Hassan kills his wife and "the face of Muslim news" is unveiled rather more literally, detached from her corpse at his TV studios, it's all he can do to make the local press—page 26 of Newsday, plus The Buffalo News, and a very oddly angled piece in the usually gung-ho New York Post, "Buffalo Beheading: Money Woe Spurred Slay."

Did the tepid press coverage signal a deproblematization of Muslims in the American press?

Two days prior to the publication of "Headless Body in Gutless Press," in the same outlet, Steyn had penned a piece rebuking the British government for not allowing Dutch politician Geert Wilders into the country to make a scheduled presentation to Parliament. Wilders had risen to prominence on anti-Muslim sentiment, which he fed with anti-Muslim rhetoric and his very controversial film, *Fitna*. Wilders had been invited by a right-wing MP, but British officials became concerned about keeping the peace in London in the face of Muslim protests.

Within ten days of his ejection from Heathrow and Steyn's rebuke of British officials, Wilders appeared on the widely viewed American television show, *The O'Reilly Factor*. This, for a Dutch public figure, is seen as the height of glory. Europe's television arena is small potatoes by comparison; America is the golden ticket.

The upstate New York beheading that, as Steyn pointed out, didn't make much of an impression on the American press, was never mentioned on *The Factor*. Instead, the notoriously conservative host, Bill O'Reilly, and Wilders focused on the difference in European and American attitudes toward Islam. Wilders was barred from the United Kingdom, but he was allowed into the United States and appeared on one of the country's most popular talk shows. O'Reilly and Wilders commented on America's tradition of free speech, and they tacitly agreed that much of the world's terrorism is driven by Islam. Wilders said of Europeans: "They are afraid and—of the reality. If I tell you that, even today in the European country, Great Britain, in the country that banned me and sent me away after paying me for a few hours, we have already today, when it comes to family law, Sharia laws functioning."

The individualistic lens of the beheading of a very real, individual Muslim woman had seemingly been passed over in the press in favor of Wilders's broad lens, a macroview of an entire population. To be sure, there are ghastly examples of Muslim criminality, and the beheading in New York offered a prime example, but they are exceptions to the rule. Wilders's view, instead of seeking to hold the exceptions up to the light, seeks to reduce all Muslims to merely parts of a larger, sinister whole. His approach—which is also the approach of Ayaan Hirsi Ali—is a critical cog in the machine of the trifecta of coercion, which assembles dangerous fanatics from the shards of the individuals it shatters, individuals who would otherwise be capable of making courageous decisions for the sake of a better life in an enlightened society—as did Aasiya Hassan, a Muslim woman who filed for divorce from an abusive husband.

The Importance of Empowering Moderates

One day in January 2008, I took refuge in the home of Imam Mansour Ben Ouled from the cold wind that whipped the town of Watergrafsmeer. Over hot mint tea, he told me of his grave concerns regarding the unrest that he felt would be unleashed with the much-heralded release of the film *Fitna*. That, coupled with the pending enlargement of the EU, which he said would allow the Dutch to give jobs currently occupied by Muslims to Polish migrants, made him feel particularly pessimistic about the future of his community.

Mansour could not be described as a fundamentalist by any stretch of the imagination. In early 2002, he had accompanied me to a Gay Pride rally, where he spoke against homophobia in the Muslim community. Yet, these more recent developments had prompted concerns that are very much like those of more conservative imams. He sees the danger of intentionally provocative projects like *Fitna*. He knows the social impact of economic shifts. But imams like Mansour are rarely portrayed in the media. Because they are moderate, they lack the polarizing qualities sought by the media, which rely on conflict to generate interest in news. This polarization ensures conflict and thus greater interest (and market) for the news. The predictable result is that much of the real story is lost.

Mansour and imams like him have played a key role in my studies and in the formation of this book.

My intention was to explore the historical, geographical, political, cultural, and sociological context very often missing from reports on ethnic tensions in Europe—missing from reports by the media as well as from scholarly treatises in academia—because of the increasing visibility of Islam in the public sphere in European societies. I sought to do this by using a model I call the trifecta of coercion, a model that illustrates how Muslim communities in Europe are shaped by, and respond to, coercion from below, from within, and from above.

Coercion from below is a product of universal pressures common to all of humanity—the pressure to make a living, to succeed in one's profession, to have a place in one's community. I noted the peculiar traits characteristic of coercion from below among a particular group—the Dutch Muslim imams of the 1990s—and how their particular methods of dealing with coercion would have an impact on their congregations and communities for many years to come. The second part of the trifecta is coercion from within, which refers to the pressure within the Muslim European individual, as well as within his or her community. This coercive pressure is produced by the conflict of messages put forth by the larger society and by the Muslim religious establishment. Coercion from above, the third part of the trifecta, is exerted by official Islam through embassies and government programs, as well as by radical unofficial Islam through a message of Muslim transnationalism and anti-Western activism. In the middle of all this tension is an individual who, like all human beings, is for the most part just trying to make a life for himself or herself. The trifecta of coercion acts as a machine wherein all this combined pressure pulverizes the individual who happens to be Muslim and spits out a reconstituted entity—someone whose sense of self has been replaced with a sense of being only a part of a larger, alienated, monolithic entity, in this case the "Muslim threat." It is entirely possible to dismantle the trifecta of coercion simply by removing or substantially alleviating any one of the three sources of coercion, for example, by reducing the conflict between the religious message and the message of the larger society or by diminishing the pressure exerted by radical unofficial Islam. Any lessening of the coercions within the trifecta is like snipping a connecting wire in a bomb. Alleviate the pressure, and we can dismantle this apparatus that turns individuals who happen to be Muslim into people who see themselves—and who are primarily seen as—merely parts of a larger alienated whole.

My reflections have been based on a narrative thread of details that, taken together, reveal three major developments since the 1960s that have enabled the trifecta of coercion: (1) the growing visibility of what happens inside the mosque or the movement from inside to outside the mosque and the emergence of more "pertinent" or consistent claims of Muslims in the public sphere; (2) the crisis of models of integration and incorporation in Europe, complicated by Europe's own integration within an enlarged EU configuration (the fear of new EU migrants from Poland coincided with national debates about the fear of Turkey joining the EU);[1] and (3) the globalization of Europe's Muslim problem. All three processes have one overarching aspect in common: the media as facilitator.

The religious expressions of Muslim guest workers in Europe in the 1960s, 1970s, and 1980s in the public sphere can be characterized by a kind of agoraphobia.[2] They were little seen and less heard. The 1990s can be described as the decade that prompted them to explore the European society beyond the door of the mosque and to enter the public space to gain visibility. This process of intensification of religious expression in the public sphere created new challenges for Europe's secular societies, a process described by many observers as the return or revival of religion in the public sphere.[3] But this particular revival is unprecedented because the religion in question is Islam, which missed the Enlightenment experience that Christianity and Judaism had shared in Europe in the seventeenth century. Consequently, Islam is seen as incompatible with European societies.

Discussions of the Enlightenment are not merely tangential to the topic of Muslim individuals in European societies.

What Europeans call the Enlightenment was a series of events that occurred over more than a century in different ways in different countries. It was sparked to a great extent by the question of faith: who holds authority for faith? The individual? Or the church? Or the state? The Thirty Years' War in Western Europe, Galileo's feud with the pope, and the rise of Protestantism all pointed more and more to the widening schism between church and state. Descartes' exploration of the separation of body and soul suggested to some that there must be a similar separation reflected in the relationship of the temporal and spiritual worlds: the power that ruled one did not necessarily rule the other. Into this widening crack between church and state shone the light of the intellect, as Europe's burgeoning middle class sought to find their way independently of those who claimed to rule by divine right. The burghers and bourgeoisie increasingly rejected the notion that God chose who should rule and, in their attempts to rule themselves, developed a voracious appetite for reason.

If the Arabic world, at that time dominated by the Ottoman Empire, did not participate, it was in large part because it didn't have to. Europe seemed to be an exercise in fragility—with states constantly breaking apart and realigning between Catholicism and Protestantism. The Ottoman Empire, on the other hand, was expanding from the fifteenth century through the seventeenth, and as it expanded to three continents and converted its new citizens, the question was not one of faith, but one of political power. By the mid-seventeenth century, as the Europeans found new trade routes to the East, thereby increasingly cutting the Arab middlemen out of their commerce, the Arab world had begun to shrink. Thus, the need to bolster the Muslim royal houses' claim to shrinking tax coffers became critical. This necessitated laying claim to the same divine right that Europe's growing middle class was increasingly rejecting.

This was only one part of the two worlds' diverging paths. As Ann Thompson explains in *Barbary and Enlightenment: European Attitudes toward the Maghreb in the 18th Century*, when the Enlightenment developed in Europe, attitudes toward the Islamic world were already well established. Thompson points to the European translations of the Koran that occurred at this time as evidence of how the Enlightenment opened the European mind to the Arabic world, but notes that "at the same time there persisted an image of Moslems as fanatics."[4]

Centuries later, this vision has persisted. Today, much of the discussion of European and Arab relations focuses on guest workers and their children, the multiplication of mosques, Islamic schools, and communitarian claims through the end of the 1990s and into the new millennium.[5] It's still about "Moslems as fanatics."

After 9/11, all Muslim migrants, regardless of their varying ethnic origins and national traditions, became fodder for the trifecta of coercion. They were reduced to only a single, one-dimensional aspect of their identities: their Muslimness. Even second- and third-generation descendants of Muslim guest workers in Europe continue to be seen as foreign or as being from their parents' homeland or are simply cast, monolithically, as Muslims. Being a European-born citizen with a European passport does not guarantee that one is seen as part of a European nation. Citizenship is still defined in legalistic terms without being anchored in the experience of civic and national cultures. A number of factors have played a role in magnifying the religious aspect, aside from the multiplication of mosques and Islamic schools, among them the growing numbers of Muslims in urban areas (distinctive clothing has made them especially visible, as has the media's overexposure of problematic Muslim youngsters), the failure of secular organizations of migrants to be successful spokespeople for these changing communities, and the resulting rise of religious leaders as an efficient alternative. Religious leaders and imams have formulated an identity based on their sense of pride in being Muslim as a defense against feelings of discrimination and exclusion. To do this, they have intensified their religious expression in the public sphere.

Along with the rise of European Islamic religious leadership, the immediate question that arises is whether this leadership is also part of the civil society. Specifically, we know that, at least for a couple of centuries now, Europe's secular leadership has dominated its religious leadership. In the case of migrant organizations, this model has been reversed: the secular leadership has lost out to the religious leadership. In the Netherlands and France, rather ironically, the state created new political structures to contain the different leaders of the Muslim organizations or mosques: councils that represent Muslim communities. In Holland, council members are appointed, and in France, they are elected according to a difficult formula involving a measurement in square meters of area represented. Polarization was the result in both countries. Nobody feels represented by these councils. In France, newspapers and secular Muslims claimed that the national council was hijacked by fundamentalists. The goal of the secular states that created these councils is to channel all the demands and needs of all Muslims through one voice that supposedly represents and speaks on behalf of different groups of Muslims. This paradoxical policy of highly secular countries like France poses fundamental questions regarding the old separation between church and state. Not only France but also countries like Belgium and Holland upended their secular state in an attempt to structure Islamic representation. The councils' inefficacy may be explained in part by the sheer number of Muslims on European soil.

On one hand, the governments certainly need a way to hear from these individuals, but they have set up a channel that makes Muslims less a group of individuals and more a voting bloc. In a sense, Europe has objectified Islam. Peter Mandaville argues for "a non-essentialist definition of Islam, focusing more on Muslim subjectivity and less on some objectified entity called Islam."[6]

Europeans need to interact with their Muslim fellow citizens, but they are afraid of how much power interaction may give to the Muslims. The Peruvian writer Mario Vargas Llosa used the term *paranoid* to describe the attitude of some European countries: on one hand, they need migration; on the other hand, they are terrified of it.[7] The organization of the Muslim councils was a sort of unhappy compromise.

By implementing a fully formed trifecta of coercion through such measures, secular and religious Muslims are lumped together. This has aided the media and politicians in the construction of an imagined Umma that incorporates the religious and the secular without distinction. It is a given that European secularism has many expressions in different countries, and the levels of state neutrality are not always consistent. European societies are in an almost daily cultural war, in no small part because school policies and the influence of parents vary within the EU. In France, it's the state that determines what constitutes a religious symbol, like the headscarf. In the Netherlands, parents are allowed to choose the kind of school they want their children to attend and the kind of dress they want them to wear, based on their religious beliefs. The school rules then define what's acceptable and what's not. Even if the Netherlands doesn't have the kind of problems with the scarf that the French have, Dutch politicians have succeeded in banning burkas, a measure that some observers said amounted to shooting an ant with a cannon. The mixing of religion and politics by the secular states of Europe has compromised the state's neutrality. This is most evident in the organization of the official Muslim councils discussed previously. This loss of neutrality of the state raises the problem of the so-called cultural exception for both the French and the Dutch, which feature quite different exceptions. The French exception is characterized in the concept of *laïcité*, which was seen as an ideal and final solution to the problem of spiritual power, as August Comte used to say,[8] but now it is challenged as being too exclusive, as shutting out religious citizens. The Dutch exception resides in being a socially progressive country that finds social solutions to the problems associated with drugs, euthanasia, and prostitution and did, in fact, give voting rights to migrants at the municipal level—yet still cannot overcome social exclusiveness to function as Europe's "big emancipation machine."

Crisis of the European Models of Integration

The two historically powerful models of integration of foreigners in Europe are provided by the countries of Descartes and Spinoza: France and the Netherlands. These two models, a communitarian-based one in the Netherlands and an intensely individualistic secular-based one in France, started to erode for three reasons: (1) the rise of populism and far right politics, (2) the intensification of the drumbeat of the media, and (3) the increased coercion from within. This coercion from within—part of the trifecta of coercion—was possible only in the free haven Europe provided for transnational fundamentalist Islamic groups. This coercion from within, the conflict that Muslim individuals feel when the messages sent by their religious establishment conflict with the messages sent by the larger society, was bolstered by the introduction of media programming

CONCLUSION: THE VANISHING MUSLIM INDIVIDUAL   225

from non-Western countries in the late 1990s, thanks to satellite dishes and to the growing Islamization in cyberspace.

The rise of the far right is surprisingly parallel in the two countries. In France, Jean Marie Le Pen made it to the second round of the presidential elections against President Jacques Chirac on April 21, 2002, and in Holland, in May of that year, Pim Fortuyn, who was shot dead a week before the elections, almost became prime minister as his upstart party ascended to being the second most powerful in the country. The pressure of the far right in Europe made political parties move to the center until it became an "extreme center." One of the consequences of this move to the center is the erosion of socially established rights like social, cultural, and health care entitlements. The return of the question of the veil in the French public arena is a sign of the victory of the far right,[9] which has also gained ground in Italy, Germany, Denmark, and Sweden. Pierre Bourdieu suggests that when we ask the question, "Should the Islamic veil be accepted at school?" that another question then must be raised: "Should the migrants from North Africa be accepted in France?"[10] Ironically, since 1989, the number of pupils wearing the scarf or the veil at school has remained stable, a total of about two thousand students in all French schools combined, even as the number of incidents or conflicts during the polemics leading to the ban of the veil in 2003 were declining.[11] This shows there was no urgent and pressing problem that needed to be solved immediately. The affair of the veil in France is often compared in its impact to the Dreyfus affair.

In both countries, the media helped in framing the issues the way politicians defined them until the politicians themselves had been backed into a corner by their statements in the press. One of the consequences of the media's negative framing of Islam and migrants is that diversity and multiculturalism were rejected by politicians in the EU and by many Europeans. The rejection of the EU constitution can be seen also as a nationalist withdrawal. The rejection of the EU led to more repressive legislation than had been seen in the past.

In the case of the veil, for example, Bourdieu says the media "contribute to staging fear, generating the irrationality that a number of French feel towards this reality. They [media] do nothing but delay the moment when the need to give the migrants, who are very often de-islamized and de-culturalized (most are unaware of everything, even their language and culture of origin), the possibility of fully affirming their dignity as mankind and citizen is mobilized."[12]

The same thing happened with the movie *Submission*, which was overwhelmingly covered in the European media and triggered controversies in the European Parliament and the blogosphere. This had happened previously, of course, Bourdieu noted "the grip of the media looking for the sensational, the empire of survey that helped transform the false problems into objects of 'democratic' consultation."[13]

Stigmatizations of, and discrimination against, "Arab-Muslims" in France work to the advantage of the far right and to the development of political Islam ideologies.[14] Political Islam found fertile ground in some of the disoriented second- and third-generation Europeans of migrant origin. The media and politicians were not interested in the question asked by the Algerian-French sociologist Abdelmalek Sayad:[15] Why do people want to resemble or differ from mainstream citizens? Instead of finding or reporting about the process of socialization, people talk about enemies from within, sleeper cells, and terrorist networks and say that the suburbs of big cities in Europe are becoming like Kandahar in the time of the Taliban. It is legitimate to talk about all these things happening because it's the security of the state and society that is at stake, but equating political Islam and law-abiding Muslim citizens in Europe is counterproductive. Extreme stigmatization leads to disempowerment of individuals who can't get free from the stigma.

Peter O'Brien, a professor of political science at Trinity University in San Antonio, Texas, has said that the media concentrate on fundamentalist fanatics among Europe's Muslims and do not discuss more reasoned Muslim critics. The European establishment, he says, including the media, is based on a liberalism that assumes "that all persons properly exposed to liberalism will in due time embrace it. Opponents are expected to convert to the universality of liberalism. The failure of Muslims to convert leads to a loss of faith in liberalism and adoption of illiberalism."[16]

Europe's Muslim Problem Globalized: The Secular Malaise

Many of Europe's citizens are now discovering that they and their children will never be considered real Europeans, even if they were born on European soil, hold a European passport, and speak the language as well as natives. To paraphrase one comment written in Dutch on a Web site used by many young people with Maghrebian heritage in Holland (http://www.magreb.nl): "They don't see you as a citizen or a neighbor, they see you only as a Muslim, because once you are born Muslim, you always remain Muslim." David Rieff put it this way: "A great many of Europe's Muslims don't fit in, and won't."[17]

When the media decontextualizes what's happening in a society and recontextualizes it for a broader global audience, the historical context and its genesis disappear. To decontextualize and recontextualize is to make an inventory of facts without revealing how those facts came to be. The background is erased to construct an almost transcendental meaning that equals the "truth" systems of religions. This creation of independent facts as objects of meaning leads to a loss of meaning from the original context. That is how the creation of myths begins. If the media write the first draft of history, then it is time to study the limits of simplicity in the daily work of the media. "Keep it simple" may work for a while, but when individuals are seen only as part of a group and judged as a group regardless of the individuals' desires to be part of the larger society, it becomes a civic duty for journalists to reflect on the consequences of their work.

The Dutch case is very relevant in this respect. Because of the difficulty foreign journalists have in understanding the Dutch language, what is reported is a superficial knowledge of facts and the duplication of biased information and analyses about Muslims in that country. A more general example is the argument of Karen Armstrong, that the label of "Catholic terror" was never used to talk about the IRA in Ireland:

> Like the Bible, the Qur'an has its share of aggressive texts, but like all the great religions, its main thrust is towards kindliness and compassion. Islamic law outlaws war against any country in which Muslims are allowed to practice their religion freely, and forbids the use of fire, the destruction of buildings and the killing of innocent civilians in a military campaign. So although Muslims, like Christians or Jews, have all too often failed to live up to their ideals, it is not because of the religion per se. We rarely, if ever, called the IRA bombings "Catholic" terrorism because we knew enough to realise that this was not essentially a religious campaign.[18]

Or as Naftali Brawer concludes: "The story of Elijah teaches us that God is not found in the drama of zealotry, in the earthquakes and fires of religious radicalism, but rather in the still small voice imbued with sensitivity and compassion. Our challenge as religious leaders is to reclaim that still small voice by reducing the shrill and angry sounds of hatred all around us. God's voice is speaking to us even now, desperately urging us to respect each other. All that is required of us is the humility to listen."[19]

Muslims have scrutinized their own religion for such zealotry, but their examinations have been wrested from their hands and used by the media to inflate the perception of the otherness of Islam.

An Intellectual Impasse

In his efforts to go beyond his book *Critique of Islamic Reason*, the liberal philosopher of Islamic thought Mohammed Arkoun[20] draws a parallel between media intellectuals in France, Italy, and the Netherlands and Muslim scholars, who for centuries worked on the edifice of mythical history and mythical ideology of Islam. In other words, the media intellectuals created another "intellectual impasse," a kind of space of unthought and the unthinkable, which is beyond north and south and west and east, which is Islam no longer entrenched in the Orient, as Edward Said wrote, but, more harmful and lethal, an imagined Islam that is essentially and forever opposed to the West.[21] This binary opposition is becoming a moral template used by journalists, public intellectuals, and scholars and therefore the public at large. Arkoun reiterates: "So long as this fictional dualism remains in place, the intellectual impasse, which is thereby engendered, is destined to remain irresolvable."[22] He makes a plea for a double liberation of Islam and the West, which are subject to mythical and hidden appropriations, mainly about Islam as a religion and a culture. In his early work, the famous liberal philosopher of Islamic thought insisted on questioning the cognitive status of what has been taken uncritically and for granted by Muslim theologians, exegetes, historians, and jurists as revelation. This nonreflexive tradition has been perpetuated from the classical age of Islam up to now. And it has "resorted to the strategy of sanctifying classical, textual definitions of Islam, turning these effectively into the ultimate bedrock of legitimacy and authority for its own axioms and proclamations."[23] Arkoun's radical critique was necessary to formulate a solution for the impasse created by the Islamic mythical construct itself. Arkoun's antireformist perspective is calculated to counter the overidealization and mythologization of Islamic texts.

The same approach, he writes, can be applied to the concept of the "West's understanding of itself. This understanding is the other, if hidden, side of the West's current discourse on Islam" in the "recent flood of publications on Islam."[24] Arkoun questions why there is only one single dominant interpretation after the tragic events in New York, Casablanca, Egypt, Indonesia, Madrid, and London, which has to do with "collective psyche, which has not yet been emancipated from a mytho-historical mode. This mentality is further encumbered by mytho-ideological procedures of thought and perception designed to exploit this way of thinking so as to produce spurious impressions of legitimacy."[25]

Holding a mirror to only the European media would be an egregious error. The media market is becoming extremely competitive and so globalized that it is important to talk about networks. I explained in a recent study that although much of the extant literature, for example, on Al-Jazeera describes it as the "CNN of the Arab world," it is more like an Islamic version of CBN (Christian Broadcasting Network) than like the secular or nonreligious Cable Network News because of the time it devotes to the views of Islamic religious leaders and the ways in which it promotes Islamic practices. Al-Jazeera is not a "liberal" or "neutral" channel; it is a religious and news channel that allows other programs that are liberal or neutral to be shown occasionally. If the news broadcast on Al-Jazeera is pluralist, the religious message that it disseminates almost daily is monodenominational. Al-Jazeera, in fact, is using the issue of the veil in France to influence viewers in France and Europe and to build a global Muslim identity, mobilize a shared public opinion, and construct an imagined transnational Muslim community—a guaranteed market for itself. Not only Al Jazeera but also many other media outlets from the Islamic world are focusing on Europe. For example, the Danish cartoon question exploded from a tiny incident in 2005 in a country of 5 million inhabitants to become a worldwide phenomenon endangering the social cohesion of many societies, thanks almost entirely to Al Jazeera.

As long as the European media and politicians continue the drumbeat against part of their citizenry, stressing Muslimness as the boundary separating modernity from backwardness and reiterating that Islam and modernity or Europeanness are incompatible forever, the forces of transnational, extremist Islam will persist as a seductive alternative for young Muslims who feel alienated. Islamic televangelism via satellite dishes and cyberspace, in addition to distribution channels on the ground of recordings, CDs, and DVDs, will continue to flourish. Islamic iPods are already available to download sermons and songs. That's why the European media have to be more nuanced in singling out the problem with religious expression and stop generalizing. Such generalization leads to the orthodoxization of Islam in Europe, that is, playing the game of transnational Islam. Orthodoxization is a discourse that doesn't distinguish between religion and politics, simulating the dominant discourse in many Islamic countries where the political structure uses the religious structure to run the unit as a whole. Orthodoxization can lead some isolated communities to call for their own sharia institutions, as is the case for Muslim communities in the United Kingdom and Canada.

As Arkoun pointed out to me during a conversation in 2005, both the European media and the transnational Islamic media via satellite and the Internet help create a phantasmagorical reality regarding what is called Islamic law and the doctrinal content of this law. These phantasmagorical realities can create catastrophes and disorder as a result, because the ideological pressure will produce utopian claims that can only be made by people who identify themselves with these phantasmagorical realities. An inclusive citizenship that stresses the primacy of the individual is one way to solve the growing artificial schism between *autochtones* and *allochtones*—those who do not adapt and those who do. That inclusive feeling has the power to convince Muslim citizens of

Europe to reject the polarizing discourse of televangelists because their own experience would be proof of a reality the televangelists do not present.

Europe has to transgress the religious, philosophical, cultural, and political boundaries that are now paradoxically trapping Europe because of political reasons that have to do with exclusion more than inclusion. In my view, the secular question in Europe is something beyond the veil question in France, Hirsi Ali and Van Gogh or Pim Fortuyn in the Netherlands, or the Danish cartoons question. Dramatization means framing the existing social problems in terms of a conflict with citizens from Islamic descent (non-Europeans, Muslims, and potential "enemies from within"). It also means reducing Islam to fundamentalism and fundamentalism to Islam. If Europe wants to be a union of civilization in the sense of De Tocqueville and Michelet, it has to reconnect with its philosophy of liberty and freedom and use its grand humanism to tackle and solve the problems through education, art, and economic measures, not by merely resorting to verbal and physical violence. Europe can save the democratic state through a new civilizing process that gives political and scientific means for the emergence of a modern European Islam that fits harmoniously with the grand secular design of Europe while maintaining its faith. A secular Islam is possible, not only in Turkey but also elsewhere. According to Arkoun, reading Averroës is a good start; Averroës gave primacy to reason. Arkoun stresses that a study of the humanism realized within the Islamic cities of the fourth and fifth centuries of the Islamic calendar serves as a reliable model of this. Provocative questions, including questions about the creation of the Koran, were asked in that highly reflexive and philosophical period. Everything was subject to the *disputatio*, or public discussions between peers. That period is a formidable base from which to approach the question of the separation between state and religion. But since that enlightened century of humanism, the door of *Ijtihad* [intellectual endeavor] has been closed repeatedly by successive governments until now. It is important to teach history at schools from a comparative perspective so that students, both Muslim and non-Muslim, understand the anxiety now associated with being a Muslim in Europe and also elsewhere.

Europe's Muslim "problem" is the result of the trifecta of coercion, the construction of which has been greatly aided by the media. This doesn't mean that there are no problems with Muslims in Europe but that Muslims as a group don't exist. The democratic state deals with individuals, and a Muslim group is constructed only for the purpose of assigning guilt to that particular group. It is evident that some people want to adhere to a certain cultural identity, but that doesn't mean that all the people who share that denominator are homogeneous.

The voices usually absent from this discussion are those of the new generation of European citizens, descendants of Muslim guest workers, who will

CONCLUSION: THE VANISHING MUSLIM INDIVIDUAL 231

serve as intellectual and cultural mediators between European cultures and the cultures within the immigrant communities. They will help bring into view a new horizon of citizenship that is inclusive and European.

By focusing on the establishment process of guest workers from Islamic countries, we shed more light on the roots of racial, ethnic, religious, and class dynamics. We see the framing of migrants (still called migrants, even if they have lived in Europe more than forty years and their children have been born there) as permanent outsiders and permanent representatives of Islam. "Muslim" is an imposed nominal that leads to the collapse of the very concept of the individual. Thanks to the efficiency of the trifecta of coercion, the Muslim individual doesn't exist in the new world order of Europe. Muslimness is a broad brush stroke that erases individual responsibility and replaces it with a collective self.

A study of the failures of Islam to live up to the challenges of modernity is already present in the work of Muslim classical thinkers, and these works can counter the wild imaginings and false conflicts that have been established between Europe and the Islamic shore of the Mediterranean world. Norbert Elias states the importance of the long-term historical processes to understand the present is why history can help solve some mysteries such as "the backwardness" of Islam, as many politicians and media in Europe want to call it. Or as Bernard Lewis eloquently frames the conundrum, "What went wrong?" but without giving hope to the possibility of an enlightened practice of Islam.

The name of this book, *In the House of War: Dutch Islam Observed*, holds at least a small part of the answer. "In the house of war" is a literal translation of *Dar al Harb*, an Arabic phrase colloquially used as "the land of the unbelievers." That was indeed the feeling among many of the imams I studied in the 1990s, and that was the way that Muslim attitudes were perceived by many non-Muslims after September 11, 2001. It is also fair to say that there were many rank-and-file Muslims themselves who felt this way.

However, as I write this, we are indeed at the beginning of a new century, a hundred years of changes lie ahead of us, and there is absolutely no reason why those changes cannot be for the good not only of Muslims and the Netherlands but also the world. It is possible to dismantle the trifecta of coercion, and if we're going to save the individuality that our rapidly developing world will so desperately need to escape fascism, violence, and inequality, we have to alleviate the pressures that perfect that trifecta.

Only an *inclusive* "we" can lead to higher levels of integration without destroying the individual. Elias says: "As a human being an individual has rights that even the state cannot deny him or her."[26]

Notes

INTRODUCTION

1. Geert Mak, *Gedoemd tot Kwetsbaarheid* [Damned to Vulnerability] (Amsterdam: Atlas, 2005).
2. Rachid Mimouni, *De la barbarie en général et de l'intégrisme en particulier* (Paris: Le Pré aux Clercs-Belfond, 1992).
3. Oussama Cherribi, "De borrelpraat van pim Fortuyn. Bespreking van Tegen de islamisering van Nederland," *Liberaal Reveil* 38 (1987): 3.
4. Mohammed Arkoun, *Lectures du Coran*, 2nd ed. (Tunis, 1991); Qadâyâ fî naqd al-'aql al-dînî, *Kayfa nafhamu-l-islâm al-yawm* (Beyrouth: Dâr al-talî'a, 1998); *Al-fikr al-usûlî wal-stihâlat al-ta'sîl* (Beyrouth: Dâr al-sâqî, 1999); *A paraître: The Unthought in Contemporary Islamic Thought* (London, 2000); *Combats pour l'humanisme en contextes islamiques* (Paris, 2000); *Penser l'islam aujourd'hui* (Paris, 2000).
5. Interview of Gayatri Spivak in the summer of 1992 at Columbia University in New York.
6. *Laïcité* sometimes connotes an antireligious tone, as the debate on the veil demonstrated in France, where religion is reduced to symbolism.
7. Salman Rushdie press conference, Emory University, March 2007.
8. Clifford Geertz, *Islam Observed: Religious Developments in Morocco and Indonesia* (London: University of Chicago Press, 1968), 18.
9. Philippe Brachet, *Descartes n'est pas Marocain* (Paris: Pensée Universelle, 1982).
10. Kees Schuyt, "Steunberen van de samenleving," *Sociologische Essays* (Amsterdam: Amsterdam University Press, 2006), 266.
11. Oussama Cherribi, "Ik ben een niet onverdienstelijk houtbewerker," Exclusief interview met Jimmy Carter: Missionaris, militair en meubelmaker.

De Groene Amsterdammer. ["I am not an undeserving carpenter," exclusive interview with Jimmy Carter: Missionary, soldier, and furniture maker.] [Interview with Jimmy Carter. Moral Leadership], May 25, 2006, 23–25.

12. Bernard Henri Levy, *American Vertigo: Traveling in the Footsteps of de Tocqueville* (New York: Random House, 2006).

13. Abdullahi Ahmed An-Na'im, *The Future of Shari'a Law* (Cambridge, Mass.: Harvard University Press: 2008).

14. Jean Paul Sartre, *L'Existentialisme est un Humanisme* (Paris: Nagel, 1946).

15. Oussama Cherribi, *Les Imams D'Amsterdam* (Amsterdam: University of Amsterdam, 2000).

CHAPTER 1

1. AlJazeera.com, "The Growing Islamization of Europe," in *Modernizing Islam: Religion in the Public Sphere in Europe and the Middle East*, ed. John L. Esposito and Francois Burgat (Newark, N.J.: Rutgers University Press and London: Hurst, 2003), 193–214.

2. Christopher Gladwell, "Islamic Europe," *Weekly Standard*, October 4, 2004.

3. Ibid.

4. Frank Lechner, *The Netherlands: Globalization and National Identity* (New York: Routledge, 2008), 281.

5. Alain Touraine, *Le Monde des Femmes* (Paris: Fayard, 2006), 163.

6. Ibid., 73.

7. Yamin Makri, 'Quelle contribution cityenne des associations musulmanes de France ?' in Alain Gresh. *Islam de France, Islams d'Europe*. Paris: L'Harmattan, 2004, 51–58.

8. Michèle Lamont, *The Dignity of Working Men: Morality and the Boundaries of Race, Class, and Immigration* (Cambridge, Mass.: Harvard University Press, 2000), 2.

9. Mathijs Kalmijn, quoted in ibid., 192; Kalmijn, Mathijs, "Status Homogamy in the United States," *American Journal of Sociology* 97, (1991): 496–523.

10. Lamont, *Dignity of Working Men*, 4.

11. Ibid.?

12. "Een eind op weg naar apartheid," *NRC*, November 29, 2004, 6.

13. Steven Vertovec and Ceri Peach, eds., *Islam in Europe, the Politics of Religion and Community* (New York: St. Martin's), 1997; Yvonne Yazbeck Haddad and Jane I. Smith, eds., *Muslim Minorities in the West: Visible and Invisible* (Walnut Creek, Calif.: Altamira), 2002; Thomas Gerholm and Yngve Georg Litman, eds., *The New Islamic Presence in Western Europe* (London: Mansell), 1990; (eds)Brigitte Marechal, Stephano Alievi, Felice Dassetto and Jorgen Nielsen, Muslims in the Enlarged Europe: Religion and Society, Leiden: Brill, 2003 Jytte Klausen: The Islamic Challenge: Politics and religion in Western Europe. Oxford University Press, 2005.

14. Mohammed Arkoun, ed., *Histoire de L'Islam et des Musulmans en France, du Moyen Age a nos jours* (Paris: Michel Albin, 2006), ix; Jorgen Nielsen, "L'Islam en Grande-Bretagne," in Alain Gresh, *Islam de France, Islams d'Europe* (Paris: L'Harmattan, 2004), 59–64; *Emancipatie Monitor*, 2006, http://ww.cbs.nl.

15. Columnists and politicians are predicting the worst for Europe. In the Netherlands, the radical right spoke about expecting an Islamic tsunami in the future and compared Islam to Nazism in the 1930s in Germany in that the government did nothing to stop Nazism. Even a mainstream and respected columnist like Ivan Rioufol of *Le Figaro* spoke about "Islam as a ticking bomb" ("Islam bombe a retardement"), *Le Figaro*, October 27, 2006.

16. Paul R. Brewer and Clyde Wilcox, "Trends: Same-Sex Marriage and Civil Unions," *Public Opinion Quarterly* 69 (2005): 599–616; Craig A. Rimmerman, Kenneth D. Wald, and Clyde Wilcox, eds., *The Politics of Gay Rights* (Chicago: University of Chicago Press, 2007).

17. Nulifer Guler, "La question de la femme et Le republicanisme et la laicité. Regards croisés entre la Turquie et la France," in Gresh (2004): 107.

18. Ronald Inglehart and Pippa Norris, *Rising Tide* (Cambridge: Cambridge University Press, 2003).

19. Ibid., chapter 3.

20. And understandably, these changes would not have been picked up in national surveys. Even now, national survey samples in most European countries usually do not include a sufficient number of ethnic minorities to conduct reliable analyses on the basis of race or religion. Moreover, in many European countries, surveys do not ask about religion. Even the census in many countries fails to ask a question about religion, thus making it difficult, for example, to estimate the number of Muslims in the United Kingdom or France. See Mohammed Arkoun, *Histoire de L'Islam et des Musulmans en France, du Moyen age a nos jours* (Paris: Michel Albin, 2007); Xavier Ternisien, *La France des mosquées* (Paris: Albin Miche, 2002).

21. See, for example, Jack Goody, *Islam in Europe* (Cambridge, England: Polity, 2004); Nezar Alsayyad and Manuel Castells, *Muslim Europe or Euro-Islam: Politics, Culture, and Citizenship in the Age of Globalization* (Lanham, Md.: Lexington, 2002). Although these are valuable in their own right, they remain superficial and sometimes even misleading because of the lack of depth in the country studies.

22. The three governments led by Prime Minister Lubbers, the first and second Purple Coalition governments led by Wim Kok, and the first and second governments led by Jan Peter Balkenende.

23. All had been in Germany, Netherlands, Belgium, or Denmark for at least five years. Their status as temporary refugees in these European countries was never in dispute, but when the time came to actually send them back, there were many calls to change their status because of their exemplary integration and the difficult economic hardships they would face by returning to their country of origin. The news media featured many personalized accounts of Muslim families, mothers and children, who were being sent back to Bosnia because the area had become safe again.

24. Pippa Norris, *Radical Right: Parties and Electoral Competition* (New York: Cambridge University Press, 2005).

25. Stefaan Walgrave and Peter van Aelst, "The Contingent Nature of Agenda-setting: Different Agenda-setting Dynamics in Election and Non-Election Times?" Paper presented at 3rd annual pre-APSA Conference on Political Communication: Faith, Fun and Futuramas, 2004.

26. Julianne Stewart Mazzoleni and Bruce Horsfield, *The Media and Neo-Populism: A Contemporary Comparative Analysis* (Westport, Conn.: Praeger, 2003), 24.

27. Ternisien, *La France des mosquées*, 42.

28. There has been no tradition in Islamic countries of measuring religiosity—the frequency of attending services at the mosque, for example—until very recently.

29. Alain Boyer, quoted in "Haut Conseil a l'integration, L'Islam dans la Republique," *La Documentation Francaise*, November 2000, quoted in Ternisien, *La France des mosquées*, 43.

30. *The Encyclopaedia of Islam*, CD-ROM, version 1.0 (Leiden, the Netherlands: Koninklijke Brill NV, 1999).

31. Ternisien, *La France des mosquées*, 43 and Brigitte Marechal, "The Question of belonging" pp5–18 in *Muslims in the Enlarged Europe* ed.by Brigitte Marechal, Stephano Allievi, Felice Dacetto and Jorgen Nielsen.Leiden:Brill,2003,5.

32. Ibid., 44, based on *Le Monde*, October 5, 2001.

33. Institut National de la Statistique et des Études Économiques, accessed November 7, 2009, at http://www.insee.fr/fr/insee_regions/bourgogne/rfc/docs/demographie_dossier_41.pdf.
For the history of the migrations' flows in one region of France, see National de la Statistique et des Études Économiques, accessed November 7, 2009, at http://www.insee.fr/fr/insee_regions/Champagne-Ardenne/publi/Atlas_flux_2004.pdf.
According to the BBC, there are 12 million Muslims in Europe. Magdi Abdelhadi, "European Muslims Search for Identity," *BBC News*, accessed November 7, 2009, at http://news.bbc.co.uk/2/hi/europe/3665779.stm.

34. Sources: Statistics Netherlands, http://www.cbs.nl, 2005 figures; Italian National Statistical Institute, http://www.istat.it, 2004 figures; Statistics Sweden, 2005 figures; Spanish National Institute of Statistics, http://www.ine.es, 2005 figures; U.S. State Department, http://www.state.gov, all accessed November 7, 2009.

35. I use a pseudonym to protect their identity.

36. Another area of private life in which transnational disputes occur concerns home ownership in Morocco. This became an issue in 2001 in the Netherlands because some immigrant Dutch citizens send their children back to Morocco to live with other family members in a home they purchased for that purpose, and they also send their child benefit payments to Morocco to support their children. The issue became a topic of national debate when the Labour minister of social affairs described this practice as "fraud" and then said that these people should be required to sell any assets they own in Morocco before receiving child benefits (which are paid to everyone regardless of income) and any forms of welfare or public assistance. From the perspective of those Euro-Moroccan homeowners, however, this new legislation was very threatening because the Dutch government requested that the Moroccan government cooperate fully to look into their files to determine who on welfare owns assets abroad.

37. This means that a French Moroccan man can take his wife and children on holiday to Morocco and then while there repudiate her. This will be recognized by Moroccan officials as a divorce, as well as by France. The new Moroccan king wanted

to change the civil law on this point—to liberalize the divorce laws in Morocco to improve the situation of women. But this process was slowed down and may never result in what the king originally intended because many Moroccan imams in Europe joined with the fundamentalist opposition in Morocco to collect signatures of thousands of Moroccans to petition the Moroccan government not to liberalize the law.

38. In the Netherlands, in the year 2000, some 3,000 Moroccan women were in the following situation: divorced under Dutch law from their Moroccan husbands without having this divorce accepted by Morocco, they can travel to Morocco and find that the Moroccan ex-husband retains certain rights, such as the right to insist that she return to him and to her home with him. If she does not agree, she may have to face consequences such as a fine, as well as public humiliation. This becomes even more problematic when she remarries under Dutch law and has children with her new spouse, because in Morocco she nevertheless continues to be seen as legally married to her first husband. See http://www.mvvn.nl/index.php?option=com_content&task=view&id=23&Itemid=51, accessed November 7, 2009.

39. Defined as those built by members of Moroccan communities and/or funded and run by a majority of those from the Moroccan community.

40. Ternisien, *La France des mosquées*, 44.

41. *Volkskrant* story; Fortuyn claimed later that he was misquoted or set up by the newspaper's interviewer and that he is not against Muslims but against the religion, which was against homosexuality.

42. Paul Sniderman et al., *The Outsider: Prejudice and Politics in Italy* (Princeton, N.J.: Princeton University Press, 2002.

43. Veit Bader, "The Cultural Conditions of Transnational Citizenship: On the Interpretation of Political and Ethnic Cultures," *Political Theory* 25 (1997): 771–813; Rogers Brubaker, *Citizenship and Nationhood in France and Germany* (Cambridge, Mass.: Harvard University Press, 1992); Mark J. Miller, *Foreign Workers in Western Europe: An Emerging Political Force?* (New York: Praeger, 1981); Mark J. Miller, "The Political Impact of Foreign Labour," *International Migration Review* 16 (1982): 27–60; J. Goytisolo, "Strangers among Us (Europe's Long-Held Fear of Islam)," *Index on Censorship* 28 (1999): 60–65; Randall Hansen and Patrick Weil, *Dual Nationality, Social Rights and Federal Citizenship in the U.S. and Europe: The Reinvention of Citizenship* (London: Berghahn, 2002); Ruud Koopmans, "Explaining the Rise of Racist and Extreme Right Violence in Western Europe: Grievances or Opportunities," *European Journal of Political Research* 30 (1996): 185–216; Ruud Koopmans, "Germany and Its Immigrants: An Ambivalent Relationship," *Journal of Ethnic and Migration Studies* 24 (1999): 627–647; Rey Koslowski, *Migrants and Citizens: Demographic Change in the European State System* (Ithaca, N.Y.: Cornell University Press, 2002); David Kyle and Rey Koslowski, eds., *Global Human Smuggling: Comparative Perspectives* (Baltimore, Md.: Johns Hopkins University Press, 2001); Aristide R. Zolberg and Peter Benda, eds., *Global Migrants, Global Refugees: Problems and Solutions* (London: Berghahn, 2001); Michael Dummett, *On Immigration and Refugees (Thinking in Action)* (London: Routledge, 2001); Saskia Sassen, *Guests and Aliens* (New York: New Press, 1999).

44. Caroline Brettell and James Frank Hollifield, eds., *Migration Theory: Talking across the Disciplines* (London: Routledge, 2000); Patrick Ireland, *The Policy Challenge of Ethnic Diversity: Immigrant Politics in France and Switzerland* (Cambridge, Mass.: Harvard University Press, 1994); Will Kymlicka, *Multicultural Citizenship: A Liberal Theory of Minority Rights* (Oxford: Clarendon, 1995).

45. Saskia Sassen, "Regulating Immigration in a Global Age: A New Policy Landscape," *Annals of the American Academy of Political and Social Sciences* 570 (2000): 65–77.

46. Christian Joppke, *Immigration and the Nation-State: The United States, Germany, and Great Britain* (Oxford: Oxford University Press, 2000).

47. Rey Koslowski, *Migrants and Citizens: Demographic Change in the European States System* (Ithaca, N.Y.: Cornell University Press, 2000).

48. "Spain Launches Immigrant Amnesty," BBC News, February 7, 2005, accessed November 7, 2005, at http://news.bbc.co.uk/2/hi/europe/4242411.stm.

49. I interviewed Mohammed Arkoun in Paris, June 2002.

50. Bourdieu, Pierre, *Sociologie de l'Algérie*, Paris, PUF, coll. « Que sais-je ? », 1958 [2002 (8ᵉ éd.)], 59–70.

51. Sniderman et al., *The Outsider*, 26. Sniderman more recently coauthored, with Louk Hagendoorn, *When Ways of Life Collide: Multiculturalism and Its Discontents in the Netherlands* (Princeton, N.J.: Princeton University Press, 2007). Though it is a very informative work that mentions Pim Fortuyn and others who played roles in Dutch society since 2002, I have not referred to it in this book because it is based on a survey conducted between January and April 1998, well before most of the events it discusses—events also discussed in this book. Additionally, the survey had a response rate of only 37 percent, which compromises its significance.

52. Sniderman et al., *The Outsider*, 24.

53. Ibid., 25.

54. Ibid., 15.

55. Ibid., 41.

56. Ibid., 82.

57. Ibid., 81–82.

58. Ibid., 138.

59. Ibid.

60. Ibid., 140.

61. Gary P. Freeman, "The Consequence of Immigration Policies for Immigrant Status: A British and French Comparison," in *Ethnic and Racial Minorities in Advanced Industrial Democracies*, ed. by Anthony Messina, L. Fraga, L. Rhodebeck, and F. Wright (New York: Greenwood, 1992).

62. Gary P. Freeman, "Can Liberal States Control Unwanted Migration?" *Annals of the American Academy of Politics and Social Sciences* 534 (1994): 17.

63. Ibid.

64. Gary P. Freeman, "Modes of Immigration Politics in Liberal Democratic States," *International Migration Review* 29 (1995): 881–902; Gary P. Freeman, "The Decline of Sovereignty? Politics and Immigration Restriction in Liberal States," in

Challenge to the Nation-State: Immigration in Western Europe and the United States, ed. by Christian Joppke (Oxford: Oxford University Press, 1998), 103.

65. Freeman, *Challenge to the Nation-State*, 103.

66. Norbert Elias and John L. Scotson, *The Established and the Outsiders: A Sociological Enquiry into Community Problems* (London: Frank Cass, 1965).

67. Nabil I. Matar, *Islam in Britain, 1558–1685* (Cambridge, England: Cambridge University Press, 1998); Ansari Humayun, *The Infidel Within: Muslims in Britain since 1800* (London: C. Hurst, 2004); and the indispensable Bernard Lewis, *Cultures in Conflict: Christians, Muslims and Jews in the Age* of Discovery (New York: Oxford University Press, 1995).

68. Phillip Lewis, "Beyond Victimhood: From the Global to the Local, a British Case Study," in Cersari J., (ed.) European Muslims and the Secular State in a comparative perspective: final symposium report, 30 June and July 1 2003, Network on Comparative Research on Islam and Muslims and Europe, 82 http://www.euro-islam.info/PDFs/Final_ICDEI_Symposium.pdf.

CHAPTER 2

1. http://benjebangvoormij.nl/ November 5, 2002.
2. Michèle Lamont, *The Dignity of Working Men: Morality and the Boundaries of Race, Class, and Immigration* (Cambridge, Mass.: Harvard University Press, 2000), 174.
3. Ibid.
4. Ibid., 171.
5. Ibid., 179.
6. Ibid., 184.
7. Barry van Driel, *Confronting Islamophobia in Educational Practice* (Stoke-on-Trent, England: Trentham, 2004).
8. Mohammed Arkoun, ed., *Histoire de L'Islam et des Musulmans en France, du Moyen age a nos jours* (Paris: Michel Albin, 2007).
9. Loïc Wacquant, *Urban Outcasts: A Comparative Sociology of Advanced Marginality* (Cambridge, England: Polity, 2007). See also Loïc Wacquant and Sébastien Chauvin, *Parias urbains : Ghetto, banlieues, Etat (*Paris: La Découverte, 2006).
10. "La galère des jeunes blacks et beurs face à l'emploi," *Lien Social*, May 15, 2003; accessed November 7, 2009, at http://www.lien-social.com/spip.php?article306&id_groupe=4.
11. Arkoun, *Histoire de L'Islam*, xix.
12. Abram de Swaan, *Bakens in Niemandsland, Opstellen over massaal geweld* (Amsterdam: Uitgeverij Bert Bakker, 2007); Jean Muttapa, "Avant propos de l'editeur" in ibid, ix.
13. Gilles Kepel, *The War for Muslim Minds: Islam and the West* (Cambridge, Mass: Belknap, 2006).
14. Talal Assad, *Formations of the Secular: Christianity, Islam, Modernity* (Stanford, Calif.: Stanford University Press, 2003), 159.
15. Alain Boyer in Arkou, *Histoire de L'Islam*, 763.

16. Arkoun, *Histoire de L'Islam*, 745–749.

17. Jack Goody, *Islam in Europe* (Cambridge, England: Polity, 2004), 14.

18. Ibid., 17.

19. Dale Eickelman, "Clifford Geertz and Islam," in *Clifford Geertz by His Colleagues*, ed. by Richard A Shweder and Bryon Good (Chicago: University of Chicago Press, 2005), 63–75.

20. Ruud Koopmans and Paul Statham, "Migration and Ethnic Relations as Field of Political Contention: An Opportunity Structure Approach," in *Challenging Immigration and Ethnic Relations Politics: Comparative European Perspectives*, ed. by R. Koopmans and P. Statham (Oxford: Oxford University Press, 2000), 19.

21. Ibid., 19.

22. Ibid., 20.

23. Ibid.

24. Ibid., 22–29.

25. Ibid., 27–28.

26. See also Dietrich Thranhardt, "Conflict, Consensus, and Policy Outcomes: Immigration, and Integration in Germany and The Netherlands," in Koopmans and Statham, *Challenging Immigration*, 162–186.

27. Koopman and Statham, 28–29.

28. Henri Mechoulan, *Amsterdam au temps de Spinoza* (Paris: PUF, 1990); Jonathan Israel, *Radical Enlightenment: Philosophy and the Making of Modernity 1650–1750* (Oxford: Oxford University Press, 2002).

29. Clifford Geertz, *Islam observed: Religious development in Morocco and Indonesia* (New Haven, Conn.: Yale University Press, 1968).

30. (Jacques Waardenburg, *L'Islam dans le miroir de l'Occident* (The Hague and Paris: Mouton, 1961), 20.

31. Ibid., 25.

32. Ibid.

33. Paul Pascon, "L'émigration des chleuhs du Souss, Les Ait-Quadrim à Jerada," *Bulletin Economique et Social du Maroc* 2 (1987): 155–156.

34. Dale Eickelman, *Moroccan Islam* (Austin: University of Texas Press, 1976).

35. Arend Lijphart, *The Politics of Accommodation: Pluralism and Democracy in the Netherlands* (Berkeley: University of California Press, 1968).

36. The importance of this stimulus to the emigration from Morocco can be found in the number of annual departures of Moroccans to Europe. In 1960, four years after Morocco's independence from France, there were 10,000 emigrants to Europe per year up to 1962, when it began to increase and peaked ultimately at 29,000 a year in 1970 to 1972. Already in 1965, there were 5,500 Moroccans officially registered in the Netherlands, at a time when it was not common to register officially (so this does not take account of those who did not register). Many Moroccans followed a complex migratory trajectory. They went first to Algeria, then to France, and then to Holland. The Dutch first recruited the Italians, who came in 1959 to Limburg to work in the mines. The Dutch recruited Spaniards in 1961 and Greeks in 1964. The Moroccans and Tunisians were the last to be recruited to the country. In 1963, Dutch

recruitment of unskilled laborers officially ended, but the immigration from Morocco and Turkey continued through family reunions and marriage. The different regulations of the migration flows influenced the public image of guest workers. It is worth noting that boys were more likely to be brought over for family reunions than girls, because the fathers put the boys to work so that more money could be sent home to the families. The consequence was that when these boys wanted to marry, they returned to Morocco, and after they did so, they brought their wives back to the Netherlands. In 1981, the majority of the children emigrating were male, between 15 and 19 years old. From 1983, the Dutch established an obligatory visa for Moroccans and an upper age limit of 18 for candidates for family reunion, and this led to a considerable decline in numbers arriving. Between 1980 and 1990, the Moroccan population in the Netherlands increased by 106 percent, from 71,760 to 147,975. This increase was particularly youthful in the age group 10–34. The Dutch began to encourage people to take payments to return to their home countries, and although this approach succeeded with many migrants from other European countries, only 10 percent of the Moroccans took this offer.

37. I interviewed Gijs von der Fuhr in Café Het Paleis in Amsterdam, June 1999.

38. *De Molukken*, accessed November 7, 2009, at http://www.nrc.nl/W2/Lab/Profiel/Molukken/historie.html.

39. Interviews conduted by the author in *Les Imams D'Amsterdam, A travers L'exemple de la diaspora marocaine.Amsterdam:University of Amsterdam,2000,53.*

40. For more analysis about the process of integration of organizations of migrants in the Netherlands and the impact of the integration policy of the Dutch government, see Jan Willem Duyvendak and R. Rijkschroeff, "De bronnen van het integratiebeleid," *Sociologische Gids* 51 (2004): 3–17; and Jan Willem Duyvendak and R. Rijkschroeff, "De omstreden betekenis van zelforganisaties," *Sociologische Gids* 51 (2004): 18–35.

41. Paolo de Mas in a talk at Le Maroc et la Hollande, Colloque (University of Amsterdam, 1986). In *Le Maroc et la Hollande. Actes du IVe rencontre universitaire maroco-neerlandaise* (Colloques et Seminaires 39).

42. Michel Laguerre, *Minoritized Space: An Inquiry into the Spatial Order of Things* (Berkeley, Calif.: Institute of Governmental Studies Press, 1999); Jan Rath, "Minorisering: De sociale constructie van 'etnische minderheden'" (thesis, University of Utrecht, 1991).

43. See L. Van Zoonen, "De maatschappelijke betekenis van populaire cultuur," 1999 in J. van Cuilenburg, ed., "Media in overvloed. Over verdwijnende loyaliteiten en wisselende mediacontacten." Speciaal nummer van *Mens & Maatschappij* (1999).

44. Lotty van den Berg-Eldering, *Marokkaanse gezinnen in Nederland* (Alphen aan de Rijn: Samsom, 1978); Lotty van den Berg-Eldering, *Van gastarbeider tot immigrant. Marokkanen en Turken in Nederland* (Alphen an den Rijn: Samsom, 1986).

45. Gilles Kepel, *The War for Muslim Minds: Islam and the West* (Cambridge. Mass.: Belknap, 2006).

CHAPTER 3

1. Marisca Milikowski, "Exploring a Model of De-Ethnicization: The Case of Turkish Television in the Netherlands," *European Journal of Communication* 15 (2000): 443–468.

2. John Esposito with Francois Burgat, *Modernizing Islam: Religion in the Public Sphere in the Middle East and Europe* (London: Hurst; New Brunswick, N.J.: Rutgers University Press, 2003); Mohammed Arkoun, *L'Islam, morale et politique* (Paris: Desclée de Brouwer/UNESCO, 1986); Mohammed Arkoun and Joseph Maila, *De Manhattan à Bagdad. Au-delà du bien et du mal* (Paris: Desclée de Brouwer, 2003).

3. Pierre Bourdieu, *La Distinction. Critique sociale du jugement* (Paris: Minuit, 1979); *Le Sens pratique* (Paris: Minuit, 1980); discussion of Bourdieu, *La Distinction*, accessed November 7, 2009, at http://fr.wikipedia.org/wiki/La_distinction; Bourdieu, *Les Règles de l'art. Genèse et structure du champ littéraire* (Paris: Seuil, 1992); Bourdieu, *La Domination masculine* (Paris: Seuil, 1998), and discussion of it, accessed November 9, 2009, at http://fr.wikipedia.org/wiki/La_Domination_masculine; Elias and Scotson, *The Established and the Outsiders*.

4. In another manuscript, I draw extensively on the full range of concepts in Bourdieu's theoretical arsenal: habitus; different forms of capital such as social, cultural, symbolic, positions, and dispositions; and the prise de positions. I also draw on the long-term historical perspective of Elias, his interdependency theories, and his use of the concept of habitus. The theoretical framework of my larger study (see Cherribi, *Les imams d'Amsterdam*. Amsterdam: University of Amsterdam, 2000) is informed by a number of concepts and theories. It is primarily intellectually indebted to Pierre Bourdieu, for his theory of reflexive sociology and for his seminal research on writers in France, which serves as a basis for this study of imams in Amsterdam. I also drew on the historical sociological perspective of Norbert Elias, whose theory on interdependencies serves as a basis for studying the transnational configuration of Moroccan imams in Amsterdam and the sociogenesis of the mosques. The work of Mohammed Arkoun provides a basis for understanding the sermons of the imams and their theological and historical contexts, and the work of Abram de Swaan provides the basis for understanding the spheres of identification of the imams within society and within a transnational perspective.

5. Edward Said, *Covering Islam*, 1981.

6. Gilles Kepel, *Les banlieues de l'islam: Naissance d'une religion en France* (Paris: Seuil, 1987).

7. ACB (Amsterdam Center for Foreigners) Nieuwsbrief, Amsterdam, February 2001.

8. The corpus of sermons and interviews with the imams of Amsterdam I collected in the early 1990s is in Cherribi, *Les imams d'Amsterdam* (Amsterdam: University of Amsterdam, 2000).

9. Peter van der Veer, *Religious Nationalism. Hindus and Muslims in India* (Los Angeles: University of California Press), 1994.

10. Ibid.

11. Frits Bolkestein, *Moslem in de Polder* (Amsterdam: Contact, 1997) (I conducted these interviews with Frits Bolkestein and drafted the manuscript).

12. Jacques Wardenburg, "Integratie, moslims en Islam:een verkenning." In K.Wachtendonk,[ed] Islam in *Nederland, Islam op school*. Muidenberg: Coutinho, 1987, 31–48.

13. Leaflet acquired and translated by the author, August, 1992.

14. Marcel Gauchet, *Le désenchantement du Monde: une histoire politique de la religion* (Paris: Gallimard, 1985).

15. Interviews conducted by the author, 2000, 67.

16. Dale Eickelman, *Moroccan Islam: Tradition and Society in a Pilgrimage Center*, Modern Middle East Series (Austin: University of Texas Press, 1976).

17. Buijs, F., *Een moskee in de wijk: de vestiging van de Kocatepe moskee in Rotterdam-Zuid*, Amsterdam: Het Spinhuis.1998; Ruud Strijp, Om de Moskee; Het Religieuze Leven van Marokkaanse Migranten in een Provinciestad. Amsterdam:Thesis,1998 and Xavier Ternsien, La France des mosquées (Paris: Albin Michel, 2002).

18. Nico Landman, *Van mat tot minaret, De institutionalisering van de islam in Nederland* (Amsterdam: VU, 1992).

19. Xavier Ternisien, *La France des mosquées* (Paris: Albin Michel, 2002).

20. Kepel, *Les Banlieues de l'Islam*.

21. Uri Rubin, *The Eye of the Beholder: The Life of Muhammad as Viewed by the Early Muslims, A Textual Analysis* (Princeton, N.J.: Darwin, 1995).

22. *New York Times*, March 13, 2000.

23. Visit this Web link to watch the program: http://weblogs.vpro.nl/villa-achterwerk?s=ik+wil+een+meisje+zijn.

24. Soheib Bencheikh, *Marianne et le prophète, l'islam dans la France laïque* (Paris: Grasset, 1998).

CHAPTER 4

1. Jacques Julliard, lecture about Turkey and Europe at the Halle Institute, Emory University, March 2005; Nezar AlSayyad and Manuel Castells, *Muslim Europe or Euro Islam: Politics, Culture and Citizenship in the Age of Globalization* (Lanham, Md.: Lexington, 2001).

2. Hans Sinnema, "Kiesrecht," ACB report, Amsterdam, 1986.

3. Clifford Geertz, *Islam Observed, Religious Development in Morocco and Indonesia* (Chicago: University of Chicago Press, 1968).

4. Pierre Bourdieu, *Esquisse d'une théorie de la pratique*, précédé de *Trois études d'ethnologie kabyle* (Geneva: Droz, 1972).

5. Pierre Bourdieu et al., *La misère du monde* (Paris: Seuil, 1993).

6. Gilles Kepel, Le Prophete et Pharaon:les mouvements islamistes dans l'Egypte contemporaine. Paris : La Decouverte 1984.

7. Ibid,165.

8. Tayob, Abdolkader, *Islam in South Africa: Mosques, Imams and Sermons.* (Miami: University of Florida Press, 1999).

CHAPTER 5

1. The morning of the day of his death, the Intomart survey director was quoted in the *Volkskrant* as saying that the LPF would gain "38 seats," which would have made it the largest party in the Parliament, and therefore Fortuyn would have been called on by the queen to form the next government.

2. Dick Pels, "Populism is niet alleen slecht," *Vrij Nederland,* May 3, 2003, 35–37.

3. Marcel Roele, "Vacature: Fortuyn," *HP/De Tijd,* May 3, 2003, 23.

4. I am currently working on an article devoted to the developments on the issue of Islam in the year after Pim's death.

5. For an analysis of the impact of visuals on learning, recall, and emotional response, see Doris A. Graber, *Processing Politics: Learning from Television in the Internet Age* (Chicago: University of Chicago Press, 2001).

6. Stan de Jong and Joost Niemoller, "Fortuyns beveiliging: een bloody shame," *HP de Tijd,* May 2, 2003, 30–38.

7. I appreciate the comments of some of my colleagues in other countries who reminded me of this.

8. See Gianpietro Mazzoleni, "The Media and the Growth of Neo-Populism in Contemporary Democracies," in *The Media and Neo-Populism: A Contemporary Comparative Analysis,* ed. by Gianpietro Mazzoleni, Julianne Stewart, and Bruce Horsfeld (Westport, Conn.: Praeger, 2003), 1–20; Julianne Stewart, Gianpietro Mazzoleni, and Brusce Horsfeld, "Conclusion: Power to the Media Managers" in ibid., 217–237.

9. See Gianpietro Mazzoleni, "The Media and the Growth of Neo-Populism."

10. Stewart et al., "Conclusion," 221.

11. Mazzoleni, "The Media and the Growth of Neo-Populism," 21–24.

12. Stefaan Walgrave, "The Making of the (Issues of the) Vlaams Blok." Paper presented at the annual meeting of the American Political Science Association, August 28, 2002.

13. See, for example, David Snow and Robert D. Benford, "Ideology, Frame Resonance and Participant Mobilization," *International Social Movement Research* 1 (1988): 197–217. The work of Erving Goffman put forward the concept of frame analysis; see Erving Goffman, *Frame Analysis* (San Francisco: Harper Colophon, 1974). The concept of media framing and framing effects has been the subject of much scholarly research. For a review of studies see, for example, Holli A. Semetko and Patti M. Valkenburg, "Framing European Politics: A Content Analysis of Press and Television News," *Journal of Communication* 50 (2000): 93–109.

14. Robert M. Entman and Andrew Rojecki, *The Black Image in the White Mind: Media and Race in America* (Chicago: University of Chicago Press, 2001).

15. Rogers Brubaker, "Ethnicity without Groups," *European Journal of Sociology (Archives Europeenes de Sociologie)* 43, no. 2 (2002): 163–189; the material I refer to is on pages 173–175.

16. William A. Gamson, *Talking Politics* (New York: Cambridge University Press, 1992); William A. Gamson and Andre Modigliani, "The Changing Culture of Affirmative Action," *Research in Political Sociology* 3 (1987): 37–77.

17. Entman and Rojecki, *The Black Image in the White Mind*, 120.

18. Benedict Anderson, *Imagined Communities: Reflections on the Origin and Spread of Nationalism* (London: Verso, 1991).

19. Pierre Bourdieu, *La distinction, critique sociale du jugement* (Paris: Editions Minuit, 1979), 554.

20. Ibid., 489.

21. Research on ethnic claims making has been inspired by studies of social movements; see Sidney Tarrow, *Democracy and Disorder: Protest and Politics in Italy 1963–1975* (Oxford: Clarendon, 1989); Sidney Tarrow, *Power in Movement: Social Movements, Collective Action and Politics* (Cambridge, England: Cambridge University Press, 1994); Charles Tilly, *From Mobilisation to Revolution* (Reading, Mass.: Addison-Wesley, 1978); Charles Tilly, Louise Tilly, and Richard Tilly, *The Rebellious Century 1830–1930* (Cambridge, Mass.: Harvard University Press, 1975).

22. Jos van der Linden, "Rassenwaan: De Amerikaanse obsessie met discriminatie en segregatie," *De Academische Boekengids* 2 (2003): 13–15.

23. Sniderman, Paul, et al., *The Outsider: Prejudice and Politics in Italy*. Princeton, N.J.: Princeton University Press, 2002.

24. See Teun van Dijk, *Communicating Racism: Ethnic Prejudice in Thought and Talk* (London: Sage, 1989); Teun van Dijk, *Elite Discourse and Racism* (London: Sage, 1993); as well as various contributions in Philmena Essed and David Theo Goldberg, eds., *Race Critical Theories: Text and Context* (London: Blackwell, 2001).

25. W. Lance Bennett, *News: The Politics of Illusion*, 4th ed. (New York: Addison-Wesley Longman, 2001).

26. Ibid.

27. Michael Schudson, *The Sociology of News* (New York: W. W. Norton, 2003).

28. Ibid., 2.

29. Ibid., 71.

30. See, for example, Kees Aarts and Holli A. Semetko, "The Divided Electorate: Media Use and Political Involvement," *Journal of Politics* 65 (2003): 759–784.

31. See Schudson, *Sociology of News*. Also see Jay G. Blumler and Michael Gurevitch, *The Crisis in Public Communication* (London: Routledge, 1995).

32. Benedict Anderson, *Imagined Communities: Reflections on the Origin and Spread of Nationalism* (London: Verso, 1983).

33. Mahammed El-Nawawy and Adel Iskandar, *Al-Jazeera: How the Free Arab News Network Scooped the World and Changed the Middle East* (Cambridge, Mass.: Westview, 2003).

34. Hent de Vries and Samuel Weber, eds., *Religion and Media* (Stanford, Calif.: Stanford University Press, 2001), 17.

35. Hent de Vries, "In Media Res: Global Religion, Public Spheres, and the Task of Contemporary Comparative Religious Studies," in ibid., 21.

36. Edward Said, *Orientalism* (New York: Vintage, 1979).

37. Edward Said, *Covering Islam* (London: Vintage, 1997).

38. This information was given to me by close associates of the imam.

39. This information was provided by several individuals working in gay newspapers and interest groups whom I interviewed.

40. Rudy B. Andeweg and Galen A. Irwin, *Governance and Politics of the Netherlands* (New York: Palgrave Macmillan, 2002), 17–40.

41. Jonathan Israel, *The Dutch Republic and the Hispanic World, 1606–1661* (New York: Oxford University Press, 1982); Jonathan Israel, The *Dutch Republic: Its Rise, Greatness and Fall 1477–1806* (Oxford: Clarendon, 1995); Jonathan Israel, *Radical Enlightenment: Philosophy and the Making of Modernity* (Oxford: Oxford University Press, 2001).

42. Public discussion in De Balie, Amsterdam, between Alan Touraine and Abram De Swaan, moderated by Paul Scheffer, June 28, 2001.

43. Personal discussion with the author.

44. Pim Fortuyn, *Aan het Volk van Nederland: de contractmaatschappij, een politiek economische zedenschets* (Amsterdam: Contact, 1992).

45. Pim Fortuyn, *Het Zakenkabinet Fortuyn* (Utrecht: Bruna, 1994).

46. Pim Fortuyn, *Tegen de Islamisering van Nederland* (Uithoorn: Karakter Uitgevers, 1997). A revised version of this book was published six months before the 2002 election with a new title and including an epiloge/postface by Imam Abdullah Hazelhoef; see Pim Fortuyn, *De Islamisiering van Nederland: Nederlands identiteit als fundament* (Uithoorn: Karakter Uitgevers, 2001).

47. Pim Fortuyn, *De Puinhopen van Acht Jaar Paars* (Rotterdam: Karakter Uitgevers, 2002).

48. This was the headline of the news story on the front page in *Algemeen Dagblad*, January 18, 2002.

49. I looked at a random sample of ten articles per year over this period and identified the tone toward Moroccans, which was negative in most cases. This is admittedly a small sample, and so my conclusions must be seen as tentative. That said, the current affairs program *Netwerk* on May 8, 2003, drew this same conclusion after asking people on the street what comes to mind when they hear the word "Moroccans." Answers included crime, theft, street gangs, wife-beating, and veils. The reporter described this as negative.

50. See Pels, "Populism."

51. This material from the video shown in the documentary was quoted in the article Patrick Meershoek, "Blumder van de eeuw op video [Blunder of the century on video]," *Het Parool*, May 6, 2003, 16.

52. See the table on page 24 of Andeweg and Irwin, *Governance and Politics of the Netherlands*.

53. See, for example, Liesbet van Zoonen, "After Dallas and Dynasty, We Have . . . Democracy. The Soap Factor in Politics," in *Restyling politics*, ed. by J. Corner and D. Pels (London: Sage, 2003); Liesbet van Zoonen, ed., "Popular Culture as Political Communication," special issue of *Javnost/The Public*, in press; Liesbet van Zoonen and Christina Holtz-Bacha, "Personalization in Dutch and German Politics: The Case of

the Talkshow," *Javnost/The Public*, Vol. 7, February 2000, 45–56. ; Liesbet van Zoonen, "De talkshow: personalisering als politieke strategie," in *Tussen beeld en inhoud: politiek en media in de verkiezingen van 1998*, ed. by Kees Brants and Phillip van Praag (Amsterdam: Het Spinhuis, 2000); Liesbet van Zoonen, "Broken Hearts, Broken Dreams: Politicians and Their Families in the Dutch Gossip Press," in *Gender, Politics and Communication*, ed. by Anabelle Sreberny and Liesbet van Zoonen (Cresskill, N.J.: Hampton, 2000), 101–121; Liesbet van Zoonen, ed., "Making Politics Popular," special issue of *Media, Culture and Society* 20, no. 2 (1998); Liesbet van Zoonen, "A Day at the Zoo: Politicians, Pigs and Popular Culture," *Media, Culture and Society* 20, no. 2 (1998): 183–200; Liesbet van Zoonen, "Finally I Have My Mother Back: Male and Female Politicians in Popular Culture," *Harvard International Journal of Press/Politics* 3, no. 1 (1998): 48–64.

54. Rosenmöller accused Pim of becoming theatrical every time an issue became difficult.

55. Jan Kleinnijenhuis, Dirk Oegema, Jan de Ridder, Anita van Hoof, and Rens Vliegenthard, *De puinhopen in het nieuws: De rol van de media bij de Tweede-Kamerverkiezingen van 2002* (Alphen aan den Rijn-Mechelen: Kluwer, 2002).

56. Wouter van der Brug, "How the LPF fuelled Discontent: Empirical Tests of Explanations of LPF-support." Acta Politica (2003)38(1): 89–106.

57. Ibid. The connection between news, political cynicism and non-voting is made in Thomas E. Patterson, *The Vanishing Voter* (New York: Knopf, 2002).

58. Kleinnijenhuis et al., *De puinhopen in het nieuws*, 136–138.

59. I discuss this in greater detail in my book *European Islam Observed: Contested Issues in the Public Space*, forthcoming.

60. *Trouw*, May 2, 2003, 3.

CHAPTER 6

1. "Aboujahjah stelt moslimhaat gelijk aan jodenhaat,"De Telegraaf, March 8, 2003, 1, accessed November 7, 2009, at www.detelegraaf.nl.

2. He debated Philip Dewinter, leader of the Vlaams Blok (since 2004 Vlaams Belang), on Belgian Public Television in November 2002; accessed November 7, 2009, at http://forum.politics.be/archive/index.php/t-452.html.

3. Kustaw Bessems and Helene Butijn, "deVerdieping: Abou Jahjah heft altijd een antwoord," *Trouw*, March 8, 2003, 15.

4. The Dutch media star who likes to think of himself as the Jeremy Paxman of the Low Countries, with *Nova* the closest the Dutch come to the BBC's *Newsnight*.

5. *Nederland Kiest*, January 25, 2003. See also "Biografie: Dyab Abou Jahjah," accessed November 7, 2009, at http://www.novatv.nl/index.cfm?ln=nl&fuseaction=artikelen.details&achtergrond_id=1082.

6. Radio One, March 6.

7. The traditional Dutch holiday celebrated on December 5 describes *Zwarte Piet* as black characters helping Saint Nicholas.

8. Radio One, March 6.

9. Dyab Abou Jahjah and Zohra Othman, "Resist! Veel meer dan een cultuurschok, Opgetekend door Han Soete & Christophe Callewaert van Indymedia," Berchem, EPA, 2003, 34.

10. Ibid.

11. Interview with Abou Jahjah on Radio One, 9–10 A.M., March 6, 2003.

12. *Volkskrant*, March 8, 2003, 1.

13. Abou Jahjah and Othman, "Resist!" 23.

14. Paul Brill, "Messiaans visioen [messianic vision]," *Volkskrant*, March 4, 2003.

15. *Trouw*, March 8, 2003, 15.

16. A content analysis of all 279 articles in five Dutch newspapers that mentioned Abou Jahjah or his AEL in March, April, and May 2003 found that while Abou Jahjah himself was overall evaluated slightly negatively in March, slightly positively in April, and slightly negatively in May, AEL was evaluated more negatively each month, and this pattern held for each of the newspapers. Nearly two-thirds of these evaluations came from journalists themselves. The newspapers are *NRC, Volkskrant, Trouw, Algemeen Dagblad*, and *Het Parool*. See Karin Hommen, "The AEL in the Press: A Content Analysis of the Dutch Newspaper Coverage of the Arab European League," unpublished paper prepared for Professor Semetko's course on news and public opinion, University of Amsterdam, June 2003.

17. Abou Jahjah and Othman, "Resist!" 41.

18. Ibid., 43.

19. Ibid., 44.

20. Ibid.

21. "Geen vervolging Oudkerk wegens 'kut-Marokkanen,'" Het Parool, April 9, 2002.

22. Kut Marokkaan lyrics by De Raymtzer, translated to English by the author.

23. This might be changing, however, according to academic Philomena Essed, whose observation of the Zwarte Piet characters in the Dutch dime store HEMA suggests that the displays and characters are getting smaller or becoming less visible over the years, shrinking like the Confederate flag in Georgia's state flag prior to 2003.

24. *Het Parool*, June 3, 2002.

25. *New York Times*. November 9, 2002 (Behind the Veil: A Muslim Woman Sepeaks Out).

26. *The Age* [Melbourne], November 29, 2002.

27. "Ayaan Hirsi Ali," *Trouw*, August 15, 2005; accessed November 7, 2009, at http://www.trouw.nl/achtergrond/Dossiers/article1431856.ece.

28. A. Hirsi Ali, *De zoontjesfabriek: over vrouwen, Islam en integratie* (Amsterdam: Bol, 2002).

29. *Het Parool*, October 24, 2002; See also *Vrij Nederland* that same week.

30. Andrew Osborn, "Unlikely Martyr Who Battled the Mullahs Forced to Flee for Her life," *Observer*, November 10, 2002.

31. http://www.tegenwicht.org/30_multicult/manifest.htm January 16, 2003.

32. "Wispelturige kiezer zoekt beschutting, Gerrit Voerman en Paul Lucardie," *Trouw*, January 24, 2003, 17.

33. "Landen eisen excuus Hirsi Ali," *Trouw*, June 29, 2006; accessed November 7, 2009, at http://www.trouw.nl/archief/article365150.ece/Landen_eisen_excuus_Hirsi_Ali.

34. "Hirsi Ali roept op tot een derde feministische golf," *Trouw*, March 10, 2003, 1.

35. The play was the Lira Fonds, Stichting Doen, the VSB fonds and the city of Almere. The play is a Dutch version of the *Vagina Monologues*, which is a rip-off of the American production of the same name. See SOQ Archives, accessed November 7, 2009, at http://www.bostheaterproducties.nl/default.asp?keuze=producties&productie=25&archief=true.

36. These translate as: 'I get a wet cunt from Allah. I masturbate with my vagina toward the East." Ronald Giphart, *Gala* (Amsterdam: Podium, 2003), 35.

37. Imad El Kaka and Hatice Kursun, *Mijn geloof, Mijn geluk* (Amsterdam, 2002).

38. "De kogel is door de moskee," *Wij Amsterdammers*, November 6, 2002.

39. Interviews with five students in Amsterdam on March 11, 2003.

40. I interviewed the journalist of Moroccan descent on March 3, 2003.

41. Interview on local Amsterdam TV for minorities with a prominent KMAN member, Mr. Maroufi, in Amsterdam on March 1, 2003.

42. Abou Jahjah, Radio One interview, March 6, 2003.

43. Personal discussion with author, June 17, 2003.

44. Hans van der Beek, "Met Cheppih wordt AEL een stuk geloviger," *Het Parool*, April 12, 2003, 3.

45. Achmed T. Olgun, "Men wil alleen horen dat de Islam fout is," *NRC Handelsblad*, April 12, 2003, 8.

46. A scandal involving a member of the board of the Dutch AEL, who was accused of stealing computers, led to a lot of negative publicity for the organization and its leadership in the months of May and June 2003.

47. "Immigranten niet meer welkom" [Immigrants Are Not Welcome Anymore], *Algemeen Dagblad*, March 16, 1992.

48. "Bolkestein versus Trouw, Willem Breedveld and Jan Kuuk," *Trouw*, August 29, 1992.

49. This comes from the 1994 VVD manifesto: Investing in the Future.

50. Dick Pels, *De geest van Pim. Het gedachtegoed van een politieke dandy* (Amsterdam: Anthos, 2003); Dick Pels, *Een Zwak voor Nederland. Ideeën voor een nieuwe politiek* (Amsterdam: Anthos, 2005).

51. Liesbet van Zoonen, 2003, "After Dallas and Dynasty, We Have . . . Democracy. The Soap Factor in Politics," in J. Corner and D. Pels, eds., *Restyling Politics* (London: Sage, 2003); Liesbet van Zoonen, ed., "Popular Culture as Political Communication," special issue of *Javnost/The Public*, 2000; Liesbet van Zoonen and Christina Holtz-Bacha, "Personalization in Dutch and German Politics: The Case of the Talkshow," *Javnost/The Public*, 2000; Liesbet van Zoonen, "De talkshow: personalisering als politieke strategie," in Kees Brants and Phillip van Praag, eds., *Tussen beeld en inhoud: politiek en media in de verkiezingen van 1998* (Amsterdam: Het Spinhuis, 2000); Liesbet van Zoonen, "Broken Hearts, Broken Dreams: Politicians and Their Families in the Dutch Gossip Press," in *Gender, Politics and Communication*, ed. by Anabelle Sreberny and Liesbet van Zoonen (Cresskill, N.J.: Hampton, 2000), 101–121.

52. Wouter van der Brug, "How the LPF Fuelled Discontent: Empirical Tests of Explanations of LPF-Support," *Acta Politic International Journal of Political Science* 38, no. 1 (2003): 89–106. Research conducted by Philip van Praag also confirms this. Van der Brug's findings are based on Dutch National Election Study data; van Praags's are based on polls conducted over the course of the campaign by NIPO, which were published in the *Volkskrant* newspaper during the campaign.

53. I draw this conclusion based on my conversations with more than two dozen intellectuals (university faculty and prominent journalists), as well as local and national politicians who expressed sympathy with Hirsi Ali and her viewpoints on Islam and gender issues. Many of the left-wing intellectuals with whom I spoke volunteered that they would be voting for her, in other words, casting a personal vote for a candidate on a party list that they normally would avoid (the VVD party list) because of her outspoken stands against Islam.

54. There are also at least half a dozen journalists and other older (above age thirty-five) members of the media-political elite who see Abou Jahjah in a favourable light, as a needed counterbalance to the "overwhelming negativity of the Dutch media toward the Muslim communities," especially the Arab Muslim communities, based on conversations with me in June 2003.

55. The number of MPs of Muslim origin in the elections of 1994 was two; in 1998, this was five, two of whom were the same as 1994; and in 2003, this was five, only three of whom were the same as in 1998. John Jansen van Gaal in *Het Parool* criticized the political parties for not giving ethnic minority MPs the opportunity to build seniority in Parliament, while this was not the case for many Dutch MPs, who remained on party lists for three or more four-year terms. Even in the left-wing Green Left party, it appeared that the place on the list held by a two-term very accomplished MP of Muslim origin was handed to a younger candidate of Muslim origin, although this did not increase the number of ethnic minorities in the top ten places on the Green Left list for Parliament in May 2002.

56. Anil Ramdas, column titled "Zomaar," *NRC*, April 29, 2002.

57. Pimmel refers to somebome who embodies the ideas of Pim Fortuyn.

58. In the world such as Robert Kagan's *Paradise and Power: America & Europe in the New World Order*, Bernard Lewis's The *Crisis of Islam: Holy War and Unholy Terror*, Charles Tripp's *History of Iraq*.

CHAPTER 7

1. *Vrij Nederland*, Summer 2002.

2. Christopher Caldwell, "Daughter of the Enlightenment," *New York Times*, April 3, 2005, Section 6, p. 26.

3. *Trouw*, January 6, 2006.

4. "Hirsi Ali Botst met VVD over taken," *NRC*, June 2, 2003, 1.

5. I interviewed with Clemens Cornielje in The Hague, February 2004.

6. Geert Mak, *Gedoemd tot Kwetsbaarheid* [*Damned to Vulnerability*] (Amsterdam: Atlas, 2005); see also Jacques van Doorn, "De bruske herondekking van de islam," *Podium*, October 5, 2001.

7. Pippa Norris, *Radical Right: Voters and Parties in the Electoral Market* (New York: Cambridge University Press, 2005).

8. Zwarte Voltaire, "Linkse Pim," accessed November 7, 2009, at http://www.nrc.nl/geslotendossiers/ayaan_hirsi_ali/achtergronden/article60552.ece/Paniek_en_roem.

9. See "Dossier Hirsi Ali," *Elsevier*, accessed November 7, 2009, at http://www.elsevier.nl.

10. Koopmans and Rens Vliegenthart, "De schijn van Heiligheid: onderzoek naar de politieke invloed van Hirsi Ali," *NRC Handelsblad*, July 7, 2006, Zaterdag Bijvoegsel, 35.

11. Interview with a Muslim teacher (woman) May 15, 2005, in Amsterdam.

12. Ian Buruma, *Murder in Amsterdam: The Death of Theo van Gogh and the Limits of Tolerance* (London: Penguin, 2006).

13. Annelies Moors, "*Submission*," *Sim Review* 15 (2005): 9.

14. *Ethics: Treatise on the Emendation of the Intellect and Selected Letters* (Indianapolis, Ind.: Hackett, 1992).

15. I met Ayaan Hirsi Ali twice: once in April 2002 at a working dinner hosted by the French ambassador in The Hague on Islam and Laicite, and the second time during the Liberal Party Congress in March 2004.

16. *NRC*, May 6, 2006.

17. Ayaan Hirsi Ali, *Submission* (Amsterdam: Uitgeverij Augustus 2005), 25.

18. Ibid.

19. "They killed a Van Gogh, how can we ever erase this horrible killing from the Dutch memory." The Netherlands as an export or tourist destination draws a lot on Vincent van Gogh's artistic heritage. Ads and promotional material are very often based on the monumental work of Vincent. Vincent is more than an icon. The name Van Gogh is inscribed in Dutch culture and psyche. Van Gogh is not high culture any more—it's part of the Dutch popular culture, and it has many expressions in the public sphere. Killing a Van Gogh is a direct attack on Dutch popular culture. It is a war declaration on the Dutch, a popular culture that was already aroused by the murder of the popular Pim Fortuyn, who wanted to give back the power of *het torentje* to the people and to serve, as captured in his highly effective sound bite, "at your service." Theo van Gogh, a relative of Vincent, is popular and famous for his provocative films, talk shows, and statement "*Hij neemt geen blad voor z'n mond*," a saying that characterizes the no-nonsense popular culture, with its straightforward approach of frankness and saying what you think, even if it is politically incorrect. In fact, Pim Fortuyn and subsequently his movement were opened, discovered, and launched in this new era of frankness and *bloed und Fulk*, even it hurts. Hurting the other is a way to go to *polder*, socially and culturally. It was the start of this big delta works with a waterfront and sluices to reshape the Dutch culture as the waterworks have been done for centuries with geometric precision. In the words of Theo van Gogh, his aim was to write "*pamflet-achtige* film." "Het draait allemaal om een dialoog met Allah." "Ik ga deze film ook opsturen naar Al-Jazeera." His popular pamphlet book called *Allah weet het beter* didn't make it to any Arab media outlets except the Moroccan, Turkish, and other Muslim-based Web sites in the Netherlands and Belgium.

20. Hirsi Ali, *Zomergasten*, accessed November 7, 2009, at http://www.vpro.nl/programma/zomergasten/afleveringen/17869746/items/18934598/.

21. In *Brieven aan Ayaan Hirsi Ali* [Letters to Hirsi Ali] (Amsterdam: Prometheus, 2005), 90.

22. Ibid., 139–142.

23. Ibid., 127–132.

24. Ibid., 123–126.

25. Ibid., 69–71.

26. Minister Brinkhorst in *Vrij Nederland*, December 18, cited in "Hoe nu verder? 42 visies op de toekomst van Nederland na de moord op Theo van Gogh," *Ton van Luin* (Utrecht: Spectrum, 2005), 15; Paul Cliteur, "De eigen schuld theorie."

27. Brinkhorst, 16.

28. Maarten van Rossem, *Nederland in Crisis*, 20.

29. Ibid.

30. Ibid., 21.

31. Ibid., 23.

32. I interviewed a female Muslim teacher in July 2005 in Amsterdam.

33. See the many publications in which different people talk about the problematic atmosphere in the Netherlands after the killing of van Gogh and the movie *Submission*: "Hoe nu verder," *42 visies op de toekomst van Nederland na de moord op Theo van Gogh* (Utrecht: Spectrum, 2005); Steve Austen Kaaskoppen "Twintig jonge landgenotenover de toekomst van Nederland," *Cossee* (Amsterdam, 2005); Guido Dereksen, *Hutspot Holland: Gesprekken over de multi ethnische staat van Nederland* (Amsterdam: Atlas, 2005); *Brieven aan Ayaan Hirsi Ali* (Amsterdam: Prometeus, 2005).

34. Edward Said, *Covering Islam* (London: Vintage, 1997).

35. Christine Timmerman, Dirk Hutsebaut, Sara Mels, Walter Nonneman, and Walter Van Herk, eds., *Faith-based Radicalism: Christianity, Islam and Judaism between Constructive Activism and Destructive Fanaticism* (Brussels: Peter Lang, 2007), 115.

36. Sniderman et al., *The Outsider*, 26.

37. Sam Cherribi, "Framing Controversy on Al-Jazeera: From Cartoons to the Pope." Paper presented at the annual meetings of the International Communication Association, May 24–28, 2007, San Francisco, Calif.

38. Scholten et al, "*Fitna* and the Media: An Investigation of Attention and Role Patterns," *Netherlands News Monitor*, April 2008.

39. Ruud Koopmans and Rens Vliegenthart, "De schijn van Heiligheid: onderzoek naar de politieke invloed van Hirsi Ali," *NRC Handelsbald*, July 7, 2006, Zaterdag Bijvoegsel, 35.

40. Irshad Nanji, *The Trouble with Islam: A Muslim's Call for Reform in Her Faith* (Toronto: Random House, 2003), 3.

41. Ibid., 2.

42. Fatima Mernissi, *Beyond the Veil: Male and Female Dynamics in Modern Muslim Societies* (Bloomington: Indiana University Press, 1975).

43. I interviewed Nawal Sadawi for Dutch Radio NOS in October 1986.

44. See Leila Ahmed, *Women and Gender in Islam: Historical Roots of a Modern Debate* (New Haven, Conn.: Yale University Press, 1992); Margot Badran and Mirian

Cooke, eds., *Opening the Gates: A Century of Arab Feminist Writing* (London: Virago, 1990); Inge Boer, "The World beyond Our Window: Nomads, Traveling Theories and the Function of Boundaries," *Parallax* 3 (1996): 7–26; Homa Hoodfar, "The Veil in Their Minds and on Our Heads: The Persistence of Colonial Images of Muslim Women," *Resources for Feminist Research* 22 (2003): 5–18; David Lloyd and Lisa Lowe, eds., *The Politics of Culture in the Shadow of Capital* (Durham, N.C.: Duke University Press, 1997); Abdelkebir Khatibi, *Maghreb Pluriel* (Paris: Denoël, 1983); Marnia Lazreg, "Feminism and Difference: The Perils of Writing as a Woman on Women in Algeria," in *Conflicts in Feminism*, ed. by Marianne Hirsch and Evelyn Fox Keller (New York: Routledge, 1990), 326–349; Margot Badran, *Feminists, Islam and Nation: Gender and the Making of Modern Egypt* (Princeton, N.J.: Princeton University Press, 1995); Malika Mehdid, "A Western Invention of Arab Womanhood: The 'Oriental' Female," in *Women in the Middle East: Perceptions, Realities and Struggle for Liberation*, ed. by Halej Afshar and Samia Mehrez (London: Macmillan, 1993); Fatima Mernissi, *Le harem politique: Le Prophète et les femmes* (Paris:Albin Michel, 1987); Fatima Mernissi, *Sultanes oubliées: Femmes chefs d'Etat en Islam* (Paris, 1990); Fatna Ait Sabah, *Woman in the Muslim Unconscious*, trans. by Mary Jo Lakeland (New York: Pergamon, 1984).

45. Alain Touraine, *Le Monade Des Femmes* (Paris: Fayard, 2006).
46. Ibid., 159.
47. Ibid., 160.
48. Ibid., 163.
49. Ronald Inglehart and Pippa Norris, *Rising Tide* (Cambridge: Cambridge University Press, 2003).
50. Ibid., chapter 3.
51. *Time Magazine*.
52. Reuters. *Saudi wants Dutch MP apology for Islam offence-paper*. February 18, 2007.
53. Geert Mak, *Gedoemd*.
54. Benedictus de Spinoza, Samuel Shirley and Seymour Feldman. *The Ethics; Treatise on the Emendation of the Intellect; Selected letters*. Translated by Samuel Shirley. Hackett Publishing, 1992.
55. See International Federation for Human Rights, "Intolerance and Discrimination against Muslims in the EU," accessed November 7, 2009, at http://www.ihf-hr.org/viewbinary/viewdocument.php?download=1&doc_id=6237.
56. Robert Kaplan. *Hog Pilots, Blue Water Grunts: The American Military in the Air, at Sea, and on the Ground*. Random House, 2008.
57. Bernard Lewis, *Islam and the West* (New York: Oxford University Press, 1993), 186.

CONCLUSION

1. Sam D. Huber, Hubert Tworzecki, and Sam Cherribi, "Political Campaigning in the Enlarged Europe: Party Strategies in the June 2004 European Parliament Elections" (Article under review for publication in *European Union Politics*).
2. Abram de Swaan, "Uitgaansbeperking en uitgaansangst. Over de de verschuiving van bevelshuishouding naar onderhandelingshuishouding," in *De mens is de mens een zorg* (Amsterdam: Meulenhof, 1989), 33–50.

3. Gilles Kepel, *The War for Muslim Minds: Islam and the West* (Cambridge, Mass.: Belknap, 2004); Michèle Lamont, *The Dignity of Working Men* (Cambridge, Mass.: Harvard University Press, 2000); John Esposito, "The Muslim Diaspora and Islamic World," in *Islam in Europe: The New Social and Cultural, and Political Landscape*, ed. by Shireen T. Hunter (Westport, Conn.: Greenwood, 2002).

4. Ann Thompson, *Barbary and Enlightenment: European Attitudes toward the Maghreb in the 18th Century* (Leiden: E. J. Brill, 1987).

5. Sam Cherribi, "Politicians' Perceptions of the 'Muslim Problem': The Dutch Example in European Context," in *Democracy and the New Religious Pluralism*, ed. by Thomas Banchoff (Oxford: Oxford University Press, 2007), 113–132.

6. Peter Mandaville, *Transnational Muslim Politics: Re-imagining the Umma* (London: Routledge, 2001), 188.

7. Sam Cherribi, "Mario Vargas Llosa: Reading Is Not a Luxurious Pastime," *Global Vision* 6 (2006): 32–33.

8. Etienne Balibar, "Dissonances dans la laicite," in *Le Foulard islamique en question*, ed. by Charlotte Nordmann (Amsterdam: Editions, 2004), 16.

9. Nordmann, 42.

10. Pierre Bourdieu, "Un probleme peut en cacher un autre" in Nordmann, *Foulard islamique en question*, 45.

11. Said Bouamama, "Ethicisation et construction idéologique d'un bouc émissaire" in Nordmann, *Le Foulard islamique en question*, 37–44.

12. Bourdieu, "Un probleme," 46.

13. Ibid., 45.

14. Etienne Balibar, "Dissonances," 16.

15. Abdelmalek Sayad, *The Suffering of the Immigrant* (Cambridge, England: Polity, 2004).

16. O'Brien during a lecture at UCLA sponsored by the Center for European and Eurasian Studies and the Center for Near Eastern Studies and cosponsored by the Southern California Consortium on International Studies, as quoted in the *UCLA International Institute Newsletter* by Leslie Evans in May 2004.

17. David Rieff, writing in the *New York Times Magazine* (August 14, 2005, 11), put it this way: "A great many of Europe's Muslims don't fit in, and won't."

18. Karen Armstrong, "The Label of Catholic Terror Was Never Used about the IRA," *Guardian*, July 11, 2005.

19. Naftali Brawer, in " (Eds) Christine Timmerman, Dirk Hutsebaut, Sara Mels, Walter Nonneman & Walter Van Herk, *Faith-based Radicalism: Christianity, Islam and Judaism between Constructive Activism an Destructive Fanaticism*, Brussels, P.I.E Peter Lang s.a., 2007,12.

20. M. Arkoun and Joseph Maila, *De Manhattan à Bagdad: Au-delà Bien et du Mal* (Paris: Desclée de Brouwer, 2003); See also Arkoun, *Humanisme et Islam: Combats et Propositions* (Paris: Vrin, 2005).

21. Mohammed Arkoun, *The Unthought in Contemporary Islamic Thought* (London: Saqi, 2002), 10–28; from the new unpublished preface to the second edition of this book; Mohammed Arkoun allowed me to cite from it before publication.

22. Ibid.; see also Mohammed Arkoun, *Pour Une critique de la raison islamique* (Paris: Maisonneuve et Larose, 1984), 361.
23. Ibid.
24. Ibid.
25. Ibid.
26. Elias and Scotson, *The Established and the Outsiders*, 233.

Bibliography

Aarts, Kees, and Holli A. Semetko, "The Divided Electorate: Media Use and Political Involvement," *Journal of Politics*, 65 (2003): 759–784.
Ahmed, Leila, *Women and Gender in Islam: Historical Roots of a Modern Debate*. New Haven, Conn.: Yale University Press, 1992.
Ait Sabah, Fatna, *Woman in the Muslim Unconscious*. New York: Pergamon, 1984.
Ali, Ayaan Hirsi, *Brieven aan Ayaan Hirsi Ali* [Letters to Hirsi Ali]. Amsterdam: Prometheus, 2005.
Ali, Ayaan Hirsi. *Submission*. Amsterdam: Uitgeverij Augustus, 2005.
Ali, Ayaan Hirsi, *De zoontjesfabriek: over vrouwen, Islam en integratie*. Amsterdam: Bol., 2002.
AlSayyad, Nezar, and Castells, Manuel, *Muslim Europe or Euro Islam: Politics, Culture and Citizenship in the Age of Globalization*. Lanham, Md.: Lexington, 2001.
Anderson, Benedict, *Imagined Communities: Reflections on the Origin and Spread of Nationalism*. London: Verso, 1991.
Andeweg, Rudy B., and Galen A. Irwin, *Governance and Politics of the Netherlands*. New York: Palgrave Macmillan, 2002.
An-Na'im, Abdullahi Ahmed, *Islam and the Secular State: Negotiating the Future of Shari'a*. Cambridge, Mass.: Harvard University Press, 2008.
Ansari, Humayun, *The Infidel Within: Muslims in Britain since 1800*. London: C. Hurst, 2004.
Arkoun (ed.). *La France et ses musulmans: Un siècle de politique Musulmane 1895–2005* (Fayard, 2006), 344.
Arkoun, Mohammed, *Histoire de L'Islam et des Musulmans en France, du Moyen age a nos jours*. Paris: Michel Albin, 2007.
Arkoun, Mohammed, *Humanisme et Islam: Combats et Propositions*. Paris: Vrin, 2005.

Arkoun, Mohammed, *The Unthought in Contemporary Islamic Thought*. London: Saqi, 2002.
Arkoun, Mohammed, Interview. Paris: June 2002.
Arkoun, Mohammed, *Lectures du Coran*, 2nd ed. Tunis: Alif: 1991.
Arkoun, Mohammed, *L'Islam, morale et politique*. Paris: Desclée de Brouwer, 1986.
Arkoun, Mohammed, *Pour une critique de la raison islamique*. Paris: Maisonneuve et Larose: 1984.
Arkoun, Mohammed, and Joseph Maila, *De Manhattan à Bagdad. Au-delà du bien et du mal*. Paris: Desclée de Brouwer, 2003.
Armstrong, Karen, "The Label of Catholic Terror Was Never Used about the IRA," *Guardian*, July 11, 2005.
Assad, Talal, "*Formations of the Secular: Christianity, Islam, Modernity*," Stanford: Calif.: Stanford University Press: 2003. 159.
Austen, Steve, Kaaskoppen, *Twintig jonge landgenotenover de toekomst van Nederland. Cossee* Amsterdam, 2005.
Bader, Veit, "The Cultural Conditions of Transnational Citizenship: On the Interpretation of Political and Ethnic Cultures," *Political Theory* 25 (1997): 771–813.
Badran, Margot, *Feminists, Islam and Nation: Gender and the Making of Modern Egypt*. Princeton, N.J.: Princeton University Press, 1995.
Badran, Margot, and Miriam Cooke, *Opening the Gates: A Century of Arab Feminist Writing*. London: Virago, 1990.
Balibar, Etienne, "Dissonances dans la laïcité," in *Le Foulard islamique en question*, ed. by Charlotte Nordmann. Amsterdam: Editions, 2004. 15–27.
Bencheikh, Soheib, *Marianne et le prophète, l'islam dans la France laïque*. Paris: Grasset, 1998.
Bennett, W. Lance, *News: The Politics of Illusion*, 4th ed. New York: Addison-Wesley Longman, 2001.
Bessems, Kustaw, and Helene Butijin, "de Verdieping: Abou Jahjah heft altijd een antwoord," *Trouw*, March 8, 2003, p. 15.
Blumler, Jay G., and Michael Gurevitch, *The Crisis in Public Communication*. London: Routledge, 1995.
Boer, Inge, "The World beyond Our Window: Nomads, Traveling Theories and the Function of Boundaries," *Parallax* 3 (1996): 7–26.
Bolkenstein, Frits, *Moslem in de Polder*. Amsterdam: Contact, 1997.
Bouamama, Said, "Ethicisation et construction idéologique d'un bouc émissaire" in *Le Foulard islamique en question*, ed. by Charlotte Nordmann. Amsterdam: Editions, 2004, 37–44.
Bourdieu, Pierre, "Un probleme peut en cacher un autre," in *Le Foulard islamique en question*, ed. by Charlotte Nordmann. Amsterdam: Editions, 2004.
Bourdieu, Pierre, *La Domination masculine*. Paris: Seuil, 1998.
Bourdieu, Pierre, *Les Règles de l'art. Genèse et structure du champ littéraire*. Paris: Seuil, 1992.
Bourdieu, Pierre, *Le Sens pratique*. Paris: Minuit, 1980.
Bourdieu, Pierre, *La Distinction. Critique sociale du jugement*. Paris: Minuit, 1979.
Bourdieu, Pierre, *Esquisse d'une théorie de la pratique*, précédé de *Trois études d'ethnologie kabyle*. Geneva: Droz, 1972.

Bourdieu, Pierre, *Sociologie de l'Algérie*, Paris, PUF, coll. « Que sais-je ? », 1958 [2002 (8ᵉ éd.)].
Bourdieu, Pierre, et al., *La misère du monde*. Paris: Seuil: 1993
Brachet, Philippe, *Descartes n'est pas Marocain*. Paris: Pensée Universelle, 1982.
Naftali Brawer in (Eds) Christine Timmerman, Dirk Hutsebaut, Sara Mels, Walter Nonneman &Walter Van Herk. "Faith-based Radicalism: Christianity, Islam and Judaism between Constructive Activism an Destructive Fanaticism," Brussels, P.I.E Peter Lang s.a., 2007.
Brettell, Caroline, and James Frank Hollifield, *Migration Theory: Talking across the Disciplines*. London: Routledge, 2000.
Brewer, Paul R., and Clyde Wilcox, "Trends: Same-Sex Marriage and Civil Unions," *Public Opinion Quarterly* 69 (2005): 599–616.
Brinkhorst, Laurens Jan "Hoe nu verder? 42 visies op de toekomst van Nederland na de moord op Theo van Gogh," in *Ton van Luin*. Utrecht: Spectrum, 2005.
Brubaker, Rogers, *Citizenship and Nationhood in France and Germany*. Cambridge, Mass.: Harvard University Press, 1992.
Brubaker, Rogers. "Ethnicity without groups," *European Journal of Sociology (Archives Europeenes de Sociologie)* 43 (2002): 173–175.
Buruma, Ian, *Murder in Amsterdam, the Death of Theo van Gogh and the Limits of Tolerance*. London: Penguin Press, 2006.
Buijs, F., *Een moskee in de wijk: de vestiging van de Kocatepe moskee in Rotterdam-Zuid*, Amsterdam: Het Spinhuis.1998.
Caldwell, Christopher, "Daughter of the Enlightenment," *New York Times*, April 3, 2005, p. 26.
Cherribi, Sam, "Politicians' Perceptions of the 'Muslim Problem': The Dutch Example in European Context," in *Democracy and the New Religious Pluralism*, ed. by Thomas Banchoff. New York: Oxford University Press, 2007.
Cherribi, Sam, "Framing Controversy on Al-Jazeera: From Cartoons to the Pope." Paper presented at the annual meetings of the International Communication Association, May 24–28, 2007, San Francisco, Calif.
Cherribi, Sam, "Mario Vargas Llosa: Reading Is Not a Luxurious Pastime." *Global Vision* 6 (2006): 32–33.
Cherribi, Sam, *Les imams d'Amsterdam*. Amsterdam: University of Amsterdam, 2000.
Cherribi, Oussama. *Les Imams D'Amsterdam*. Amsterdam: University of Amsterdam, 2000.
Cherribi, Oussama, "De borrelpraat van Pim Fortuyn. Bespreking van Tegen de islammisering van Nederland," *Liberaal Reveil* 38 (1987): 3.
De Mas, Paolo. "Dynamique récente de la migration marocaine vers les Pays-Bas: spécificité régionale et réseau rifain." In *Le Maroc et la Hollande. Actes du IVe rencontre universitaire maroco-neerlandaise* (Colloques et Séminaires 39). Rabat: Universite Mohammed V, 1995, pp. 213–228.
De Tocqueville, Alexis. "De la colonie en Algérie," Report of the Parliamentary Commission of 1847 (Paris: Editions Complexe, 1988);

Dereksen, Guido, *Hutspot Holland: Gesprekken over de multi ethnische staat van Nederland*. Amsterdam: Atlas, 2005.
Dummett, Michael, *On Immigration and Refugees (Thinking in Action)*. London: Routledge, 2001.
Duyvendak, Jan Willem, and R. Rijkschroeff, "De bronnen van het integratiebeleid," *Sociologische Gids* 51 (2004).
Duyvendak, Jan Willem, and R. Rijkschroeff, "De omstreden betekenis van zelforganisaties," *Sociologische Gids* 51 (2004).
Eickelman, Dale, "Clifford Geertz and Islam," in *Richard Clifford Geertz by His Colleagues*, ed. by Richard A. Shweder and Byron Good. Chicago: University of Chicago Press, 2005, pp. 63–75.
Eickelman, Dale, *Moroccan Islam: Tradition and Society in a Pilgrimage Center*. Austin: University of Texas Press, 1976.
Elias, Norbert, and John L. Scotson, *The Established and the Outsiders: A Sociological Enquiry into Community Problems*. London: Frank Cass, 1965.
El Kaka, Imad, and Hatice Kursun, *Mijn geloof, Mijn geluk*. Amsterdam: Schorerstichting, 2002.
El-Nawawy, Mahammed, and Adel Iskandar, *Al-Jazeera: How the Free Arab News Network Scooped the World and Changed the Middle East*. Boulder, Colo.: Westview, 2003.
Emanticpatie Monitor, 2006, http://www.cbs.nl/NR/rdonlyres/74B6DC34-B135-45CE-A34D-98147FB681AD/0/Emancipatiemonitor_2006.pdf.
Entman, Robert M., and Andrew Rojecki, *The Black Image in the White Mind: Media and Race in America*. Chicago: University of Chicago Press, 2001.
Esposito, John, "The Muslim Diaspora and Islamic World," in *Islam in Europe: The New Social, Cultural, and Political Landscape*, ed. by Shireen T. Hunter. Westport, Conn.: Greenwood, 2002.
Esposito, John, and Francois Burgat, *Modernizing Islam: Religion in the Public Sphere in the Middle East and Europe*. London: Hurst and New Brunswick, N.J.: Rutgers University Press, 2003.
Fortuyn, Pim, *De Puinhopen van Acht Jaar Paars*. Rotterdam: Karakter Uitgevers, 2002.
Fortuyn, Pim, *De Islamisiering van Nederland: Nederlands identiteit als fundament*. Uithoorn: Karakter Uitgevers, 2001.
Fortuyn, Pim, *Tegen de Islamisering van Nederland*. Uithoorn: Karakter Uitgevers, 1997.
Fortuyn, Pim, *Het Zakenkabinet Fortuyn*. Utrecht: Bruna, 1994.
Fortuyn, Pim, *Aan het Volk van Nederland: de contractmaatschappij, een politiek economische zedenschets*. Amsterdam: Contact, 1992.
Freeman Gary P. "The Decline of Sovereignty? Politics and Immigration Restriction in Liberal States," *Challenge to the Nation-State: Immigration in Western Europe and the United States*, ed. by Christian Joppke. New York: Oxford University Press, 1998.
Freeman, Gary P., "Modes of Immigration Politics in Liberal Democratic States," *International Migration Review* 29 (1995): 881–902.

Freeman, Gary P., "Can Liberal States Control Unwanted Migration?" *Annals of the American Academy of Politics and Social Sciences* 534 (1994): 17–30.
Freeman, Gary P., "The Consequence of Immigration Policies for Immigrant Status: A British and French Comparison," Ethnic and Racial Minorities in Advanced Industrial Democracies., ed. Anthony Messina, Luis Fraga, Laurie RhodeBeck, and Frederick Wright (New York: Greenwood, 1992).
Gamson, William A., *Talking Politics*. New York: Cambridge University Press, 1992.
Gauchet, Marcel, *Le désenchantement du Monde: une histoire politique de la religion*. Paris: Gallimard, 1985.
Geertz, Clifford, *Islam Observed: Religious Developments in Morocco and Indonesia*. London: University of Chicago Press, 1968.
Gerholm, Thomas, and Yngve Georg Litman, *The New Islamic Presence in Western Europe*. London: Mansell, 1990.
Giphart, Ronald, *Gala*. Amsterdam: Podium, 2003.
Gladwell, Christopher, "Islamic Europe," *Weekly Standard*, October 4, 2004.
Goffman, Erving, *Frame Analysis*. San Francisco, Calif.: Harper Colophon, 1974.
Goody, Jack, *Islam in Europe*. Cambridge, England: Polity, 2004.
Goytisolo, J., "Strangers among Us (Europe's Long-Held Fear of Islam)," *Index on Censorship* 28 (1999): 60–65.
Graber, Doris A., *Processing Politics: Learning from Television in the Internet Age*. Chicago: University of Chicago Press, 2001.
Gresh, Alain, *Islam de France, Islams d'Europe*. Paris: L'Harmattan, 2004.
Guler, Nulifer, "La question de la femme et Le republicanisme et la laïcité. Regards croisés entre la Turquie et la France," *Gresh* (2004): 599–616.
Haddad, Yvonne Yazbeck, and Jane I. Smith, *Muslim Minorities in the West: Visible and Invisible*. Walnut Creek, Calif.: Altamira, 2002.
Hagendoom, Louk, and Paul Sniderman, *When Ways of Life Collide: Multiculturalism and Its Discontents in the Netherlands*. Princeton, N.J.: Princeton University Press, 2007.
Hansen, Randall, and Patrick Weil, *Dual Nationality, Social Rights and Federal Citizenship in the U.S. and Europe: The Reinvention of Citizenship*. London: Berghahn, 2002.
Hervieu-Léger, Danièle "Islam and the Republic: The French Case", in *Democracy and the New Religious Pluralism*, ed. by Thomas Banchoff. New York: Oxford University Press, 2007, pp 203–222.
Hoodfar, Homa, "The Veil in Their Minds and on Our Heads: The Persistence of Colonial Images of Muslim." *Resources for Feminist Research* 22 (2003): 5–18.
Huber, Sam D., Hubert Tworzecki, and Sam Cherribi, "Political Campaigning in the Enlarged Europe: Party Strategies in the June 2004 European Parliament Elections." Presentation at the 3rd Annual Pre-APSA Conference on Political Communication: Faith, Fun and Futuramas, Chicago.
Inglehart, Ronald, and Pippa Norris, *Rising Tide: Gender Equality and Cultural Change*. Cambridge, England: Cambridge University Press, 2003.

Ireland, Patrick, *The Policy Challenge of Ethnic Diversity: Immigrant Politics in France and Switzerland*. Cambridge, Mass.: Harvard University Press, 1994.
Israel, Jonathan, *Radical Enlightenment: Philosophy and the Making of Modernity*. Oxford, England: Oxford University Press, 2001.
Israel, Jonathan, *The Dutch Republic: Its Rise, Greatness and Fall 1477–1806*. Oxford, England: Clarendon, 1995.
Israel, Jonathan, *The Dutch Republic and the Hispanic World, 1606–1661*. New York: Oxford University Press, 1982.
Jahjah, Dyab Ahou, and Zohra Othman, "Resist! Veel meer dan een cultuurschok, Opgetekend door Han Soete & Christophe Callewaert van Indymedia," Berchem: EPA, 2003.
Joppke, Christian, *Immigration and the Nation-State: The United States, Germany, and Great Britain*. Oxford: Oxford University Press, 2000.
Kalmijn, Mathijs, "Status Homogamy in the United States," *American Journal of Sociology* 97, (1991): 496–523.
Kepel, Gilles, *The War for Muslim Minds: Islam and the West*. Cambridge, Mass.: Belknap Press, 2006.
Kepel, Gilles, *Les banlieues de L'Islam: Naissance d'une religion en France*. Paris: Seuil, 1987.
Kepel, Gilles, Le Prophete et Pharaon: les mouvements islamistes dans l'Egypte contemporaine. Paris: La Decouverte, 1984.
Khatibi, Abdelkebir, *Maghreb Pluriel*. Paris: Denoël, 1983.
Klausen, Klausen, "Taking a Cue from the Danish Cartoon Scandal" in *Spiegel* on March 28, 2008 accessed on March 30 http://www.spiegel.de/international/europe/0,1518,druck-543378,00.html
Klausen, Jytte, *The **Islamic Challenge**: Politics and Religion in Western Europe*. Oxford University Press. 2005
Kleinnijenhuis, Jan, et al., *De puinhopen in het nieuws: De rol van de media bij de Tweede Kamerverkiezingen van 2002*. Alphen aan den Rijn-Mechelen: Kluwer, 2002.
Koopmans, Ruud, "Germany and Its Immigrants: An Ambivalent Relationship," *Journal of Ethnic and Migration Studies* 24 (1999): 627–647.
Koopmans, Ruud, "Explaining the Rise of Racist and Extreme Right Violence in Western Europe: Grievances or Opportunities," *European Journal of Political Research* 30 (1996): 185–216.
Koopmans, Ruud, and Paul Statham, "Migration and Ethnic Relations as Field of Political Contention: An Opportunity Structure Approach," *Challenging Immigration and Ethnic Relations Politics: Comparative European Perspectives*, edited by Ruud Koopmans and Paul Statham. Oxford: Oxford University Press, 2000, pp. 13–56.
Koopmans, Ruud, and Rens Vliegenthart, "De schijn van Heiligheid: onderzoek naar de politieke invloed van Hirsi Ali," *NRC Handelsblad*, July 7, 2006, p. 35.

Koslowski, Rey. *Migrants and Citizens: Demographic Change in the European State System*. Ithaca, N.Y.: Cornell University Press, 2002.

Kressel, Neil J, *Bad Faith: The Danger of Religious Extremism*. Amherst, N.Y.: Prometheus, 2007.

Kyle, David, and Rey Koslowski, eds., *Global Human Smuggling: Comparative Perspectives*. Baltimore, Md.: Johns Hopkins University Press, 2001.

Kymlicka, Will, *Multicultural Citizenship: A Liberal Theory of Minority Rights*. Oxford, England: Clarendon, 1995.

Laguerre, Michel, *Minoritized Space: An Inquiry into the Spatial Order of Things*. Berkeley, Calif.: Institute of Governmental Studies Press, 1999.

Lamont, Michèle, *The Dignity of Working Men: Morality and the Boundaries of Race, Class, and Immigration*. Cambridge, Mass.: Harvard University Press, 2000.

Lamont, Michèle,- Money, Morals, and Manners:The Culture of the French and the American Upper-Middle Class. Chicago: University of Chicago Press, 1992.

Landman, Nico, *Van mat tot minaret: De institutionalisering van de Islam in Nederland*. Amsterdam: VU, 1992.

Lazreg, Marnia, "Feminism and Difference: The Perils of Writing as a Woman on Women in Algeria," in *Conflicts in Feminism*, ed. by Marianne Hirsch and Evelyn Fox Keller. New York: Routledge, 1990, pp. 326–349.

Lechner, Frank, *The Netherlands: Globalization and National Identity*. New York: Routledge, 2008.

Levy, Bernard Henri, *American Vertigo: Traveling in the Footsteps of de Tocqueville*. New York: Random House, 2006.

Lewis, Bernard, *Cultures in Conflict: Christians, Muslims and Jews in the Age of Discovery*. New York: Oxford University Press, 1995.

Lewis, Bernard, *Islam and the West*. New York: Oxford University Press, 1993.

Lewis, Bernard, and Dominique Schnapper, *Muslims in Europe*. London: Pinter, 1994.

Phillip Lewis, "Beyond Victimhood: From the Global to the Local, a British Case Study," in Cersari J., (ed.) European Muslims and the Secular State in a comparative perspective: final symposium report, 30 June and July 1 2003.

Lijphart, Arend, *The Politics of Accommodation: Pluralism and Democracy in the Netherlands*. Berkeley: University of California Press, 1968.

Lowe, Lisa, and David Lloyd, *The Politics of Culture in the Shadow of Capital*. Durham, N.C.: Duke University Press, 1997.

Mak, Geert, *Gedoemd tot Kwetsbaarheid [Damned to vulnerability]*. Amsterdam: Atlas, 2005.

Brigitte Marechal, Stephano Alievi, Felice Dassetto and Jorgen Nielsen(eds), Muslims in the Enlarged Europe: Religion and Society, Leiden: Brill, 2003.

Matar, Nabil I., *Islam in Britain, 1558–1685* (Cambridge, England: Cambridge University Press, 1998),

Mazzoleni, Gianpietro, Julianne Stewart, and Bruce Horsfield, eds., *The Media and Neo-Populism: A Contemporary Comparative Analysis*. Westport, Conn.: Praeger, 2003.

Mechoulan, Henri, *Amsterdam au temps de Spinoza*. Paris: PUF, 1990.
Meershoek, Patrick, "Blunder van de eeuw op video [*Blunder of the century on video*]," *Het Parool*, May 6, 2003, p. 16.
Mehdid, Malika, "A Western Invention of Arab Womanhood: The 'Oriental' Female," in *Women in the Middle East: Perceptions, Realities and Struggle for Liberation*, ed. by Haleh Afshar. London: Macmillan, 1993.
Mernissi, Fatima, *Sultanes oubliées: Femmes chefs d'Etat en Islam*. Paris: Albin Michel, 1990.
Mernissi, Fatima, *Le harem politique: Le Prophète et les femmes*. Paris: Albin Michel, 1987.
Mernissi, Fatima, *Beyond the Veil: Male and Female Dynamics in Modern Muslim Societies*. Bloomington: Indiana University Press, 1975.
Milikowski, Marisca, "Exploring a Model of De-Ethnicization: The Case of Turkish Television in the Netherlands," *European Journal of Communication* 15 (2000): 443–468.
Miller, Mark J., "The Political Impact of Foreign Labour," *International Migration Revie* 16 (1982): 27–60.
Miller, Mark J., *Foreign Workers in Western Europe: An Emerging Political Force?* New York: Praeger, 1981.
Mimouni, Rachid, *De la barbarie en général et de l'intégrisme en particulier*. Paris: Le Pré aux Clercs-Belfond, 1992.
Moors, Annelies, "*Submission*," *Review* 15 (Spring 2005): 9.
Nanji, Irshad, *The Trouble with Islam: A Muslim's Call for Reform in Her Faith*. Toronto: Random House, 2003.
Nielsen, Jorgen, "L'Islam en Grande-Bretagne," in *Islam de France, Islams d'Europe*, ed. by Alain Gresh. Paris: L'Harmattan, 2004.
Norris, Pippa, *Radical Right: Parties and Electoral Competition*. New York: Cambridge University Press, 2005.
O'Brien, Peter, Lecture. University of California, Los Angeles, May 2004.
Olgun, Achmed T., "Men will alleen horen dat de Islam fout is," *NRC Handelsblad*, April 12, 2003, p. 8.
Olgun, Achmed T.,"Immigranten niet meer welkom [Immigrants Are Not Welcome Any More]," *Algemeen Dagblad*, March 16, 2003.
Patterson. Thomas E., *The Vanishing Voter*. New York: Knopf, 2002.
Pels, Dick, *Een Zwak voor Nederland. Ideeën voor een nieuwe politiek*. Amsterdam: Anthos, 2005.
Pels, Dick, *De geest van Pim. Het gedachtegoed van een politieke dandy*. Amsterdam: Anthos, 2003.
Pels, Dick, "Populism is niet alleen slecht," *Vrij Nederland*, May 3, 2003, pp. 35–37.
Ramdas, Anil, "Somaar," *NRC*, April 29, 2002.
Rath, Jan, *Minorisering: de sociale constructie van "etnische minderheden*." Amsterdam: Sua, 1991.
Rimmerman, Craig A., Kenneth D. Wald, and Clyde Wilcox, *The Politics of Gay Rights*. Chicago: University of Chicago Press, 2005.

Roele, Marcel, "Vacature: Fortuyn," *HP de Tijd*, May 3, 2003, p. 23.
Rubin, Uri, *The Eye of the Beholder: The Life of Muhammad as Viewed by the Early Muslims, A Textual Analysis*. Princeton, N.J.: Darwin, 1995.
Sadawi, Nawal, Interview, Dutch Radio NOS, October 1986.
Said, Edward, *Covering Islam*. London: Vintage, 1997.
Said, Edward, *Orientalism*. New York: Vintage, 1979.
Sartre, Jean Paul, *L'Existentialisme est un Humanisme*. Paris: Nagel, 1946.
Sassen, Saskia, "Regulating Immigration in a Global Age: A New Policy Landscape," *Annals of the American Academy of Political and Social Sciences* 570 (2000): 65–77.
Sassen, Saskia, *Guests and Aliens*. New York: New Press, 1999.
Sayad, Abdelmalek, *The Suffering of the Immigrant*. Cambridge, England: Polity, 2004.
Shirley, Samuel, Ethics, Treatise on the Emendation of the Intellect and Selected Letters. Indianapolis, Ind.: Hackett: 1992.
Scholten, Otto., Nel Ruitgrok, Martijn Krijt, Joep Schaper and Hester Paanakker "Fitna and the Media: An Investigation of Attention and Role Patterns," Netherlands News Monitor, April 2008.
Schudson, Michael, *The Sociology of News*. New York: W. W. Norton, 2003.
Schuyt, Kees, "Steunberen van de samenleving," in *Sociologische Essays*. Amsterdam: Amsterdam University Press, 2006.
Semetko, Holli A., and Patti M. Valkenburg, "Framing European Politics: A Content Analysis of Press and Television News," *Journal of Communication* 50 (2000): 93–109.
Sinnema, Hans, "Kiesrecht," *ACB Report*, 1986.
Sniderman, Paul, and Louk Hagendoorn, *When Ways of Life Collide: Multiculturalism and Its Discontents in The Netherlands*. Princeton, N.J.: Princeton University Press, 2007.
Sniderman, Paul, et al., *The Outsider: Prejudice and Politics in Italy*. Princeton, N.J.: Princeton University Press, 2002.
Snow, David, and Robert D. Benford, "Ideology, Frame Resonance and Participant Mobilization," *International Social Movement Research* 1 (1988): 197–217.
"Spain Launches Immigrant Amnesty," *BBC News*, February 7, 2005, accessed November 4, 2009, at http://news.bbc.co.uk/2/hi/europe/4242411.stm.
Stewart, Julianne, and Bruce Horsfield, "Conclusion: Power to the Media Managers," in *The Media and Neo-Populism: A Contemporary Comparative Analysis*, ed. by Gianpietro Mazzoleni, Julianne Stewart, and Bruce Horsfield. Westport, Conn.: Praeger, 2003.
Strijp, Ruud, *Om de Moskee. Het religieuze leven van Marokkaanse Migranten in een Nederlandse Provinciestad*. Amsterdam: Thesis.1998.
Swaan, Abram de, *Bakens in niemandsland: Opstellen over massaal geweld*. Amsterdam: Uitgeverij Bert Bakker, 2007.
Swaan, Abram de, "Uitgaansbeperking en uitgaansangst. Over de de verschuiving van bevelshuishouding naar onderhandelingshuishouding," in *De mens is de mens een zorg*. Amsterdam: Meulenhof, 1989.
Tarrow, Sidney, *Power in Movement: Social Movements, Collective Action and Politics*. Cambridge, England: Cambridge University Press, 1994.

Tarrow, Sidney, *Democracy and Disorder: Protest and Politics in Italy 1963–1975*. Oxford: Clarendon, 1989.
Tayob, Abdolkader, Islam in South africa: Mosques, Imams and Sermons.Miami: University of florida Press, 1999.
Ternisien, Xavier, *La France des mosquées*. Paris: Albin Miche, 2002.
Thompson, Ann, *Barbary and Enlightenment: European Attitudes toward the Maghreb in the 18th Century*. Leiden: E. J. Brill, 1987.
Thranhardt, Dietrich, "Conflict, Consensus, and Policy Outcomes: Immigration and Integration in Germany and the Netherlands," in *Challenging Immigration and Ethnic Relations Politics: Comparative European Perspectives*, ed. by Ruud Koopmans and Paul Statham. Oxford: Oxford University Press, 2000, pp. 162–186.
Tilly, Charles, *From Mobilisation to Revolution*. Reading, Mass.: Addison-Wesley, 1978.
Tilly, Charles, Louise Tilly, and Richard Tilly, *The Rebellious Century 1830–1930*. Cambridge, Mass.: Harvard University Press, 1975.
Timmerman, Christine, Dirk Hutsebaut, Sara Mels, Walter Nonneman, and Walter Van Herk, eds., *Faith-based Radicalism: Christianity, Islam and Judaism between Constructive Activism and Destructive Fanaticism*. Brussels: Peter Lang, 2007.
Touraine, Alain, *Le Monde des Femmes*. Paris: Fayard, 2006.
Touraine, Alan, and Abram de Swaan, Public lecture about Tolerance, moderated by Paul Scheffer, June 28, 2001 in the Amsterdam Political and cultural Center: De Balie Amsterdam.
Van der Beek, Hans, "Met Cheppih wordt AEL een stuk geloviger," *Het Parool*, April 12, 2003, p. 3.
Van den Berg-Eldring, Lotty, *Van gastarbeider tot immigrant. Marokkanen en Turken in Nederland*. Alphen an den Rijn: Samsom, 1986.
Van den Berg-Eldring, Lotty, *Marokkaanse gezinnen in Nederland*. Alphen an de Rijn: Samsom, 1978.
Van der Brug, Wouter, "How the LPF Fuelled Discontent," *Acta Politica: International Journal of Political Science* 38 (2003): 89–106.
Van der Linden, Jos, "Rassenwaan: De Amerikaanse obsessie met discriminatie en segregatie," *De Academische Boekengids* 2 (2003): 13–15.
Van der Veer, Peter, *Religious Nationalism. Hindus and Muslims in India*. Los Angeles: University of California Press, 1994.
Van Dijk, Teun, *Elite Discourse and Racism*. London: Sage, 1993.
Van Dijk, Teun, *Communicating Racism: Ethnic Prejudice in Thought and Talk*. London: Sage, 1989.
Van Doorn, Jacques, "De bruske herondekking van de Islam," *Podium*, October 5, 2001.
Van Driel, Barry, *Confronting Islamophobia in Educational Practice*. Stoke-on-Trent, England: Trentham, 2004.
Van Zoonen, Liesbet, "After *Dallas* and *Dynasty*, We Have . . . Democracy. The Soap Factor in Politics," in *Restyling Politics*, ed. by J. Corner and D. Pels. London: Sage, 2003.

Van Zoonen, Liesbet, "Popular Culture as Political Communication," *Javnost/The Public* 7(2) (2000), 5–18.
Van Zoonen, Liesbet, "Broken Hearts, Broken Dreams: Politicians and Their Families in the Dutch Gossip Press," in *Gender, Politics and Communication*, ed. by A. Sreberny and L. van Zoonen. Cresskill, N.J.: Hampton, 2000, pp. 101–121.
Van Zoonen, Liesbet, "De talkshow: personalisering als politieke strategie," in *Beeld en Inhoud: politiek en media in de verkiezingen van 1998*, ed. by K. Brants and P. van Praag. Amsterdam: Het Spinhuis, 2000.
Van Zoonen, Liesbet, "A Day at the Zoo: Politicians, Pigs and Popular Culture," *Media, Culture and Society* 20 (1998): 183–200.
Van Zoonen, Liesbet, "Finally I Have My Mother Back: Male and Female Politicians in Popular Culture," *Harvard International Journal of Press/Politics* 3 (1998): 48–64.
Van Zoonen, Liesbet, "Making Politics Popular," *Media, Culture and Society* 20(2) (1998): 183–200.
Van Zoonen, Liesbet, and Christina Holtz-Bacha, "Personalization in Dutch and German Politics: The Case of the Talkshow," *Javnost/The Public* (2000), 45–57.
Vertovec, Steven, and Ceri Peach, *Islam in Europe, the Politics of Religion and Community*. New York: St. Martin's, 1999.
Voerman, Gerrit, and Paul Lucardie, "Wispelturige kiezer zoekt beschutting," Trouw, January 24, 2003, p. 17.
Von der Fuhr, Gijs, Interview. Café Het Paleis in Amsterdam, June 1999.
Vries, Hent de, "In Media Res: Global Religion, Public Spheres, and the Task of Contemporary Comparative Religious Studies," in Vries, Hent de, and Samuel Weber, eds., Religion and Media. Stanford, Calif.A: Stanford University Press, 2001. pp 3–42.
Vries, Hent de, and Samuel Weber, eds., *Religion and Media*. Stanford, Calif.: Stanford University Press, 2001.
Wacquant, Loïc, and Sébastien Chauvin, *Parias urbains: Ghetto, banlieues, Etat*. Paris: La Découverte, 2006.
Walgrave, Stefaan, *The Making of the (Issues of the) Vlaams Blok*, paper presented at the annual meeting of the American Political Science Association, 2002.
Walgrave, Stefaan, and Peter van Aelst, "The Contingent Nature of Agenda-Setting: Different Agenda-Setting Dynamic in Elections and Non-Election Times?" Paper presented at 3rd Annual Pre-APSA Conference on Political Communication: Faith, Fun and Futuramas, 2004.
Waardenburg, Jacques, *L'Islam dans le miroir de l'Occident*. The Hague: Mouton, 1961.
Waardenburg, Jacques, "Integratie, moslims en Islam:een verkenning". In K. Wachtendonk, [ed] Islam in *Nederland, Islam op school*. Muidenberg: Coutinho, 1987, 31–48.
Zolberg, Aristide R., and Peter Benda, eds., *Global Migrants, Global Refugees: Problems and Solutions*. London: Berghahn, 2001.

Index

Aarts, Kees, 245, 257
Aartsen, Jozias van, 191, 192
Abd al-Ghaffar, 64, 65
Abou Jahjah, Dyab, 155, 156, 157, 158, 159, 160, 161, 165, 171, 173, 178, 179, 180, 181, 182, 183, 184, 185, 247, 248, 249, 250, 258
AEL, 155, 156, 157, 158, 159, 160, 161, 180, 181, 183, 184, 248, 249, 266
Agenda-setting, 235, 267
Alarabiya, 205
Al-Jazeera, 141, 205, 206, 228, 229, 245, 251, 252, 259, 260
Albin Michel, 243, 253, 264
Algemeen Dagblad, 148, 150, 246, 248, 249, 264
Algeria, 7, 8, 13, 27, 28, 30, 33, 39, 42, 46, 47, 48, 49, 60, 67, 95, 120, 205, 212, 226, 240, 253, 263
Algerians, 7, 8, 28, 33, 39, 42, 46, 95
Ali, 184, 196, 249, 257
Allah, 15, 71, 87, 88, 89, 98, 112, 113, 127, 177, 202, 203, 209, 249, 251
  house of, 87, 88, 91
Alphen, 241, 247, 262, 266

Amicales, 28, 29, 69, 70, 71, 72, 73, 75, 76
Amsterdam, city of, 86, 159, 161
Amsterdam Center for Foreigners, 8, 242
Anderson, Benedict, 138, 141, 245, 257
An-Na'iem, Abdulahi, 20, 234, 257
Anti-immigrant, 50, 142, 169, 184
Anti-immigrant message, 151, 184
Anti-Islam, 153, 182
Anti-Muslim, 207, 218
Antwerp, 40, 155, 156, 179, 180, 181
Arab countries, 39, 158
Arab media, 205, 206
Arab street, 205
Arabic-speaking imams, 17, 25, 108
Arabs, 6, 11, 12, 15, 33, 55, 123, 157, 178
Arkoun, Mohammed, vii, 6, 17, 46, 59, 60, 64, 227, 228, 229, 230, 233, 234, 235, 238, 239, 240, 242, 254, 255, 257, 258
Armstrong, Karen, 227, 254, 258
Assad, Talal, 57, 60, 176, 187, 239, 251, 258
Assimilation, 17, 58, 61, 62, 89, 102, 103, 139

Attacom, 57, 58
Austria, 38, 39, 40, 134, 136

Balibar, Etienne, 254, 258
Balkenende, Jan Peter, 171, 172,
  173, 175, 189, 191, 197, 209, 235
Banlieues, 18, 59, 239, 242, 243, 262,
  267
Banlieusisation, 32, 174
Barend en Van Dorp, 136, 146, 165, 166
BBC, 134, 146, 236, 238, 247, 265
  Jemery Paxman, 10
Beckett, Samuel, 3, 133
Belgium, 6, 18, 37, 39, 41, 61, 75, 120,
  137, 155, 156, 157, 158, 159, 178,
  179, 181, 183, 185, 223, 235, 251
Bennett, Lance, 245, 248
Berbers, 41, 64, 65, 77, 78, 119, 120, 122,
  125, 157, 178, 202
Berkeley, 240, 241, 263
Bible, 19, 145, 204, 227
Blogosphere, 255
Blumler, Jay, 245, 258
Bolkestein, Frits, viii, 25, 149, 181, 182,
  243, 249
Bos, Wouter, 168, 169, 171, 172
Bouamama, Said, 254, 258
Boundaries, 32, 45, 212, 229, 253, 258
  orthodox Islam, 14
  geografic, 30
  symbolic, 30, 31
  socioeconomic, 31
  moral, 31
  cultural, 31
  disciplinairy, 61
  racial, 137
  party, 188
  race class immigration, 205, 234, 239,
    263
  European society, 205
Bourdieu, Pierre, vii, 4, 8, 10, 11, 17, 30,
  46, 47, 48, 85, 114, 118, 128, 138,
  225, 238, 242, 243, 245, 254, 258,
  259
Brinkhorst, Laurens Jan, 200, 252, 259
Britain, 45, 54, 55, 62, 191, 239, 257, 263

British Muslims, 54, 55, 56
British society, 54, 55
Browning, 32
Brubaker, Rogers, 137, 237, 244, 259
Brussels, 40, 61, 111, 112, 120, 192, 252,
  254, 259, 266
Buitenhof, 145, 147
Burgat, Francois, 234, 242, 260
Buruma, Ian, 194, 195, 209, 251, 259

Calvinism and Islam, 65
Capital, 71, 113, 114, 129, 242, 253, 263
  symbolic, 96
  religious, 101, 114, 127, 128, 129, 130,
    131
  economic, 101, 121, 128, 129, 130
  linguistic, 104
  of notoriety, 124
Carter, Jimmy, 233, 234
Cartoons, 205, 206, 207, 208, 252, 259
Casablanca, 65, 67, 78, 100, 121, 228
Castels, Manuel, 235, 243, 257
Catholic, 17, 79, 90, 139, 145, 174, 222,
  227, 254, 258
Catholicism, 222
CDA (Christian Democratic Appel), 134,
  169, 172, 173, 175, 183
Cheppih, Mohammed, 180, 181, 183, 249,
  266
Cherribi, Sam, 233, 234, 240, 253, 254,
  259, 260, 261
Christen Unie (CU), 169
Christian, 11, 12, 15, 17, 19, 20, 26, 43, 52,
  54, 64, 69, 71, 106, 134, 145, 169,
  173, 191, 204, 205, 215, 228, 238,
  239, 260, 262
Christianity, 15, 57, 204, 215, 221, 239,
  252, 254, 258, 259, 266
Claims, 4, 18, 33, 51, 79, 114, 157, 209,
  221, 222, 229, 245
Cliteur, Paul, 199
CNN, 163, 208
Coercion, 4, 5, 6, 29, 118, 220, 223, 224
Cohen, Job, 161, 176
Colonial, 14, 27, 46, 47, 63, 64, 65, 205,
  211, 253, 261

Colonialism, 13, 98
Communities
  gay, 43
  imagined, 138, 141, 245, 257
  migrant, 30, 46, 86, 97, 98
Comparative European Perspectives, 240, 262, 266
Composite, ix, 3, 16, 207
Conflict, internal, 72, 93, 94
Confronting Islamophobia in Educational Practice, 239, 266
Context, 4, 5, 29, 34, 43, 44, 46, 47, 55, 59, 61, 70, 97, 122, 130, 137, 138, 139, 148, 161, 179, 204, 220, 233, 242, 245, 254, 259
  decontextualisation, 101, 226
  recontextualisation, 101, 226
Council of Churches, 70
Countries, majority-Muslim, 39
Covering Islam, 142, 242, 246, 252, 265

D66, 78, 134, 181, 191, 192
Danish cartoons, 207, 209
Darod, 196
Denmark, 37, 39, 40, 95, 170, 205, 206, 208, 225, 235
Derrida, Jacques, 13, 47, 48
Descartes, René, 8, 15, 17, 21, 221, 224, 233, 259
Desclée, 242, 254, 258
Dewinter, Filip, 37
Diaspora, 25, 27, 39, 40, 41, 57, 87, 94, 138, 241, 254, 260
Divorce, 33, 42, 99, 100, 212, 218, 219, 236, 237
Djma'a, 89, 91, 93, 111, 114, 124
Doorn, Jacques van, 250, 266
Dreyfus affair, 225
Drugs, 43, 100, 172, 173, 224
Dutch Muslim, 90, 167, 178, 198, 220
Dutch news media, 143, 146, 148, 183
Duyvendak, Jan-Willem, 241, 260
Dutch organizations, 72, 73, 76, 77, 81
Dutch politics, 146, 150, 154, 190
Dutch Republic, 246, 262

Eastern Europe, 39, 49
ECAME, 85, 87, 89, 91, 93, 95, 97, 99, 101, 103
Economic capital, 101, 121, 128–30
Effects, 37, 38, 151, 244
Egypt, 13, 30, 95, 108, 122, 126, 158, 211, 212, 228
Eickelman, Dale, 240, 243, 260
Elias, Norbert, 17, 31, 53, 85, 217, 231, 239, 242, 255, 260
El-Moumni, Ghalil, 131, 143, 144, 145, 148, 154, 164, 182
Elsevier, 133, 189, 251
Emancipation, 27, 32, 65, 78–9, 200, 211, 212, 215
Enlarged Europe, 234, 236, 253, 261, 263
Enlightenment, 101, 221–2, 254, 266
Entman, Robert, 137, 138, 244, 245, 260
Entrepreneur,
  iman, 26, 40, 80, 120, 121, 126, 128, 130, 134, 166
Esposito, John, 234, 242, 254, 260
Etzioni, Amitai, vii
EU countries, 45, 158
Eurabia, 25
Euro, 23, 24, 39, 156
Euro Islam, 243, 257
European Attitudes, 52, 222, 254, 266
European citizenship, 184, 185
European cultures, 11, 34, 60, 231
European environment, 40, 48, 59, 61, 107
European identity, 32, 106
European media, 84, 140, 225, 228–9
European Muslims, 5, 17, 55, 141, 239, 263
European Parliament Elections, 253, 261
Europe's Muslims, 4, 5, 27, 221, 226, 230, 254
Exile, 28, 30, 60, 77, 163

Fatwa, 82, 98, 112
Feminism, 253, 263
Feminist, 34, 176, 177, 211, 213, 253, 258, 261

272   INDEX

Field, 110, 240, 262
Figaro, le, 190, 235
Fitna, 206–9, 218, 220, 252, 265
Fkih, 118, 119, 120, 121, 127, 128, 130
Flemish, 156, 158, 180
Foreign Workers in Western Europe, 237, 264
Fortuyn, Pim, ix, 4, 6, 9, 10, 19, 36, 37, 40, 44, 50, 108, 131, 133, 134, 135, 136, 139, 142, 146, 147, 148, 149, 150, 151, 152, 153, 154, 155, 157, 159, 160, 162, 166, 168, 169, 170, 175, 178, 182, 183, 184, 193, 197, 225, 233, 237, 238, 244, 246, 250, 251, 259, 260, 265
 the legacy 153
 Fortuynism, 183
 career, 192
Framing, 137, 141, 181, 210, 225, 230, 231, 252, 265
 effects, 244
 European politics, 244
Freeman, Gary P., 51, 238, 260, 261
Friday sermons, 86, 109, 111, 119, 123
Fundamentalist Islam, 217, 218

Gamson, William, 137, 245, 261
Gardian, the, 55
Gauchet, Marcel, 93, 243, 261
Geertz, Clifford, 16, 61, 64, 113, 233, 240, 243, 260, 261
Gender equality, 34–5, 213
Gender equity, 211–12
Germany, 37, 39, 40, 41, 45, 52, 53, 54, 55, 56, 60, 61, 63, 95, 97, 143, 146, 225, 235, 237, 238, 240, 259, 262, 266
Gianpietro Mazzoleni, 244, 265
Goffman, Erving, 244, 261
Goody, Jack, 23, 61, 235, 240, 261
Goudsblom, Johan, vii
Graber, Doris, vii, 244, 261
Groen Links (Green Left), 77, 78, 168, 169, 170, 171, 172
Groene Amsterdammer, 58, 234
Groups, ethnic, 67, 85, 90, 137, 138
Guilders, 23, 91, 93, 128, 145

Guler, Nulifer, 235, 261
Gurewitch, Michael, 245, 258

Habitus, 118, 242
Haddad, Yvonne, 234, 261
Halsema, Femke, 172
Hate, 10, 157, 162, 163, 200, 214
Headscarf, 29, 33, 34, 61, 143, 224
Hervieu-Léger, Danièlle, 9, 261
Het Parool, 148, 176, 246, 248, 249, 250, 264, 266
Hidjra, 66, 67, 97, 98, 101, 183
Hierarchy, 73, 92, 109, 113
Hindus and Muslims in India, 242, 266
Hirsi Ali, Ayaan, 4, 6, 159, 166, 168, 176, 178, 181, 184, 185, 187, 188, 189, 190, 191, 192, 193, 194, 195, 196, 197, 198, 199, 200, 201, 202, 203, 209, 210, 213, 214, 215, 219, 230, 248, 249, 250, 251, 252, 257, 262
 personal story, 167
 Times 100, 190
 Submission, 86, 189, 194, 197, 198, 199, 200, 201, 202, 203, 204, 207, 209, 210, 213, 225, 251, 252, 257, 264
Homosexuality, 26, 33, 44, 100, 143, 144, 145, 237
 homosexual, 26, 43, 44, 74, 84, 143, 145, 146, 148, 176, 177, 184, 211
Horsfield, Bruce, 236, 263, 265
HP/De Tijd, 134, 199, 244, 265
Hurgronje, Snouck, 64, 65

Identity, 14, 23, 29, 43, 48, 77, 82, 85, 86, 87, 89, 97, 103, 178, 215, 223, 229,
 non-identity, 24
 European Union, 24
 muslimaized, 25
 alienated, 30
 European, 32, 106,
 religious, 32, 38, 78, 81
 Islamic, 32, 33, 81, 106, 138
 misogynist, 34

secular society, 38
sexual, 38, 100
national, 58, 234, 263
cultural, 63, 74, 80, 142, 230
group, 79
transnational, 79
ethnic, 79
Holland, 90
public, 138
racial, 138
stigmatized, 138
Imam, 5, 17, 25, 28, 42, 44, 56, 60, 66, 71, 72, 81, 86, 87, 88, 89, 91, 92, 93, 94, 95, 96, 97, 100, 102, 103, 104, 105, 106, 107, 109, 111, 112, 113, 114, 116, 117, 118, 119, 124, 125, 127, 129, 130, 133, 143, 144, 152, 167, 170, 177, 178, 180, 182, 183, 201, 206, 207, 214, 220, 223, 231, 237, 242, 246, 259
radical, 6
tenth century Bagdad, 21
in London and Amsterdam, 21
Dutch language, 25
revolutionary, 26
prisoners in their own mosques, 26
European tenure, 26
entrepreneur, 26
gay pride, 26
social work, 26
isolated, 27
alienation, 29
deputized by their home country, 29
European media, 84
sermons, 98
on women, 99
interpreters of a new social reality, 101
Saudi Arabia and the Gulf, 108
imported legally and illegally, 110
Islamic countries, 115
oratory skills, 115
freelance, 120
village, 121
neo-imam, 122
shaykh, 123
kichk, 126
low religious capital, 128

economic capital, 128
moderate, 131
orthodox, 131
El-Moumni, Ghalil, 131, 143, 144, 145, 148, 154, 164, 182
conservative, 219
India, 27, 30, 54, 60, 211, 212, 242, 266
Indonesia, 64, 65, 211, 228, 233, 240, 243, 261
Indonesian, 27, 64
Integration, 5, 17, 18, 38, 53, 54, 61, 66, 74, 80, 84, 98, 102, 144, 148, 149, 153, 154, 167, 169, 170, 172, 175, 184, 191, 197, 201, 221, 224, 231, 235, 236, 240, 241, 266
European, ix, 4, 23, 47
anti integration ideology, 29
ethnic disintegration, 35
successful, 37
Britain, Germany and the US, 45
economic, 51
policies, 52
national, 52
Islamic Diaspora's, 57
France and the US, 62
Dutch society, 101
Muslims, 103
socio-political, 142
burka, 171
forced, 173
minorities, 181, 188
cultural, 215
Internet, 82, 205, 206, 207, 209, 229, 244, 261
Iraq, 160, 161, 185, 250
Islamization, 9, 59, 60, 81, 87, 89, 131, 142, 146, 147, 150, 181, 183, 208, 225, 234
Israel, 156, 158, 159, 181, 195, 215
Israelis, 211
Israel, Jonathan, 262
Issues, ix, 50, 75, 83, 92, 97, 99, 107, 134, 137, 148, 153, 165, 167, 169, 225, 244, 250, 267
contested, 33, 43, 45, 183, 185
immigration, 48, 175, 182, 197

Issues (*continued*)
  Islamic, 64, 123
  social, 71, 101, 103, 108, 191
  sexual identity, 100
  identity, 103,
  conflict, 140
  Pim Fortuyn, 146, 147
  political, 184
Italy, 37, 39, 40, 48, 49, 67, 69, 145, 153, 185, 205, 225, 228, 237, 245, 265, 266

Jansen van Galen, John, 166, 250
Jews, 17, 26, 36, 43, 54, 55, 90, 159, 181, 198, 227, 239, 263
Jewish, 17, 41, 159, 162, 174, 179, 195

Kepel, Gilles, 82, 97, 126, 239, 241, 242, 243, 254, 262
Khatibi, Abdelkebir, 13, 253, 262
Kichk (Egyptian preacher), 123, 125, 126, 127
King of Morocco, 24, 28, 70, 71, 76, 82, 100, 107, 108, 115, 126, 236, 237
Klausen, Jytte, 207, 208, 262
Kleinnijenhuis, Jan, 152, 247, 262
KMAN, 69, 70, 71, 72, 73, 75, 76, 77, 180, 249
Kok, Wim, 153, 181, 235
Koran, 13, 14, 19, 30, 44, 88, 89, 94, 96, 99, 100, 102, 105, 106, 108, 111, 113, 119, 120, 121, 122, 124, 125, 126, 127, 130, 157, 194, 198, 202, 203, 206, 208, 209, 211, 213, 214, 222, 230
Koopmans, Ruud, 61, 62, 63, 209, 210, 237, 240, 251, 252, 262, 266

Laguerre, Michel, vii, 79, 241, 263
Laïcité, 233, 235, 251, 254, 261
Lamont, Michèle, 30, 31, 58, 205, 234, 239, 254, 263
Leefbaar Nederland (LN), 44, 136, 147, 148, 150
Legner, Frank, vii, 234, 263
Libanon, 30, 156, 158, 211, 212
Lijbhart, Arend, 240, 263

Lewis, Bernard, 12, 14, 25, 54, 215, 239, 250, 253
LPF (List Pim Fortuyn), 36, 37, 44, 108, 134, 136, 142, 147, 148, 149, 150, 151, 152, 153, 165, 166, 168, 169, 170, 175, 183, 184, 185, 244, 247, 250, 266

Marijnissen, Jan, 169, 170, 172
Malcolm X, 151, 157
Mas, Paolo de, 67, 78, 241, 259
Mazzoleni, Gianpietro, 136, 151, 236, 244, 263, 265
Mechoulan, Henri, 240, 264
Media, 4, 9, 11, 19, 20, 24, 25, 26, 32, 33, 44, 45, 52, 58, 59, 66, 75, 79, 84, 85, 98, 121, 123, 131, 134, 135, 138, 142, 143, 144, 148, 152, 160, 163, 179, 181, 182, 191, 199, 201, 204, 207, 208, 209, 215, 218, 220, 221, 223, 224, 226, 227, 228, 230, 231, 235, 241, 247, 248, 251, 252, 257, 260, 262, 267
  conflict, ix, 146
  EU constitution, 39
  public policy, 37
  coverage of immigrants, 48
  gays, 133
  Neopopulism, 136, 236, 244, 263, 265
  Europe's imagined Muslim community, 137
  Islam, 139
  markets, 140
  Pim as a Brand, 146
  personalization of politics, 150
  media effects, 151
  verbal extremism, 151,
  framing Islam as a problem, 154
  Dutch, 156, 250
  obsession, 156
  the Netherlands, 159
  El-Moumni, 164
  Arabic, 176
  frenzy, 180, 193, 205
  Abou Jahjah, 180
  bias, 183

Flemish, 183
  elite, 188, 190, 250
  system, 188
  columnists, 188
  Dutch print, 189
  validation, 190
  intellectuals, 196
  international, 197
  Al-Jazeera, 205
  Abou Laban, 206
  Fitna, 206
  political establishment, 210
  western, 211, 212
  September 11, 214
  overexposure, 222
  programming, 225
  European, 229
  Islamic, 229
  framing, 244
  effects, 244
Mernissi, Fatima, 13, 211, 252, 253, 264
Mierlo, Hans van, 181
Migration, 13, 16, 40, 45, 46, 47, 51, 53, 61, 62, 66, 67, 68, 71, 79, 90, 97, 98, 101, 211, 237, 238, 240, 241, 259, 260, 261, 262, 264
  illegal, 51, 66
  post-colonial migration, 63
  Berbers, 65
  migration of male guest workers, 66
  migration to Medina, 97
  family reunion, 122
  migration trajectory, 126
  migration and Islam, 190, 191
  migration and Asylum, 199
Milli Gürüs, 86
Mobilization, 73, 97, 137, 138, 139, 154, 165, 174, 244, 265
Monde, le, 38, 211, 234, 236, 266
Moors, Annelies, 195, 251, 264
Morocco, 6, 7, 8, 11, 12, 13, 14, 16, 17, 24, 27, 28, 29, 30, 40, 41, 42, 43, 49, 60, 64, 65, 66, 67, 68, 71, 75, 77, 78, 80, 82, 90, 93, 95, 98, 100, 105, 106, 107, 108, 111, 115, 116, 117, 118, 119, 120, 121, 122, 128, 129, 157, 163, 164, 170, 177, 178, 184, 210, 211, 212, 233, 236, 237, 240, 241, 243, 261
Mosque, 4, 6, 26, 27, 28, 33, 40, 52, 59, 60, 71, 72, 73, 76, 81, 82, 83, 87, 88, 89, 90, 91, 92, 93, 94, 97, 99, 101, 104, 105, 107, 108, 109, 110, 111, 113, 114, 115, 116, 117, 118, 119, 120, 121, 122, 123, 124, 126, 127, 128, 129, 130, 131, 140, 141, 143, 145, 146, 152, 160, 167, 179, 180, 183, 184, 189, 204, 221, 222, 223, 235, 236, 237, 242, 243, 249, 266
  source of separatism, 29
  source of identity, 29
  symbol of alienated identity, 30
  in Europe, 42
  in the Netherlands, 66
  of Amsterdam, 84
  Bouyeri (Van Gogh murderer), 86
  daw'a, 95
  Javanese mosque, 96
  community, 96
  Turkish, 96
  hidjra, 98

Nanji, Irshad, 211, 213, 252, 264
Netherlands, the, 3, 4, 6, 8, 9, 10, 11, 17, 18, 19, 23, 24, 27, 31, 32, 36, 37, 39, 40, 41, 42, 43, 44, 50, 60, 61, 62, 63, 64, 66, 67, 68, 69, 71, 72, 75, 77, 78, 79, 80, 84, 86, 87, 89, 90, 93, 95, 96, 97, 98, 99, 100, 101, 103, 105, 107, 109, 110, 114, 118, 134, 138, 142, 143, 146, 147, 150, 152, 153, 154, 155, 156, 157, 158, 159, 161, 163, 165, 166, 167, 168, 171, 172, 173, 176, 177, 178, 180, 181, 182, 183, 184, 188, 190, 192, 194, 198, 199, 201, 202, 208, 209, 210, 214, 223, 224, 228, 230, 231, 234, 235, 236, 237, 238, 240, 241, 246, 251, 252, 257, 261, 263, 264, 265, 266
Nielsen, Jorgen, 234, 236, 263, 264
NIOD (Netherlands Institute for War Documentation), 36

Norris, Pippa, 34, 35, 212, 213, 235, 251, 253, 261, 264
NOS, 252, 265
NRC, 148, 149, 150, 156, 192, 207, 234, 241, 248, 249, 250, 251, 252, 262, 264

Olgun, Achmed, 249, 264
Orthodox, 27
  Islam, 14
  Militants, 102
  Imam, 131
Orthodoxization, 229
Outsiders, ix, 23, 31, 36, 48, 49, 50, 53, 81, 87, 101, 137, 139, 205, 231, 237, 238, 239, 242, 245, 252, 255, 260, 265

Pakistan, 7, 27, 30, 33, 54, 60, 86, 95, 138, 140, 200, 206, 207, 213
Palestine, 179
Parliament, 8, 9, 10, 11, 17, 34, 36, 48, 50, 64, 77, 85, 87, 91, 102, 103, 134, 136, 144, 152, 153, 154, 155, 156, 165, 166, 168, 169, 174, 180, 181, 182, 184, 185, 187, 188, 189, 190, 191, 192, 196, 197, 198, 210, 218, 225, 244, 250, 253, 259, 261
  parliamentary, 192, 197, 214, 253
  parliamentarian, 206, 209
Pascon, Paul, 16, 65, 240
Pels, Dick, 244, 246, 249, 264, 266
Politics of the sacred, 99
Populism, 10, 149, 224, 236, 244, 246, 263, 264, 265
Praag, Philip van, 250
Prejudice, 48, 49, 50, 139, 157, 164, 205, 237, 245, 265, 266
Principles of hierarchy, 113
Prisoners of the mosque, 9, 26, 105, 114, 115, 116, 117, 118, 119, 120, 126, 129, 130
Protestant, 17, 43, 79, 139, 145, 159, 174, 221, 222
Protestantism, 221, 222
Purple coalition, 134, 146, 147, 151, 152, 168, 169, 175, 181, 235

PvdA (Labor party), 77, 78, 134, 149, 150, 153, 171, 172, 175, 180

Queen, 135, 159, 244

Radical, 5, 47, 63, 156, 183, 188, 190, 192, 214, 220, 235, 251
  radical and official Islam, 5, 6, 29, 156
  radical imams, 6, 131, 201
  radical secularism, 16
  radical form of islamization 47
  radical ideology of Islam, 86
  radical Islamic group, 161
  radical critique, 228
  radical enlightenment, 240, 246, 262, 264
Ramadan, 19, 44, 58, 72, 81, 89, 93, 140
Ramdas, Anil, vii, 250, 264
Rap, 58, 162, 167
Rapper, 162, 163, 164, 165, 166
Raymzter, Moroccan, rapper, 162, 163, 164, 165, 166
Religion, 13, 14, 15, 17, 18, 19, 20, 21, 26, 31, 33, 34, 38, 43, 44, 45, 46, 50, 51, 57, 61, 65, 70, 79, 82, 84, 85, 86, 87, 90, 96, 105, 106, 107, 108, 122, 139, 142, 146, 148, 149, 154, 160, 173, 184, 191, 195, 196, 202, 204, 209, 213, 214, 215, 217, 221, 224, 227, 228, 229, 230, 233, 234, 235, 237, 242, 243, 245, 260, 261, 263, 267
  religion and media, 142
Revolutionary, 99, 127
  ideals, 15
  imam, 26, 120, 123, 126, 127, 128, 130
Rif, 41, 67, 78, 96, 105, 119, 121, 122, 125, 163, 164, 183
Rojecki, Andrew, 137, 138, 244, 245, 260
Rosenmöller, Paul, 151
RTL4, 136, 146
Rubin, Uri, 243, 265
Rushdie, Salman, 15, 47, 82, 167, 177, 200, 233

Sadawi, Nawal, 211, 252, 265
Sartre, Jean Paul, 21, 234, 265

Said, Edward, 85, 142, 204, 228, 242, 245, 246, 252
Sayed, Abdelmalek, 67, 226, 254, 265
Scarf, 58, 99, 171, 176, 224, 225
Scheffer, Paul, 149, 246, 266
Scholten, Otto, 208, 252, 265
Schudson, Michael, 141, 245, 265
Schuyt, Kees, vii, 233, 265
Secular, 8, 17, 32, 38, 57, 60, 61, 68, 72, 75, 77, 81, 85, 87, 107, 108, 131, 206, 215, 221, 223, 224, 228, 230
hyper secular, 11
   secularism, 14, 15, 18, 20, 21, 28, 34, 215
   in the media, 215
   ethics, 15
   secularization, 15
   utopia, 15
   laïcité, 15
   societies, 18
   American counterparts, 20
   Europe, 20
   Muslims, 51
   public space, 213
   politics, 214
   the secular question in Europe, 230
   secular design of Europe, 230
   secular Islam is possible, 230
Secularism, ix, 14, 15, 16, 18, 20, 21, 28, 34, 83, 213, 215, 224
Semetko, Holli, vii, 244, 245, 248, 257, 265
Sex, 43, 100, 146, 177, 178
Sexuality, 17, 27, 43, 146
Shaykh, 113, 122, 123, 125, 126, 127
Sheikh, 92
SMT (Samenwerking Marokkanen en Tunesiërs), 75, 76
SMR (The Urban Moroccan council), 75, 76
Sniderman, Paul, 48, 49, 50, 139, 205, 237, 238, 245, 252, 261, 265
Spain, 16, 39, 40, 41, 42, 46, 52, 55, 67, 69, 238, 265
Sociogenesis, 60, 96, 242
   of a mosque, 87
Somali, 138, 166, 167, 168, 210
   Somalia, 166, 167

SP, 169, 170, 172
Spiegel, der, 206, 207, 262
Spinoza, Baruch, 16, 17, 187, 195, 214, 224, 240, 253, 264
Spivak, Gayatri, vii, 15, 233
Srebrenica, 35, 36, 153
Stigmatization, 47, 48, 138, 139, 142, 165, 178, 179, 226
Sunna, 89, 91, 127
Swaan, Abram de, v, 8, 17, 23, 239, 242, 246, 253, 265, 266
Sweden, 39, 40, 201, 225, 236
Syria, 122, 206, 211, 212
Syrians, 42

Taboo, 160, 177, 183, 210
Tarrow, Sidney, 245, 265, 266
Tayob, Abdolkader, 244, 266
Telegraaf, de, 159, 247
Tilly, Charles, 245, 266
Tocqueville, Alexis de, 105, 234, 259, 263
Touraine, Alain, 27, 211, 212, 234, 246, 253, 266
Trifecta of coercion, 4, 5, 6, 29, 58, 156, 219, 220, 221, 222, 223, 224, 230, 231
Trouw, 10, 148, 150, 151, 160, 176, 190, 247, 248, 249, 250, 258, 267
Tunesia, 7, 27, 28, 30, 33, 39, 42, 49, 75, 98, 212, 240
Turkey, 25, 27, 28, 29, 30, 34, 37, 39, 42, 69, 71, 90, 95, 106, 148, 170, 192, 210, 221, 230, 241, 243

Ulama, 64, 87, 98, 110
Umma, 52, 84, 87, 89, 122, 203, 224, 254
   transnational Islamic identity, 110
UMMON (Union of Moroccan mosques in the Netherlands), 72, 75, 76, 77
UMP
United States of America, 4, 5, 6, 8, 11, 19, 20, 21, 25, 30, 31, 34, 37, 45, 49, 62, 137, 167, 170, 173, 180, 188, 208, 211, 219, 234, 238, 239, 260, 262

2Vandaag, 162
Van den Berg-Eldering, Lotty, 80, 241, 266

Van der Brug, Wouter, 247, 250, 266
Van Dijk, Teun, viii, 245, 266
Van Dijke, Leen, 145
Van Gogh, Theo, 4, 6, 10, 32, 40, 86, 189, 194, 198, 199, 201, 210, 230, 251, 252, 259
Van der Veer, Peter, 89, 242, 266
Veil, 34, 83, 99, 171, 198, 225, 229, 230, 233, 248, 252, 253, 261, 264
Verkleuring, 32
Virginity
  Virginity cults, 177
  Virginity in Islam, 211, 212
Volkskrant, 147, 148, 174, 237, 244, 248, 250
Von der Fuhr, Gijs, 73, 241, 267
VPRO, 243, 252
Vries, Hent de, 142, 245, 267
Vrij Nederland, 168, 187, 198, 244, 248, 250, 252, 264
VVD, (free-market liberal party), 44, 77, 78, 134, 149, 150, 159, 160, 165, 167, 168, 169, 171, 176, 181, 187, 188, 190, 191, 192, 193, 197, 210, 249, 250

Waardenburg, Jacques, 240, 243, 267
Wacqant, Loïc, vii, 239, 267
Walgrave, Stefaan, 180, 244
Western, 5, 7, 12, 17, 25, 26, 29, 34, 35, 37, 39, 49, 53, 55, 84, 85, 86, 100, 102, 131, 139, 142, 156, 160, 161, 173, 188, 195, 196, 199, 200, 204, 209, 211, 212, 213, 214, 218, 220, 225, 234, 237, 239, 253, 260, 261, 262, 264

Wilders, Geert, 4, 6, 152, 192, 206, 207, 208, 214, 218, 219,
  Fitna, 209
  Koran, 209
Witteman, Paul, 150
Women, ix, 16, 26, 27, 33, 34, 35, 42, 43, 53, 55, 58, 66, 83, 84, 91, 94, 98, 99, 100, 102, 111, 116, 144, 148, 160, 162, 166, 167, 168, 171, 176, 177, 179, 182, 184, 187, 196, 201, 202, 203, 206, 210, 211, 212, 213, 214, 237, 252, 253, 257
women's day, 176
women in Morocco, 177
women in the Netherlands, 178, 202
muslim women, 178, 188, 194, 198
women's submission, 198, 200
women in Saudi Arabia, 198
women's emancipation, 199
women in patriarchal Islamic societies, 211
women in Europe, 211, 212
women and men, 211
women in France, 212
women in Algeria, 253, 263
women in the Middle East, 253, 264

Xenophobia, 19, 149

Yugoslavia, 35, 37, 71

Zalm, Gerrit, 168, 171, 176, 181, 191
Zionists, 181,
Zolberg, Aristide, 237, 267
Zomergasten, 197, 252
Zoonen, Liesbet van, 79, 184, 241, 246, 247, 249, 266, 267

www.ingramcontent.com/pod-product-compliance
Ingram Content Group UK Ltd.
Pitfield, Milton Keynes, MK11 3LW, UK
UKHW021317180426
11947UKWH00015B/1289